Achieving Dynamism in an Anaemic Europe

Luigi Paganetto
Editor

Achieving Dynamism in an Anaemic Europe

Springer

Editor
Luigi Paganetto
FUET, Economics Foundation
University of Rome Tor Vergata
Rome
Italy

ISBN 978-3-319-38624-9 ISBN 978-3-319-14099-5 (eBook)
DOI 10.1007/978-3-319-14099-5

Springer Cham Heidelberg New York Dordrecht London

Softcover reprint of the hardcover 1st edition 2015

Printed on acid-free paper

Springer International Publishing AG Switzerland is part of Springer Science+Business Media (www.springer.com)

Contents

Perspectives on Growth, Trade, and Social Agenda Expenditures in the Eurozone During the Rest of this Decade, With and Without the EU-US Transatlantic Trade and Investment Partnership (TTIP)

Fred Campano, Lucio Laureti and Dominick Salvatore

Abstract The Euro Zone countries have been experiencing slow growth of real GDP during the last decade. Without the increase in exports and national income estimated to result from a successful EU-US Transatlantic Trade and Investment Partnership (TTIP) now being negotiated, most members of the Eurozone would be unable to maintain the same *share* of government expenditures in gross domestic product and finance their social agenda in the same degree during the rest of this decade, as they did during the last decade. In this paper, we project the trends in GDP growth, national savings, household consumption and import demand for the seventeen countries that comprised the Eurozone in 2013. The exports of Eurozone members are determined by their share of the import demand of their most important trading partners and the rest of the world. We find that without TTIP, most members of the Eurozone would be unable to maintain the same *share* of government expenditures in gross domestic product and finance their social agenda in the same degree during the rest of this decade, as they did during the last decade. This conclusion would change with a successful TTIP. Even without a successful TTIP, however, most member nations would still be able to increase the *absolute* amount of government expenditure and social expenditures even as their *shares* decline.

F. Campano
Department of Economics, Fordham University at Lincoln Center, New York, NY, USA
e-mail: campano@fordham.edu

L. Laureti
Dipartimento di Economia, Università LUM Jean Monnet, Casamassima, BA, Italy
e-mail: laureti@lum.it

D. Salvatore (✉)
Department of Economics, Fordham University, New York, NY, USA
e-mail: salvatore@fordham.edu

L. Paganetto (ed.), *Achieving Dynamism in an Anaemic Europe*,
DOI 10.1007/978-3-319-14099-5_1

1 Introduction

The member countries of the European Monetary Union (EMU) or Eurozone have been experiencing slow growth of real GDP for at least a decade. Without TTIP, our projections of real GDP are somewhat pessimistic with an average GDP growth rate of 1.46 % over the period from 2012 and 2020. This is slightly higher than the 2000–2012 growth rate which was 1.13 %, but a bit lower than the 1995–2012 rate of 1.65 %. The projections were made at the country level and added to get the EMU totals. Figure 1 shows the projected trends. The model uses GDP projections to drive household expenditure and import demand, but the trade balance is constrained by borrowings. We argue that the marginal propensities to consume (and save) are not easy to alter and they should remain in line with past experience. However, exports depend upon demand in the markets of their trading partners, which is an exogenous input. For the purpose of this exercise we constructed a 23 by 23 trade matrix based on the data of 2012. Included are 17 countries of the Euro Zone, China, USA, Japan and the UK. The 22nd place in the matrix is occupied by the rest of the world, and the 23rd place is the world total. We looked at the scenario of constant export shares, that is, each exporter in the matrix would have the same share of all the other markets as it had in 2012. It is a plausible scenario for the EMU countries because they export "quality" goods (and services). By this we mean goods that have an income elasticity of demand greater than one and thus see a proportionately rising demand in emerging economies as these economies become more affluent. In any case, we would not expect to see diminishing shares for EMU exports.

2 The Economic Model

In projecting the supply side of the economy, we will make the assumption that labor is not a constraint in the region. That is, there is a surplus of labor in almost any country and the only real constraint to production is capital. In this case, the Harrod-Domar production function is a good stand-in for the more commonly used constant elasticity of substitution (CES) type of function, such as the Cobb-Douglas, which uses capital as well as labor as inputs. The identities and equations of the model are based on the expenditure table of the national accounts, as follows:

Identities: $Y = C + G + I + X - M$,

where Y is GDP, C is household consumption, G government expenditure, I is gross capital formation, X is exports, and M is imports.
$S = Y - DA$, where S is national savings and DC is domestic absorption
$X - M$ = net exports, which equals $S - I$
$B = M - X = I - S$ = national borrowings

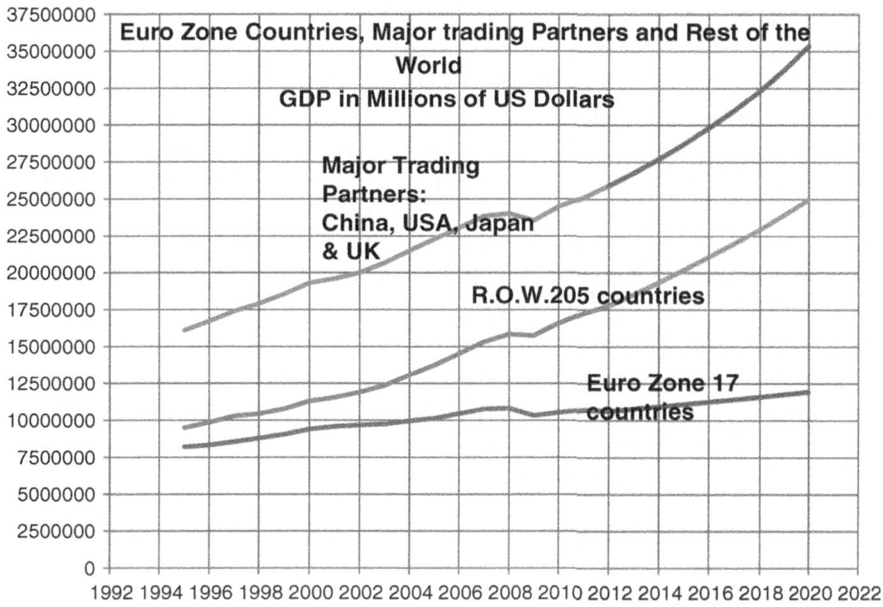

Fig. 1 Historical and projected GDP of the Euro Zone as compared to its major trading partners

Behavioral: C = a + b Y, S = a + bY and M = a + bX + cY
Harrod-Domar: $Y_{t+1} = a + b\sum I_t$
Investment trend: I_t/Y_t = a + b Year

The estimated parameters and further details regarding the estimates will be provided by the authors upon request. The projection of GDP for region as a whole is shown in Fig. 1. The projected trend reflects recovery path from the 2008 recession when each country moves back on its 1995–2012 trend.

As mentioned above, the trade is built-up from the individual member countries. The data are taken from the COMTRADE data bank of the United Nation. This allowed us to construct the bilateral trade between the 21 individual countries of the matrix as well as the aggregate for the rest of the world. This is an approach that is used primarily for short-term forecasting, but is also useful for long-term projections (see Klein and Asher 1979; Klein and Dominick 2013).

3 The Outcome for GDP by Expenditure

The historical and projected levels of the real GDP expenditure components are shown in Table 1. Gross Domestic Product rises from $10.6 trillion in 2012 to $11.9 trillion in 2020. While this rise is modest, the per capita GDP for the region is still quite high.

Table 1 Euro zone aggregate (millions of 2005 US dollars)

Year	Y	C	G	I	X	M
1995	8,196,184	4,726,192	1,729,133	1,639,513	2,135,131	2,033,785
1996	8,325,438	4,814,505	1,758,975	1,631,564	2,238,121	2,117,727
1997	8,545,081	4,905,557	1,783,035	1,697,273	2,483,963	2,324,747
1998	8,786,837	5,053,332	1,807,706	1,824,575	2,663,905	2,562,681
1999	9,045,023	5,216,743	1,840,274	1,932,745	2,814,555	2,759,294
2000	9,391,477	5,379,935	1,884,831	2,037,387	3,175,824	3,086,500
2001	9,580,007	5,481,756	1,925,993	2,030,790	3,300,570	3,159,102
2002	9,670,118	5,533,615	1,972,289	1,977,819	3,363,434	3,177,039
2003	9,742,147	5,594,587	2,006,799	2,011,457	3,404,576	3,275,272
2004	9,957,773	5,685,654	2,039,748	2,073,612	3,669,840	3,511,081
2005	10,129,161	5,787,628	2,072,050	2,120,931	3,860,526	3,711,974
2006	10,458,490	5,910,054	2,116,398	2,263,182	4,205,281	4,036,425
2007	10,770,808	6,006,301	2,162,364	2,406,430	4,484,075	4,288,362
2008	10,811,295	6,032,135	2,212,413	2,361,478	4,534,115	4,328,846
2009	10,331,494	5,978,626	2,269,767	1,969,389	3,967,798	3,854,086
2010	10,536,527	6,039,328	2,284,706	2,022,532	4,434,200	4,244,239
2011	10,706,506	6,052,579	2,283,204	2,083,216	4,719,379	4,431,872
2012	10,635,038	5,974,376	2,269,955	1,947,681	4,832,831	4,389,805
Projected						
2013	10,788,317	6,096,017	2,279,075	2,131,898	4,594,803	4,313,480
2014	10,944,425	6,172,227	2,293,639	2,167,647	4,946,270	4,635,357
2015	11,103,435	6,249,881	2,306,911	2,204,144	5,326,624	4,984,123
2016	11,265,408	6,329,008	2,318,639	2,241,418	5,739,566	5,363,227
2017	11,430,409	6,409,645	2,328,534	2,279,485	6,189,401	5,776,656
2018	11,598,510	6,491,828	2,336,253	2,318,366	6,681,128	6,229,061
2019	11,769,785	6,575,588	2,341,382	2,358,083	7,220,573	6,725,844
2020	11,944,306	6,660,969	2,343,437	2,398,661	7,814,554	7,273,317

Table 2 shows the expenditure components expressed in terms of shares of GDP. In both the historical and the periods, net exports remain positive.

While the projections of GDP are based on historical trends and thus a bit pessimistic, the population projections which are the medium variant of the United Nations Population Division are growing at even a lower rate. As a result, the per capita projections show an increasing trend (see Fig. 2) for the Euro Zone as a group. However, as we see in Fig. 3, the per capita gains vary from country to country. Under the assumptions of this scenario, Greece will have a marginal real decline in per capita GDP in 2020 as compared to 2010 and Italy and Portugal will only have a marginal increase. But still, as compared to most parts of the world, the per capita incomes are comfortably high. Slovakia, Estonia and Malta are projected to have the lowest per capita incomes in 2020, but they will all be over $15,000.

Table 2 Shares in GDP

Year	Y	C	G	I	X	M	X-M
1995	100.0	57.7	21.1	20.0	26.1	24.8	1.2
1996	100.0	57.8	21.1	19.6	26.9	25.4	1.4
1997	100.0	57.4	20.9	19.9	29.1	27.2	1.9
1998	100.0	57.5	20.6	20.8	30.3	29.2	1.2
1999	100.0	57.7	20.3	21.4	31.1	30.5	0.6
2000	100.0	57.3	20.1	21.7	33.8	32.9	1.0
2001	100.0	57.2	20.1	21.2	34.5	33.0	1.5
2002	100.0	57.2	20.4	20.5	34.8	32.9	1.9
2003	100.0	57.4	20.6	20.6	34.9	33.6	1.3
2004	100.0	57.1	20.5	20.8	36.9	35.3	1.6
2005	100.0	57.1	20.5	20.9	38.1	36.6	1.5
2006	100.0	56.5	20.2	21.6	40.2	38.6	1.6
2007	100.0	55.8	20.1	22.3	41.6	39.8	1.8
2008	100.0	55.8	20.5	21.8	41.9	40.0	1.9
2009	100.0	57.9	22.0	19.1	38.4	37.3	1.1
2010	100.0	57.3	21.7	19.2	42.1	40.3	1.8
2011	100.0	56.5	21.3	19.5	44.1	41.4	2.7
2012	100.0	56.2	21.3	18.3	45.4	41.3	4.2
Projected							
2013	100.0	56.5	21.1	19.8	42.6	40.0	2.6
2014	100.0	56.4	21.0	19.8	45.2	42.4	2.8
2015	100.0	56.3	20.8	19.9	48.0	44.9	3.1
2016	100.0	56.2	20.6	19.9	50.9	47.6	3.3
2017	100.0	56.1	20.4	19.9	54.1	50.5	3.6
2018	100.0	56.0	20.1	20.0	57.6	53.7	3.9
2019	100.0	55.9	19.9	20.0	61.3	57.1	4.2
2020	100.0	55.8	19.6	20.1	65.4	60.9	4.5

Comparing projected per capita GDP in 2020 with the major trading partners of the EMU, we notice in Fig. 4 that China, which is one of the fastest growing countries and the world's largest exporter, is only expected to have a per capita income of less than $8000 (2005 US%) when 2020 arrives—a little over one-half of what is projected for Slovakia, Estonia and Malta. Furthermore, the rest of the world (ROW) per capita is projected to be $4613 in 2020 as compared to $3512 in 2010 which is much lower than Slovakia, Estonia and Malta. However, the differences between countries in the ROW are very large with Norway having a per capita income greater than the United States and many developing countries with per capita incomes below $1000. Hence, we would argue that even under less than desirable growth rates of GDP, the member countries of the Euro Zone will be much better off than most of the world.

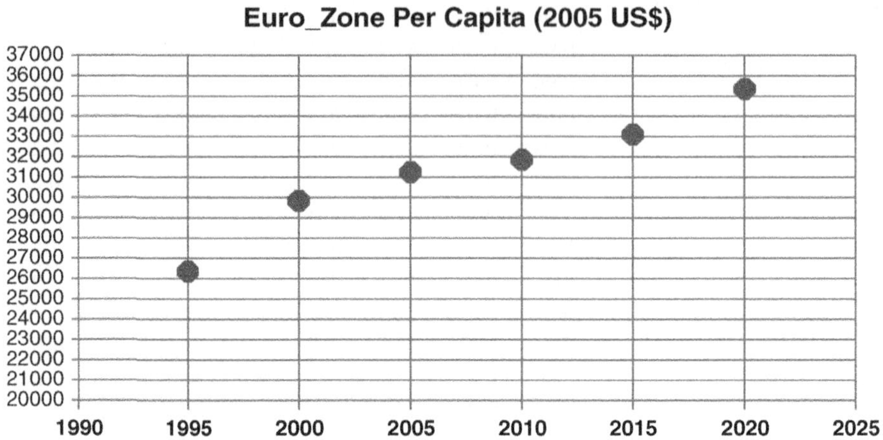

Fig. 2 Historical and projected pre capita income for the aggregate of the Euro Zone

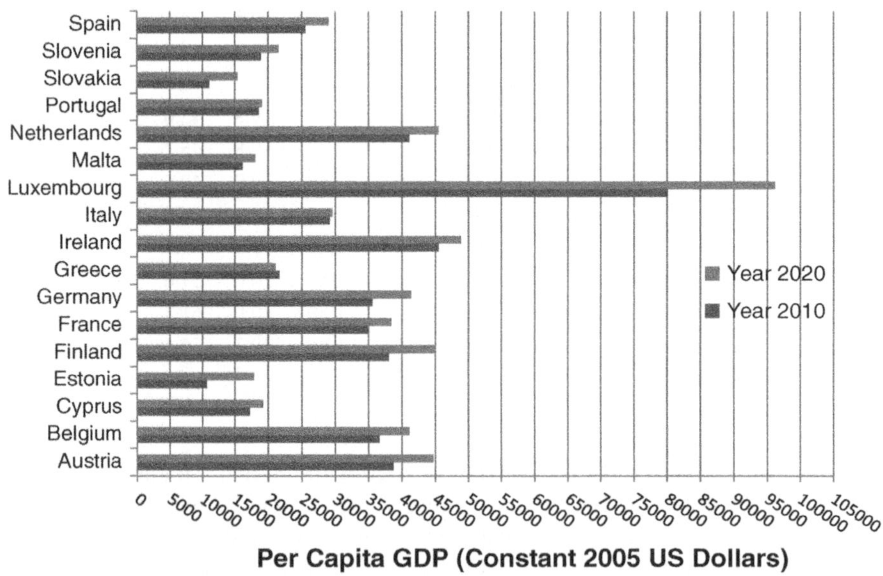

Fig. 3 Comparison between 2010 and 2020 per capita GDP

4 Projections of the National Savings Share in GDP

Figure 5 shows that the model maintained a consistent, though not exact, propensity to save for each of the member countries in the Euro Zone. This is one of the basic assumptions of the exercise.

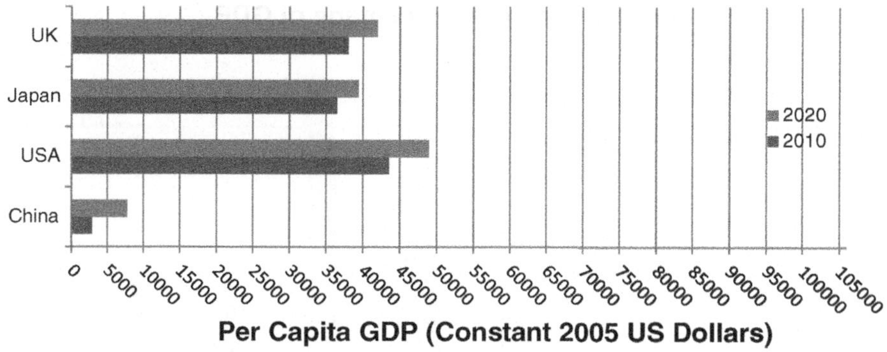

Fig. 4 Euro zone major trading partners per capita GDP

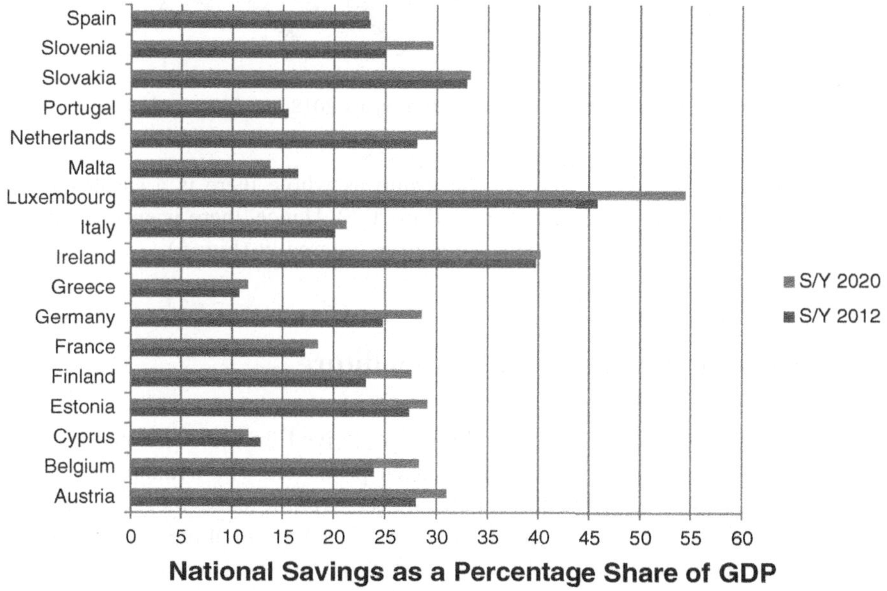

Fig. 5 Projections of the national savings as a share of GDP

5 Projections of Net Exports as a Share in GDP

For most countries in the group, net-exports remains positive, thereby, providing the possibility for those individual governments to increase discretionary spending. For a few countries, net-exports is a negative percentage of GDP that exceeds 7 %. These countries have less flexibility in their government budgets and are dependent

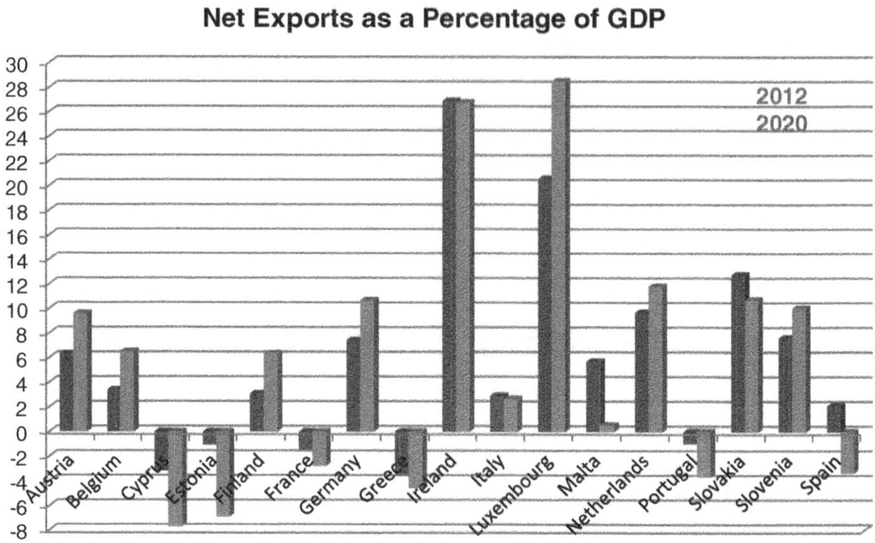

Fig. 6 Net exports as a percentage share in GDP in years 2012 and 2020

on external financing. However, for the group as whole there is a surplus which reaches about 4.5 % of the aggregate GDP in 2020. Hence, there is enough surplus within the EMU to finance the deficit countries internally (Fig. 6).

6 Projections of Government Expenditure

The projections of government expenditure are derived from the national accounts identity after the other components have been projected. The availability of government expenditure is therefore dependent on exports since they are the only variable which is not tied to domestic GDP. Keeping in mind the underlying assumptions that investment and GDP will follow historical trends and that consumption and savings propensities are cultural and do not change very much—then exports become the determinant of the government spending. In Fig. 7 we see that the projected share of government spending is in line with the historical shares. The projected shares show a gradual decline for most countries, but no major changes. They reflect the gradual decline already started in the historical period. In level terms (real 2005 US dollars) most of these countries (see Table 3) are actually increasing government expenditure. We would argue that these are achievable targets for government expenditure for these countries and no further reductions in government spending are necessary.

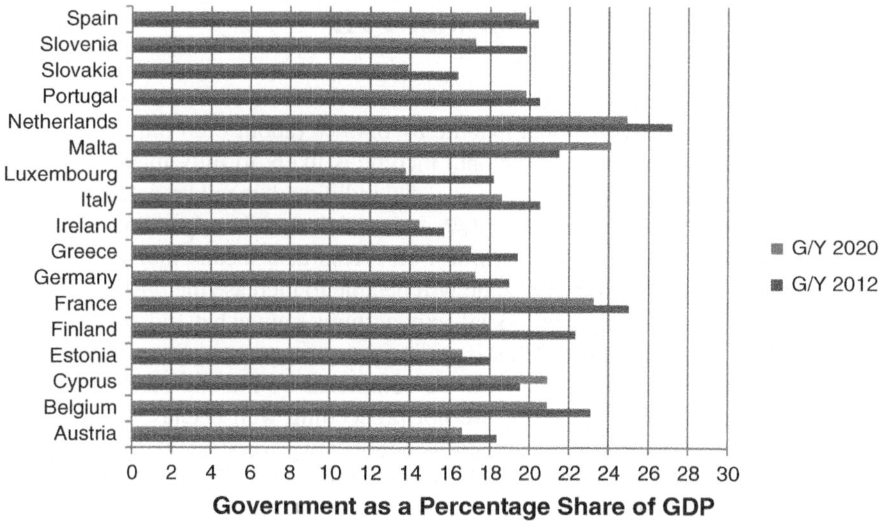

Fig. 7 Government expenditure as a percentage share of GDP

Table 3 Government expenditure as a share of GDP and in 2005 US dollars

	G/Y 2012	G/Y 2020	G 2012	G 2020
Austria	18.35	16.60	61,974	64,754
Belgium	23.10	20.89	94,023	97,565
Cyprus	19.53	20.90	3647	4899
Estonia	17.97	16.62	2844	3750
Finland	22.32	18.00	46,414	44,951
France	25.01	23.25	562,496	594,471
Germany	18.97	17.25	582,991	584,482
Greece	19.40	17.02	40,646	39,818
Ireland	15.70	14.46	32,660	35,070
Italy	20.53	18.60	354,717	337,529
Luxembourg	18.19	13.77	7530	7638
Malta	21.50	24.11	1513	1901
Netherlands	27.17	24.92	184,984	193,113
Portugal	20.50	19.80	38,621	39,926
Slovakia	16.38	13.89	10,334	11,725
Slovenia	19.83	17.25	7585	7784
Spain	20.42	19.78	236,976	274,061

7 Potential Trade Expansion with TTIP

The EU Commission (2013) estimated that a successful TTIP would increase EU exports by 28 % and EU national income by 0.48 % (about € 86 billion) by 2027. Such an increase in exports and national income is likely to fully make up, for the EU and Eurozone as a whole and for most individual member nations, for the shortfall in government *shares* in GDP and social agenda expenditures that we estimated to result without a successful TTIP. This also means that in real terms most members of the EU and Eurozone will be able to increase the *absolute* amount of government expenditure and social expenditures somewhat more with a successful TTIP that without one. This is an important reason to pursue the negotiations for TTIP, which are scheduled to be completed by the end of 2015.

Negotiations of TTIP, however, are not proceeding well because (1) Germany and some other Northern European nations oppose investor-state dispute settlement regulations, (2) of the U.S. decision to exclude financial regulations from the negotiations, (3) of the inability of President Obama to obtain "Fast Track" trade authority from the US Congress, (4) the recent EU election in which some anti-establishment parties (such as Le Pen's in France) oppose TTIP, and (5) the recent U.S. National Security Agency spying on European leaders (including Angela Merkel) makes it difficult to negotiate free transatlantic data flow. This means that TTIP may in fact be concluded after 2015 and its effect be delayed.

8 Conclusions

The trade surplus in the Eurozone countries plays an important role in making possible a social agenda financed by government expenditure. Using a world trade matrix for the Eurozone members which includes entries for their major trading partners, we have shown that there is no need to make drastic cuts in government expenditure, even in the face of slow GDP growth for the foreseeable future. The export surplus, which historically has been the rule rather than the exception, should provide the balance in the macro economy to continue government programs without interruption at the same level as before and even increase them for most Eurozone members (even as the *share* of government expenditures in gross domestic product and social agenda expenditures decline slightly during the rest of this decade relative to the last decade without TTIP). The increase in the trade surplus and real GDP in the Eurozone with a successful TTIP will make the absolute increase in social welfare expenditures even greater.

References

European Commission. 2013. Impact Assessment Report on the future of EU-US relations (2013). Commission Staff Report 68, 3 Dec 2013.

Klein, Lawrence R., and Asher, Tishler. 1979. Long-run projections of the LINK world trade model. In *Modelling the international transmission mechanism*, ed. John A. Sawer, 73–84. New York: North-Holland.

Klein, Lawrence R., and Dominick Salvatore. 2013. Shift in the world economic center of g Gravity from G7 to G20. *Journal of Policy Modeling* 2013: 416–424.

Can Trade Become Again an Engine of Growth for Europe and the World?

Moreno Bertoldi and Christopher Mc Innes

Abstract Global trade collapsed in dramatic fashion in 2009, after growing exponentially in the two decades prior to the crisis. In recent years it has failed to regain its pre-crisis dynamism. At a time when the G20 is trying to provide new momentum to global growth, a critical issue is whether trade can become, once again, one of its engines. While the conditions to conclude ambitious multilateral trade negotiations are not in place, there is room and political capital to finalise 'super' Free Trade Agreements (FTA) (like TTIP) that can unlock the trade potential and support GDP growth in the future. Should this happen, trade can become again one of the major engines of growth of the global economy. The main challenge ahead will be to ensure that, as they come close to conclusion, super-FTA negotiations are not watered down and keep an adequate level of ambition. Once this has happened, it will then be important to find ways to effectively and comprehensively multilateralise the progress FTAs will have made on regulatory convergence and other non-tariff related issues. In this respect the EU can play a critical role, given its weight in the global trade system, the FTA negotiations it is carrying out with key partners, and its commitment to the development of a multilateral trade system. The EU has a strong incentive to move in this direction. With the European recovery stalling, the EU has a lot to gain from successful FTA agreements and further positive developments at multilateral level (and a lot to lose from the current lacklustre global trade performance).

The authors are grateful to Peter Bekx, Malgorzata Galar, Sandra Gallina, Istvan Jakab, Norbert Wunner and Przemyslaw Wozniak for their valuable comments. The views expressed here are those of the authors and they should not be attributed to the European Commission.

M. Bertoldi (✉) · C. Mc Innes
European Commission, Brussels, Belgium
e-mail: Moreno.BERTOLDI@ec.europa.eu

C. Mc Innes
e-mail: Christopher.MC-INNES@ec.europa.eu

L. Paganetto (ed.), *Achieving Dynamism in an Anaemic Europe*,
DOI 10.1007/978-3-319-14099-5_2

1 Introduction

The recovery from the global financial crisis of 2008–2009 has been weak and uneven. World trade, which in past recoveries was a key driver of growth, has remained subdued this time. While trade collapsed in 2009 on a greater scale than during the Great Recession, a "Kindleberger Spiral", i.e. a self-reinforcing spiral of continuously falling international trade fuelled by increasingly protectionist trade policies (Bown 2011), was avoided, not least thanks to decisive commitments taken in the G20 framework and by the rule enforcing role played by the WTO. Nevertheless, trade seems to have lost its pre-crisis dynamism and its ability to support higher GDP growth. At a time when the G20 is trying to provide new momentum to global growth,[1] a key issue is whether trade can become, once again, one of its engines. Trade is also crucial for the recovery in Europe, where, in presence of weak domestic demand and the need to reduce the high levels of public debt, trade agreements can create demand for European companies by opening new markets, boost investor confidence and raise household disposable income.

2 Trade as an Engine of Global Growth

Global trade has historically been an engine of growth. It has been able to do so thanks to its inherent benefits such as enhancing consumer choice and increasing competition, which in turn leads to enhanced firm efficiency and lower prices, specialisation in line with comparative advantages and economies of scale and scope. Crucially, it can enable the efficient allocation of resources across the international economy. Trade today supports millions of jobs, channels large amounts in productive investments and serves as a vector for economic growth and development (WTO 2013).

As a result, the level of world trade is over 10 times higher today than in 1970, compared to world GDP levels only four times higher today than in 1970, as shown in Fig. 1. World trade grew twice as fast on average as world GDP in the 1990s and almost 50 % faster than GDP from 2000 to 2008. The recent boost to trade came from the growing integration of emerging markets into the world economy, declining transport costs, and trade liberalisation. A gradual shift in the structure of the international trade system in order to accommodate growing Global Value Chains (GVC) was also behind this remarkable performance.

[1]In the Sydney G20 Communique, Ministers of Finance and Central Bank Governors committed to the development of "ambitious but realistic policies with the aim to lift our collective GDP by more than 2 % above the trajectory implied by current policies over the coming 5 years. To achieve this we will take concrete actions across the G20, including to (…) enhance trade". Trade is in fact one of the four priority areas to in the Comprehensive Growth Strategies that will form the basis of the G20 Brisbane Action Plan.

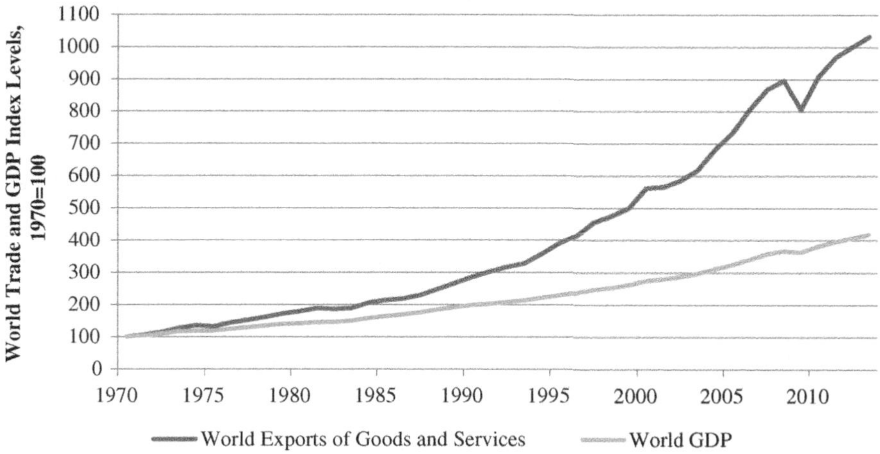

Fig. 1 World trade and GDP levels, 1970–2013. *Source* OECD

Due to its policies in favour of openness, the EU greatly benefitted from trade in the past and has historically been a staunch supporter of trade liberalisation. Its commitment to openness has also served it well in the period that followed the global financial crisis. In particular during the sovereign debt crisis, in presence of declining consumption and investment in a number of countries, trade proved to be the most important source of growth for the Euro area economy, contributing as much as 1 and 1.5 % to GDP growth in 2011 and 2012 respectively, mitigating significantly the impact of the recession (see Fig. 2). This positive impulse was even stronger for vulnerable countries where contributions were as high as 2 and 2.5 % in 2011 and 2012 respectively.[2]

Looking forward, trade has the potential to put Europe on a higher growth path, with positive effects on the rest of the world, creating a win-win situation. In fact, the strengthening of European growth can have positive spillovers on world GDP. According to the IMF Spillover Report (2014a), each additional percentage point of growth in the EU can, on average, lead to 0.13 % additional GDP growth for the rest of the world. ECFIN estimates corroborate the IMF's findings, with each percentage point of EU GDP growth above the baseline potentially contributing between 0.1 and 0.2 % additional GDP growth for the rest of the world.

[2]It is important to note that the significant contribution to growth by trade in the EU/EA was also due to cyclical factors, notably depressed economic demand triggered by the recession, and efforts to regain competitiveness in the vulnerable economies, which moved from large deficit positions to surplus positions. Therefore, the EU/EA is not a special case and would probably have benefitted more from the external sector had trade elasticities remained at their pre-crisis levels. In addition, EU growth can be boosted also by a further increase of the intra-EU trade through the completion of the Single Market. This issue is not developed further in this article, which treats the EU as a single entity in the global economy and therefore looks exclusively at the extra-EU trade.

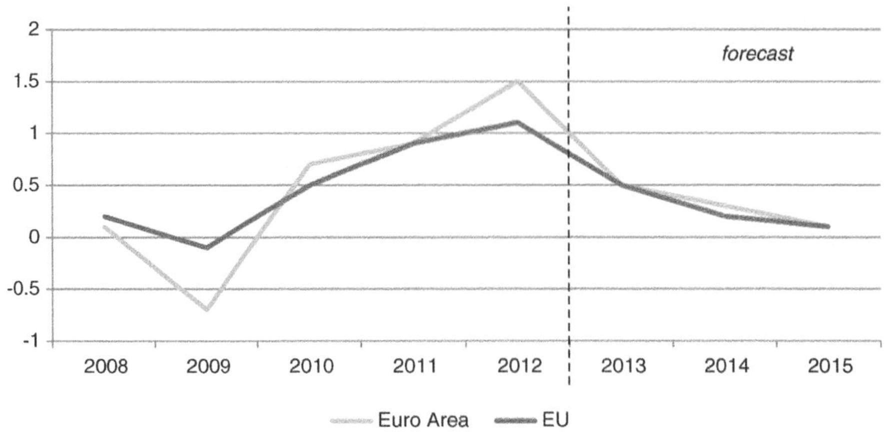

Fig. 2 Contribution of net exports to GDP growth, 2008–2015. *Source* European Commission

The EU's ability to affect world GDP growth positively rests on its centrality in the international trade system, since it is the first trading partner of a large number of countries, over 80 compared to 20 for the US, including the majority of developed countries (EC 2012).[3]

3 The Puzzle of Lower Trade Elasticities

Trade growth has slowed markedly since the start of the crisis, and has even been slightly outpaced by world GDP growth in 2012 and 2013. As a result, the share of trade in world GDP has declined as well. According to Baldwin (2009), trade in past recoveries regained its pre-crisis path within 2–4 quarters, meaning trade should have recovered and continued its upward trajectory in 2010, which has not been the case. Concerted and comprehensive policy action can create new momentum to revive its contribution to growth.

The elasticity of trade has remained below 1 in 2012 and 2013 and is expected to remain low in 2014 as well. This is in stark contrast to elasticity values prior to the economic crisis of 2.2 in the 1990s and 1.5 from 2000 to 2008 (Fig. 3).[4] Such trade growth dynamics in relation to GDP growth suggests that trade has so far failed to show its full potential as a driver of GDP growth is failing to be a positive contributor to GDP growth. It may even imply that trade held global GDP growth back over that period.

---

[3]The EU has a 20 % share of world exports not far from 20 % and retains close to 28 % of global income generated by the production of manufactured goods (European Commission 2013).

[4]A trade elasticity value of less than one indicates that GDP growth outstripped international trade growth. Here, trade elasticity, or intensity, is taken as trade growth over GDP growth.

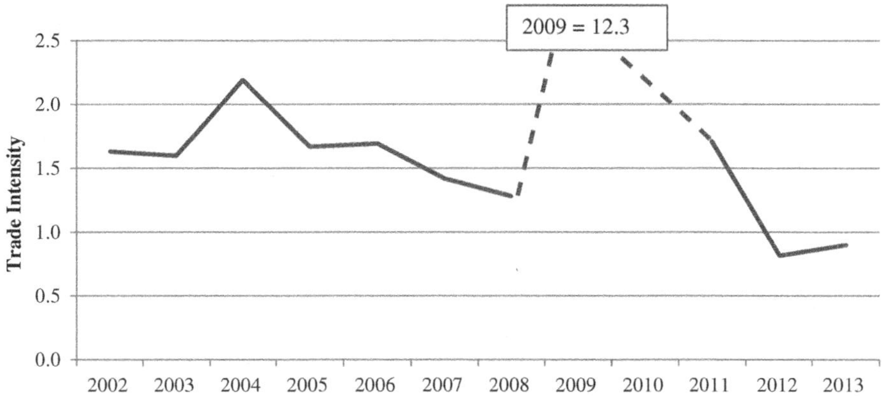

Fig. 3 World trade intensity, 2002–2013. *Source* European commission

As a corollary, international trade as a share of world GDP has failed to regain its pre-crisis dynamism and has declined slightly to around 31 % of world GDP in 2013 after almost returning to its pre-crisis level in 2010. Trade as a share of world GDP rose gradually from 17 to 24 % during the 1986–2000 period and accelerated from 2000 to 2008 to reach a pre-crisis peak of 32 %. The crisis caused trade to drop abruptly to 27 %. It recovered some of the lost ground rapidly, yet has flat lined since 2011 (IMF 2014a, b).

This stagnation of trade at global level can be explained by several factors, although at this stage it is difficult to come up with a fully satisfactory explanation. Baldwin (2009) dwelled extensively on the reasons behind the collapse in trade, notably on the potential negative impact of global supply chains acting as channels for the economic crisis. The uptick and subsequent stagnation in international trade still has not found a fully convincing explanation and a combination of factors seem to interact, although it is difficult to disentangle precisely their relative weight.

Composition effects may have been at play. A weak global recovery in investment levels is one such cause as investment is considered the most trade intensive component of GDP. Advanced countries are the most open economies to export and import investment goods and represent a major share of international trade. Therefore, low investment levels in advanced economies that have failed to regain their pre-crisis trajectory can partly explain the lowering of trade elasticities (Fig. 4).

Against this background, should investment levels pick up again, especially in advanced economies, the trade intensity of global growth could improve markedly. If instead investment takes a long time to recover because of the lingering effects of the financial crisis (Reinhard and Rogoff 2009; Blanchard et al. 2014), then it cannot be excluded that trade elasticities will remain low and trade growth in the coming years will be sluggish.

The reduction in transport costs, which in the past was also a driver in international trade, has recently levelled off. New technologies such the use of the

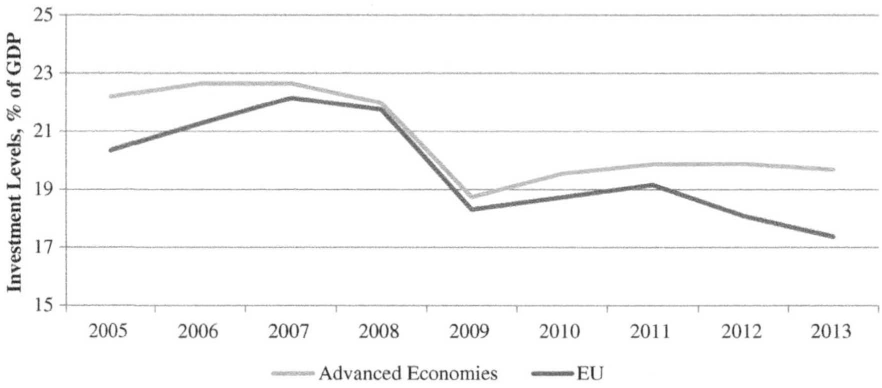

Fig. 4 Investment levels for EU and advanced economies, 2005–2013. *Source* IMF

Internet in the fields of logistics and communication slashed the cost of distance and, as pointed out by Lamy (2014) "[i]t costs less today to ship a container from Marseille to Shanghai than it does to shift to Avignon." Still, these innovations came into fruition in the 1990s and in the early 2000s and a new wave of innovations able to slash further already very low transport costs looks unlikely in the short-term.

International trade has also been weakened by increased uncertainty related to natural disasters and geopolitical uncertainties. As a result, some manufacturers have sought to reduce their exposure to disruptions in the production chains. For instance, the March 2011 earthquake in Japan has shifted some productions back (or closer) to, domestic markets as a form of insurance. The global economic crisis also contributed to the partial unravelling of global supply chains as producers sought to hedge against the risk of regional economic breakdowns, which could negatively affect their supply chain. In addition, global uncertainty related to the global financial crisis has increased the home bias both in terms of production chains and in terms of markets where products are sold.

Lastly, in the wake of the global economic crisis, a number of countries turned to limited protectionist trade policies in an attempt to shield some of their markets from competition and from adverse effects stemming from the crisis. These measures are thought to have affected only 0.6 % of total international trade, but 80 % of these measures were still in place after the worst of the crisis was over (Dadush et al. 2011) It has also been reported that an increasing number of countries have been resorting to 'stealth' or 'murky' protectionism, which flout the spirit of WTO agreements without necessarily breaking the rules (Evenett 2013; Cernat and Madsen 2011). Trade liberalisation and further integration, which has guided trade policy thus far, has therefore been negatively affected. Although there has not been a fully-fledged roll-back in trade liberalisation, in many areas and regions it has stalled.

4 Unlocking the Trade Potential

The inability of trade to regain its pre-crisis dynamism calls for determined policy action. In the remaining part of the article we shall focus on trade policy actions that could provide new momentum to trade growth and make it again an engine of growth for the global economy in general and the EU in particular. Ideally, the preferred and best option would be the finalisation of multilateral trade agreements, *in primis* the Doha Development Round. Historically, first through the GATT and then through the WTO, multilateral trade agreements have proven effective in considerably reducing tariffs across the board, providing a significant boost to international trade.

Yet, the ability of traditional multilateral trade policies to fuel higher growth has plateaued. Tariffs, whose reductions over the previous decade fuelled large increases in international trade, are already at an all-time low (under 5 % on average), and further decreases—already difficult to attain—are unlikely to provide a big boost to international trade. Interestingly, the reduction of administrative constraints and immobilisation at the borders (which was the main deliverable of the deal reached in Bali in December 2013) had a higher potential since on average their cost is twice as high as the cost of custom duties (Lamy 2014).

Therefore, at present, further tariff-based multilateral liberalisation, while certainly useful, does not seem able to move international trade on a significantly higher growth path. In this respect, traditional trade policies based mainly on tariff reduction seem to be approaching (although they are not there yet) the policy equivalent of the zero lower bound in monetary policy, in particular in advanced economies.[5] As a result, returns from further tariff cuts are likely to be limited and show decreasing returns.[6]

While showing (and maybe because of) decreasing returns, the WTO system has also had to face the inability/unwillingness of the various players to agree on an agenda reflecting "new balances, particularly among agricultural disciplines, the reduction of tariffs in the industrial sphere and the opening up of the services market" (Lamy 2014, p. 9). A striking element of this inability or unwillingness to reach a compromise despite strong political guidance in favour of it can be found in the ineffectiveness of G20 Leaders' statements in 2009–2010 urging a rapid conclusion of the Doha Round,[7] at a time when trade revitalisation could have provided a significant boost to desperately needed global growth.

---

[5]Average tariff level in the US is about 2 and 3 % in the EU.

[6]These developments call for a rethinking of the multilateral trade system, which should evolve towards a WTO 2.0 (Baldwin 2012) more able to take into account the supply dimension of international trade and be more focus on regulatory and non-tariff barriers.

[7]At the London Summit in London in April 2009, G20 Leaders stated: "We remain committed to reaching an ambitious and balanced conclusion of the Doha Development Round, which is urgently needed. This could boost the global economy by at least $150 billion per annum. To achieve this we are committed to building on the progress already made, including with regard to modalities". The importance of concluding the Doha Round was restated in the Pittsburgh G20

Against this background, it is clear that the setback on the conclusion of the Round has deep roots related both to the consequences related to the shift of political and economic weight in the global economy and, even more importantly, the changing nature of the trade system. As pointed out by Baldwin (2014), "the trade system is being used to make goods, rather than simply sell them. The resulting transformation of international commerce and commercial policy triggered a paradigm shift." Global value chains have increasingly come to dominate and shape the current international trade system and new trade rules have appeared (Galar 2012). "[T]hese supply-chain trade rules have been, and continue to be, written outside the WTO. The supply chain governance gap is being filled by uncoordinated developments in deep regional trade agreements, bilateral investment treaties, and autonomous reforms in emerging economies. In particular, the existing deep RTAs signed by the big outsourcing nations—especially the US, Japan and the EU—have set a template for the sort of disciplines that seem necessary. Mega-regionals like TPP are trying to harmonise the rules across a broad range of nations… Even if TPP ultimately fails or slips into limbo, the TPP negotiations have already strongly conditioned the shape of harmonised rules that will eventually emerge" (Baldwin 2012, p. 10).

As such, bilateral and regional free trade agreements have become large countries' preferred policy for further trade liberalisation. Since 2000, 199 FTAs came into force, from a total of 377 FTAs in force (WTO 2014). FTAs cover 60 % of international trade. Recently, a number of "super" FTAs have started to be negotiated: the Transatlantic Trade and Investment Partnership (TTIP), the Transpacific Partnership (TPP), the Regional Comprehensive Economic Partnership (CEP). Some important FTAs have already been concluded, such as the EU-South Korea Free Trade Agreement and the US-South Korea Free Trade Agreement or are in the final stages of adoption, such as the EU-Canada Comprehensive Economic and Trade Agreement.

However, there is the risk that the gradual rise in prominence of FTAs as the preferred tool of trade liberalisation will have negative effects that might overshadow their potential benefit. According to standard international trade economics this type of trade arrangement is considered a second best, which has important negative side

(Footnote 7 continued)
Leaders' Communique of September 2009: "We are committed to bringing the Doha Round to a successful conclusion in 2010" and in the Toronto Communique of June 2010: "We are committed to bringing the Doha Round to a successful conclusion in 2010. We therefore reiterate our support for bringing the WTO Doha Development Round to a balanced and ambitious conclusion as soon as possible, consistent with its mandate and based on the progress already made". Finally, in Seoul in November 2010 G20 Leaders used an even stronger language: "Our strong commitment to direct our negotiations to engage in across-the-board negotiations to promptly bring the Doha Development Round to a successful, ambitious, comprehensive and balanced conclusion consistent with the mandate of the Doha Development Round and built on the progress already achieved. We recognise that 2011 is a critical window of opportunity, albeit narrow, and that engagement among our representatives must intensify and expand. We now need to complete the end game", to no avail.

effects, such as exclusion and trade diversion. Therefore, countries that are not part of a trade agreement might see their trade performance negatively affected as trade is rerouted to countries that are part of FTAs.

In addition, a proliferation of FTAs might lead to a "spaghetti-bowl" international trade architecture (Baghwati 1995). As a result, FTAs' might start overlapping, creating inefficiencies between competing agreements. This type of architecture might make the multilateral harmonisation of standards more difficult, as standards diverge and multiply, undermining multilateral harmonisation efforts altogether. Last but not least, Baldwin (2012) sees the growing trend in value chain tailored FTAs posing the risk of fragmenting international trade, as not all WTO members are actively part of global value chains.

Still, in the current situation characterised by a political stalemate on the Doha Development Round, FTAs may also present significant advantages. FTAs have the ability to pioneer the future of the international trade system.[8] They focus on 21st century trade policy issues, notably taking into account the development of global supply chains, which have come to define and explain the boom in international trade since the mid-1990s. In this respect, regional FTAs can lay the groundwork for regulatory standards that can then be more easily adopted at the multilateral level (Cernat 2013; Acharya 2013).

By pioneering these issues on a smaller, regional or bilateral scale, they can serve as platforms for improved multilateral trade conditions. Moreover, non-members can in fact benefit from rather positive spillovers stemming from FTAs in their region (DeRosa and Hufbauer 2007). In addition, it has been found that global supply chains are more accurately described as regional value chains: supply chains are much more sensitive to distance than trade in final goods. International supply chains require machine and personnel interaction, which itself requires extensive travel, restricting the geographical scope of supply chain development (Baldwin 2012).

An additional significant advantage of FTAs is their ability to accommodate the 21st century imperatives of international trade, going beyond the simple focus on tariffs (OECD, WTO and UNCTAD 2013). FTAs today still focus on tariffs but also on sanitary and phytosanitary and technical barriers to trade issues, regulatory cooperation, services, investment, and public procurement markets, amongst many other areas. FTAs have a much broader scope and can therefore better accommodate an international trade system that has shifted from a "produce to trade" approach to a "trade to produce" reality.

[8]This role cannot be filled at the moment by the WTO. As noted by Baldwin (2012), "Without a conclusion to the Round, it seems politically impossible for the WTO to move on to new issues, i.e., to address the deeper disciplines needed to underpin supply-chain trade. The reason is that few WTO members have a significant stake in supply-chain trade and many have a stake in setting market access and agriculture issues. The latter fear that talk of 'new issues' is another way for rich nations to (once again) avoid opening their markets to the goods in which developing nations have their comparative advantage" (p. 10).

Sooner or later, WTO members will have to address the issue of how the proliferation of RTAs and FTAs can be partially reconciled and try to find at least a partial reconciliation with the multilateral trade system. Otherwise it will become increasingly difficult to avoid the "spaghetti-bowl effect" preconized by Baghwati and, even more importantly, the fragmentation of the global trade governance system. RTAs and FTAs should not become an alternative to the multilateral trade system, which has still the potential to play a leading role in developing a coherent framework for 21st century trade (Baldwin 2012; Hoekman 2014; Lamy 2014).

5 The Transatlantic Trade and Investment Partnership (TTIP): A 21st Century Trade Agreement?

The broad scope of Regional Trade Agreements (RTAs) between large economies, with a particular focus on regulatory convergence across many different product and service markets, has certainly a higher potential than tariff reduction to provide new momentum to international trade. In addition, it tackles issues relevant to today's digital economy, where non-tariff barriers hamper flows of goods, services and capital between the two sides of the Atlantic. Against this background, and in presence of a global slow-down in trade and the gridlock in multilateral trade negotiations, the currently negotiated agreement between the EU and the United States stands out—together with the Trans-Pacific Partnership—as the most ambitious venture in regional trade liberalisation. Its successful completion would create the largest free trade area in the world. Therefore, it is not by chance that TTIP has from day one been billed as a "21st century" trade agreement.

Still, since its launch the TTIP has been faced with strong opposition. Many consider it neither feasible nor desirable, since they consider that (i) it weakens the multilateral trade system; (ii) it is overambitious, lacks focus and the rules of the game are not clear; (iii) it lacks transparency; (iv) it could trigger a race to the bottom, in particular in the areas of labour standards and safety regulations; (v) it deals with issues that should not be part of trade negotiations and that should be changed only as there is a political consensus and not because of a trade agreement. It is understandable that the nature and scope of the trade agreement currently negotiated raises concerns that need to be addressed on both sides of the Atlantic. In particular, it is important to make sure that the negotiations do not impinge on what belongs to the realm of domestic political choices and that therefore cannot be part of a trade deal.[9]

---

[9]An excellent review of the criticism addressed to TTIP and its cost and benefits of TTIP is included in the UK House of Lords Report "The Transatlantic Trade and Investment Partnership" published on 13 May 2014. A critical assessment of the challenges that the new type of negotiations implied by the TTIP specific nature can be found in Fabry et al. (2014), "TTIP: Une negociation a la Pirandello", Notre Europe and in Defraigne (2014), "Departing from TTIP and going plurilateral", Madariaga-College of Europe Foundation, October.

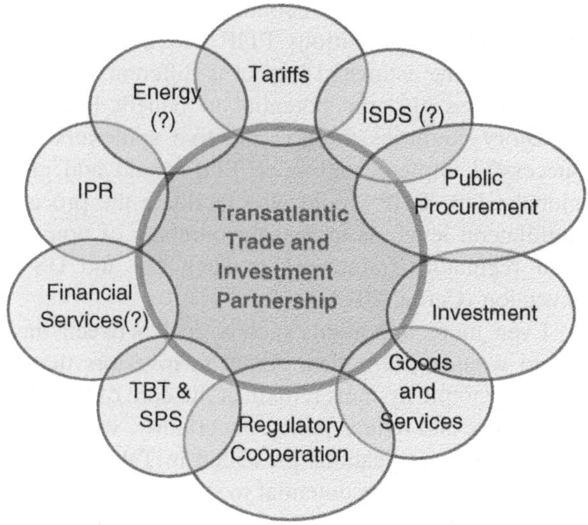

Fig. 5 TTIP and its ingredients. *Source* Authors

In addition, the focus on non-tariff barriers to trade has left open the issue of what should be included in the agreement and what should be kept out (Fig. 5). For instance the EU was strongly in favour of having financial services in TTIP, while the US was reluctant to achieve strong regulatory convergence in this area. On the other hand, some European countries (as well as NGOs) have strong reservations in putting in place a framework for the investor-state dispute settlement (ISDS) mechanism, since it is feared that it would trigger costly litigation disputes between EU countries and US companies, and become a tool for big corporations to challenge domestic regulations.

Despite these concerns and agenda setting problems, TTIP represents nevertheless a substantial opportunity to bring back trade to the central stage. First of all, TTIP has the potential to have a significant, positive economic impact on the EU and US economies. Because it aims to impact both supply and demand on both sides of the Atlantic, TTIP can be a powerful tool to boost growth both in the short and in the medium-term (Fontagne et al. 2013; Galar 2013). Table 1 presents

Table 1 EU and US GDP and trade forecasts from selected publications

	ECORYS	EC (CEPR)	BIS (CEPR)	CEPII
Benchmark year	2018	2027	2027	2025
Change in US GDP (%)	0.30	0.40	0.40	0.30
Change in EU GDP (%)	0.70	0.50	0.70	0.30
Change in total US exports (%)	6.10	8	7.50	10.10
Change in total EU exports (%)	2.10	5.00	n.a.	2.30

Source European Commission, ECORYS, BIS, CEPII, CEPR

various estimates of the economic impact on the EU and the US of a successful conclusion of an ambitious TTIP. The models used are not the same and therefore the size of the estimated impact is different, but in all cases is far from negligible.

TTIP has also the potential to benefit both GDP and trade growth of non-signatory countries through positive spillovers. According to one estimate, the successful implementation of TTIP could add an additional €100 billion to the global GDP. TTIP would also facilitate the process of regulatory convergence at multilateral level, as increasing numbers of non-signatory countries seek to align their regulatory framework to keep EU and US markets open and avoid trade diversion (Cernat 2013).

Even more important, such a deal between the two largest economies in the world would send a clear signal to investors that the principles of free trade and open economic systems remain at the core of the global economy. This would boost confidence and reduce policy uncertainty, with positive spillovers that would come above the quantifications presented in Table 1.

TTIP has also the potential to strengthen the domestic pro-growth policy agenda in the US and in the EU. In the US, where, according to impact assessment studies, exports would be boosted to a larger extent than in the EU (see Table 1) this would strengthen the private sector-led recovery under way, contribute to the rebalancing of the US economy and support the revitalisation of the manufacturing sector (which would be among the major beneficiaries of a successful conclusion of TTIP negotiations—see Francois et al. 2013). In the case of the EU, the agreement would create additional demand for the export sector, with positive spillovers on private investment. TTIP would also support the strategy to raise investment in the period 2015–2017 through a number of policy actions at national and European level. Last but not least, Euro area vulnerable countries, which regained competitiveness through difficult and painful structural reforms, would probably be among the main beneficiaries of a successful TTIP agreement and this would translate in stronger growth and employment. Therefore, if TTIP[10] becomes part of a coherent set of policy measures aimed at strengthening both the demand and the supply side of the European economy, its dividends can be particularly important and contribute to move the EU on a badly needed higher growth path.

Lastly, through regulatory convergence, trade related costs should fall for both the EU and US, as well as for third countries. By reducing the cost of compliance for firms across the free trade area and beyond, TTIP offers a way to keep the downward pressure on trade related costs alive, after tariff and transport reductions seemingly levelled off in recent years. Should TTIP lead to a comprehensive multilateral convergence push, these costs will be reduced across the international

[10]These considerations also apply to other trade and investment agreement under negotiations, e.g., the EU-Japan Free Trade Agreement or the EU-China Investment Agreement.

trade system, with the potential to kick start trade growth once again, especially considering its appropriateness for the further development of global value chains.

Against this background, TTIP could become a game changer in the international trade system. On the one hand, it can set a high standard precedent for future trade and investment agreements, thereby unlocking the existing potential for trade liberalisation. On the other hand, if implemented in a non-exclusionary manner, it also has the potential to give multilateral trade negotiations much needed momentum and could contribute to eventually bringing the Doha round to a successful conclusion (Galar 2013). However, to keep its promise, TTIP must produce an ambitious agreement. Should this not be the case, some of the expected positive impacts could move into reverse. For instance an agreement that would disappoint expectations would weaken confidence and increase policy uncertainty, since investors would question the strength of EU and US commitments to free trade and to boost further international trade in future.

6 Conclusions

In recent years the contribution of international trade to global growth has weakened. Several economic factors have affected this unsatisfactory performance: weak investment, levelling off of transport costs, partial reversal of global value chains. In addition, even if during the crisis damaging protectionist policies have been avoided, policymakers failed to conclude the WTO Doha Development Round and to promote further multilateral trade liberalisation. Still, these developments do not imply that policy tools are not available to reverse the trend.

While the conditions to conclude ambitious multilateral trade negotiations are not in place, there is room and political capital to finalise 'super' FTAs (like TTIP) that can unlock the trade potential and support GDP growth in the future. Should this happen, trade can become again one of the major engines of growth of the global economy. It is not by chance that in the G20 growth strategies trade was identified, together with investment, competition and employment, as a crucial growth pillar. The main challenge ahead will be to ensure that, as they come close to conclusion, super-FTA negotiations are not watered down and keep an adequate level of ambition. Once this has happened, it will then be important to find ways to effectively and comprehensively multilateralise the progress FTAs will have made on regulatory convergence and other non-tariff related issues.

In this respect the EU can play a critical role, given its weight in the global trade system, the FTA trade and investment negotiations it is carrying out with key partners (US, Japan, China, etc.) and its commitment to the development of a multilateral trade system. The EU has also a strong incentive to move in this direction. With the European recovery stalling, the EU has a lot to gain from successful FTAs agreements and further positive developments at multilateral level (and a lot to lose from the current lacklustre global trade performance).

References

Acharya, R. 2013. Multilateralisation of trade agreement. In *The future of the world trading system: Asian perspectives*, ed. R. Baldwin, M. Kawai, and G. Wignaraja, 155–160. London: Vox Ebook.

Baldwin, R. 2014. Multilateralising 21st Century Regionalism. Voxeu.org.

Baldwin, R. 2009. The Great Trade Collapse: What Caused It And What Does It Mean? Voxeu.org.

Baldwin, R. 2012. WTO 2.0: Global governance of supply-chain trade. CEPR Policy Insight No. 64. Centre for Economic Policy Research.

Bhagwati, J. 1995. US Trade Policy: The Infatuation with FTAs. Columbia University Discussion Paper Series 726.

Blanchard, O., D. Furceri, and A. Pescatori. 2014. A prolonged period of low real interest rates? In *Secular stagnation: facts, causes and cures*, ed. C. Teuligns, and R. Baldwin, 101–110. London: Vox Ebook.

Bown, C. 2011. Import Protection and the Great Recession. Voxeu.org.

Centre for Economic Policy Research. 2013. Estimating the Economic Impact on the UK of Transatlantic Partnership Agreement Between the European Union and the United States. CEPR Report prepared for the Department for Business, Innovation and Skills.

Cernat, L., and M.R. Madsen. 2011. "Murky Protectionism" and Behind-the-Border Barriers: How Big an Issue? The €100 Billion Question. Voxeu.org.

Cernat, L. 2013. TPP, TTIP and Multilateralism: Stepping Stones or Oceans Apart? Voxeu.org.

Dadush, U., S. Ali, and R. Esplin Odell. 2011. Is Protectionism Dying? Voxeu.org.

Defraigne, P. 2014. Departing from TTIP and going plurilateral. Madariaga-College of Europe Foundation, October.

DeRosa, D.A., and G.C. Hufbauer. (2007). What Do Gravity Models Tell Us About PTAs Impact on Trade Flows: More Creation or More Diversion? Voxeu.org.

Ecorys. 2009. Non-Tariff Measures in EU-US Trade and Investment—An Economic Analysis. Report prepared by K. Berden, J.F. Francois, S. Tamminen, M. Thelle, and P. Wymenga for the European Commission.

European Commission. 2012. Why the European Union is an essential Trade Partner.

European Commission. 2013. Trade: A key Source of growth and Jobs for the EU. Commission Contribution to the European Council of 7–9 Feb 2013.

European Commission. 2014. Spring 2014 European Economic Forecast.

Evenett, S.J. 2013. Protectionism's Quiet Return: GTA's Pre-G8 Summit Report. Global Trade Alert and Centre for Economic Policy Research.

Fabry, E., G. Garbasso, and R. Pardo. 2014. TTIP: Une Negociation a la Pirandello. Synthese. Notre Europe.

Francois, J., Manchin, M., Norberg, H., O. Pindyuk, and P. Tomberger. 2013. Reducing Transatlantic Barriers to Trade and Investment: An Economic Assessment. Centre for Economic Policy Research.

Fontagne, L., J. Gourdon, and S. Jean. 2013. Transatlantic Trade: Whither Partnership, Which Economic Consequence. CEPII Policy Brief No. 1. Centre d'Etudes Prospectives et d'Informations Internationales.

Galar M. 2012. Competing within global value chains. ECFIN Economic Brief, n. 17.

Galar M. 2013. EU Trade Negotiations from a Global Chain Perspective. ECFIN Economic Brief, n. 28.

Hoekman, B. 2014. Supply chains, mega-regionals and the WTO: New CEPR book. Voxeu.org.

IMF. 2014a. Spillover Report, Washington DC.

IMF. 2014b. World Economic Outlook Statistical Database, Washington DC.

House of Lords. 2014. The Transatlantic Trade and Investment Partnership. Authority of the House of Lords.

Lamy, P. 2014. The World Trade Organisation: New Issues, New Challenges. Policy Paper 117. Notre Europe.

OECD Statistical Database.

OECD, WTO and UNCTAD. 2013. Implications of Global Value Chains for Trade, I Investment, Development and Jobs. Report Prepared for the G-20 Leaders Summit Saint Petersburg.

Reinhart, C., and K. Rogoff. 2009. *This time is different: eight centuries of financial folly*. Princeton: Princeton University Press.

WTO. 2013. The Future of Trade: The Challenges of Convergence. Report of the Panel on Defining the Future of Trade convened by WTO Director-General Pascal Lamy.

WTO. 2014. Regional Trade Agreements Information System.

Trade Margins and Exchange Rate Regimes: New Evidence from a Panel VARX Model

Lilia Cavallari and Stefano D'Addona

Abstract This paper studies the dynamics of output and export margins in the aftermath of external shocks in fixed and floating exchange rate regimes. Using a panel VARX model, it traces the mean responses of output, terms of trade, extensive and intensive margins to real and nominal shocks in 22 developed economies over the period 1988–2011. It finds remarkable differences in the transmission of shocks depending on the exchange rate regimes. Overall, our findings provide novel evidence in support of the stabilization advantages of flexible exchange rates based on their ability to smooth extensive margins. These findings are consistent with the predictions of theoretical models with firm entry.

1 Introduction

It is a well-established fact that a relevant fraction of the growth in trade volumes occurs at the extensive margin, with exports of new products and previously non-traded goods (see Kehoe and Ruhl 2013). The relevance of product creation and destruction for overall production is amply documented. Bernard et al. (2010) show that the value of new products represents 34 % of US output over a 5-year horizon and the lost value from product destruction over the same period is 30 %. The importance of product creation and destruction is confirmed by Broda and Weinstein (2010), who use the finest possible level of disaggregation: the product barcode. In addition, they report that product creation is strongly pro-cyclical at quarterly business cycle frequency. Inspired by these facts, a new generation of DSGE models has emerged stressing the business cycle implications of product

L. Cavallari · S. D'Addona (✉)
Department of Political Science, University of Rome 3, Via G. Chiabrera, 199, 00145 Rome, Italy
e-mail: daddona@uniroma3.it

L. Cavallari
e-mail: lilia.cavallari@uniroma3.it

L. Paganetto (ed.), *Achieving Dynamism in an Anaemic Europe*,
DOI 10.1007/978-3-319-14099-5_3

creation and destruction.[1] In these models, product creation (destruction) is proxied by firm entry (exit). In open economies, exports of new products and previously non-traded goods may affect the propagation of shocks worldwide in important dimensions. Yet evidence on the role of trade margins for the transmission of shocks is still very limited. This paper aims to bridge the gap.

The paper provides a description of the dynamics of output and trade in the aftermath of external shocks in fixed and floating exchange rate regimes. It traces the responses of output, terms of trade, intensive and extensive export margins to real and nominal shocks in twenty-two developed economies over the period 1988–2011. Its purpose is to study the role of trade margins in the propagation of shocks and their implications for the stabilization properties of flexible exchange rates. In departing from previous studies, the paper allows trade flows to adjust at the extensive and the intensive margin. Extensive margins reflect trade of new products and previously non-traded goods while intensive margins represent trade of previously traded goods.

The study is based on a panel VARX model with country pair fixed effects. The vector of endogenous variables includes real output, terms of trade and export margins, measured on a country pair basis. The exogenous variables vector, common to all country pairs, comprises US output, US consumer prices, energy prices and the Federal funds rate. The model is semi-structural: external shocks are identified by means of a recursive ordering of the exogenous variables while domestic shocks are left unidentified. Using a bootstrap-bias corrected estimator as in Pesaran and Zhao (1999), we trace the mean responses of the dependent variables to external shocks in the full sample. In order to study the role of the exchange rate regime, we estimate the model separately for the samples of peggers and floaters and provide a formal test of heterogeneity across exchange rate regimes.

This paper makes two main contributions to the literature. First, it provides new evidence in support of the stabilization properties of flexible exchange rates. Since Friedman (1953), an advantage typically attributed to flexible exchange rates over fixed regimes is their ability to insulate the economy against real shocks. In a world with sticky prices, changes in the nominal exchange rate allow for larger movements in relative prices that help to smooth adjustment of output to real shocks. An empirical implication of this theory is that the responses to real shocks should differ across exchange rate regimes: flexible regimes should have smoother output (quantity) responses and quicker adjustments in relative prices compared to fixed regimes. Advocates of fixed exchange rates, on the other side, point out that exchange rate variability exacerbates business cycle fluctuations in the wake of nominal shocks. More importantly, it may discourage trade flows. One of the major reason for adopting fixed exchange rates, especially hard pegs, in the first place is

[1]Non-exhaustive examples include Ghironi and Melitz (2005), Corsetti et al. (2007, 2013) and Bilbiie et al. (2012).

their ability to promote trade.[2] The stabilization advantages of flexible exchange rates may be more than offset by trade diversion towards countries with fixed exchange rates. Recent studies document that fixed exchange rates have indeed had a positive effect on the creation of new export varieties, i.e. on extensive margins.[3] This adds a new dimension to the old debate on the choice of the exchange rate regime: as long as fixed exchange rates help to smooth extensive margins, one might observe smoother quantity responses and quicker adjustment in relative prices in fixed regimes in contrast to the Friedman's hypothesis. As far as we know, this paper is the first attempt to gauge the role of trade margins for output stabilization. We find that the mean responses of output in the sample of peggers are significantly larger than in the sample of floaters for all the shocks considered, supporting the Friedman's hypothesis. The finding rests on the extreme reactivity of extensive margins in fixed regimes: the mean responses of extensive margins in fixed regimes are between twice and four times as large as the responses in floating regimes depending on the type of shock. In addition, these responses are fairly persistent.

Second, the paper helps to bring to the data the predictions of international business cycle models with firm entry.[4] As is now well-understood, entry and the creation of new varieties affect the transmission of shocks along a number of dimensions. Investments at the extensive margin act as a business cycle amplifier and help to improve the performance of these models at replicating key facts in the data. Cavallari (2013) shows that entry provides a channel for positive international comovements: a business cycle expansion in one country leads to the creation of new varieties in the trading partner's market. One should therefore observe a positive response of extensive margins to external output shocks. We find that this is indeed the case in our data. In addition, these models suggest that exchange rate variability may affect the extent to which exporters adjust trade at the extensive and the intensive margin. First-time entry in foreign markets and the creation of new products entail sunk entry costs, implying a much longer horizon and a greater exposure to exchange rate risk than investments at the intensive margin. Fixed exchange rate regimes should therefore be associated with a high volatility of extensive margins. In the model of Bergin and Lin (2012), all of the adjustment of trade occurs at the extensive margin when exchange rate uncertainty is completely and permanently eliminated. A comparison of responses in the samples of peggers and floaters confirms this prediction.

[2]Despite a long history of failures to find a robust relation between exchange rate variability and trade, Rose (1999) has revived the debate by showing that the adoption of a currency union raises bilateral trade by a large amount. Subsequent research has supported the statistical significance, if not the magnitude of this result.

[3]See, among others, Bergin and Lin (2012) and Auray et al. (2012).

[4]Since the seminal study of Melitz (2003), a number of papers have investigated the implications of entry for the international business cycle. Open economy models with firm entry include, among others, Bergin and Glick (2007), Ghironi and Melitz (2005), Cavallari (2007, 2010, 2013) and Corsetti et al. (2007, 2013).

The remainder of the paper is organized as follows. Section 2 describes the data and presents the econometric methodology. Section 3 discusses the main results and Sect. 4 concludes.

2 Empirical Strategy

2.1 Data

We use annual data for 23 OECD countries over the period 1988–2011.[5] This is dictated by the frequency of trade data. Output—which accounts for the general macroeconomic conditions—is proxied by year-on-year GDP growth rates. Prices are proxied by inflation (GDP deflator, CPI and energy prices). US monetary policy is captured by the Federal funds rate. All these data are from the OECD StatExtracts database. The terms of trade are from the IFS-IMF database or the World Bank upon availability. These are defined as the price of a country's exports towards the world divided by the price of its imports from the world. An increase in the terms of trade is therefore an appreciation.

Trade margins are from the UN Comtrade database.[6] They are calculated from bilateral trade measures at the four-digit Standard International Trade Classification. Following Hummels and Klenow (2005), the extensive margin of exports from country j to country m is defined as:

$$XM_m^j = \frac{\sum_{i \in I_m^j} X_{m,i}^W}{X_m^W} \tag{1}$$

where $X_{m,i}^W$ is the export value from the world to country m of category i, I_m^j is the set of observable categories in which country j has positive exports to country m, and X_m^W is the aggregate value of world exports to country m. The extensive margin is a weighted sum of country j's exported categories relative to all categories exported to country m, where the categories are weighted by their importance in world's exports to country m. XM_m^j is a positive index between 0 and 1, where higher values of the index reflect a larger variety of categories exported.

The intensive margin of exports from country j to country m is defined as:

$$IM_m^j = \frac{X_m^j}{\sum_{i \in I_m^j} X_{m,i}^W} \tag{2}$$

---

[5]The countries included are: Australia, Belgium, Canada, Czech Republic, Denmark, Finland, France, Germany, Iceland, Italy, Japan, Korea, Luxembourg, Netherlands, Portugal, Spain, Sweden, Mexico, New Zealand, Norway, Switzerland, United Kingdom and the United States.

[6]http://wits.worldbank.org/wits/.

where X_m^j is the total export value from country j to country m. The intensive margin is the value of j's exports to country m relative to the weighted categories in which country j exports to country m. IM_m^j is a positive index between 0 and infinity, where 0 means that country j has not previously exported to country m, and where higher values of the index reflect a larger volume of exports within previously traded goods. By definition, the country j's share of world exports to country m is given by the product of the intensive and extensive margins:

$$Sh_m^j = \frac{X_m^j}{X_{m,i}^W} = XM_m^j IM_m^j \tag{3}$$

The measurement implies that for a given level of a country j's share in world exports to country m, the extensive margin would be higher if country j exports many different categories of products to country m whereas the intensive margin would be higher if it only export a few categories of products.

2.2 Panel VARX

The analysis is based on a multivariate dynamic panel data model, i.e. a panel VAR model, which includes macroeconomic and trade time series by country pairs. The model takes the following form:

$$Y_{it} = \alpha_i + \beta(L)Y_{it-1} + \gamma(L)X_t + \varepsilon_{it} \tag{4}$$

$$X_t = a + b(L)X_{t-1} + e_t \tag{5}$$

for each country pair $i = j \times m$ and time t.[7] The vector of endogenous variables Y_{it} contains output, terms of trade and any one of the extensive and intensive margin, i.e. $Y_{it} = (\Delta \log TOT_{it}, \Delta \log GDP_{it}, XM_{it})$ or $Y_{it} = (\Delta \log TOT_{it}, \Delta \log GDP_{it}, IM_{it})$ where Δ denotes the first-difference operator. α_i is a vector of country pair fixed effects; $\beta(L)$ and $\gamma(L)$ are matrix polynomials of slopes in the lag operator; ε_{it} is the vector of errors in the system. The exogenous variables vector X_t, common to all country pairs, includes US output, US consumer prices, energy prices and the Federal funds rate, i.e. $X_t = (\Delta \log GDP_t^{US}, \Delta \log CPI_t^{US}, \Delta \log Energy_t, FFR_t)$. a is a vector of intercepts, $b(L)$ is a matrix polynomial in the lag operator; e_t is the vector of exogenous errors with variance $E(e_t e_t') = \Sigma$ for all t.[8]

The analysis focuses on the transmission of common shocks to output and export margins. We also include in the VAR model the terms of trade and energy prices as

[7]In our notation $j = 1, 2, \ldots, N$ is the exporting country, $m = 1, 2, \ldots, M$ with $m \neq j$ denotes the destination country. The total number of country pairs is 22×22 as the set of destination countries includes the US.

[8]The exogenous VAR model is estimated over the period 1970–2011 in order to improve efficiency.

additional controls for substantial country heterogeneity regarding trade openness and the capacity to affect prices in global markets. Moreover, they represent global forces that might influence the dependent variables and omitting them can lead to serious estimation bias (see Forni and Reichlin 1998). Based on a formal test of exogeneity, we include the terms of trade among endogenous variables while energy prices are considered exogenous. The presence of energy prices in the vector of exogenous variables has an additional advantage. Energy prices typically belong to the information set of central banks and omitting them can cause a price puzzle, i.e., a counter-factual increase in inflation after a rise in the monetary policy rate.

In Eq. (4) we assume the homogeneous error structure $E(\varepsilon_{it}\varepsilon'_{it}) = \Omega$ for all i and t. Furthermore, we assume independence of the errors within the equations, $E(\varepsilon_{is}\varepsilon'_{it}) = 0$ for $s \neq t$, and across equations, $E(\varepsilon_{is}\varepsilon'_{ht}) = 0$ for any s and t when $i \neq h$. These assumptions are less restrictive that it might appear at first. Variance homogeneity, i.e. the fact that the shocks hitting different countries have the same magnitude, and the assumption that the shocks are not correlated across countries are inconsequential for the scope of the analysis, which is focused on the transmission of common shocks more than on spillovers across countries. In our analysis, it is more important to allow for slope heterogeneity, so that countries may respond differently to a common shock. In the estimation, we allow the slopes and the contemporaneous impact matrix to be different for the two sets of countries that we consider (peggers and floaters) and we restrict them to be common within each set of countries. This implies that Eq. (4) changes as follows:

$$Y_{r,it} = \alpha_{r,i} + \beta_{r,i}(L)Y_{r,it-1} + \gamma_{r,i}(L)X_t + \varepsilon_{r,it} \tag{6}$$

where $r = p$ or f indicates a regime of pegged of floating exchange rates. For each regime r, we estimate the model with country pair fixed effects. Over a short time span, this framework provides a convenient balance between pooling diverse information from all countries and controlling for the required level of heterogeneity. The group of "peggers" includes all country pairs with a fixed exchange rate regime (i.e., to be included in the sample of peggers both origin and destination countries must adopt a fixed exchange rate regime in our classification). It contains European country pairs and reflects intra-EMU trade. The sample of " floaters" includes pairs with a flexible exchange rate (i.e. to be included among the floaters at least one country must adopt a flexible exchange rate regime in our classification). We test the null of parameter homogeneity across the two groups of countries against the alternative assumed by our specification in Eq. (6) using the bootstrapping methods in Born et al. (2013).

After controlling for fixed effects, the multiplier form of the model can be written as:

$$Y_{it} = (I - \beta(L))^{-1}\gamma(L)X_t + \beta(L)^{-1}\varepsilon_{it} \tag{7}$$

$$Y_{r,it} = \left(I - \beta_{r,i}(L)\right)^{-1}\gamma_{r,i}(L)X_t + \beta_{r,t}(L)^{-1}\varepsilon_{r,it}$$

in, respectively, the full sample and the two sub-samples.

The mean responses to external shocks are captured by the lag polynomial $(I - \beta(L))^{-1}\gamma(L)$. As pointed out by Nickell (1981), the least-squares dummy variable (LSDV) estimator or within (fixed-effect) estimator is inconsistent in dynamic models with small T, even if the number of countries goes to infinity, and the bias decreases as T grows. Given the limited time span in our data, we employ the bootstrap-bias corrected estimator (BSBC) in Pesaran and Zhao (1999). As stressed by these authors, a bootstrap strategy is appealing compared to analytical corrections for a number of reasons. First and foremost, it does not require theoretical assumptions on the model. Specifically, analytical corrections imply assumptions on the short-run coefficients of the model that may be hard to reconcile with non-linear responses. Second, the bootstrap approach provides a direct correction of the mean responses while analytical corrections use short-run coefficients. We follow Fomby et al. (2013) in adapting the bootstrap algorithm of Pesaran and Zhao (1999) to our unbalanced panel.

For the sake of imposing minimum restrictions and in accord with the scope of the analysis, which is focused on common shocks, we leave country-specific shocks unidentified.[9] Identification of external shocks is achieved by assuming a contemporaneous recursive ordering where exogenous variables are ordered as given in the definition of X_t. This entails the assumption that US output does not react to a contemporaneous innovation in the Federal funds rate either directly or through the effect of the policy rate on energy and consumer prices. The Federal funds rate, on the contrary, reacts to a contemporaneous change in any other variable in the system. Zero contemporaneous restrictions of this type are standard in structural VAR models (see Christiano et al. 1999). We have experimented alternative identification strategies, based on long-run and sign restrictions, with no major consequences for the results.

2.3 Diagnostic Tests

The model in the previous section rests on the assumption of stationarity of the variables. Before we can proceed to estimate the model, we need to determine the stationary form of the variables that will be used. To this end we perform individual and panel unit root tests on the following variables: the log of output, the log of the terms of trade, the level of external and internal margins, the level of the Federal funds rate and the log of energy and consumer prices. We use the log transformation whenever possible for two reasons. The first is the well-known variance stabilizing property of the log transformation. The second is that if a unit root is

[9]We tried several recursive orderings of the endogenous vector in the VARX model. This did not significantly change our results.

contained in the logged variables, then differencing them provides a straightforward interpretation of the differenced data as percentage change.

The individual unit root tests are the Augmented Dickey-Fuller (ADF) test and the Phillips-Perron (PP) test applied on a series-by-series basis. The panel unit root test is the ADF test in the model with individual country effects as in Levin et al. (2002). All these unit root tests are dependent on the specification of the deterministic part of the unit root (auto-regressive) equations. We test the significance of the trend in all variables by testing the significance of the intercept in the following AR(2) equation for each variable, country by country:

$$\Delta Z_{it} = \alpha_i + \phi_i Z_{it-1} + \varphi_i \Delta Z_{it-1} + \epsilon_{it}$$

In the case that the null $H_0 : \alpha_i = 0$ is not rejected, we conclude that the data do not have a time trend. The hypothesis that the data do not have a time trend is supported for extensive margins, intensive margins and the Federal funds rate. The null hypothesis is rejected for the remaining variables. Therefore, in applying the unit root tests we treat the data for output, terms of trade and prices as having a trend. In the remaining data, the ADF equations include an intercept.

Individual unit root tests could not reject the existence of a unit root in the time series for output, the terms of trade and prices in almost all countries.[10] The hypothesis of a unit root is rejected when differenced data for these variables are considered. These results are confirmed by the panel unit root tests. We therefore conclude that output, terms of trade and prices are I(1). Individual and panel unit root tests allow to reject the null hypothesis of a unit root in all remaining data. We conclude that extensive margins, intensive margins and the Federal funds rate are I(0).

The presence of non-stationary variables raises the question whether an error correcting specification, i.e. a VECM model, might be more appropriate for describing the dynamics in the data. A linear combination of output and the terms of trade, the cointegrating vector, might be stationary implying the existence of a long-run relation between these variables. We provide a formal test of cointegration for output and the terms of trade based on the Westerlund ECM panel cointegration test. The null hypothesis of no cointegration could not be rejected against the alternative hypothesis that a cointegrating relation between output and the terms of trade exists for at least one country in the sample. Consequently, estimating the VARX model in first differences for output and the terms of trade without imposing any cointegrating relation between these two variables is a good approximation.

Before estimating the VARX model, we need to know how many lags of the dependent and the exogenous variables need to be included. As is standard practice, we use the Akaike Information Criterion (AIC) and the Schwartz's Bayesian information criterion (SBC). In all panels, these criteria suggest including either one or two lags. We use a parsimonious one-lag specification for our VARX model,

[10]Details on these statistics are available upon request.

though we checked that using two lags would not lead to different conclusions. In the exogenous VAR model standard criteria suggest including 2 lags.

A key assumption in the VARX model (4) is block exogeneity of US variables and energy prices, namely the assumption that these variables are exogenous in the time series sense with respect to the dependent variables (Y_{it} cannot help forecast X_t). In principle, large economies as those included in our dataset might exert a non-negligible influence on external variables. For instance, energy producers might influence energy prices in world markets. In practice, however, we will soon show that such an influence has no significant impact on the predictability of the exogenous variables in our data. This in turn suggests that the bias eventually introduced by assuming that US variables and energy prices are exogenous is small. We test the hypothesis that the vector X_t is block exogenous in the model (4) using the panel Granger-non causality test of Dumitrescu and Hurlin (2012). The test is a Wald statistic and is applied to all country pairs. The null hypothesis that the dependent variables do not Granger-cause the exogenous variables is not rejected at the 1 % significance level in almost all country pairs. Precisely, the null is rejected only in 9 % of all country pairs. Excluding these country pairs from the estimation has no major consequences for the results.

3 Results

We now discuss the main results on the impact of external shocks. We organize the presentation by type of shock: a real shock is a one-standard deviation increase in US output growth; a monetary policy shock is a one-standard deviation increase in the Federal funds rate and the energy price shock is a one-standard deviation increase in energy inflation (we overlook US inflation shocks). For each of them, we consider the dynamic effect on output, terms of trade and export margins in the full sample. Then, we estimate these effects separately for the samples of peggers and floaters.

Since we are interested in tracing out the dynamic path of adjustment in the aftermath of external shocks, we consider the mean responses of the dependent variables to a given shock for each year since the shock occurred. As explained before, these mean responses combine the conditional effects of external shocks on the dependent variables with their own auto-regressive process. Since the effects of the shocks dye out in approximately 6 years we consider the mean responses for years 0–6. In addition, we report 10 % confidence intervals generated by Monte Carlo simulations with 1000 replications.

The main results for the full sample are presented in Figs. 1 and 2 for the model with, respectively, extensive and intensive margins. In order to assess the stabilization advantages of the exchange rate regime, we then compare the mean responses in the sample of peggers with those in the sample of floaters. In this exercise, we focus on US output and monetary policy shocks. Figures 3 and 4 display the mean responses to output shocks in the model with extensive and intensive margins respectively. Figures 7 and 8 do the same for monetary policy shocks.

For ease of interpretation, we report below the expected signs of the responses.

	GDP^{US}	FFR	*Energy*
GDP_i	+	±	−
TOT_i	±	±	−
XM_i	+	±	−
IM_i	±	±	−

External output shocks are expected to have positive spillovers through the trade channel: a business cycle expansion in the US leads to higher US imports, which in turn boost demand and output in US trading partners. In principle, output spillovers may be associated with any combination of extensive and intensive margins. In traditional business cycle models, all of the adjustment takes place at the intensive margin: exporters increase the volume of previously traded goods whenever business conditions are favourable. We should therefore observe a positive response of intensive margins to external output shocks. Entry models predict that exporters will react to a favourable business environment by creating new products and trading previously non-traded goods. The expected response of extensive margins is

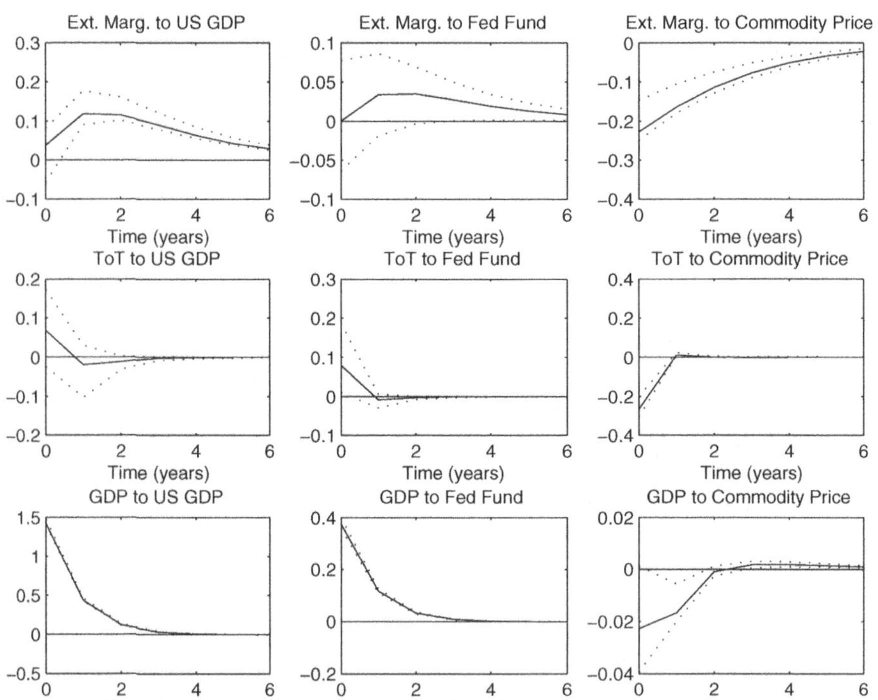

Fig. 1 Mean responses in the model with extensive margins. Full sample

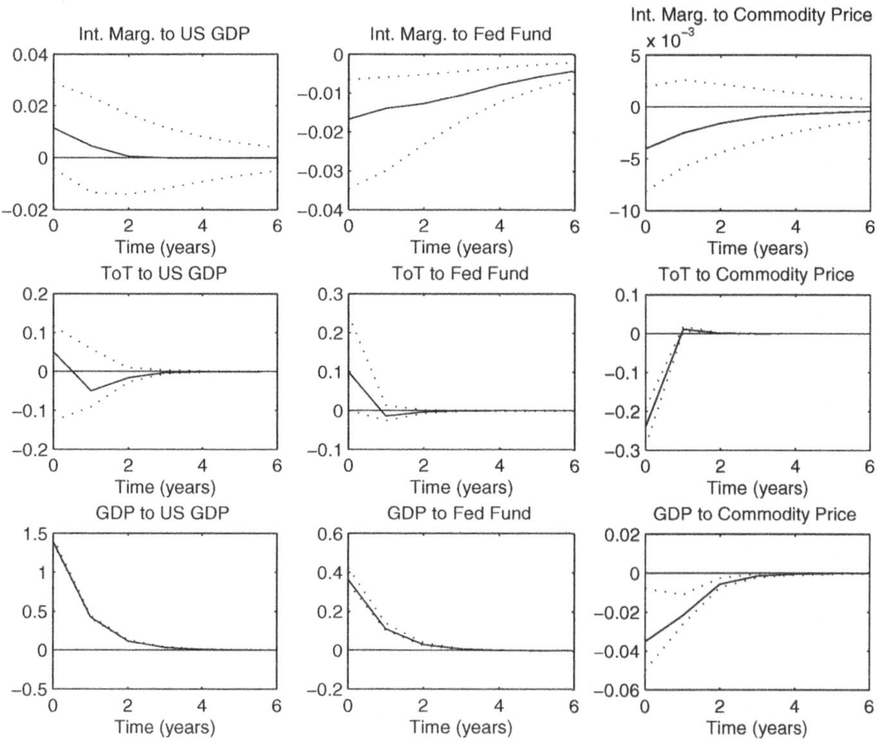

Fig. 2 Mean responses in the model with intensive margins. Full sample

therefore positive. In these models trade of new products may come at the expense of previously traded goods: when a large number of new firms enters the export market the average size of incumbents may decline. As a consequence, the response of intensive margins may turn negative. As it will be clear soon, adjustment to output shocks seems to take place mostly along the extensive margin and particularly so in fixed exchange rate regimes.

The response of the terms of trade is in principle ambiguous as it depends on the extent to which US output shocks affect the price of US imports, the price of substitutes of US exports and US dollar exchange rates. These prices in turn depend on the structure of trade of each country with respect to the US and the rest of the world. To get an intuitive account consider for example a situation where prices are fixed in the currency of consumers. A business cycle expansion in the US—a positive output shock in our model—will appreciate the US currency and improve the terms of trade of countries that export substitutes of US exports. Export prices will in fact rise in domestic currency and the more so the higher the switch of world demand away from US products. By the same token, the US dollar appreciation deteriorates the terms of trade of countries that import substitutes of US goods.

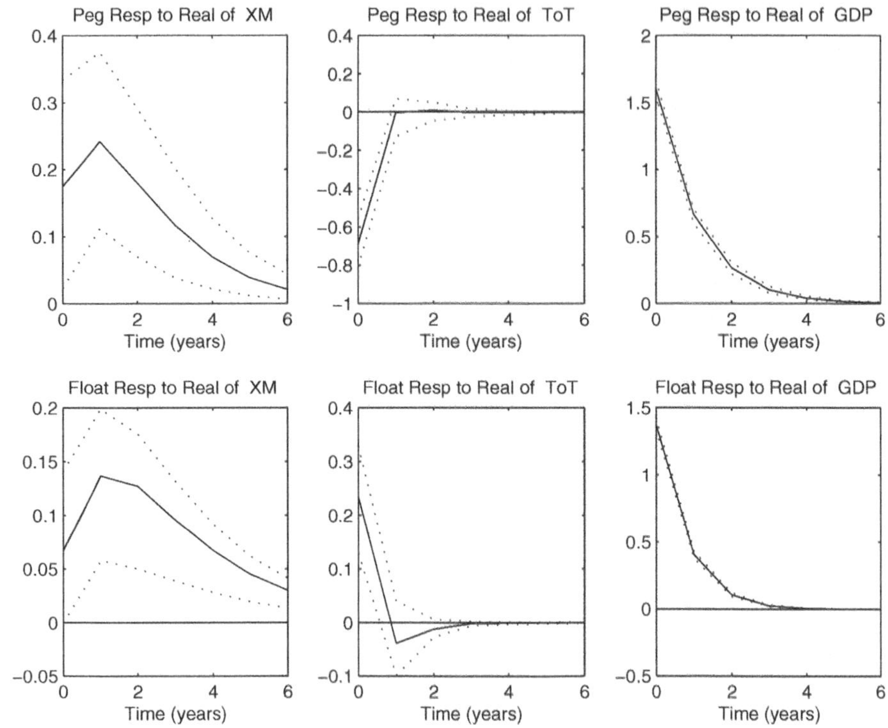

Fig. 3 Mean responses in the model with extensive margins. Mean responses to real shocks in the model with extensive margins in the sample of peggers (*first row*) and in the sample of floaters (*second row*)

External monetary policy shocks have two opposing effects on the trade channel. First, a monetary tightening in the US reduces US imports (the income effect), thereby generating negative output spillovers in US trading partners. These spillovers are large especially in countries for which the US represent a major export market. Second, it appreciates the US dollar, making US products less competitive in global markets and switching world demand towards the products of US trading partners (the substitution effect). Output spillovers are clearly positive in this case. Which one of these two effects prevails depends on the elasticity of demand for US imports and for the substitutes of US exports as well as on the relevance of US products in a country's overall trade. For given elasticities, the larger the share of substitutes of US products in a country's trade the larger the substitution effect. As we will see, there are remarkable differences in the transmission of monetary policy shocks in fixed and floating exchange rate regimes.

Energy price shocks are expected to have negative effects on all variables. In particular, a negative response of the terms of trade reflects the fact that our sample includes only a limited number of energy producers so that an eventual appreciation of their terms of trade has a negligible impact on the mean response.

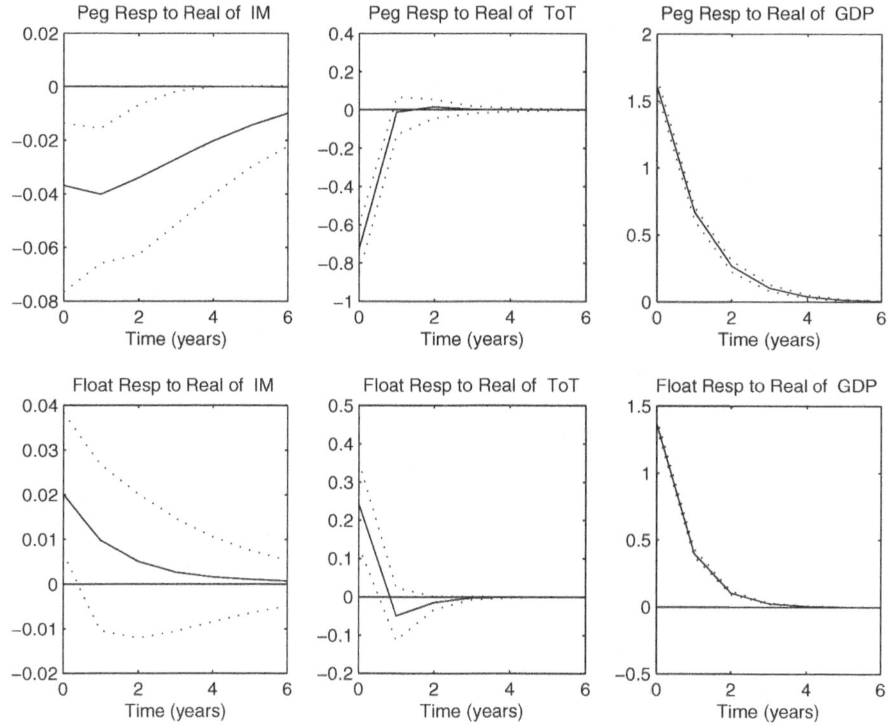

Fig. 4 Mean responses in the model with intensive margins. Mean responses to real shocks in the model with extensive margins in the sample of peggers (*first row*) and in the sample of floaters (*second row*)

3.1 Real Shocks

In the full sample, US output shocks have positive spillovers on output and export margins as expected. The mean response of output is high on impact then it gradually declines and dyes out completely after three years. The cumulated average increase in output growth in the aftermath of a US output shock is about 2 % in both models.

The mean response of trade margins is positive, although only extensive margins are significant. The response of extensive margins is persistent throughout the transition and reverts to the mean in approximately 8 years (not shown in Fig. 1). It is hump-shaped with a peak after one year and a half while intensive margins display a gradual decline after the initial impulse. We stress that the behaviour of extensive margins is consistent with the predictions of international business cycle models with firm entry. As pointed out by Cavallari (2013), entry generates positive comovements across countries: a business cycle expansion in one country leads to export of new products (i.e., a rise in the extensive margin) in the trading partner's market.

Comparing mean responses in the samples of peggers and floaters reveals a number of interesting features. A visual inspection of Figs. 3 and 4 shows that there are remarkable differences in the transmission of output shocks. First, the mean response of output is higher in the sample of peggers than in the sample of floaters: the difference in the cumulated response is as large as 0.78 (0.79) in the model with extensive (intensive) margins. This accords with the Friedman's hypothesis that flexible exchange rates help to smooth output in the wake of real shocks.

Second, adjustment seems to occur mainly at the extensive margin and particularly so in fixed regimes. The mean response of extensive margins in the sample of peggers is almost 4 times as high as the response among floaters. By contrast, the responses of intensive margins are similar in quantitative terms yet opposite in sign. The behaviour of export margins is consistent with the findings of recent studies showing that trade flows vary mostly along the extensive margin in fixed regimes.[11] A novel contribution of our study is to clarify the role of trade margins for the transmission of shocks. A business cycle expansion abroad implies positive output spillovers through the trade channel in any exchange rate regime. Yet in the sample of peggers, trade switches from previously traded goods towards new products and previously non-traded goods (the so-called variety effect). A strong variety effect in turn exacerbates output fluctuations. A possible reason why variety effects are stronger in fixed regimes is stressed in models with firm entry as Bergin and Lin (2012). Here the absence of exchange rate fluctuations reduces the sunk costs of first-time entry in foreign markets and provides a strong incentive to trade new products and previously non-traded goods. Flexible exchange rates, on the contrary, allow a quicker adjustment in relative prices, included the price for investments. Quantity (trade margins) responses are therefore smoother compared to fixed regimes. The finding that flexible regimes smooth the responses of extensive margins strengthens the traditional argument in favour of the stabilization property of these regimes.

Finally, consider the responses of the terms of trade. In the sample of peggers, the terms of trade depreciate on impact, then gradually appreciate before reverting to the trend in approximately 2 years. The terms of trade of floaters move in the opposite direction. Since all countries in our dataset have flexible exchange rates with the US dollar, these responses reflect differences in the structure of trade between peggers and floaters. In order to see why, consider an appreciation of the US dollar. US products become less competitive in global markets and this tends to improve the terms of trade of countries that export substitutes of US products. By the same token, the appreciation deteriorates the terms of trade of countries that import substitutes of US products. Which one of these opposing effects prevails

[11]In panel regressions for European countries, Bergin and Lin (2012) show that extensive margins have responded aggressively to the implementation of the Economic and Monetary Union in Europe (EMU). They find a statistically significant rise in extensive margins already four years ahead of actual EMU adoption, and ahead of any rise in overall trade. The estimated effect of the adoption of the Euro on the intensive margin of trade is, on the contrary, negligible. See also Auray et al. (2012).

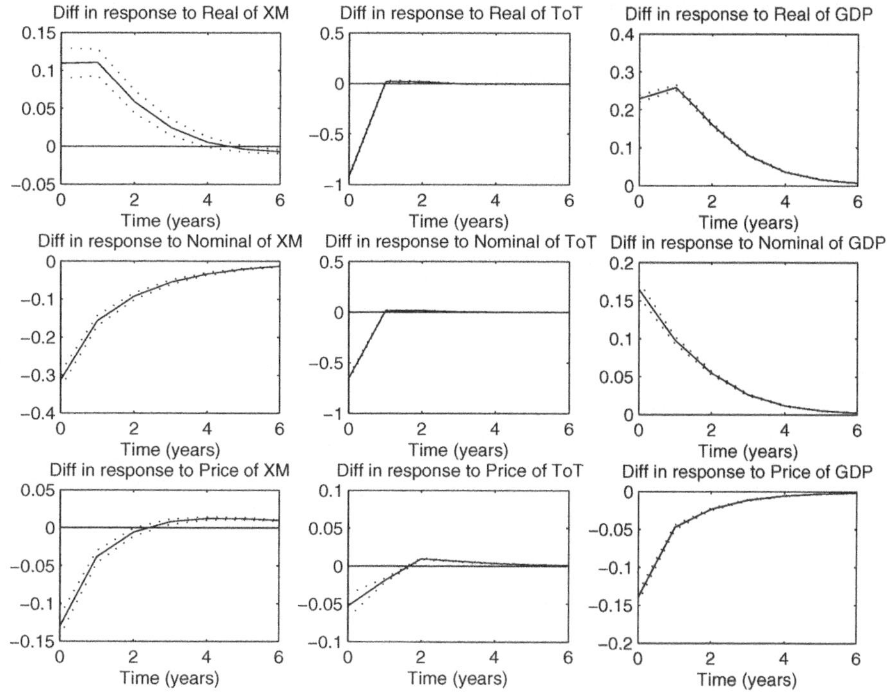

Fig. 5 Difference in the mean responses of peggers and floaters in the model with extensive margins

depends on the structure of trade as well as on the degree of exchange rate pass-through in import and export prices. In the sample of peggers, that includes Euro-zone countries in our dataset, the latter effect dominates.

In order to test the statistical significance of the impact of the exchange rate regime, Figs. 5 and 6 depict the difference in the mean responses of peggers and floaters together with 10 % confidence intervals in the model with, respectively, extensive and intensive margins. Confidence intervals are computed by bootstrapping methods as in Born et al. (2013).[12] All differences are statistically significant. Heterogeneity in the responses of the terms of trade is high on impact then rapidly declines and vanishes completely after 1 year and a half. The reason is easy to grasp: the advantages of flexible exchange rates hinge on price stickiness, i.e. on their ability to affect relative prices when nominal prices are sticky. Over time, as prices adjust, the impact of the exchange rate regime becomes negligible. Slope heterogeneity for output and trade margins is instead persistent up to 5 years.

[12]Confidence intervals for the difference of the mean responses in the sample of peggers and floaters reflect differences in the variance of the estimated coefficients equation by equation (i.e., differences in the variance structure of floaters and peggers) as well as across equations (i.e. difference in the covariance structure between floaters and peggers).

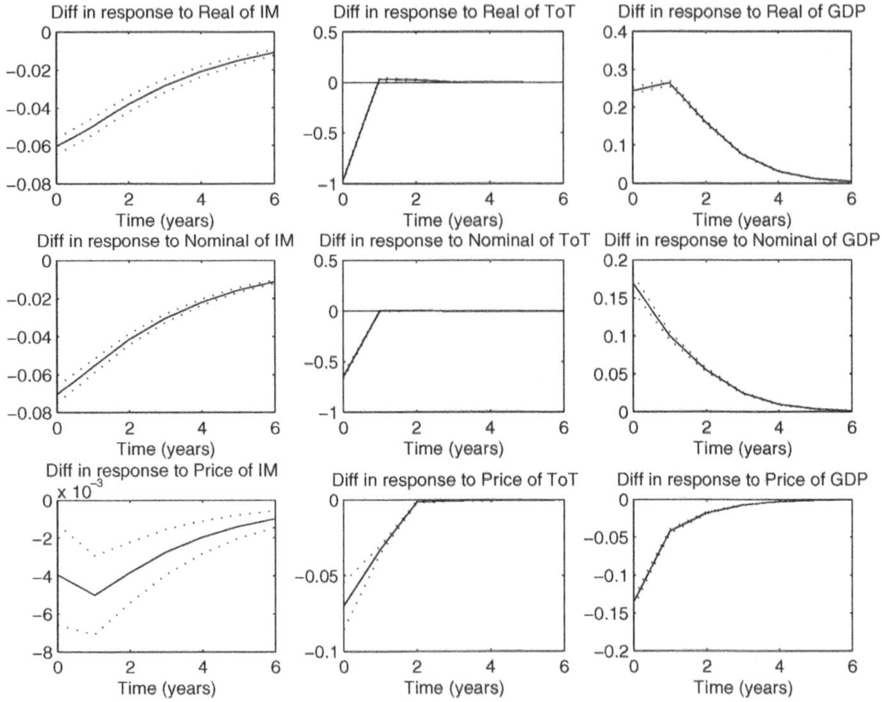

Fig. 6 Difference in the mean responses of peggers and floaters in the model with intensive margins

3.2 Monetary Policy Shocks

In the full sample, the mean response of output to a US monetary restriction is positive. As is discussed above, positive spillovers reflect a switch of world demand towards substitutes of US products when the US dollar appreciates. It is worth noticing that trade adjusts positively at the extensive margin and negatively at the intensive margin: trade shifts from previously traded goods to new products and previously non-traded goods. The possibility that volume and variety of exports move in opposite direction is stressed in models with firm entry. It reflects movements in the relative price of investments in new products (the extensive margin) and investments in existing capacity (the intensive margin) in response to business cycle fluctuations. A, say, monetary policy shock may well alter the attractiveness of exporting new products compared to previously traded goods. In line with this argument, our findings can be interpreted as evidence that the creation of new products provides an important channel for the transmission of monetary policy shocks worldwide.

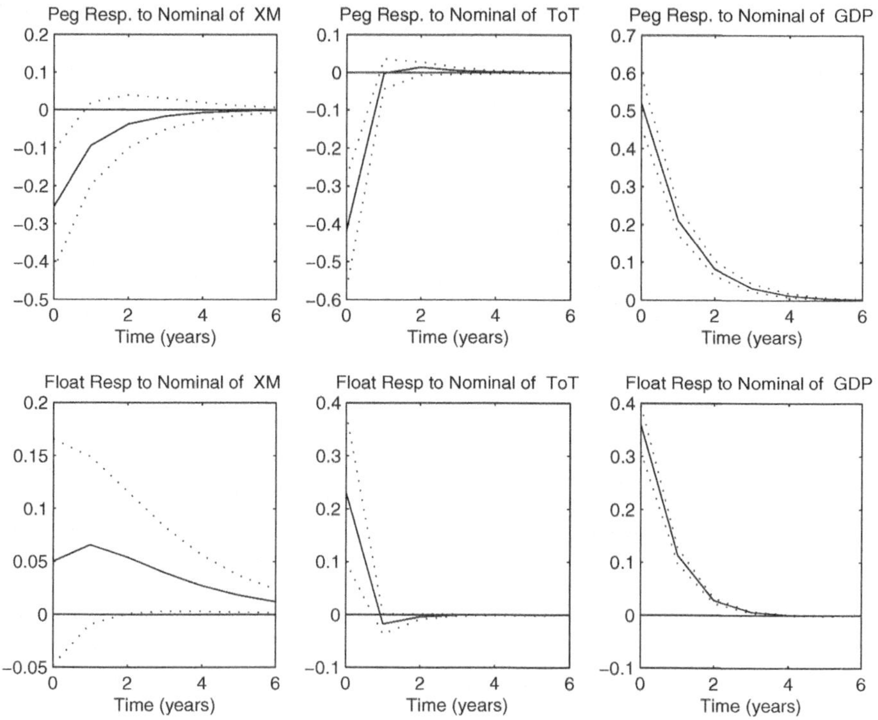

Fig. 7 Mean responses to nominal shocks. Model with extensive margins in the sample of peggers (*first row*) and in the sample of floaters (*second row*)

Comparing mean responses across exchange rate regimes reveals interesting insights on the transmission of monetary policy shocks. Output spillovers are higher in the sample of peggers: the responses of output in Figs. 7 and 8 are almost twice as large for peggers than for floaters. In addition, trade spillovers are higher in fixed regimes. While intensive margins decline in both samples and the more so for peggers, extensive margins increase in the sample of floaters.

These results are in contrast with the view that fixed exchange rates help to smooth the effects of nominal shocks: since Poole (1970) an advantage typically attributed to fixed exchange rates is their ability to insulate the economy from external nominal shocks. Our findings support an alternative explanation: flexible exchange rates, by allowing a quicker adjustment in the price of investments, help to smooth extensive margins. This in turn facilitates output stabilization. As before, we test the significance of differences in the mean responses in the sample of peggers and floaters. The responses in the bottom row of Figs. 5 and 6 show that all differences are significant.

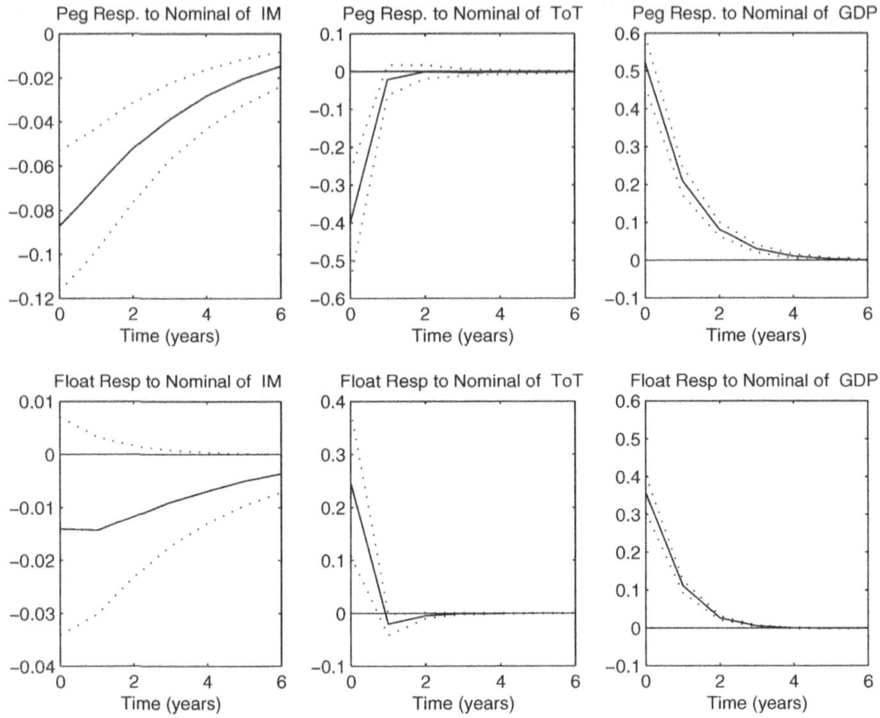

Fig. 8 Mean responses to nominal shocks. Model with intensive margins in the sample of peggers (*first row*) and in the sample of floaters (*second row*)

4 Conclusions

This paper studied the dynamics of output and export margins in the wake of external shocks in fixed and floating exchange rate regimes. The objective of the analysis is twofold. First, it verifies the predictions of international business cycle models about the behaviour of export margins over the cycle and across exchange rate regimes. Second, it re-assesses the stabilization properties of flexible exchange rates when trade is allowed to adjusts also at the extensive margin.

Using a panel VARX model, the paper traces the mean responses of output, terms of trade and export margins to external output and monetary policy shocks in twenty-two developed economies over the period 1988–2011. We find that the mean responses of output in the sample of peggers are larger than in the sample of floaters independently of the type of shock considered. An important contribution of our study is to clarify the role of trade margins for the transmission of shocks. A business cycle expansion abroad implies positive output spillovers through the trade channel in any exchange rate regime. Yet in the sample of peggers, there is a switch from trade of previously traded goods towards trade of new products and previously non-traded goods (the so-called variety effect). A strong variety effect in turn exacerbates output fluctuations.

Overall, our findings provide novel evidence in support of the stabilization advantages of flexible exchange rates based on their ability to smooth extensive margins. These findings are consistent with the predictions of theoretical models with firm entry.

References

Auray, Stphane, Aurlien Eyquem, and Jean-Christophe Poutineau. 2012. The effect of a common currency on the volatility of the extensive margin of trade. *Journal of International Money and Finance* 31(5): 1156–1179.

Bergin, Paul, and Reuven Glick. 2007. A Model of endogenous nontradability and its implications for the current account. *Review of International Economics* 15(5): 916–931.

Bergin, Paul R., and Ching-Yi Lin. 2012. The dynamic effects of a currency union on trade. *Journal of International Economics* 87(2): 191–204.

Bernard, Andrew B., Stephen J. Redding, and Peter K. Schott. 2010. Multiple-product firms and product switching. *American Economic Review* 100(1): 70–97.

Bilbiie, Florin O., Fabio Ghironi, and Marc J. Melitz. 2012. Endogenous entry, product variety, and business cycles. *Journal of Political Economy* 120(2): 304–345.

Born, Benjamin, Falko Juessen, and Gernot J. Mller. 2013. Exchange rate regimes and fiscal multipliers. *Journal of Economic Dynamics and Control* 37(2): 446–465.

Broda, Christian, and David E. Weinstein. 2010. Product creation and destruction: Evidence and price implications. *American Economic Review* 100(3): 691–723.

Cavallari, Lilia. 2007. A macroeconomic model of entry with exporters and multinationals. *The B. E. Journal of Macroeconomics* 7(1): 446–465.

Cavallari, Lilia. 2010. Exports and foreign direct investments in an endogenous-entry model with real and nominal uncertainty. *Journal of Macroeconomics* 32(1): 300–313.

Cavallari, Lilia. 2013. Firms' entry, monetary policy and the international business cycle. *Journal of International Economics* 91: 263–274.

Christiano, Lawrence J., Martin Eichenbaum, and Charles L. Evans. 1999. Monetary policy shocks: What have we learned and to what end? In *Part A of handbook of macroeconomics*, vol. 1, ed. John B. Taylor, and Michael Woodford, 65–148. Amsterdam: Elsevier.

Corsetti, Giancarlo, Philippe Martin, and Paolo Pesenti. 2007. Productivity, terms of trade and the home market effect. *Journal of International Economics* 73(1): 99–127.

Corsetti, Giancarlo, Philippe Martin, and Paolo Pesenti. 2013. Varieties and the transfer problem. *Journal of International Economics* 89(1): 1–12.

Dumitrescu, Elena-Ivona, and Christopher Hurlin. 2012. Testing for granger non-causality in heterogeneous panels. *Economic Modelling* 29(4): 1450–1460.

Fomby, Thomas, Yuki Ikeda, and Norman V. Loayza. 2013. The growth aftermath of natural disasters. *Journal of Applied Econometrics* 28(3): 412–434.

Forni, Mario, and Lucrezia Reichlin. 1998. Let's get real: A factor analytical approach to disaggregated business cycle dynamics. *The Review of Economic Studies* 65(3): 453–473.

Friedman, M. 1953. The case for flexible exchange rates. In *Essays in positive economics*, ed. Milton Friedman. Chicago, IL: University of Chicago Press.

Ghironi, Fabio, and M.J. Melitz. 2005. International trade and macroeconomic dynamics with heterogeneous firms. *The Quarterly Journal of Economics* 120(3): 865–915.

Hummels, David, and Peter J. Klenow. 2005. The variety and quality of a nation's exports. *American Economic Review* 95(3): 704–723.

Kehoe, Timothy J., and Kim J. Ruhl. 2013. How important is the new goods margin in international trade? *Journal of Political Economy* 121(2): 358–392.

Levin, Andrew, Chien-Fu Lin, and Chia-Shang James Chu. 2002. Unit root tests in panel data: asymptotic and finite-sample properties. *Journal of Econometrics* 108(1): 1–24.

Melitz, Marc J. 2003. The impact of trade on intra-industry reallocations and aggregate industry productivity. *Econometrica* 71(6): 1695–1725.

Nickell, Stephen J. 1981. Biases in dynamic models with fixed effects. *Econometrica* 49(6): 1417–1426.

Pesaran, M.Hashem, and Zhirong Zhao. 1999. Bias reduction in estimating long-run relationships from dynamic heterogeneous panels. In *Analysis of panels and limited dependent variable models*, ed. C. Hsiao, M.Hashem Pesaran, Kajal Lahiri, and Lung Fei Lee, 297–322. Cambridge, UK: Cambridge University Press.

Poole, William. 1970. Optimal choice of monetary instruments in a simple stochastic macromodel. *The Quarterly Journal of Economics* 84(2): 197–216.

Rose, Andrew K. 1999. One money, one market: estimating the effect of common currencies on trade. NBER Working Papers 7432, National Bureau of Economic Research, Inc.

Rebalancing and the Euro

Paul van den Noord

Abstract Pushing down the euro is seen by many as a solution to stagnation and 'lowflation' in the euro area, but this paper argues it needs to be supported by a fiscal expansion, in particular in Germany. Unfortunately the incentives for Germany to embark on fiscal stimulus are weak. Yet without a fiscal expansion the current account surplus would widen further in response to exchange rate depreciation, thus exacerbating the current imbalances—excess saving in Germany alongside indispensable deleveraging in southern Europe. It would risk producing a protracted slump that feeds onto itself, with (core) inflation declining further and the risk of outright deflation increasing. If that risk were to materialise the ECB may have to be called to rescue the euro again, as it did in 2012 with the introduction of Outright Monetary Transactions (OMT). And it would have to do so persuasively or else Europe risks ending up in a Japanese conundrum. It is in this perspective the ECB's move towards quantitative easing should be seen.

1 Introduction

The euro area has been trapped in a low growth and low inflation environment, in which deleveraging—while necessary—remains painfully slow, activity subdued and unemployment sky-high. While the perception in financial markets is that ECB has been slow to acknowledge the extent of the problem, it has embarked on a material (further) easing of monetary policy, with the deposit rate in negative territory and liquidity injections in the banking system targeted on institutions that are able and willing to lend more. In recent meetings the ECB has also been

The views expressed in this chapter are those of the author only and cannot be attributed to Autonomy Capital or its staff.

P. van den Noord (✉)
Autonomy Capital, London, UK
e-mail: pvandennoord@autonomycapital.com

L. Paganetto (ed.), *Achieving Dynamism in an Anaemic Europe*,
DOI 10.1007/978-3-319-14099-5_4

changing its rhetoric, making explicit reference to the exchange rate as a possible trigger for further monetary policy easing so as to take out insurance against the risk of deflation (as recent disinflation has been attributed to currency appreciation and an associated fall in import prices). One option put forward by the ECB at the time of writing was to buy Asset Backed Securities (ABS) with freshly printed money to be used to shore up banks' balance sheets. More recently the ECB embarked on US/UK-style outright quantitative easing.

The change in rhetoric left observers with the impression that the euro is overvalued, and therefore needs to be driven down towards a supposedly lower equilibrium. Some observers have even been calling for outright intervention in foreign exchange markets (Feldstein 2014; Frankel 2014). The problem with this view is that calling for a depreciation of the euro in real effective terms boils down to calling for a bigger current account surplus, while in fact the area's external surplus is already at an all-time high of almost 3 % of GDP. Forex intervention in such an environment would almost certainly be perceived as 'beggar-thy-neighbour' policy. It would be hard to defend in for instance a G20 context, with prominent G20 members recurrently calling for a reduction in the area's current account surplus so as to support global demand. However, the political appetite in Europe to do so is totally absent, at least in the perception of financial markets, which may explain the strong exchange rate.

This raises three questions this paper will try to answer. The first question asks what the forces are that are driving up the current account surplus. The second question asks why the real exchange rate has been stuck at its perceived height and how this hangs together with the current account surplus. And the third question asks why it is so difficult to rein in the current account surplus, in particular from a political point of view, as opposed to calling for 'an easy way out' via forex intervention.

2 What Is Driving the Euro Area Current Account Surplus?

A striking development in the euro area immediately after the crisis has been the sudden and sizeable surge in the net saving deficit of general government, reflecting fiscal stimulus and the operation of the automatic fiscal stabilisers (upper-left panel of Fig. 1). This was more than offset, however, by a strong increase in the corporate net saving surplus as deleveraging set in, while there was no increase in the household net saving balance. As a result, the current account went into surplus after it had registered a small deficit in 2008. The current account surplus rose significantly further with the onset of the sovereign debt crisis in 2010, and has now attained roughly 3 % of GDP. As shown in the upper-left panel of Fig. 1, this is mostly a reflection of the sharp decline in government dis-saving, as budgets were consolidated, and which has so far not been offset by a commensurate fall in corporate or household net saving.

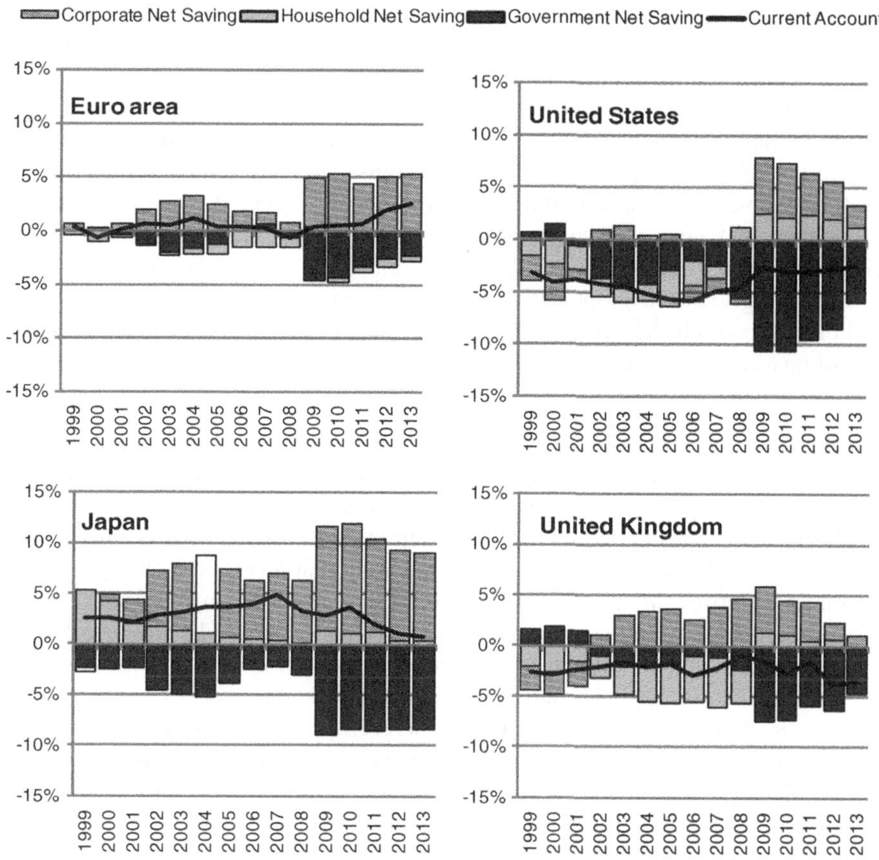

Fig. 1 Saving-investment balances by sector as a % of GDP in advanced economies. *Source* AMECO Database, European Commission

This contrasts with developments in other major advanced economies over the period 2010–2013, with a growing external deficit of the UK economy, a narrowing external surplus in Japan and a broadly stable US external deficit. The deepening UK current account deficit over this period occurred for the most part because the private sector reduced its net saving surplus, while the fall in government dissaving as the pubic budget was consolidated did not provide a full offset. So the combined public and private balance sheets have been a source of demand stimulus in the UK, much unlike the situation in the euro area.

It is interesting also to make a comparison with developments in the United States and Japan (see again Fig. 1). This shows that in the United States household net saving has been much stronger than in the euro area, though it has been coming down. And like in the United Kingdom, US corporate dissaving has been slowing down as well. But since US fiscal consolidation has been quite strong, the current account deficit did not widen. The striking feature of Japan obviously is the enormous and persistent net saving surplus of the corporate sector. Therefore, with the government saving deficit roughly constant, the recent decline in Japan's current account surplus is mostly due to lower household net saving.

So, all in all, unlike major counterparts in the advanced world, fiscal consolidation in the euro area has not been offset by a commensurate decline in the private (and especially the corporate) net saving surplus. To analyse this asymmetry, it is useful to dive into the country-by-country detail. Figure 2 shows the saving-investment and current account position in the five largest euro area countries Germany, France, Italy, Spain and the Netherlands as well as Portugal.

Interestingly, the developments in the two largest euro-area economies, Germany and France, could be hardly more contrasting. Specifically, while Germany has been recording a big and rising current account surplus, France portrays a widening current account deficit. Specifically:

- The German surplus is entirely due to a high corporate saving surplus as both the household and government sectors do not run a saving surplus to speak off. In fact the German corporate sector has been accumulating net savings since the 2001–2003 'dotcom' slump. In the run-up to the financial crisis Germany never engaged in the accumulation of corporate debt that has been a characteristic of many countries. Meanwhile, a significant share of Germany's current account and corporate saving surplus has served to finance large FDI flows to Eastern Europe and Asia to build up a global supply chain for Germany's manufacturing industry, as discussed in more detail below.
- This is sharp contrast with France, where corporate net dis-saving continues unabated, which entirely explains the country's widening current account deficit. There is reason for concern that corporate indebtedness in France proves unsustainable. The French current account deficit will need to correct, and this must happen through an increase in profitability and hence the corporate net saving surplus. This view is broadly accepted in France, but it can be achieved only through politically painful structural reforms and slashing government expenditure to boost competitiveness.

A main difference between the third and fourth largest economies Italy and Spain is that households and businesses are facing different deleveraging challenges. The challenge is very severe in Spain, where corporates and households leveraged massively in the run-up to the crisis as the housing bubble inflated. They have begun de-leveraging, as reflected in the rapid increase of the corporate net saving surplus and the concomitant move into current account surplus, but still have a long way to go. It is unlikely demand for credit in Spain will resume anytime soon, even when banks' balance sheets have healed and the ECB's Asset Quality Review (AQR) turns out favourably for Spanish banks.

Households in Italy, in contrast, never leveraged much before the crisis in the first place and since the crisis have been running a saving deficit, presumably a result of weak income growth. More recently, with a higher household saving deficit and a larger business saving surplus largely offsetting, the improvement in

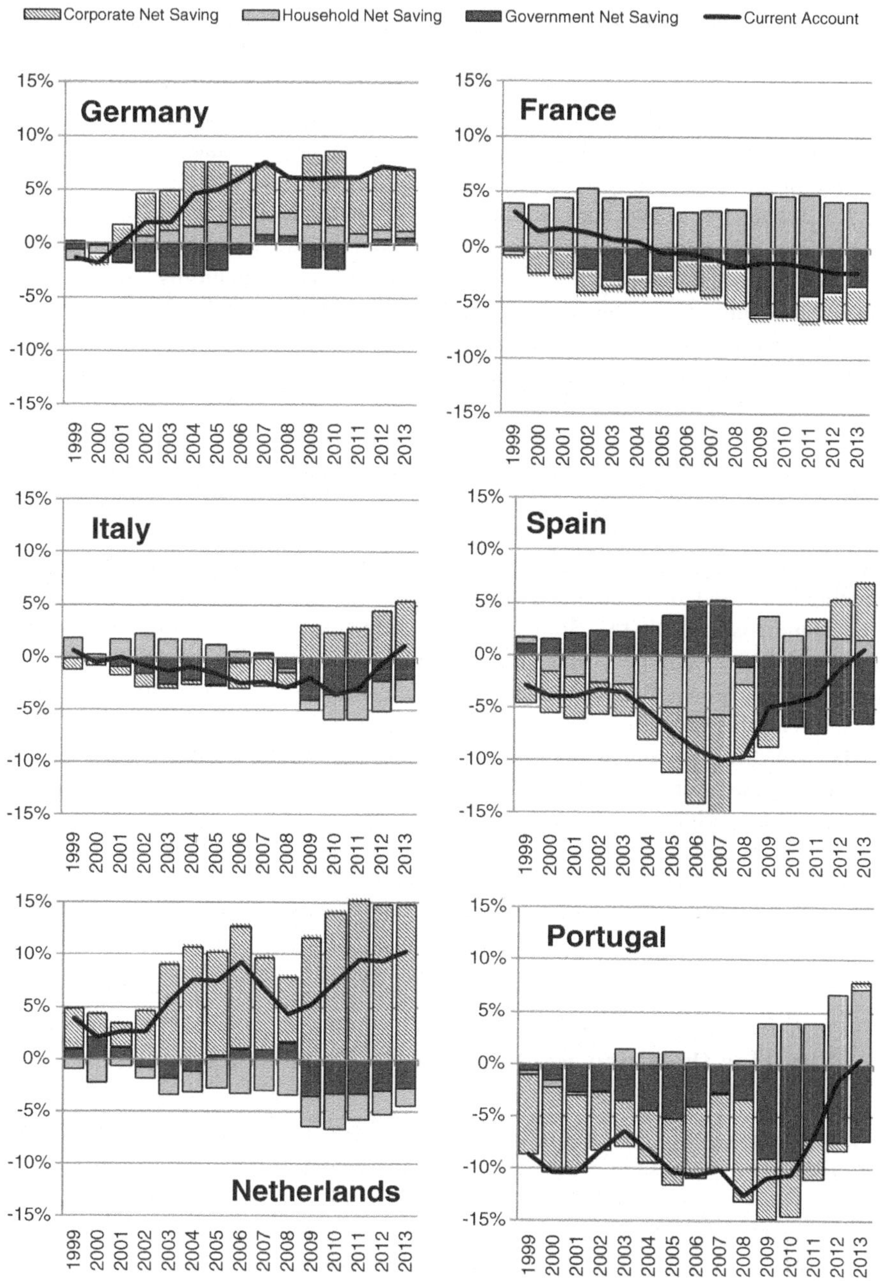

Fig. 2 Saving-investment balances by sector as a % of GDP in euro area countries. *Source* AMECO Database, European Commission

Italy's current account position is mostly a reflection of fiscal consolidation. So, understandably, the economy is still depressed. But because the corporate and households sectors were never excessively leveraged, Italy's economy does not look excessively unbalanced, and credit growth resume when banks are back into shape (and the ECB's AQR is broadly supportive of this) and political stability takes root.

It is interesting to take look at Portugal as it is unique in the sense that the sharp decline in the current account deficit is driven by increases in net saving (or decreases in net dissaving) in *all* sectors simultaneously, including the household sector as it were mostly the corporate and government sectors that have contributed most to past profligacy. So in a way the household sector is paying part of the bill left by the corporate and government sector—an unbalanced rebalancing of sorts.

Finally, the Netherlands, the country with the biggest current account surplus of the euro area (and one of the biggest in the world), has elements of both the "core" and "periphery" present in its economy. Like Germany, its corporate sector has been running massive saving surpluses ever since the early 2000s, and even more so than Germany. However, its household sector has consistently been running saving deficits, largely induced by tax incentives for household (mortgage) indebtedness and an associated housing bubble that burst at the onset of the financial crisis in 2008–09. Household dissaving has been falling in recent years as mortgage credit slumped, and so has government dissaving as the budget was consolidated. Meanwhile, corporate net saving stayed strong, and hence the current account surplus increased.

In sum, the increase in the current account surplus in the euro area since the onset of the sovereign debt crisis is attributable to falling current account deficits in the euro area periphery, driven by public and private deleveraging, not being offset by a commensurate narrowing of the German and Dutch external surpluses. Therefore, should we be surprised that the euro area's real effective exchange rate has stayed strong for so long even in the face of monetary policy easing? The answer is broadly no as the next section illustrates.

3 Why Has the Euro Exchange Rate Been so Resistant?

Figure 3 depicts the development of the euro area's real effective exchange rate (REER) and its current account, along with indicators of the area's relative stances of fiscal and monetary policies. The left-hand panel shows that in the initial three years of monetary union the REER plunged and then recovered—a phenomenon that is usually attributed to the dotcom boom and bust that affected the US dollar (first positively and then negatively). Ever since the euro REER has moved closely in line with the relative stance of monetary policy in the area (here gauged by the real short-term interest differential against a weighted average of OECD countries).

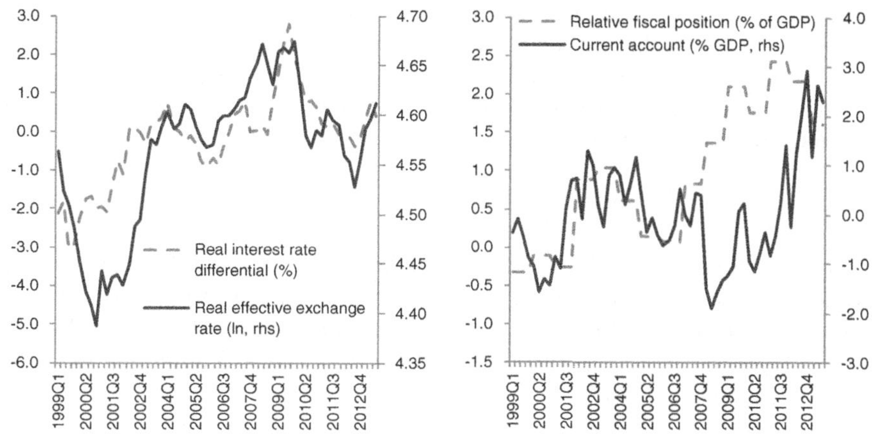

Fig. 3 Euro area REER, current account and macroeconomic policy stances. *Source* Reuters Datastream; see Appendix for definitions

Both the REER and the relative tightness of euro area monetary policy peaked around the time of the Lehman debacle. Thereafter both have been trending down until roughly President Draghi's 'whatever it takes' speech in July 2012. Since then the REER and monetary policy stance have been trending up again until very recently, though obviously financial conditions eased as sovereign bond yields came down in the periphery.

The fall in periphery sovereign yields has been supported by the splurge of fiscal consolidation, and this shows up as a relative fiscal tightening (gauged here by movements in the differential of the euro area fiscal position against that of a weighted average of OECD economies) in the period 2009–2013. The current account position of the euro area essentially followed a similar pattern, albeit with a rather long lag.

This simple analysis is obviously incomplete; the underlying economic relationships are complex with lots of feedbacks, as suggested by the econometric analysis reported in the Appendix. But overall, a combination of relative fiscal tightening and relative monetary easing is likely to have contributed to the symptoms we have observed: sharp increases in the current account surplus and the relatively inflexible REER. This can be illustrated in a stylised fashion as follows.

Let us assume that the REER (S) tends to appreciate if it is below its equilibrium level $\bar{S}$ (determined for instance by the economy's relative per capita income), or if its current account B exceeds its equilibrium $\bar{B}$:

$$\dot{S} = -a_1(S - \bar{S}) + a_2(B - \bar{B}) + M$$

The variable M is a monetary policy shock (this can be a rate increase or any form of conventional or unconventional monetary policy). Similarly, let us assume that the current account surplus will tend to increase if either the REER is below its equilibrium level (as this will tend to crowd in net exports) or if the current account itself is below its equilibrium level (this refers to the monetary approach of the balance of payment which predicts that liquidity inflows stemming from a current account surplus will induce dissaving):

$$\dot{B} = -b_1(S - \bar{S}) - b_2(B - \bar{B}) + F$$

The variable F is a shock variable that can be thought of as a deleveraging shock, like for instance a fiscal tightening (but it can also be interpreted as a deleveraging shock in the private sector). The associated fall in domestic demand will *cetiris paribus* boost net exports and hence the REER. In dynamic equilibrium ($\dot{B} = \dot{S} = 0$) these relationships read:

$$S - \bar{S} = \frac{a_2}{a_1}(B - \bar{B}) + \frac{M}{a_1}$$
$$B - \bar{B} = -\frac{b_1}{b_2}(S - \bar{S}) + \frac{F}{b_2}$$

The first of these two relationships is the condition for REER equilibrium (depicted as the upward sloping line in Fig. 4) and the second one is the condition for current account equilibrium (the downward sloping line in Fig. 4). The left-hand panel of Fig. 4 shows that a (relative) monetary policy easing will increase the current account position while reducing the REER. The right-hand panel shows that a relative tightening of fiscal policy will again increase the current account position but also the REER. Therefore, a policy mix of monetary ease and fiscal austerity (or

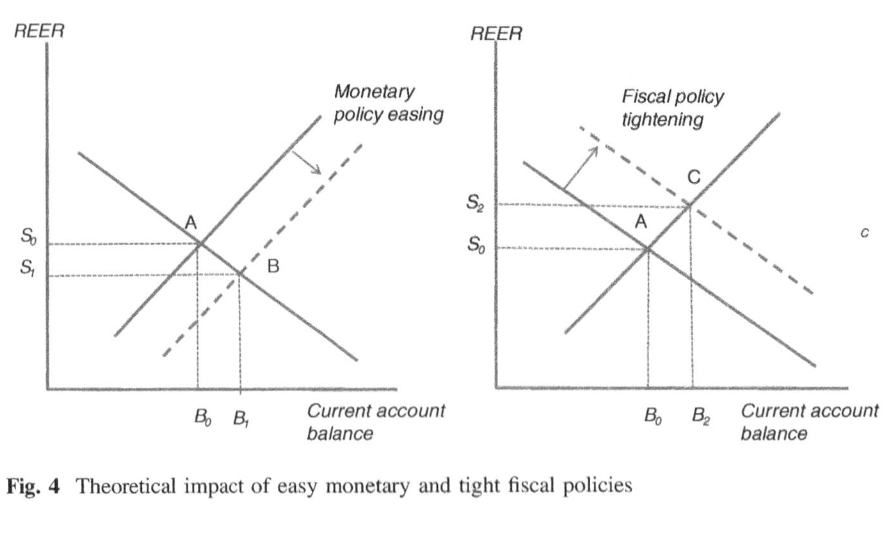

Fig. 4 Theoretical impact of easy monetary and tight fiscal policies

more broadly deleveraging) is likely to result in the constellation of developments we have been observing: the current account surplus increases while the REER hardly moves.

The Appendix reports an attempt to estimate an extended version of this stylised model on 1999–2013 quarterly data. It broadly supports the above analysis, even if the time series are short and data issues severe, so uncertainty over the precision of the parameter estimates or even the specification itself is large. Bearing that caveat in mind, it may be useful to examine the impulse responses generated with the model, reported in Fig. 5.

The results can be summarised as follows:

- An exogenous increase in the aggregate fiscal position or an exogenous shock to the aggregate current account position other than through fiscal consolidation (i.e. public and private deleveraging) both result in an appreciation in the REER and an increase in the current account surplus.
- An exogenous decrease in the real short-term interest rate differential (relative easing of monetary policy) puts downward pressure on the REER and upward pressure on the current account position. Direct foreign exchange intervention, meanwhile, generates a depreciation of the REER, though no discernible effect on the current account position.

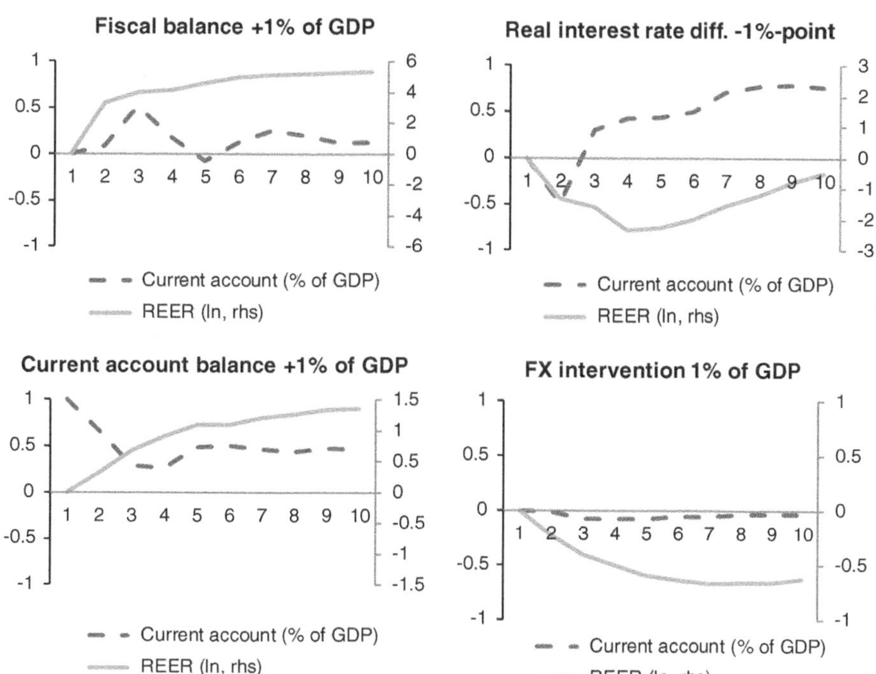

Fig. 5 Impulse responses. *Note* non-cumulative changes. *Source* see Appendix

4 Why Is It so Difficult Politically to Rein in the Current Account Surplus?

As we have seen, the increase in the euro area's current account surplus is the net effect of the German surplus staying large (6–7 % of GDP) while "austerity" has forced the current account deficit of the rest of the area to turn to a small surplus position (indeed all euro area countries, except France, are currently running an external surplus). We have also seen that this asymmetric adjustment puts upward pressure on the euro REER which monetary policy easing can only partly offset, unless monetary easing becomes very large—as it may well become as deflation risks grow.

The rebalancing that is going on in the "periphery" is necessary and unavoidable. It is an essential component of crisis resolution in the euro area. What is less obvious is why Germany should be running a current account surplus of over 7 % of GDP, as it currently does. Interestingly, the German surplus has not been found 'excessive' by the Commission's Macroeconomic Imbalances Procedure. There are undoubtedly ways to rationalise this decision, but it also suggests there are political impediments to reining in the German surplus. Where do these come from? To understand this, three observations are in order.

First, one should never forget a basic truth: Germany resisted the creation of the euro at the stage when it was created. It was a French initiative the Germans felt compelled to accept in exchange for re-unification. Germany set certain conditions, some of which were granted (ECB shaped on the Buba model, based in Frankfurt), and some of which were not granted (e.g. only "core" countries adopt the euro as the periphery was deemed not ready to give up the option of exchange rate adjustment). So when markets suddenly woke up to the non-bailout clause in the Treaty, and the sovereign debt crisis broke, Germany's basic position was (and still is): "you've only got yourself to blame".[1] Little wonder calls on German "solidarity" to" spend the euro area out of the slump" fails.

Second, the German current account surplus has become a matter of ideology. At conferences and meetings I sometimes ask German colleagues the following question: why are business leaders generally upbeat and German consumers depressed? The answer is key to understanding why the current account surplus is so large and why it has become a matter of ideology. The answer is that as German business has used the fall of the Iron Curtain as an opportunity to develop new

[1]This is not totally unfair, but only half the truth since it was Germany (and France), not Italy or Spain, who put the Excessive Deficit Procedure of the Stability and Growth Pact "in abeyance" in 2003. And Germany also happily financed these ballooning current account deficits in the south. Even so, the German vision of Europe has always been to first construct a political (federal) union, then a fiscal union and finally a monetary union (unlike France who wants a monetary union without fiscal or political union). The German position is a sensible (even textbook-like) one, but conflicting with Europe's political realities.

value chains in low-wage Eastern Europe, preparing the ground for a new *Wirtschaftswunder*, it also undermined union bargaining power in Germany. This is reflected in a massive flow of German FDI to Eastern Europe and, at a later stage, China—which is to some extent the counterpart of its current account surplus. And because union bargaining power was undermined, not all of the efficiency gains derived from the value chains has trickled down to German household earnings and consumption growth—hence imports lagged exports (any growth in imports there might have been is actually largely transit trade of intermediate or final products sent back from Eastern Europe or China to Germany).

Indeed, claims that this economic model has served Germans well in terms of jobs growth, are probably oversold. As Fig. 6 shows, in trend terms the number of employed persons has increased since the creation of the single currency, but not the number of hours worked, suggesting an increasing incidence of part-time jobs. German business leaders may well have an interest in maintaining this status quo, so it is perhaps not surprising the country's political spearheads have declared the current account surplus sacred and an economic necessity. Meanwhile the German in the street is left with little net worth (note that Germany now has the euro area's most skewed wealth distribution as shown in Fig. 7), weak bargaining power and stories about Troika programme countries asking him to pay for their party. Little wonder they sound depressed. And as fiscal policy is kept tight, a public infrastructure deficit builds up, making Germany less attractive as a business location, and spurring further FDI outflows.

Third, one should not count on France to attract attention to current account issues. I tend to describe France as "Spain in slow motion". In Spain massive capital inflows were channelled through the banking system prior to the financial crisis and went into the real estate sector where a bubble inflated. The bubble burst, sovereign spreads soared as the government picked up the tab of failing banks. Households, corporates and banks were forced to deleverage (with official aid), domestic

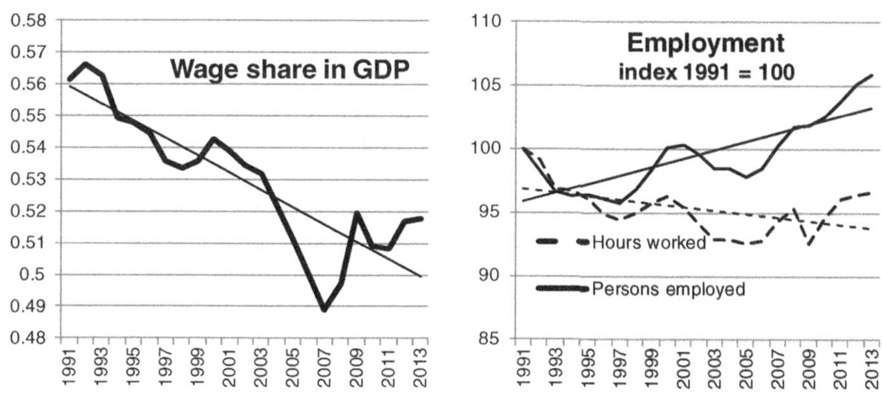

Fig. 6 Wage share and employment in Germany. *Source* AMECO Database, European Commission and Federal Statistical Office, Germany

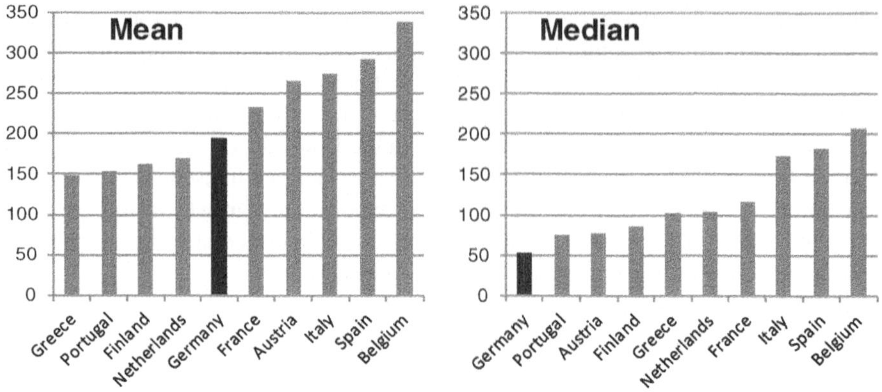

Fig. 7 Net wealth per household (× 1000€). *Source* ECB (2013), The euro system household and consumption survey

demand plummeted, unemployment soared and the current account deficit narrowed and eventually closed. France may be poised to experience the same sort of dynamics, but more gradually. As we have seen above, corporates and the government are still leveraging on the back of low interest rate. Like in Spain a housing bubble developed in the 2000s, but again low interest rates have helped it to deflate gently in what seems to be a soft landing. Yet the current account deficit is still widening as real wages keep increasing unabated. Meanwhile FDI flows into France—once a source of national pride—have all but dried up. Markets may one day wake up, but it is more likely that France is able to buy enough time to adjust on a slower track.

5 Concluding Remarks

Calls on the ECB to weaken the euro are misguided to the extent they do not address the root cause of currency strength, which is an unwillingness of external surplus countries, in particular Germany, to boost domestic investment amid a looming infrastructure deficit. Incentives for France to push Germany to do so are also weak as it is grappling with its own competitiveness problems. The result may be a French–German consensus to not adjust, while leaving it to monetary policy to do the heavy lifting. The end result may be a stalemate in which the euro area's current account surplus remains high and aggregate demand weak. That would mean that (core) inflation declined further and the risk of outright deflation increased. If that risk were to materialise the ECB may have to be called into rescue the area again, as it did in 2012 with the introduction of OMT. And it would have to do so persuasively or else Europe risks ending up in a Japanese conundrum. Quantitative easing has become all but inevitable.

Appendix: Econometrics

Methodology and Data

The aim of model is to help identify empirically for the euro area the potential links between the real effective exchange rate (*RE*), the current account position (*CA*) and the relative stances of macroeconomic policy, i.e. fiscal policy as gauged by the budget balance as a share of GDP relative to that of trading partners (*FB*) and monetary policy as gauged by the real interest rate differential (*IR*). The basic premise is that *RE, CA, FB* and *IR* are mutually dependent variables, with the direction of their dependencies in line with basic macroeconomic theory.

If we accept this premise, we can test whether—within the context of a linear vector error-correction model (VECM)—four co-integration vectors exist for the variables of interest given by:

$$RE_t = \sum_{i=1}^{n} \alpha_{RE,i} X_{i,t} + \mu_{RE,t} \tag{1}$$

$$CA_t = \sum_{i=1}^{n} \alpha_{CA,i} X_{i,t} + \mu_{CA,t} \tag{2}$$

$$FB_t = \sum_{i=1}^{n} \alpha_{FP,i} X_{i,t} + \mu_{FB,t} \tag{3}$$

$$IR_t = \sum_{i=1}^{n} \alpha_{IR,i} X_{i,t} + \mu_{IR,t} \tag{4}$$

with the following error-correction equations:

$$\Delta RE_t = \theta_{RE}\mu_{RE,t-1} + \pi_{RE}\mu_{CA,t-1} + \vartheta_{RE}\mu_{FB,t-1} + \rho_{RE}\mu_{IR,t-1} + \sum_{i=1}^{n+4} \sigma_{RE,i}\Delta Y_{i,t-1} + \varepsilon_{RE,t} \tag{5}$$

$$\Delta CA_t = \theta_{CA}\mu_{RE,t-1} + \pi_{CA}\mu_{CA,t-1} + \vartheta_{CA}\mu_{FB,t-1} + \rho_{CA}\mu_{IR,t-1} + \sum_{i=1}^{n+4} \sigma_{CA,i}\Delta Y_{i,t-1} + \varepsilon_{CA,t} \tag{6}$$

$$\Delta FB_t = \theta_{FB}\mu_{RE,t-1} + \pi_{FB}\mu_{CA,t-1} + \vartheta_{FB}\mu_{FP,t-1} + \rho_{FB}\mu_{IR,t-1} + \sum_{i=1}^{n+4} \sigma_{FB,i}\Delta Y_{i,t-1} + \varepsilon_{FB,t} \tag{7}$$

$$\Delta IR_t = \theta_{IR}\mu_{RE,t-1} + \pi_{IR}\mu_{CA,t-1} + \vartheta_{IR}\mu_{FB,t-1} + \rho_{IR}\mu_{IR,t-1} + \sum_{i=1}^{n+4} \sigma_{IR,i}\Delta Y_{i,t-1} + \varepsilon_{IR,t} \tag{8}$$

in which:

$$\Delta X_{j,t} = \sum_{i=1}^{n+4} \sigma_{X,i,j}\Delta Y_{i,t-1} + \varepsilon_{X,j,t} \tag{9}$$

where Y denotes all endogenous variables in the system, comprising the variables of interest RE, CA, FB, IR and a set of other variables X. Furthermore, μ denotes the error correction terms and ε the residuals in the error-correction equations. Note that in this system fiscal and monetary policy is endogenous. In the case of fiscal policy this could be attributed to the automatic fiscal stabilisers or, more broadly, rules-based fiscal policy responses. In the case of monetary policy this could be interpreted as policy reactions following some unspecified policy reaction function. Purely 'discretionary' fiscal and monetary policy moves are then captured by the 'innovations' $\varepsilon_{FB,t}$ and $\varepsilon_{IR,t}$. The parameters of prime interest are those on the error-correction terms in the error-correction equations, where we expect:

$$\theta_{RE} < 0,\ \theta_{CA} < 0, \pi_{RE} > 0, \pi_{CA} < 0,\ \rho_{RE} > 0, \vartheta_{FB} < 0, \vartheta_{CA} > 0 \ and\ \rho_{IR} < 0. \tag{10}$$

This effectively says that all four co-integrated variables will (by definition) converge to their long-run equilibrium, that an excessive current account surplus will over time produce an appreciation of the real exchange rate, that an overvalued real exchange rate will over time cause the current account surplus to shrink, that a fiscal policy tightening will lead the current account surplus to increase and that a tight stance of monetary policy will cause the real exchange rate to appreciate. Other relationships in the system may be more ambiguous.

The selected variables X are standard determinants of the equilibrium real effective exchange rate, comprising (for sources and definitions see Appendix):

- *TNT* = Ratio of prices of tradable to non-tradable goods (relative to trading partners)
- *TOT* = Terms of trade (relative to trading partners)
- *PROD* = Real GDP per capita (relative to trading partners)
- *NFA* = ECB net foreign assets as a share of GDP

This choice of explanatory variables will allow us to interpret *RE* as predicted by Eq. (1) as the equilibrium real effective exchange rate. The variables *TNT* and *PROD* are gauges of the Balassa-Samuelson effect, *TOT* aims to capture the impact of commodity price shocks and *NFA* captures the impact of currency intervention on *RE*. All variables are natural logarithms except for *CA*, *FB*, *NFA*, which are shares in GDP, and *IR* which is defined in percentage-points/100. The definitions and sources are:

RE = Real Effective Exchange Rate using the CPI of 37 trading partners as the deflator (Eurostat)

IR = Real short term interest rate differential (euro area—weighted average OECD, OECD)

FB = Net lending of General Government as a % of GDP, differential against OECD average, OECD)

TNT = Measured as the (EA PPI)/(EA HICP), EA PPI = Total output price index of industry excluding construction, sewerage, waste management, and remediation activities (Eurostat), EA HICP = All-items HICP (Eurostat)

TOT = Export Price Index/Import Price Index, Export Price Index of goods and services (Eurostat), Import Price Index of goods and services (Eurostat)

CA = Quarterly Current Account Surplus/Quarterly GDP (Eurostat)

$$\text{PROD} = \frac{\frac{\textit{Euro Area Real GDP}}{\textit{Capita}}}{\frac{\textit{OECD Real GDP}}{\textit{Capita}}}(\text{OECD})$$

NFA = Euro Area Central Bank Net Foreign Assets/Quarterly Euro Area GDP, Euro Area Central Bank NFA from IMF Central Bank Survey

All data is quarterly and available for the period 1999Q1 to 2013Q3.

Estimation Results

The estimation results, reported in Table 1 (based on the data reported in Table 2), are overall satisfactory in the sense that the trace test suggests the existence of four co-integration equations and that all signs are expected as in (10). Specifically,

- all coefficients on the 'self' error –correction terms in the short-term equations have the required negative sign and are significant;
- the impact of the error correction term in the current account long-run equation on the change in the real exchange rate is positive and significant;
- the impact of the error correction term in the real exchange rate long-run equation on the change in the current account is negative and significant;
- the impact of the error correction term in the fiscal balance long-run equation on the change in the current account is positive and significant; and
- the impact of the error correction term in the real interest rate differential long-run equation on the change in the real exchange rate is positive, though not significant.

Table 1 Vector error correction estimates

Cointegrating Eq	Coint Eq 1	Coint Eq 2	Coint Eq 3	CointEq 4
RE(−1)	1	0	0	0
CA(−1)	0	1	0	0
FB(−1)	0	0	1	0
IR(−1)	0	0	0	1
TNT(−1)	16.81	−1.23	2.10	2.35
	[4.52]	[−4.36]	[5.67]	[5.95]
TOT(−1)	26.48	−2.19	3.16	3.37
	[6.23]	[−6.79]	[7.46]	[7.46]
NFA(−1)	3.24	−0.22	0.18	0.27
	[3.93]	[−3.57]	[2.20]	[3.11]
PROD(−1)	−4.95	0.93	−1.03	−0.89
	[−2.09]	[5.15]	[−4.34]	[−3.54]
C	−181.51	11.48	−19.52	−22.25

Error correction	D(RE)	D(CA)	D(FB)	D(IR)	D(TNT)	D(TOT)	D(NFA)	D(PROD)
CointEq 1	−0.15	−0.05	0.01	0.00	0.02	−0.04	−0.15	−0.10
	[−3.24]	[−3.18]	[1.87]	[−0.18]	[1.02]	[−2.55]	[−2.29]	[−2.64]
CointEq 2	1.02	−0.35	−0.01	0.00	−0.25	0.12	−0.74	−0.80
	[2.93]	[−3.03]	[−0.12]	[−0.06]	[−1.57]	[0.98]	[−1.47]	[−2.94]
CointEq 3	1.30	0.47	−0.27	0.29	−0.62	0.12	−0.23	0.31
	[2.45]	[2.68]	[−3.69]	[2.45]	[−2.59]	[0.68	[−0.30]	[0.76]
CointEq 4	0.61	−0.26	0.14	−0.31	0.18	0.22	1.11	0.24
	[1.20]	[−1.55]	[1.97]	[−2.72]	[0.78]	[1.26]	[1.50]	[0.59]
D(RE(−1))	0.11	0.00	−0.03	0.01	0.08	0.01	0.03	0.09
	[0.91]	[0.07]	[−1.70]	[0.27]	[1.46]	[0.33]	[0.15]	[0.88]

(continued)

Table 1 (continued)

Error correction	D(RE)	D(CA)	D(FB)	D(IR)	D(TNT)	D(TOT)	D(NFA)	D(PROD)
D(CA(−1))	−0.70	0.02	−0.04	−0.15	0.10	0.08	0.78	1.08
	[−1.92]	[0.18]	[−0.87]	[−1.79]	[0.60]	[0.68]	[1.48]	[3.80]
D(FB(−1))	1.97	−0.38	0.07	0.46	0.19	−0.33	1.23	−0.25
	[2.21]	[−1.28]	[0.54]	[2.30]	[0.48]	[−1.07]	[0.95]	[−0.35]
D(IR(−1))	0.72	0.76	0.01	0.04	−0.69	0.31	−1.30	0.78
	[1.08]	[3.43]	[0.11]	[0.24]	[−2.33]	[1.36]	[−1.36]	[1.51]
D(TNT(−1))	1.14	0.38	−0.06	0.01	−0.28	0.05	−1.38	0.43
	[3.23]	[3.25]	[−1.27]	[0.16]	[−1.78]	[0.42]	[−2.71]	[1.56]
D(TOT(−1))	0.05	0.14	0.18	0.22	−0.44	−0.13	−0.38	−1.31
	[0.10]	[0.88]	[2.69]	[2.05]	[−2.09]	[−0.82]	[−0.57	[−3.58]
D(NFA(−1))	0.09	0.05	−0.02	0.01	0.01	−0.05	−0.05	−0.04
	[0.81]	[1.41]	[−1.01]	[0.26]	[0.19]	[−1.42]	[−0.29]	[−0.42]
D(PROD(−1))	0.36	0.22	−0.05	0.01	0.05	−0.05	0.31	−0.35
	[2.27]	[4.24]	[−2.13]	[0.19]	[0.66]	[−0.86]	[1.34]	[−2.85]
C	0.00	0.00	0.00	0.00	0.00	0.00	0.00	0.00
	[0.51]	[0.61]	[1.59]	[1.01]	[−0.35]	[−1.64]	[0.30]	[−2.14]
R-squared	0.55	0.55	0.39	0.45	0.53	0.51	0.37	0.83
Adj. R-squared	0.42	0.43	0.22	0.30	0.40	0.38	0.20	0.78
F-statistic	4.40	4.56	2.32	3.03	4.15	3.84	2.19	17.79

Note Sample: 1999Q3 2013Q3; Included observations: 57 after adjustments; t-statistics in []

Table 2 Data

	RE	NFA	TOT	TNT	PROD	IR	CA	FB
1999Q1	4.56	0.22	4.63	4.62	4.64	−2.14	−0.39	−0.33
1999Q2	4.52	0.20	4.63	4.62	4.67	−1.82	−0.10	−0.33
1999Q3	4.51	0.20	4.62	4.62	4.66	−3.03	−0.42	−0.33
1999Q4	4.49	0.21	4.61	4.62	4.68	−2.90	−0.90	−0.33
2000Q1	4.45	0.20	4.60	4.61	4.66	−2.27	−1.06	−0.11
2000Q2	4.42	0.19	4.59	4.62	4.68	−1.76	−1.59	−0.11
2000Q3	4.41	0.19	4.59	4.63	4.67	−1.68	−1.31	−0.11
2000Q4	4.39	0.17	4.58	4.64	4.70	−2.00	−1.45	−0.11
2001Q1	4.44	0.18	4.59	4.64	4.65	−1.95	−0.86	−0.26
2001Q2	4.42	0.18	4.59	4.64	4.68	−2.08	−1.11	−0.26
2001Q3	4.44	0.17	4.59	4.63	4.66	−1.39	0.13	−0.26
2001Q4	4.44	0.17	4.60	4.61	4.67	−0.76	0.69	−0.26
2002Q1	4.43	0.18	4.61	4.61	4.64	−1.09	0.74	0.89
2002Q2	4.45	0.17	4.60	4.60	4.67	0.11	−0.08	0.89
2002Q3	4.49	0.18	4.61	4.60	4.65	0.09	1.30	0.89
2002Q4	4.49	0.18	4.61	4.60	4.68	−0.05	0.99	0.89
2003Q1	4.54	0.18	4.61	4.61	4.63	−0.31	0.19	1.04
2003Q2	4.58	0.18	4.61	4.59	4.66	0.21	−0.25	1.04
2003Q3	4.57	0.18	4.62	4.59	4.64	0.24	0.79	1.04
2003Q4	4.59	0.18	4.62	4.59	4.66	0.38	0.95	1.04
2004Q1	4.60	0.19	4.62	4.59	4.62	0.73	0.79	0.61
2004Q2	4.59	0.18	4.61	4.59	4.65	0.10	0.21	0.61
2004Q3	4.59	0.18	4.61	4.60	4.63	0.00	0.63	0.61
2004Q4	4.61	0.18	4.61	4.60	4.66	−0.25	1.17	0.61
2005Q1	4.61	0.19	4.61	4.61	4.61	−0.12	0.40	0.15
2005Q2	4.59	0.19	4.61	4.60	4.65	−0.32	−0.36	0.15
2005Q3	4.57	0.19	4.59	4.61	4.63	−0.75	−0.05	0.15
2005Q4	4.57	0.19	4.59	4.61	4.65	−0.94	−0.40	0.15
2006Q1	4.57	0.19	4.58	4.63	4.62	−0.69	−0.63	0.08
2006Q2	4.59	0.19	4.58	4.63	4.64	−0.87	−0.51	0.08
2006Q3	4.60	0.20	4.58	4.63	4.62	−0.37	−0.22	0.08
2006Q4	4.60	0.20	4.59	4.63	4.66	−0.04	0.52	0.08
2007Q1	4.61	0.20	4.59	4.63	4.63	0.44	−0.01	0.83
2007Q2	4.62	0.20	4.59	4.62	4.64	0.55	−0.23	0.83
2007Q3	4.62	0.21	4.59	4.63	4.64	0.80	0.46	0.83
2007Q4	4.64	0.21	4.58	4.63	4.67	−0.01	0.39	0.83
2008Q1	4.65	0.22	4.58	4.64	4.63	0.02	−1.49	1.37
2008Q2	4.67	0.21	4.57	4.64	4.66	0.15	−1.91	1.37
2008Q3	4.65	0.14	4.56	4.66	4.65	−0.08	−1.58	1.37
2008Q4	4.63	0.07	4.58	4.63	4.67	0.81	−1.35	1.37

(continued)

Table 2 (continued)

	RE	NFA	TOT	TNT	PROD	IR	CA	FB
2009Q1	4.66	0.13	4.60	4.61	4.60	1.54	−1.23	2.10
2009Q2	4.67	0.19	4.60	4.59	4.63	2.32	−1.04	2.10
2009Q3	4.66	0.25	4.60	4.59	4.62	2.78	0.08	2.10
2009Q4	4.67	0.30	4.60	4.59	4.63	1.96	0.23	2.10
2010Q1	4.62	0.30	4.59	4.60	4.60	1.29	−0.94	1.75
2010Q2	4.58	0.32	4.58	4.61	4.62	0.78	−1.16	1.75
2010Q3	4.57	0.31	4.58	4.61	4.62	0.79	−0.78	1.75
2010Q4	4.58	0.34	4.58	4.61	4.65	0.63	−0.36	1.75
2011Q1	4.58	0.33	4.57	4.63	4.61	0.18	−0.83	2.43
2011Q2	4.61	0.36	4.56	4.63	4.63	0.14	−0.43	2.43
2011Q3	4.60	0.38	4.56	4.64	4.63	0.24	0.24	2.43
2011Q4	4.59	0.31	4.56	4.63	4.62	−0.07	1.40	2.43
2012Q1	4.56	0.35	4.56	4.64	4.61	−0.16	−0.25	2.17
2012Q2	4.55	0.31	4.55	4.63	4.60	−0.13	1.22	2.17
2012Q3	4.53	0.32	4.56	4.64	4.60	−0.37	2.04	2.17
2012Q4	4.55	0.31	4.56	4.63	4.62	−0.19	2.91	2.17
2013Q1	4.59	0.33	4.56	4.63	4.57	0.32	1.16	1.61
2013Q2	4.60	0.26	4.57	4.61	4.60	0.77	2.64	1.61
2013Q3	4.61	0.29	4.57	4.61	4.59	0.40	2.30	1.61

Source OECD Economic Outlook Database and Eurostat

Other interesting features of the estimation result regarding the long-run equations are that relative per capita income is found to exert a positive impact on the real effective exchange rate (as expected) and a negative impact on the current account balance. So everything else equal, high income economies should run a smaller current account balance and a higher real exchange rate than low income countries. Moreover, again everything else equal, high income countries run more positive fiscal positions and higher real interest rates than lower income countries per capita income.

References

Feldstein, M. 2014. A weaker Euro for a stronger Europe, Project syndicate, the worlds opinion page, April 30. http://www.project-syndicate.org/commentary/martin-feldstein-says-that-sharp-currency-depreciation-would-solve-the-eurozone-s-biggest-problems

Frankel, G. 2014. Considering QE, Mario? Buy US bonds, not Eurobonds, *VOX-EU*, March 24. http://www.voxeu.org/article/ecb-should-do-qe-forex-intervention

What Kind of Financial Integration Under Banking Union?

Mauro Grande

Abstract This paper reviews the experience of financial integration in the euro area since the start of the EMU and focuses on the possible impact that the implementation of the Banking Union (in particular the Single Supervisory Mechanism and the Single Resolution Mechanism) might have on the future process of financial integration. To that end, the paper first describes the main past developments in financial integration both at the euro area level and at a disaggregated level (e.g. in specific market segments) through a wide range of indicators. Second, it assesses the degree to which the integration process achieved the main benefits usually expected from financial integration (i.e. enhanced risk-sharing and improved capital allocation) while avoiding potential negative effects in terms of financial stability as well as it evaluates the experience of financial fragmentation during the crisis. Third, it provides some preliminary considerations on how the implementation of the Banking Union might affect some less positive elements of the past experience of financial integration if these tended to manifest themselves again in the future. Overall, the Banking Union is expected to have a positive impact by promoting a more balanced financial integration process and contributing to reducing the diffusion and negative effects of financial fragmentation in times of crisis. This enhanced quality of the financial integration process would be to a large extent the result of the Banking Union making the conduct of prudential supervision and bank resolution more effective.

Adviser to the Executive Board—European Central Bank (ECB). Views expressed in this paper do not reflect necessarily those of the institution. The author is grateful to Andreas Baumann, ECB, for his valuable research assistance.

M. Grande (✉)
European Central Bank, Frankfurt am Main, Germany
e-mail: Mauro.Grande@ecb.int

L. Paganetto (ed.), *Achieving Dynamism in an Anaemic Europe*,
DOI 10.1007/978-3-319-14099-5_5

1 Introduction

This paper reviews the experience of financial integration in the euro area since the start of the single currency and concentrates on the issue of how the financial integration process could develop in the future in particular as a consequence of the implementation of the *Banking Union*. The focus is in particular on the potential effects of the Single Supervisory Mechanism (SSM) which started on 4 November 2014 and of the Single Resolution Mechanism (SRM) which entered partially into force on 1 January 2015.[1] The possible role of a common financial backstop as an element of the Banking Union is also acknowledged where appropriate.

The issue addressed in the paper is relevant since the process of financial integration in the euro area—characterised by a significant increase in integration in the run-up to the crisis and a diffused fragmentation during the financial and sovereign crisis—has unfolded in forms which may have not fully realised the main benefits normally expected from financial integration and may have produced some negative side effects in terms of the public objectives of financial and monetary stability.

Therefore, it is timely at the current juncture—in which a slow process of recovery of financial integration in the euro area is taking place—to assess what kind of impact the Banking Union might have in case past financial integration developments tended to manifest themselves again in the future. In this respect, a general expectation is that the Banking Union might "generate a higher quality of financial integration" (Draghi 2014).

The paper is organised as follows. We first review the main benefits of financial integration as well as potential negative side effects. Secondly, we describe the main elements of the Banking Union and its main impact banking policies (supervision and resolution). Thirdly, the main past developments in financial integration at the euro area level are presented also in comparison with global trends. Fourthly, we analyse specific features of the financial integration and fragmentation processes at a disaggregated level (e.g. in main financial market segments) from the viewpoint of the main benefits (and possible negative side effects) of financial integration and provide a qualitative assessment of the potential impact of the Banking Union. We draw finally some conclusions.

2 Main Benefits of Financial Integration

While the relevant literature on financial integration highlights many benefits of financial integration, there is a widespread agreement that the two most important ones relate to *risk-sharing* and *capital allocation*.[2] While these benefits can refer to

[1]Some provisions of the SRM Regulation (e.g. on the Single Resolution Fund and bail-in mechanism) will enter into force on 1 January 2016.

[2]For a detailed review of main benefits of financial integration see Baele et al. (2004).

developments both within a country and across countries, the focus in this paper is on the cross-border dimension.

Financial integration between countries can promote *enhanced risk-sharing* in any of the countries concerned mainly through increased portfolio diversification across borders thus improving the countries' absorbing capacity to withstand shocks. This capacity would vary depending on the financial market segment which is affected by the integration process. Integration in equity markets is supposed to have a stronger effect due to the fact that shocks are immediately fully absorbed by equity owners while debt securities holders absorb shocks only when the debt servicing capacity of the securities issuers is impaired (e.g. insolvency).

The aspect of risk-sharing is particularly important in the context of *monetary unions*, such as the euro area, since countries adopting a single currency have at their disposal less policy tools to adjust to macroeconomic asymmetric shocks. In particular, these countries give up their exchange rate and country-specific monetary policy tools. Therefore, for these countries the financial diversification brought by integration can be a form of external insurance against asymmetric shocks. Van Beers et al. (2014) analyse how the various external insurance mechanisms, including through financial and banking markets, have operated until recently in the euro area also in comparison with the US experience.

Financial integration between countries can also favour *improved capital allocation* in any of the countries concerned as a result of many factors including increased availability of funds, enhanced competition among financial institutions and diffusion of financial knowledge and expertise. To the extent that financial integration allows for wider investment opportunities in a country, this could translate also into better macroeconomic performance. This could be as well the result of financial integration allowing for access to finance to economic sectors previously excluded.

Financial integration may however have also some *negative side effects* in terms of financial stability. In particular, financial integration can take forms which sow the seeds for future financial instability. This could be the case for instance of financial integration in the form of cross-border financial flows *mainly of short-term nature* which are by their very nature very volatile and thus can create financial stability problems in the recipient countries.

The reverse of financial integration, namely *fragmentation* which may arise during a crisis, has always the negative connotation of reducing the benefits gained in the precedent integration period and may take forms which are detrimental to the smooth functioning of the monetary policy function as shown by the experience of the sovereign crisis in the euro area.

Against this background, a *high quality* process of financial integration is the one able to maximise the expected benefits while keeping the potential negative side effects in terms of financial stability to a minimum. At the same time, a *not too negative* process of financial fragmentation in a crisis situation can be the one with a limited impact on the benefits gained in the integration period and limited negative side effects on the effectiveness of monetary policy. These are the metrics under which we review past developments in financial integration. This can be only a broad qualitative assessment since it is very difficult to set quantitative benchmarks. Before we do that, we consider the main elements of the Banking Union.

3 Main Elements of the Banking Union

The Banking Union is composed of the Single Supervisory Mechanism (SSM), the Single Resolution Mechanism (SRM),[3] an extended harmonisation of national regimes for deposit insurance (Deposit Guarantee Scheme Directive) and a common financial backstop in the form of the Bank Direct Recapitalisation (BDR) instrument of the European Stability Mechanism (ESM). The Banking Union represents an *enormous institutional progress* in comparison with the previous situation where responsibility for banking policies was exclusively at the national level. For the time being, it remains *incomplete* due to the lack of a Single Deposit Insurance Mechanism and the limited scope of the common financial backstop though for the latter there is a commitment of member states to develop in the future a common financial backstop also for bank resolution.[4]

The adoption of the Banking Union responded primarily to a *crisis management need*, namely to reduce the negative feedback loop between sovereign and banking risks which spread during the sovereign crisis in the euro area. In general, this loop can manifest itself in two forms:

- banking problems turning into fiscal problems due to the fact that government is the ultimate guarantor for its own banking system and under the circumstances of a weak fiscal position and a large size of the banking sector vis-à-vis the economy;
- fiscal problems turning into banking problems since the costs of government funding are the basis for the costs of bank funding and domestic sovereign bonds represent a large share of bank assets.

The Banking Union is meant to address primarily the *first dimension* of the negative loop by basically reducing to a minimum the potential for government support to banks. To that end, the SSM is to be regarded as the first step intended to *reduce the probability of banking problems* mainly through an increase of effectiveness of prudential supervision of banks. This should be achieved through various channels including a reduction in the domestic bias in the supervisory action, a convergence of supervisory practices towards the highest quality and a substantive improvement of the supervision on a consolidated basis.

---

[3]Both the SSM and the SRM are complemented by and based upon the Single Banking Rulebook (Capital Requirements Directive IV, Capital Requirements Regulation, Bank Recovery and Resolution Directive) applying to the EU as a whole.

[4]In approving the compromise with the European Parliament on the SRM on 27 March 2014, the Council stated that during the transitional phase of the Single Resolution Fund a common backstop would be developed.

Despite this expected improvement brought by the SSM, there will be nevertheless banking problems. The main objective of prudential supervision is not zero failure but rather prudent risk behaviour of banks to reduce the risk of failure to a minimum. Therefore, an effective bank resolution mechanism is also needed to manage effectively bank failure so that the potential for government intervention is reduced. This goal is first pursued by the Bank Recovery and Resolution Directive (BRRD) by introducing in all EU countries a common resolution toolkit (sale of business, bridge institution, asset separation and bail-in) and by setting up national resolution funds financed by the banking industry as well by imposing a prior use of private money to cover losses before public money could be used.[5]

The objective is further pursued by the SRM which is meant to ensure a smooth resolution process for the significant banks under the direct supervision of the ECB and cross-border banks through a centralisation at the EU level of the decision-making process (Single Resolution Board, Commission, Council) and the setting-up of a Single Resolution Fund pooling the resources of the national funds. The SRM was necessary also to ensure overall consistency of the institutional framework for banking policies: maintenance of national responsibility for bank resolution in the presence of the SSM would create misalignments of incentives between resolution authorities and the single supervisor.

Therefore, to the extent that the SSM and the SRM (together with the BRRD) are effective in practice, the likelihood that a government has to support its ailing banks would be greatly reduced but not removed completely. To that end, it is necessary to have a common financial backstop which would mutualise the residual risk for governments thus de-linking fully a domestic banking sector from its own government. In that sense, it is only once the envisaged common financial backstop for bank resolution (fiscally neutral) has been agreed and implemented that the overall framework can be regarded as addressing fully the negative loop between sovereigns and banks.

4 Financial Integration at the Euro Area Level

Main developments in financial integration in the euro area can be seen through the lenses of a new indicator developed by the ECB, notably the *Financial Integration Composite* (FINTEC) indicator.[6] The FINTEC is an aggregation of selected

[5]The BRRD provides that losses incurred by a bank first need to be covered by using the bail-in mechanism for a minimum of 8 % of the bank's total liabilities and second use can be made of the national resolution fund for a maximum of 5 % of the bank's total liabilities (experience of past banking crises indicates that governments provide on average financial support to banks in the range of 13 % of total bank assets).

[6]The FINTEC was presented for the first time on the occasion of the publication of the ECB report on Financial Integration in Europe 2014 on 28 April 2014 and details will be presented in the ECB report "Finanical Integration in Europe", April 2015.

price- and quantity-based indicators developed over time by the ECB to monitor financial integration in the main market segments of the euro area. *Price dispersions* and *cross-border holdings* are the basis for the calculation of price- and quantity-based FINTEC respectively,[7] while the monitoring process covers the money, (government and corporate) bond, equity and banking markets. The different time series (since 1995 and 1999 respectively) for the price- and the quantity-based FINTEC are due to the availability of the underlying data.

As shown in Fig. 1, the FINTEC indicates how the degree of financial integration in the euro area measured in terms both of prices and quantities varies overtime. By construction, the value of the FINTEC ranges between 0 (lack of integration) and 1 (full integration).[8] The *price-based* FINTEC indicates that the overall level of financial integration increased substantially between the introduction of the euro and the financial crisis, reflecting similar developments in the underlying market segments. At its peak, the level of integration was not far away from the defined level of full integration.[9] With the financial crisis and even more the sovereign crisis, there was a strong reversal in the process of financial integration (fragmentation) reaching a low level comparable to the one prevailing before the introduction of the euro. It is only with the announcement of the Banking Union and the ECB Outright Monetary Transactions (OMT) operations that a process of recovery of financial integration started which is still under way.

A similar pattern is shown by the *quantity-based* FINTEC though the level of integration measured through cross-border holdings tends to be lower than the one measured through price dispersions. At its peak, the quantity-based FINTEC was still far away from the defined level of full integration. In general, this bears the question of better understanding—in monitoring financial integration—the interplay between price and quantity dynamics beyond the obvious consideration that normally quantities tend to react more slowly and to a lesser degree than prices.

Developments in financial integration in the euro area should not be seen in isolation but rather against the background of the process of financial integration at the global level. Concerning equity and bond markets, Fig. 2 plots *bilateral holdings of equity and debt securities* within the euro area and among a selected

[7]The calculation of the FINTEC entails three steps: (i) homogenisation of all indicators through a transformation on the basis of the "cumulative distribution function" (CDF); (ii) definition of a theoretical benchmark of full integration; and (iii) aggregation of sub-indices through either equal weights or size weights.

[8]For the price-based FINTEC the theoretical benchmark for full integration is assumed to correspond to a value of zero for all price dispersions, while for the quantity-based FINTEC the theoretical benchmark for full integration is determined on the basis of a "market portfolio" approach (i.e. each investor replicates the market portfolio).

[9]Given that price-based indicators of financial integration are based on price dispersions which reflect also risk premiums, they may over/underestimate the degree of financial integration depending on how correctly markets price risks. If—as it is commonly assumed—in the run-up to the crisis markets were under-pricing risks, price dispersion was lower and degree of financial integration higher than in case of correct risk pricing.

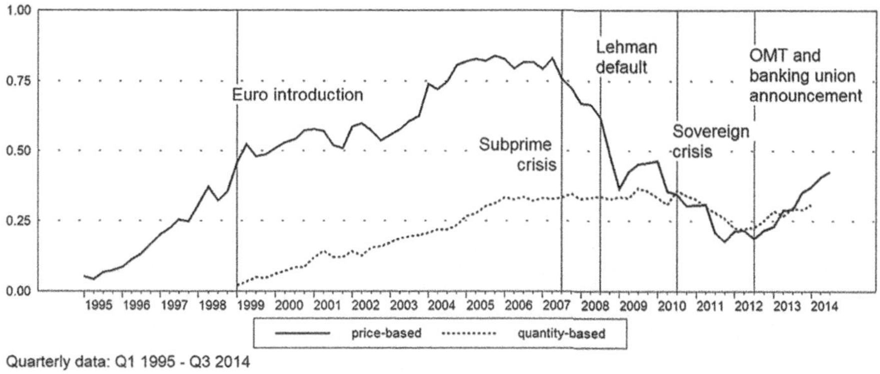

Fig. 1 Composite indicators of financial integration (*FINTECs*). *Source* ECB. *Notes* The price-based FINTEC aggregates ten indicators at the monthly frequency, covering the period Q1 1995–Q3 2014, and the quantity-based FINTEC aggregates five indicators at the quarterly frequency, covering the period Q1 1999–Q1 2014.

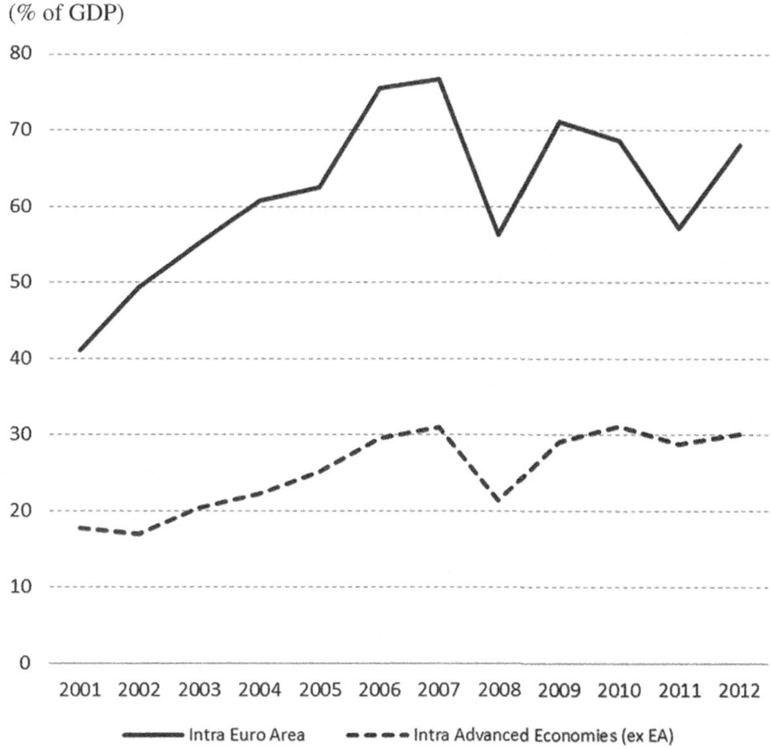

Fig. 2 Bilateral holdings of equity and debt securities (% of GDP). *Source* IMF—Coordinated Portfolio Investment Survey (CPIS), World Bank (WDI)

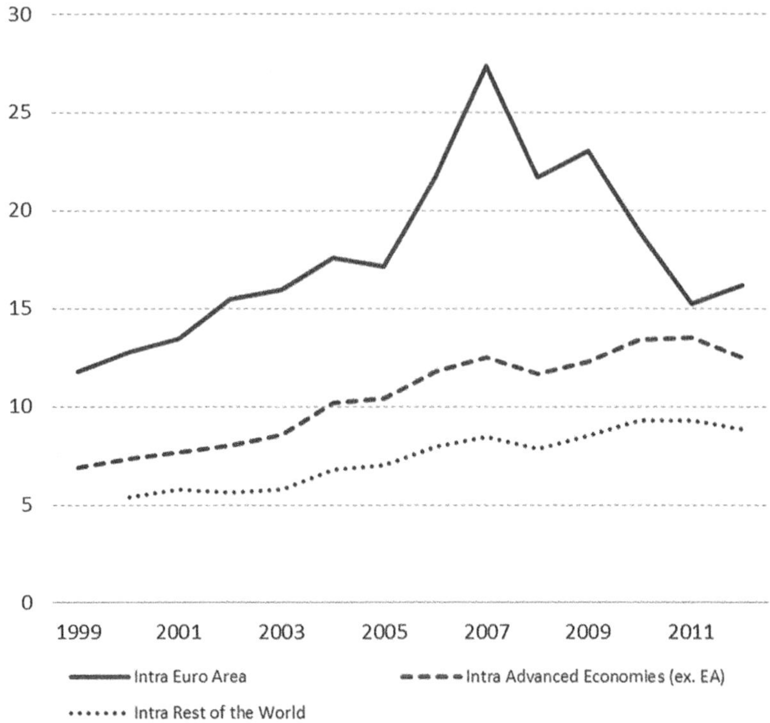

Fig. 3 Foreign bank claims (% of GDP). *Source* BIS consolidated statistics, World Bank (WDI)

sample of advanced economies (expressed as % of the respective GDP). This can be regarded as another quantity-based indicator to measure the degree of financial integration.

The figure shows that the patterns over time are similar in both geographical areas though not surprisingly the effects of the sovereign crisis were felt more in the euro area than at the global level. Interestingly the level of financial integration was normally higher in the euro area than globally reflecting the fact that a single currency provides further favourable conditions (such as disappearance of foreign exchange risk) for financial integration.

Concerning bank markets, Fig. 3 presents *bilateral foreign bank claims* for the euro area and two selected geographical samples of advanced economies and other countries (rest of the world) respectively (as % of the respective GDP). While also in these markets the level of integration in the euro area remained normally higher, the euro area has suffered the most from the financial and even more the sovereign crisis. At its bottom, the degree of banking integration in the euro area was not far away from the one among the advanced economies. This may be due to the process of reduction of cross-border activities of many euro area banks as part of a broader bank deleveraging process.

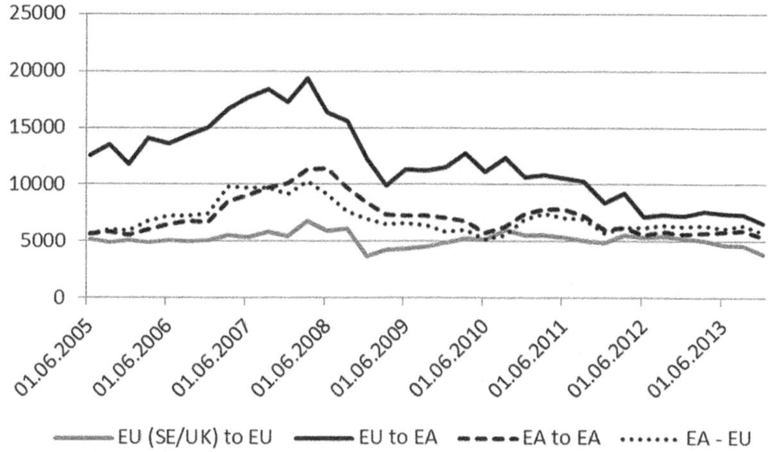

Fig. 4 Foreign bank claims within the EU (average values in US$ mn) (Average value for each category calculated as the ratio between the absolute amount and the number of counterparties). *Source* BIS consolidated banking statistics

Finally, it is interesting to compare developments in financial integration within the euro area with the rest of the European Union (EU). We confine ourselves to the banking markets. Figure 4 shows the evolution of *foreign bank claims between the EU non-EA countries* (UK and Sweden only) *and the euro area* in both directions as well as within the two areas. The figure indicates that in the run-up to the crisis there was not only a strong increase in banking integration within the euro area (see Sect. 5.1) but also in cross-border banking flows between the euro area and the rest of the EU in both directions. By contrast, the crisis determined a strong reduction of banking flows particularly from the EU non-EA countries to the euro area to very low levels. This raises the question of whether and when they will increase again.

5 Financial Integration at Disaggregated Level and Possible Impact of the Banking Union

In this section, we look at financial integration patterns at a disaggregate level (e.g. main financial market segments) with a view to providing an assessment of the quality of the integration and fragmentation processes and developing some considerations on how the past developments, if they tended to repeat themselves, could be affected by the Banking Union. We do so by distinguishing between developments occurred: (i) before the crises, where the main issue is the extent to which the process of increasing financial integration achieved the expected benefits while avoiding negative side effects on financial stability, and (ii) during the crisis, where a main aspect is the degree to which financial fragmentation triggered negative side effects in terms of monetary stability. Finally, we also highlight some structural developments.

5.1 Developments Before the Crisis

Before the crisis, as seen in Sect. 4, financial integration increased significantly at the aggregated level reflecting growing integration in the main market segments. However, the way in which this process unfolded in some segments can be regarded as not always positive from the viewpoint of the main benefits of financial integration. *Two main aspects* can be mentioned in this respect.

A first aspect relates to the *geographical composition* of financial flows within the euro area. Figures 5 and 6 show changes occurred in financial flows (bank claims and debt securities) between four regions (financial centres, euro area core and peripheral countries and others countries (rest of the word)) in the period 1997–2007.[10] The figures indicate that in the period concerned there was an increase in financial flows relating both to bank claims and, to a lesser extent, to debt securities from core to peripheral countries. In addition, core countries increased substantially their bank intermediation role between financial centres and peripheral countries. Overall, the process of increasing integration in bond and banking markets within the euro area reflected to a large degree increasing financial flows between core and peripheral countries. This development was reversed during the crisis.

While this integration process is likely to have achieved the expected benefits in terms of risk-sharing, it was possibly less advantageous in terms of capital allocation: the large amount of financial flows to peripheral countries is likely not to have been employed fully in the most efficient way as highlighted for instance by the rapid growth in some countries of bank lending to the real estate sector. It also had some negative effects in terms of financial stability for both sets of countries: in peripheral countries the banking system became excessively exposed towards certain economic sectors (again real estate), while in core countries the banking system became excessively exposed towards the peripheral countries. On balance, it is doubtful that this kind of development represents a high quality form of financial integration.

Looking forward, this type of developments is less likely to re-occur. The argument relies on the assumption that the past evolution mainly represented the *financial side of macroeconomic dynamics* within the euro area. In particular, financial integration would have allowed the current account imbalances of peripheral countries to be financed by core countries which in turn would have acted also as intermediaries for investors outside the euro area (e.g. Chen et al. 2013). Against this background, first these macroeconomic imbalances might have been just a one-off event associated with the introduction of the euro. Second, even if they tended to re-emerge, they should be more promptly detected and addressed through the new *Macroeconomic Imbalances Procedure* (MIP) agreed at the EU level.

[10]Financial centres include Canada, Denmark, Japan, Sweden, Switzerland, UK and US; core countries include Austria, Belgium, Finland, France, Germany, Netherlands and Luxembourg; peripheral countries include Greece, Ireland, Italy, Portugal and Spain.

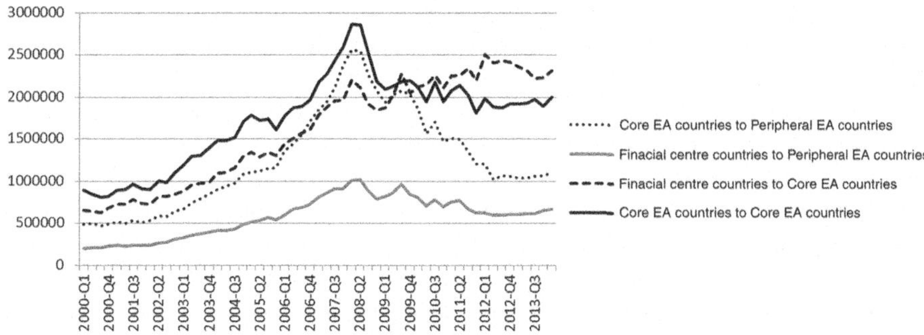

Fig. 5 Foreign bank claims in different regions (in USD millions). *Source* BIS consolidated banking statistics. *Notes* Immediate borrower basis, domestically owned banks, reporting countries: core EA countries: AT, BE, DE, FI, FR, NL; peripheral EA countries: GR, IE, IT, PT, ES; financial centre countries: CA, CH, DK, JP, SE, UK, US; counterparty countries: the same as for reporting countries, except for core countries as LU was added

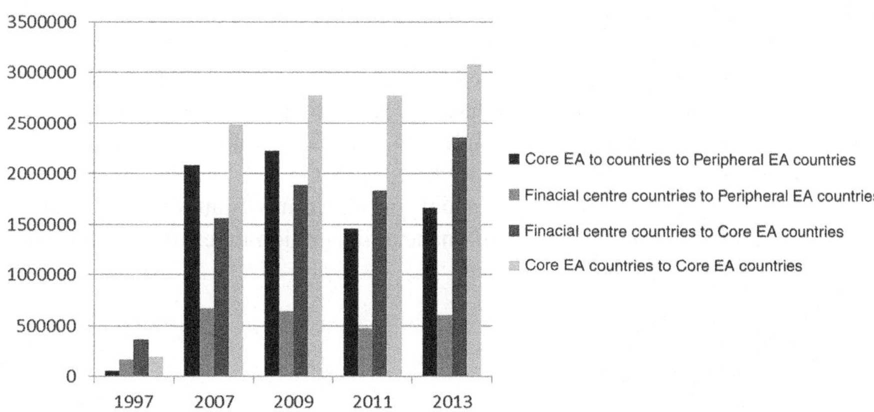

Fig. 6 Debt securities holdings in different regions (in USD millions). *Source* IMF—Coordinated Portfolio Investment Survey (CPIS). *Note* Gross portfolio debt positions reported by economies; data for GR, DE, LU and CH is not available for 1997

In addition, if imbalances were to turn out specifically in the euro area banking sector, there would be policy tools, associated with the *Banking Union*, which should help reduce the risk of financial instability. In particular, the SSM is expected to enhance the degree of effectiveness of prudential supervision thus reducing the possibility for euro area banks of building excessive risk concentrations towards economic sectors and/or countries. In addition, the new EU macro-prudential framework—laid down in the Capital Requirements Directive (CRD) IV and the Capital Requirements Regulation (CRR)—provides national authorities with specific policy tools to remediate imbalances in the banking sector. These national responsibilities are complemented in the euro area by new macro-prudential powers that the SSM Regulation assigns to the ECB so increasing the likelihood of an effective policy toolkit to address financial imbalances related to the banking system.

A second aspect relates to the main features of *banking integration*. Figure 7 shows the evolution of *banks' holdings of bank debt securities by country of issuer*.

The figure shows that between the start of the euro and the financial crisis there was a substantial reduction of domestic debt securities and a corresponding increase in the holding of securities issued by banks in other euro area countries up to 40 % of respective total holdings. During the crisis the process went into reverse to stabilise more recently with the abatement of the sovereign crisis.

Turning to lending activity, Fig. 8 provides the *share of cross-border loans for different typologies of loans*, namely interbank loans, loans to non-financial corporates and loans to households. Before the crisis the share of cross-border interbank loans increased from 25 to 35 % of the total interbank lending. By contrast, cross-border lending to non-financial corporates increased slightly before the crisis (from 5 to 7.5 % of total lending to corporates) to remain then at that low level, while cross-border lending to households has always been insignificant.

Taken together, the two figures show that the process of increasing banking integration in the euro area took place primarily through *cross-border interbank financing* in the form either of purchase of bank debt securities or of interbank lending. By contrast, cross-border lending to the real economy remained a very limited share of the overall cross-border bank activity.

A process of banking integration mainly in the form of interbank financing is likely to bring the expected benefits of financial integration in terms of risk-sharing.

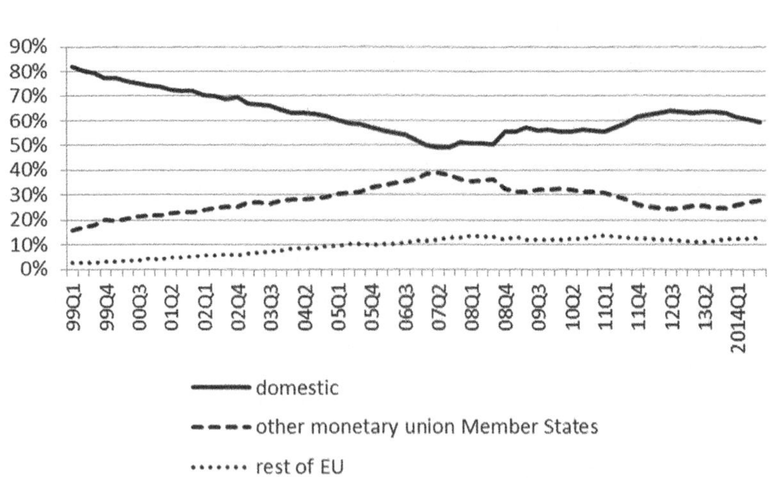

Fig. 7 Euro area banks' holdings of bank debt securities by country of issuer (% of total holdings). *Source* ECB. *Note* Outstanding amounts are classified by the residency of the issuer. Eurosystem holdings are excluded

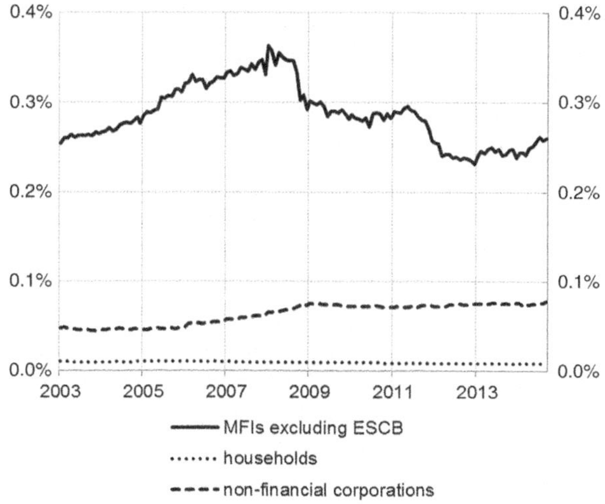

Fig. 8 Share of cross-border loans of euro area banks by typology of loans (% of respective total loans). *Source* ECB (BSI). *Notes* Cross-border loans include loans to other euro area member states for all maturities and currencies

As to capital allocation, the high share of interbank financing implies that the investment decisions in a given country fall exclusively on the domestic banking sector which may bring less efficient choices in case of very high amounts of available funds. This could be one of the reasons why some banks in the euro area became overly exposed to certain economic sectors. Whether a configuration with a higher share of direct cross-border lending to the real economy would be more efficient remains a matter for further analysis but it seems intuitive that, when capital allocation choices are shared between domestic and foreign banks, the outcome is likely to be more efficient. In addition, from the viewpoint of financial stability, cross-border interbank financing is subject to a higher degree of volatility than cross-border direct bank lending.

Overall, the process of banking integration in the run-up to the crisis had some drawbacks and it would be desirable to avoid them in the future process of financial integration. To that end, an increase in the share of direct cross-border lending to the real economy could help.

In this respect, while further analysis is needed to better understand the reasons why historically corporates and above all households resort to a very limited extent to cross-border bank financing, the Banking Union is likely to provide a positive contribution. In particular, the SSM is expected to support both the demand and the supply side of bank credit. On the demand side, the more effective supervision by the SSM would enhance the degree of confidence in the banking sector in the euro area thus possibly providing an incentive for corporates and households to resort to cross-border bank lending. On the supply side, the adoption by the SSM of a consistent approach to supervision within the euro area should remove existing hurdles to cross-border lending relating to the implementation of supervision at the national level. In addition, the SSM, being less affected by domestic bias, should not favour ring-fencing of capital and liquidity at banks within national borders. Furthermore, the SSM should promote a revamp in the cross-border consolidation of the banking system.

The SRM—together with the harmonised legal framework for bank resolution at the EU level (BRRD)—may also play a positive role. In fact effective and credible bank resolution regimes—by making bailout less likely—should exert a powerful control over the risk-taking attitude of banks. If shareholders and creditors of banks consider bank resolution (in particular the bail-in instrument) credible they will have strong incentives for monitoring effectively the risk behaviour of banks. Therefore, to the extent that the new EU bank resolution framework turns out to be effective in practice, it would assist the SSM in promoting more prudent bank behaviour thus increasing the overall level of trust in the banking system (Ignatowski and Korte 2014).

Finally, the level of confidence in the banking system could benefit also from the introduction of the envisaged common financial backstop for bank resolution.

5.2 Developments During the Crisis

During the financial and sovereign crisis, as seen in previous sections, there was a reversal in the process of financial integration with fragmentation spreading in most market (money, bond and banking) segments, while the equity markets were less affected. This process of fragmentation not only removed most of the benefits gained during the precedent period of integration but also took forms which had some negative effects in particular for the monetary policy function. In this respect, we mention three main aspects.

The first relates to integration of *money markets*. Figure 9 presents a new quantity-based indicator developed by the ECB to monitor integration in the euro area money market (*offset coefficient*).[11] The indicator measures the extent to which increases (decreases) in total liquidity autonomous factors in a country explain the inflows (outflows) from (to) other euro area countries. In other words, the coefficient measures the degree to which domestic shocks to liquidity are offset by liquidity flows across countries. The value of the indicator ranges between 0 (lack of integration) and −1 (theoretical full integration). The value of −0.66 was identified—through an econometric analysis—as the reference value for a high level of integration in the period concerned (January 2003–January 2014).

The figure shows that the coefficient has been around the reference value in the period preceding the crisis thus indicating a high level of integration. By contrast, during the crisis, the value of the coefficient moved into an area indicating

[11] The offset coefficient was introduced for the first time in the ECB report on Financial Integration in Europe 2014 (Special Feature A on "Geographical segmentation of the euro area money market: a liquidity flow approach").

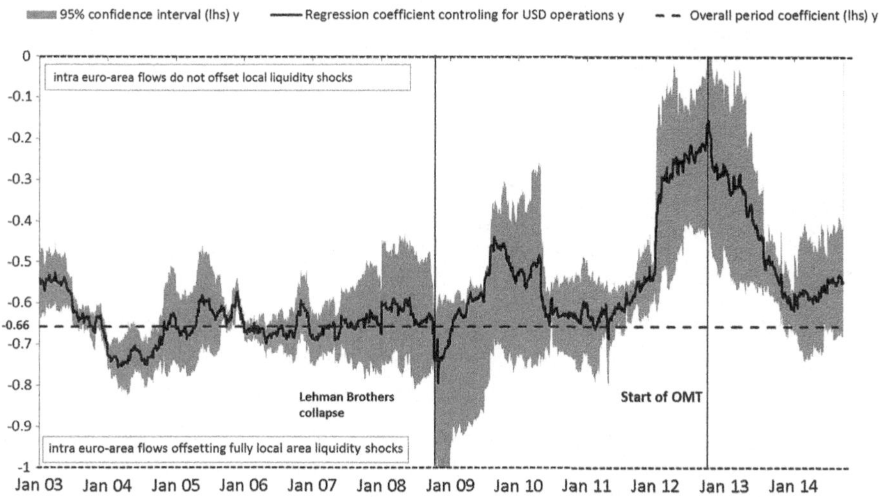

Fig. 9 Offset coefficient. *Source* ECB. *Notes* Offset coefficient measures the extent to which increases (decreases) in total autonomous factors in a country explain the inflows (outflows) from (to) other euro area countries

impairment in the cross-border re-allocation of liquidity, namely a significant reduction in the degree of integration in the euro area money market. This reduction was particularly acute during the sovereign crisis and was eased only following the announcement of the ECB OMT operations. More recently the value has stabilised close to the reference value. The reduction of cross-border liquidity flows was to a large extent the consequence of a decrease in the level of confidence among banks also as reflection of the sovereign risk.

During the crisis the process of financial fragmentation affected significantly in a negative way the effectiveness of the single monetary policy. In particular, the monetary transmission mechanism was considerably impaired as—especially during the sovereign crisis—short-term interest rates became more sensitive to domestic liquidity conditions.

The Banking Union is likely to reduce the likelihood of this negative effect in future crises for the same reasons highlighted above. The SSM and the SRM, by making prudential supervision and bank resolution more effective and promoting more prudent risk behaviour of banks, as well as the future common financial backstop for bank resolution are all likely to promote and maintain a high level of confidence within the banking sector even during crises.

A second aspect relates to integration in *bond markets*. Figure 10 shows the evolution of *banks' holdings of debt securities* (government and corporate bonds) *by residence of issuer* in the period September 1997–January 2014. Before the crisis banks increasingly substituted domestic bonds with bonds issued in other euro area countries (and partly from the rest of the EU) thus increasing integration in these markets, while during the crisis the process reverted to stabilise more recently.

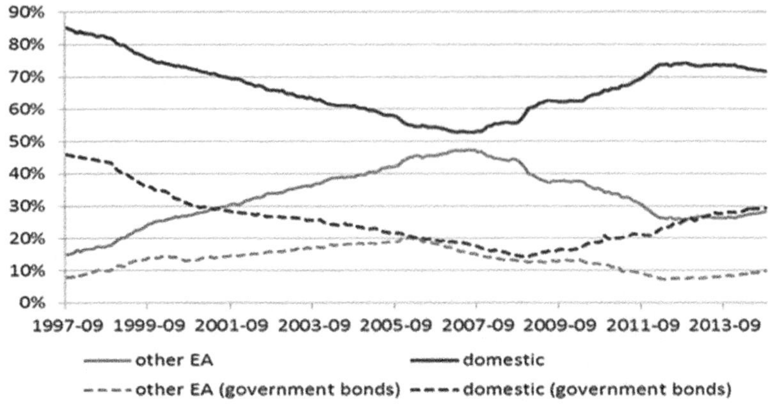

Fig. 10 Shares of euro area banks' holdings of debt securities by residence of issuer (% of total holdings, excluding Eurosystem). *Source* ECB. *Notes* Outstanding amounts are classified by the residency of the issuer. Holdings comprise sovereign and corporate debt

These developments were mainly driven by the holdings of government bonds which represent the largest share of banks' debt securities holdings.

In addition, the increasing banks' home bias for government bonds was primarily occurring in *peripheral countries*. Figure 11 shows the *banks' holdings of government bonds* as percentage of their total assets in the euro area as well as in core and peripheral countries.

The figure indicates that during the crisis the share of banks' holdings of domestic government bonds increased more in the peripheral countries reaching in April 2014 around 9 % of total banking assets versus around 2.5 % in core countries. While during the crisis the gap between the two remained lower than the one prevailing at the inception of the euro, it is an issue of concern from a financial

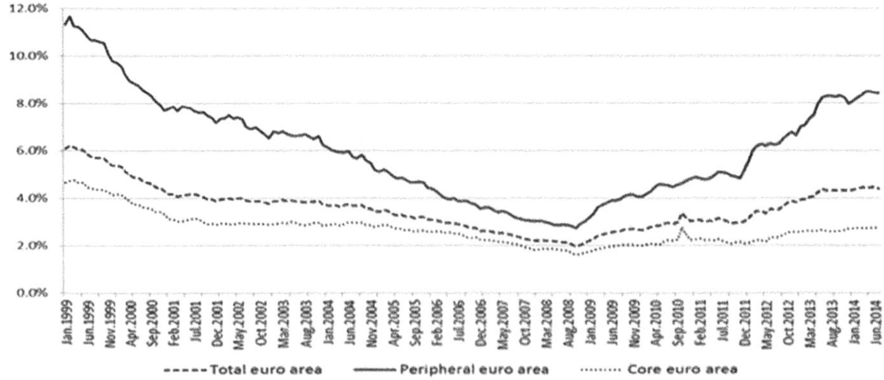

Fig. 11 Euro area banks' holdings of domestic government bonds (% of total banking assets). *Source* ECB. *Notes* Peripheral euro area countries: CY, GR, IE, IT, PT, SI and ES

stability viewpoint given that banks in peripheral countries may become excessively concentrated towards their own sovereign thus reinforcing the negative loop between them.

The increasing home bias in banks' holdings of government bonds may be the result of several factors. Battistini et al. (2014) provide evidence that, during the sovereign crisis, while all euro area banks increased their exposures to the domestic sovereign to hedge against the re-denomination risk until the ECB OMT operations, some banks in peripheral countries have increased their home bias even further as a result of various factors including: possible "moral suasion" by the respective governments, "carry trade" motivations given also their low level of capitalisation and the EU regulatory treatment of sovereign debt (e.g. risk weighting for capital requirements and large exposures regime). More in general, increasing home bias in the holding of government bonds in times of crisis may reflect a broad risk aversion attitude.

The potential impact of the Banking Union on this kind of developments is expected to be on balance positive. First, the SSM, as already mentioned, will be less affected by domestic considerations in its own action (reduction of domestic bias) and will be very attentive to developments in the concentration of sovereign risk and "carry trades" activities of banks. In addition, the SSM can be expected to play an active role when discussions on the regulatory treatment of sovereign debt develop at the EU level. Furthermore, more broadly, the Banking Union as a whole is likely to contribute to reducing the negative effects of a generalised risk aversion in the banking sector. All this should eventually reduce the home bias for sovereign debt in times of stress.

A third aspect refers to integration in *banking markets*. Figure 12 shows the pattern of the spread between lending rates of small and large loans. Small loans are assumed to be representative of loans to small and medium enterprises (SMEs). The spread is shown for the euro area as a whole and for distressed and non-distressed countries for the period Jan 2003–Mar 2014.[12] The figure shows that for the euro area as a whole the spread has been steadily decreasing before the crisis, while it has increased during the crisis. Therefore, SMEs used to pay during the crisis much higher bank lending costs than large corporates and this spread was larger in distressed countries (where it reached at the peak a value of around 200 bps).

This geographical fragmentation of the banking markets in the euro area in terms of costs of bank lending clearly affected the effectiveness of the single monetary policy with policy rates reductions not reflected in bank lending rates.[13] This development was the consequence of both demand and supply side of bank credit. On the demand side the deterioration of macro-economic conditions in distressed countries had a bearing on the demand for credit by the real economy. On the

[12]"Distressed" countries include Ireland, Greece, Spain, Italy, Cyprus, Portugal and Slovenia.

[13]These aspects are analysed in more detail in the ECB Report on Financial Integration in Europe 2014 (Special Feature B on "Divergence in financing conditions of small and medium-sized enterprises (SMEs) in the euro area").

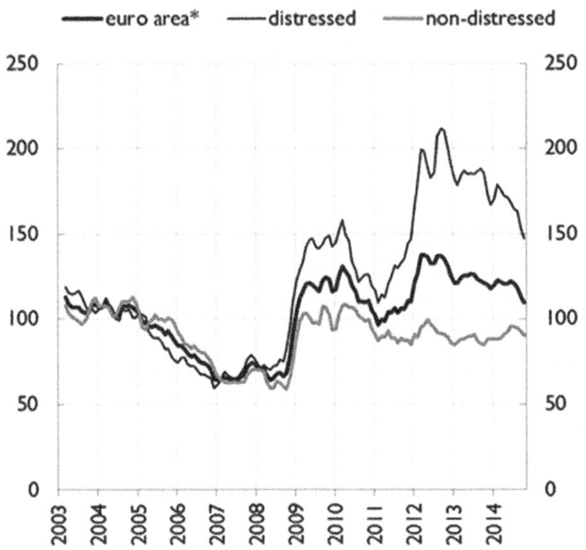

Fig. 12 Spread between small and large loans (small loans up to EUR 1 mn). *Source* ECB. *Notes* "distressed" countries are Ireland, Greece, Spain, Italy, Cyprus, Portugal and Slovenia. Small loans are loans of up to €1 million, while large loans are those above €1 million. Aggregation is based on new business volumes. *The euro area series is calculated as weighted average of country spreads

supply side, the need for banks in distressed countries to repair their balance sheet after the crisis experience as well as the high costs of funding also due to the sovereign risk contributed to a reduction in the offer of bank credit.

The Banking Union could contribute to reducing the risk of this kind of fragmentation in the banking markets in future times of crisis mainly in case of supply side issues. In that respect, the SSM is expected to promote the development and maintenance of banks' healthy financial conditions thus reducing the likelihood of balance sheet constraints as well as to induce banks (jointly with the macro-prudential authorities) to build adequate capital buffers in good times so that banks would be better able to withstand shocks in stress situations. By contrast, the SSM would be less relevant in case of financial fragmentation stemming mainly from demand side issues for which macroeconomic measures of governments and central bank interventions would be appropriate.

5.3 Developments Through the Cycle

Beyond cyclical developments, the experience of financial integration in the euro area also shows two important structural aspects. The first one was already highlighted in Sect. 5.1 above and relates to the *persistent home bias in bank lending activity to the real economy*. In that context, we have pointed to the possibility that

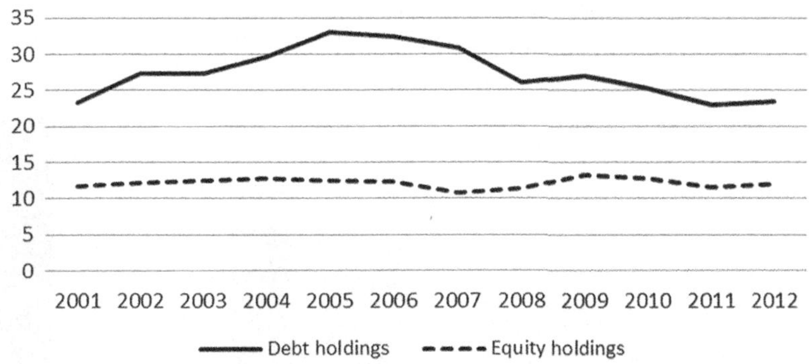

Fig. 13 Euro area bilateral equity and debt holdings (% of theoretical share of bilateral holdings). *Sources* IMF (CPIS), World Bank (WDI) and ECB calculations. *Note* The numerator is the sum of debt or equity bilateral portfolio holdings. The denominator is calculated as the sum of the products of the countries' total portfolios multiplied by the share of the partner country in the euro area debt or equity market portfolio. The sample countries include Austria, Belgium, Finland, France, Germany, Greece, Ireland, Italy, Luxembourg, Netherlands, Portugal and Spain

a larger share of direct cross-border lending to corporates and households might bring benefits in terms of capital allocation efficiency.

The second structural aspect relates to integration in *equity markets*. Figure 13 shows the ratio over time (2001–2012) between all equity and debt bilateral holdings within the euro area and the theoretical share of bilateral holdings assuming full integration.[14] As such, the indicator represents a way to compare the level of financial integration in the two markets.

In this respect, the figure highlights that the level of integration in equity markets has always been *lower* than in bonds markets though the gap has narrowed down during the crisis given the lower impact of the crisis on equity markets integration. Bearing in mind the potential benefits of financial integration, this structural element entails that there is still scope for reaping benefits in terms of risk-sharing/ shock absorbing capacity within the euro area by increasing integration of the equity versus the bond markets.

To gauge the extent to which this would be possible, we can refer to an indicator of *cross-border equity holdings*. Figure 14 provides for the period 1997–2012 the *share of equity issued in the euro area and held by residents in other euro area countries*. The figure shows that throughout the whole period the ratio has steadily increased from 12 % in 1997 to 43 % in 2012 confirming once again that equity integration was marginally affected by the crisis.

Looking forward, the Banking Union is not the primary policy tool to achieve the objective of further equity market integration. This will require specific public

[14]Calculated on the basis of a "market portfolio" approach.

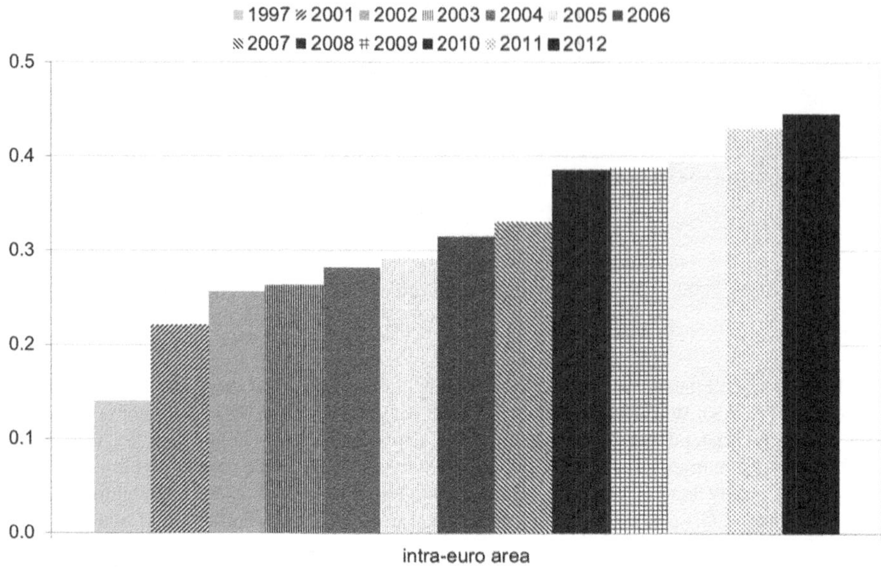

Fig. 14 Intra-euro area cross-border equity holdings (percentages). *Sources* IMF, Thomson Reuters. *Note* Intra-euro area is defined as the share of equity issued by euro area residents and held by residents of other euro area countries (excluding central banks)

actions including further legal harmonisation at the EU level in difficult fields such as corporate governance, insolvency and taxation.[15] These are likely to be main elements of the Capital Market Union project that the new Commission intends to pursue.

6 Conclusions

In this paper, we have looked at the experience of financial integration in the euro area since the introduction of the single currency. First, we reviewed the main past developments at the aggregated and disaggregated levels. Overall the euro area experienced a first full cycle of financial integration with integration increasing significantly in all market segments in the run-up to the crisis and then decreasing during the financial and sovereign crisis with spreading fragmentation covering all market segments though to a lower degree in the equity markets. Only after the announcement of the Banking Union and the ECB OMT operations there were a stabilisation and the start of a re-integration process.

[15]These aspects are analysed in Sapir and Wolff (2013) and in more detail in the ECB Report on Financial Integration in Europe 2014 (Special Feature C on "Initiatives to promote capital market integration in the European corporate bond and equity markets").

Second, we considered the extent to which the process of financial integration brought the two main expected benefits (i.e. enhanced risk-sharing and improved capital allocation) while containing potential negative side effects in terms of financial stability and the degree to which the process of financial fragmentation during the crisis had negative side effects.

In a nutshell, the result of this review is that the process of increasing financial integration seems to have brought to a large extent the expected benefit of risk-sharing, while the evidence is less conclusive in terms of improved capital allocation and it had some negative side effects in terms of financial stability. On the other side, the process of financial fragmentation during the crisis took forms which had substantial negative side effects on the monetary policy function. More specifically:

- *prior to the crisis*, it is doubtful that two main features of the process of increasing financial integration—namely the geographical composition of financial flows (mainly from core to peripheral countries) and the predominant share of interbank financing in cross-border banking flows—were conducive to efficient capital allocation. In addition, the same features may have been an important driver behind certain developments—such as high volatility of financial flows, large concentration of bank exposures towards specific economic sectors and countries and asset price inflation—raising concerns from a financial stability viewpoint;
- *during the crisis*, the process of financial fragmentation, in addition to withdrawing the main benefits gained in the previous period, was characterised—especially during the sovereign crisis—by a very high degree of home bias in money, bond and banking markets which impaired significantly the transmission mechanism of the single monetary policy.

Beyond the cyclical developments, *two structural aspects* have qualified the experience of financial integration throughout the period, namely a large degree of home bias in bank lending to the real economy (non-financial corporates and households) and a lower degree of financial integration in equity versus bond markets. The first aspect entails that a larger share of direct cross-border bank lending might bring positive effects in terms of capital allocation efficiency, while the second implies room for enhancing risk-sharing capability through higher equity market integration.

Third, we provided some preliminary qualitative considerations on the extent to which the implementation of the Banking Union, in particular the SSM and SRM (and where relevant the future common financial backstop for bank resolution), could affect the future process of financial integration if this tended to replicate past experiences. The Banking Union is expected to have a positive influence on those aspects of financial integration which are more closely affected by banking policies. In particular, the Banking Union—by pursuing the interrelated objectives of enhanced degree of effectiveness of prudential supervision and bank resolution, promotion of prudent risk behaviour of banks and maintenance of a high degree of public confidence in the banking system—is likely to contribute to:

- reducing the likelihood of unbalanced patterns of financial flows between regions of the euro area (together with the EU Macroeconomic Imbalances Procedure and the EU macro-prudential framework);
- decreasing the share of cross-border interbank financing and increasing the share of cross-border direct bank lending to the real economy;
- reducing the degree to which home bias would prevail in some market (e.g. money and bond) segments in periods of financial fragmentation.

Overall the Banking Union, to the extent it is effective in practice, should lead to a more balanced financial integration process in comparison with past experience by allowing in: (i) periods of increasing integration to reap fully the expected benefits while at the same possibly reducing potential negative side effects on financial stability and (ii) periods of crisis to reduce the intensity and impact of financial fragmentation.

By contrast, the Banking Union is less suitable to affect other developments such as cross-country differences in bank lending conditions when they reflect primarily demand side issues as well as a lower degree of integration of equity versus bond market. For the former government and central bank interventions are more appropriate, while for the latter the forthcoming project of Capital Market Union as part of the policy agenda of the new Commission is expected to play a key role.

Finally, it should be highlighted that the Banking Union, in addition to affect the possible recurrence of past developments, is also likely to trigger new dynamics in the process of financial integration which are difficult to foresee at the moment. In this respect, we mention just two possible developments. First, the SSM is likely to provide a strong momentum for banks in the euro area to carry out their capital and liquidity management on a group-wide basis and no longer along national borders thus providing further impetus to cross-border bank activities. Second, both the SSM and the SRM are likely to promote conditions for a revamp of banking flows between EU non-EA countries and the euro area in both directions.

Overall, it will be important to monitor very closely developments in financial integration in the euro area and the EU under the Banking Union.

References

Baele, L., A. Ferrando, P. Hoerdahl, E. Krylova, and C. Monnet. 2004. Measuring financial integration in the euro area. ECB Occasional Paper No 14, Apr 2004.

Battistini, N., M. Pagano, and S. Simonelli. 2014. Systemic risk, sovereign yields and bank exposures in the euro crisis. *Economic Policy* 29: 203.

Chen, R., G.M. Milesi-Ferretti, and T. Tressel. 2013. Eurozone external imbalances. *Economic Policy* 28: 101.

Draghi, M. 2014. Financial integration and banking union. Speech at the conference for the 20th anniversary of the establishment of the European Monetary Institute, Feb 2014.

European Central Bank. 2014. Financial Integration in Europe 2014, Apr 2014.

Ignatowski, M., and J. Korte. 2014. Wishful thinking or effective threat? Tightening bank resolution regimes and bank risk-taking. ECB Working Paper No 1659, Apr 2014.

Sapir, A., and G. Wolff. 2013. The neglected side of banking union: reshaping Europe's financial system, Breugel, Sep 2013.

Van Beers, N., M. Bijlsma, and G. Zwart. 2014. Cross-country insurance mechanisms in currency unions: an empirical assessment, Bruegel Working Paper No 4, Mar 2014.

Structural Reforms in the Eurozone: A Case of Self-defeating Expectations?

Luigi Bonatti and Andrea Fracasso

Abstract This work addresses the implications of agents' expectations about structural reforms in a context characterized by institutional inertia. By means of a stylized small-open economy model encompassing policy-induced barriers to entry in the non-tradable sector, the paper shows that expectations about reforms affect economic performances and alter the incentives for the authorities to implement structural reforms. Moreover, the model shows that it is possible to envisage circumstances under which no set of expectations has the potential for self-fulfillment, thereby creating self-defeating expectations traps. This model sheds light on the recent problems of the Eurozone periphery, characterized by authorities exhibiting a status quo bias against reforms and by a history of self-defeating optimistic expectations about the realization of structural reforms.

1 Introduction

The recent sovereign debt crisis in the Eurozone has ignited an intense debate about the role played by financial investors' expectations, both in the period before the introduction of the euro and after that the sovereign risk premia of some Eurozone countries (the so-called periphery) started surging because of the concerns for a possible break-up of the Economic and Monetary Union (EMU). Several observers

L. Bonatti (✉) · A. Fracasso
Department of Economics and Management and School of International Studies, University of Trento, Trento, Italy
e-mail: luigi.bonatti@unitn.it

A. Fracasso
e-mail: andrea.fracasso@unitn.it

L. Paganetto (ed.), *Achieving Dynamism in an Anaemic Europe*,
DOI 10.1007/978-3-319-14099-5_6

have questioned whether, as effectively put by Giavazzi and Spaventa (2010), the markets had been too complacent before the crisis or have displayed unwarranted pessimism during the crisis.[1]

Some scholars, such as Fernández-Villaverde et al. (2013) and Reis (2013), have convincingly pointed out that economic convergence was not just affected by expectations in the financial markets: the adoption of the euro boosted widespread confidence in the periphery countries, allowed both their government and private sectors to borrow at relatively low interest rates, and fostered investment in activities with limited productivity growth. This, in turn, lowered the incentives of the authorities to implement structural reforms. As a result, while the "Maastricht variables" converged over time and employment scores temporarily improved, productivity and unit labor costs dynamics failed to conform to those of the core countries and various structural weaknesses remained overlooked (Giavazzi and Spaventa 2010).

Consistently with this narrative, at the origin of the current problems of the Eurozone one can place, paradoxically, the widespread optimistic belief that—thanks to the euro—real convergence would have occurred between the core and the periphery countries. In retrospect, such expectations proved to be self-defeating: the elimination of nominal exchange risk and the ECB anti-inflationary credibility allowed the periphery to borrow at low interest rates, thereby creating incentives to postpone painful fiscal consolidations (Greece, Italy) and structural reforms (Greece, Italy, Portugal, Spain), or boosting aggregate demand and production thanks to the high indebtedness of the household and financial (private) sectors (Ireland, Spain). In a nutshell, the very same belief that real convergence would have occurred between the core and the periphery of the Eurozone created the conditions for the real divergence, mirrored in the large current account imbalances emerged in the last decade (Bonatti and Fracasso 2014).

This work develops a stylized analysis to capture the essence of a situation characterized by self-defeating expectations such as those outlined above. The model is kept general enough to make a point that may apply to the euro crisis but also to other situations where acting on the basis of certain expectations, especially regarding structural reforms and regime changes, creates the conditions for their falsification. The general point made by this work is that there are relevant circumstances under which it is impossible, even in principle, to have a rational expectations equilibrium, namely in which no set of expectations has the potential for self-fulfillment. In these "self-defeating expectations traps", agents have no

[1]Nominal interest rate convergence in the late 90s, the argument goes, was excessively fast and homogenous in the Eurozone, probably because of the optimistic expectations about the positive impact of the euro on the laggard countries. On the contrary, after a period in which the worldwide expansion of credit contributed to preserve low long-term interest rates, sovereign risk premia in the periphery increased by an extent that is hardly reconcilable with the observed changes in the fundamentals of these countries and that most likely reflects very pessimistic expectations. For empirical evidence on the Eurozone sovereign risk premia, see among others Aizenman et al. (2013), De Grauwe and Ji (2012, 2013), Di Cesare et al. (2012).

obvious criterion for forming their expectations about the future and have to face a high degree of indeterminacy. As we shall show, this does not stem from ad hoc assumptions about agents' cognitive biases, information problems and meta-preferences, about which we remain agnostic; rather, it relates to the uncertainty about political reforms that significantly affect the inter-temporal and inter-sectoral allocation of resources.

Moreover, the model offers an original take on the inherent problems of a monetary union among very heterogeneous members. Our model suggests that, in the presence of governments that undertake reforms ensuring real convergence only under extremely stressful circumstances (as a result of a status quo bias that characterizes actual policy-making), optimistic expectations may boost economic performance of laggard countries in early stages of the union, but ultimately undermine the prospects of real convergence and jeopardize the resilience of the union. Conversely, overly pessimistic expectations may add to existing structural problems and worsen economic conditions to a point that forces reluctant authorities to undertake reforms conducive to convergence (this was a counterfactual scenario in the history of the period leading to the crisis in the Eurozone).

This stylized model does not aspire to provide a comprehensive and detailed explanation of recent Eurozone's troubles, nor does it aim at modeling the precise mechanisms through which macroeconomic imbalances grew large in the periphery. Rather, this work aims at providing a formal representation of the rationalization of the Eurozone troubles that has been offered without full-fledge models by various influential scholars such as those mentioned above. This notwithstanding, our main findings are shown to carry over to more sophisticated versions of the model which explore various realistic extensions of the basic set up.

The remainder of the paper proceeds as follows. Section 2 contains a discussion of the relevant literature. The building blocks of the basic model are presented in Sect. 3, while the implications of alternative expectations concerning the future regulatory regimes of the sector producing (internationally) non-tradable goods are discussed in Sect. 4. Section 5 is dedicated to some extensions of the basic model. Section 6 concludes. The mathematical derivations are contained in the Appendix.

2 Relevant Literature

It is widely held that short-term credit and financial developments are affected by market sentiment, hence subject to exuberance, panic, and the like. Yet optimism and pessimism may affect a wider range of economic decisions, such as inter-temporal investment patterns and the sectoral allocation of investment. This is particularly the case when agents have to form expectations about governments' actions in the future and are uncertain about the ability and the willingness of the authorities to undertake economic reforms directed to increase long-term productivity and address structural weaknesses. This is particularly relevant during periods of profound economic transformation, such as economic transition, currency regime switches, and monetary integration.[2]

The process of designing, approving and implementing structural reforms takes time and is subject to non-economic constraints, which typically make very difficult to predict whether and to what extent reforms will be realized. Even reforms delivering aggregate benefits cannot be assumed to be costless, institutionally neutral, Pareto improving and uncontended. Reforms are "to be consistent with governments objectives outside the field of economic efficiency" and "reform processes have often met political quandaries" (Hoj et al. 2006, p. 88). The realization of reforms resembling more to regime switches than marginal changes[3] depends on discretionary decisions by the authorities who pursue a vast array of goals besides social welfare maximization and face constraints associated with various (often conflicting) concerns. For instance, incumbent authorities make decisions about reforms with a view to preserving social stability, respecting the electoral mandate (Tompson 2009), maintaining the political support of each party in a ruling coalition (Perotti and Kontopoulos 2002), appeasing powerful domestic lobbies (Olson 1965; Drazen 2000; Grossman and Helpman 2001), preventing prospective policy reversals associated with possible reform failure (Aizenman and Yi 1998), and implementing complex compensating transfers across heterogeneous citizens.[4]

Uncertainty is increased further by the fact that short-lived governments care not only for the long-run effects of structural reforms, but also for the transitory path to their full implementation; this makes the timing for implementing reforms dependent on the contingent macroeconomic environment. Hence, even when reforms are expected to produce aggregate benefits in the long run, governments tend to exhibit some institutional inertia and to preserve the status quo.[5]

---

[2]Besides monetary unification, the political economy of reforms played a key role also in the debates about economic transition (Roland 2002) and economic development (Rodrik 1996, 2005).

[3]Bianchi (2013) addresses the relationship between monetary policy regimes and agents' beliefs, where regimes differ in the degree of aggressiveness of monetary policy, as reflected in the parameters of the reaction function. Structural reforms extend further than this and impact both on the short- and long-term dynamics of the economy.

[4]Furthermore, policy-makers may face pressure from foreign peers, meet the resistance of domestic bureaucrats, and strive to frame public multi-issue debate in a consistent way.

[5]The observation that policy-making departs from the conventional assumption that the authorities maximize a (continuous) social welfare function is at the core of the field of political economy (Drazen 2000; Persson and Tabellini 2000). The literature on the political economy of reforms and on the persistence of the status quo is extremely vast (see OECD 2010 for an overview). Alesina and Drazen (1991), for instance, argue that lack of reforms may stem from the 'war of attrition' between different groups with conflicting distributional objectives. Reforms may also be hindered by the uncertainty about their aggregate and individual impact (Fernandez and Rodrik 1991; Cason and Mui 2005; Valderrama 2009) or by the authorities' inability to promise credibly compensation to the losers (Jain and Mukand 2003). Bourguignon (2011) shows that the status quo of each heterogeneous individual (Samuelson and Zeckhauser 1988) in the society affects the actual impact of reforms on aggregate welfare: this, as well as reference-dependent preferences (Tversky and

Notably, economic reforms appear extremely important in the process of real convergence among heterogeneous countries sharing the same currency. Indeed, the early debate on the desirability and feasibility of the European monetary union did touch upon the relationship between monetary unification, incentives to undertake reforms, and real economic convergence. Particular attention was attributed to the indirect effects of the prospective monetary union on the real economy through the EMU-related incentives for the authorities to operate structural reforms (see, for instance, Bean 1998a, b; Bentolila and Saint-Paul 2000). On the one hand, governments may recognize that participating in a monetary union eventually requires greater real convergence (in a sort of TINA—There Is No Alternative—argument) and market-base adjustment to asymmetric shocks. On the other hand, the union may deprive governments of some macroeconomic tools which could help to temper the negative short-term effects of reforms, thereby making the adoption of the latter less likely.[6]

As this early debate informed the literature on the costs and benefits of establishing a monetary union among heterogeneous countries, the role of agents' expectations was not directly addressed.[7] More recently, as mentioned in the Introduction, a number of scholars attributed the current worrisome state of some periphery countries to an inefficient allocation of resources due, in retrospect, to misplaced expectations (Giavazzi and Spaventa 2010; Fernandez-Villaverde et al.

(Footnote 5 continued)
Kahneman 1991; Bateman et al. 1997), complicates the analysis on the part of the authorities and favours inertia. A status quo bias is particularly likely to emerge when inaction has invisible opportunity costs whereas reforms are associated with visible upfront costs (Tompson 2009). The institutional set up can also lead to political inertia: Eterovic (2011) shows that the institutions making citizens unable to properly reward politicians tend to produce a status quo bias. Moreover, established socio-economic models are typically characterized by institutional and international complementarities (Acemoglu et al. 2012), which make difficult for the authorities to adopt isolated reforms. Finally, Abiad and Mody (2005) provide evidence that (financial) reforms are conditioned both by the occurrence of economic and political shocks (either as windows of opportunity or as extremely stressful events) and by a gradual learning process that helps dissipate uncertainty (Dewatripont and Roland 1992a, b).

[6]Empirical evidence on the issue is mixed and inconclusive (Belke et al. 2005; Duval and Elsmeskov 2006; Alesina et al. 2011; Cacciatore et al. 2012; Bouis et al. 2012). Contingent economic circumstances and country-specific social preferences have led to very different outcomes in diverse countries: the TINA argument appears to have worked in some countries but not in others.

[7]Agents' expectations did play a role in the Walters' critique to the establishment of fixed exchange rates in the European Community. Sir Alan Walters, a counselor of Ms Thatcher in the 1980s, warned about risk that the presence of nominal interest rate convergence and persistent inflation differentials (leading to diverging real interest rates) could bring about asymmetric transmission of monetary policy and a cyclical de-coupling of the high inflation countries in the union. Walters pointed out that financial market expectations about the nature of the exchange rate regime switch could be inconsistent with the expectations in the labour markets. Along similar lines, Miller and Sutherland (1991) develop a macroeconomic model that allows for a gradual convergence of initially inconsistent expectations.

2013; Reis 2013).[8] Optimism about the state of the economic fundamentals during the convergence process, political myopia and widespread rent-seeking behaviors of those operating in low productivity sectors hindered structural and institutional reforms. Even before the eruption of the debt crisis, many euro-area countries exhibit relatively low productivity levels and growth rates, which can be associated with various barriers to competition and innovation, as well as with a pervasive resource misallocation.[9] While this debate shows an increased awareness about the link between structural reforms and real economic convergence within a monetary union, the role played by agents' expectations about structural reforms has not received due attention yet.

In this work, building on the realistic tenet that governments exhibit reluctance to implement structural reforms (for any of the possible reasons illustrated in Footnote 5) and undertake them only if failing to do so risks jeopardizing social and political stability, we show that expectations about economic reforms may turn out to be self-defeating and that, when certain conditions hold, a self-defeating expectations trap may emerge. This scenario is not due to the agents' imperfect rationality, but is related to some features of the governments' choice about reform: the status quo bias, the lack of commitment devices to overcome policy inertia, and the discontinuity between reform and non-reform alternatives.

Before presenting the model, we would like to stress what distinguishes our analysis from the current debate on the problems affecting the EMU. To start, our issue is not whether financial markets were too complacent before the crisis or too pessimistic during the crisis. Rather, we focus on agents' expectations about those structural reforms that affect the inter-temporal and inter-sectoral allocation of resources and that impact on the process of real convergence among heterogeneous countries in a monetary union. Moreover, we show that self-defeating, rather than self-fulfilling, expectations may occur: if certain conditions are satisfied, the feedback between policymakers' willingness to adopt reforms and agents' expectations about these latter may lead to the disappointment of the expectations.[10]

In this work we adopt a tractable model with limited competition in the product market of the non-tradable sectors (e.g., services) and with government reluctance

[8] For a discussion of the Greek case, see Katsimi and Moutos (2010), Moutos and Pechlivanos (2013).

[9] Coudert et al. (2013) assess real exchange rate misalignments within the Eurozone and find relatively large and persistent ones in the periphery. Forni et al. (2010) and Lusinyan and Muir (2013) analyze the impact of liberalizing protected service sectors in Italy, that is the OECD country with the highest mark-ups in non-manufacturing industries and whose recent economic performance has not been affected by housing and credit bubbles.

[10] Angeletos and La'O (2013) explore the role of incomplete communication and develop a unique-equilibrium, rational expectations, macroeconomic model with individual "animal spirits". Without introducing multiple equilibria, they offer an original microfundation of the observed co-movements of market expectations and market outcomes. While Angeletos and La'O look at co-movements, we analyze the case of self-defeating expectations.

to implement structural reforms.[11] Barriers to entry and competition are still present in several countries and, according to the OECD, have a particularly negative impact on the Eurozone members lagging behind in productivity and GDP growth. Table 1 reports the OECD Regulation Impact Indicators of the barriers to entry in professional and retail services (calculated by the OECD in accordance with the method developed by Conway and Nicoletti 2006) for a number of countries.

This set-up is meant to offer a stylized and realistic analysis to capture the essence of a situation characterized by self-defeating expectations about structural reforms. Clearly, similar arguments (and model extensions) could be developed for other anticompetitive restrictions and for any policy-related market imperfection (e.g. poor financial regulation and monitoring) making the allocation of resources suboptimal (Arnold et al. 2010).[12] To keep the model tractable, we do not address the relationship between market structure and rent-seeking activities (Brou and Ruta 2013) and we exclusively focus on the direct effect of non-tradable product market regulation on the regulated market. Thus, we neglect the indirect effect of service regulation on the downstream tradable sectors (Barone and Cingano 2011) as well as the within-industry reallocation of resources (Bartelsman et al. 2013): doing so would strengthen our results, yet also add unnecessary complexity.

Finally, in the basic model we chose not to discuss the merit of the concerns inspiring the anticompetitive regulatory provisions in the non-tradable sector. Although some restrictions may well be due to agreeable public policy goals—such as tackling market imperfections, we implicitly assume that protection reflects rent-seeking vested interests. This shortcut should not suggest that we consider all anticompetitive regulations as unjustified on any economic and social terms. Yet, as such plausible concerns should be similar across countries, we argue that the observed regulatory heterogeneity across advanced countries in the EMU is likely a symptom of less noble political-economic tensions at the national level.[13]

[11]Despite a deregulation trend across the board (also reported in Duval and Elsmeskov 2006), the Mediterranean periphery countries tend to exhibit higher levels of protection in 2003 and 2008. Djankov (2009) offers an effective overview of the three main theoretical reasons (market failure theory, capture theory, tollbooth theory) to impose (more or less appropriately from a social welfare point of view) burdensome entry requirements.

[12]The range of policy and institutional factors that may limit experimentation and efficient resource allocation is indeed vast. One could think, for instance, of measures that limit the adoption of new technologies as in Krueger (1974) and Krusell and Rios-Rull (1996).

[13]The very fact that most services continued to be offered mainly by national suppliers in the European Union after the 2006 Bolkestein Directive on services provides some evidence of tensions between national regulatory frameworks and international competition (Bertola and Mola 2010). This is in line with the findings of Borchert et al. (2013) who show that although explicit discrimination against foreign providers is low, the allocation of new licenses is opaque and highly discretionary: a variety of restrictions on entry, ownership, and operations continue to affect the international trade in services.

Table 1 OECD regulation impact indicators (barriers to entry)

	Professional services												Retail		
	Accounting			Architect			Engineer			Legal					
	Entry regulations			Entry regulations			Entry regulations			Entry regulations			Barriers to entry		
	1996	2003	2008	1996	2003	2008	1996	2003	2008	1996	2003	2008	1998	2003	2008
Austria	4.4	4.4	4.4	5.3	5.3	4.1	5.3	5.3	4.0	4.5	4.4	4.4	5.5	5.5	3.6
Denmark	2.9	2.3	2.9	0.0	0.0	0.0	0.0	0.0	0.0	2.3	2.3	3.5	2.1	2.1	2.8
Finland	3.3	2.8	2.8	1.9	1.5	1.5	0.0	1.0	1.0	0.0	0.0	0.0	3.3	2.8	2.8
Germany	5.6	4.0	4.0	3.1	1.7	2.6	3.4	2.9	2.7	4.5	3.8	3.8	1.8	2.1	2.1
Netharlands	3.7	3.4	3.1	0.0	0.0	0.0	0.0	3.0	0.0	2.8	2.3	4.5	1.3	0.7	2.1
France	3.7	4.3	4.1	2.4	2.0	3.6	0.0	0.0	0.0	2.8	4.0	4.1	5.0	2.6	2.6
Greece	3.9	4.0	4.0	–	3.6	3.6	–	3.6	3.6	3.7	3.7	3.7	4.5	4.2	3.4
Italy	0.0	4.0	3.9	3.0	3.5	3.6	2.4	3.6	3.6	2.7	4.0	4.0	2.5	2.3	2.6
Portugal	2.1	3.5	3.5	2.4	3.2	3.2	3.1	3.7	3.7	3.7	3.7	3.7	3.5	3.0	2.4
Spain	3.3	2.1	2.6	3.1	3.1	3.2	3.1	3.1	3.2	3.7	3.6	3.2	3.0	3.0	3.0
Ireland	3.0	2.4	0.6	0.0	0.6	0.0	0.0	0.6	0.0	2.6	3.8	2.6	0.7	0.9	0.3
UK	4.1	4.2	4.2	0.0	0.0	0.0	0.0	0.0	0.0	3.8	3.1	0.0	3.8	2.3	2.3
US	5.2	2.6	2.6	3.5	2.3	0.0	4.8	2.6	0.0	4.9	3.1	3.1	–	3.7	3.7

Source OECD

3 The Basic Model

We model a small-open economy belonging to a currency area (the nominal exchange rate of this economy is irreversibly fixed to one).[14] Two market goods are produced in this economy: an internationally tradable good and an internationally non-tradable good. Hence, in this economy there are firms specialized in the production of tradable goods and firms specialized in the production of non-tradable goods. The tradable good is used as capital in the production of both goods and as consumption good, while the non-tradable good can be only consumed.[15] The international price of the tradable good is exogenously given and firms can freely enter this market, while firms' entry into the non-tradable market is regulated: a firm needs a license issued by the government to operate in this market. This regulatory framework is inherited from the past and, despite its sub-optimality, the government is willing to reform the regulatory framework only if the population (or a relevant portion of it) is hit by serious economic hardship because of it (more on this below).

The economy is populated by households that supply labor, buy consumer goods, accumulate productive assets (physical capital) to be rent to domestic firms, borrow from abroad (or lend abroad) at the exogenously given world interest rate and possess the licenses issued by the government for operating in the non-tradable sector. Both the workforce and the capital stock are mobile across sectors but not across countries. Wages are determined competitively but there is a reservation wage (given by the value of non-market activities) below which market wages cannot fall. Rental rates of capital are determined competitively. Also the prices at which households can cede the use of their licenses to firms that intend to operate in the non-tradable sector are determined competitively.

Time is discrete: we have the present (time 0) and the future (time 1). In period 0, only a limited number of firms are allowed to operate in the non-tradable sector (the government restricts the issuance of licenses), while in period 1 the government can maintain this regulatory regime or change it by granting licenses to everyone willing to pay a fixed fee ("liberalization" of the non-tradable sector). As anticipated, we realistically assume the existence of some institutional inertia due to a status quo bias associated with any of the various reasons illustrated in Footnote 5;

[14] Forni et al. (2010) show that structural reforms in one country of the Eurozone have negligible macroeconomic spillovers to the rest of the area. This justifies the adoption of a small-open economy framework in this work.

[15] As argued by Turnovsky (1997), there is no agreed conclusion on the share of tradables and nontradables in total investment. For some evidence on the issue, see Bems (2008). The extreme assumption that investment consists only of tradable goods is adopted here with two objectives in mind: first, to simplify the set-up, and second, to create a clearer channel through which a tradable-induced learning, as suggested by Rodrik (2008), takes place.

this implies that a regulatory regime change is implemented in period 1 only if the utility of the representative household falls below a certain minimum threshold in the absence of such a change.

Finally, there is no source of random disturbances and agents' expectations can be optimistic (in the sense that they are consistent with the assumption that the government will liberalize in the future the entry into the non-tradable sector) or pessimistic (in the sense that they are consistent with the assumption that the government will keep the initial quantitative restriction to the issuance of licenses required to operate in the non-tradable sector).

3.1 Firms Producing the (Internationally) Tradable Good

In each period t (t = 0, 1), there is a continuum (whose measure is normalized to be one) of identical firms producing the tradable good Y_{Tt} according to the following technology:

$$Y_{Tt} = A_{Tt}K_{Tt}^{1-\alpha}L_{Tt}^{\alpha}, \quad 0<\alpha<1, \tag{1}$$

where K_{Tt}, L_{Tt}, and A_{Tt} are, respectively, the capital stock, the labor input and the state of technology (total factor productivity) of the representative firm producing Y_{Tt}. Total factor productivity is a positive function of the capital installed in the tradable sector: $A_{Tt} = K_{Tt}^{\alpha}$. Consistently with this formal set-up, one can interpret technological progress as labor augmenting. This assumption combines the idea that learning-by-doing works in the tradable sector through each firm's capital investment and the idea that knowledge and productivity gains spill over instantly across all firms of this sector (see Barro and Sala-i-Martin 1995). Therefore, in accordance with Frankel (1962), it is supposed that although A_{Tt} is endogenous to the economy, each firm takes it as given, since a single firm's decisions have only a negligible impact on the aggregate stock of capital of the tradable sector.[16]

The profits of the representative firm producing tradables, π_{Tt}, are given by

$$\pi_{Tt} = Y_{Tt} - W_tL_{Tt} - R_tK_{Tt}, \quad t = 0, 1, \tag{2}$$

where W_t is the wage and R_t is the capital rental rate in period t. Notice that the price of the tradable good—which is treated as the numéraire of the system—is exogenously given and normalized to be one.

[16]This amounts to say that technological progress is endogenous to the economy, although it is an unintended by-products of firms' capital investment rather than the result of purposive R&D efforts.

3.2 Firms Producing the (Internationally) Non-tradable Good

In each period t (t = 0, 1), there is a continuum of measure N_t of identical firms producing the non-tradable good Y_{Nt}. This good is not storable and must be immediately consumed. Each firm produces the good according to the following technology:

$$Y_{Nt} = K_{Nt}^{\gamma} L_{Nt}^{\beta}, \quad 0<\gamma<1, 0<\beta<1, \gamma+\beta<1, \tag{3}$$

where K_{Nt} and L_{Nt} are, respectively, the capital stock and the labor input employed by the representative firm producing the non-tradable good. Assuming that the non-tradable sector roughly coincides with the technologically stagnant sector of the economy, we rule out the possibility that also in this sector productivity improvements can take place as a result of the positive externalities generated by each single firm's activity.

The net profit (cash flow) π_{Nt} of the representative firm producing non-tradable goods is given by:

$$\pi_{Nt} = P_{Nt} Y_{Nt} - W_t L_{Nt} - R_t K_{Nt} - Q_t, \quad t = 0, 1, \tag{4}$$

where P_{Nt} and Q_t are, respectively, the price of the non-tradable good and the price for the use of the license required to operate in the non-tradable sector at time t.

3.3 Households

There is a continuum (whose measure is normalized to be one) of households who live for two periods. In each t (t = 0, 1), the representative household produces the services C_t that it consumes by combining the tradable and the non-tradable goods according to

$$C_t = \min(\eta C_{Nt}, C_{Tt}), \quad \eta > 0, \tag{5}$$

where C_{Nt} and C_{Tt} are, respectively, the amount of non-tradable good and the amount of tradable good used by the representative household to produce consumer services in t.

In each t (t = 0, 1), the representative household determines its labor supply L_t according to the following rule:

$$L_t = \begin{cases} H & \text{if } W_t \geq \underline{W} \\ 0 & \text{otherwise,} \end{cases} \tag{6}$$

where H is the representative household's total time endowment in every period and $\underline{W}$ stays for the value of non-market activities (and acts as a reservation wage).

The lifetime utility of the representative household is given by

$$U = u_0 + \theta u_1, \quad 0<\theta<1, \tag{7}$$

where $u_t = \frac{C_t^{1-\xi}}{1-\xi}$, $0<\xi<1$ (t = 0, 1), is the household's period utility function, θ is a time-preference parameter and ξ is the coefficient of relative risk aversion.

The representative household's period budget constraint is:

$$\begin{aligned} K_{t+1} + D_t(1+r) + P_{Nt}C_{Nt} + C_{Tt} \leq R_tK_t + D_{t+1} \\ + N_t\pi_{Nt} + \pi_{Tt} + T_t + (N_tL_{Nt} + L_{Tt})W_t + N_t(Q_t - F), \\ K_0 = \overline{K}, D_0 = 0 \text{ and } N_0 = \overline{N} \text{given}, \quad D_2 \leq 0, \quad t = 0, 1, \end{aligned} \tag{8}$$

where K_t are the productive assets held by the representative household in t, D_t are the net foreign liabilities accumulated during period t – 1 by the representative household and carried over into period t with interest r (the exogenously given world interest rate), F is the fixed fee paid to the government by the representative household for each license that it holds in period t, and T_t are the net transfers that the representative household receives by the government in t. Notice that in each period the representative household can sell the right to use the licenses for operating in the non-tradable sector to the firms at a market price of Q_t per unit, and that it is entitled to receive the net profits earned by the firms as dividend payments (it is assumed that each household owns an equal share of all existing firms). Moreover, in (8) it is assumed for simplicity that capital fully depreciates every period, and that at time 0 households have zero net foreign liabilities.

3.4 Government

The government's period budget constraint is:

$$T_t = FN_t, \quad t = 0, 1. \tag{9}$$

At the beginning of period 0, the government restricts the entry into the non-tradable sector by issuing $N_0 = \overline{N}$ licenses required for operating in that sector at time 0. In the following period, the government may preserve the arrangement of the previous period, so that the households can keep $N_1 = \overline{N}$ licenses paying a fixed fee F per unit to the government, or it can liberalize the entry into the non-tradable sector by granting licenses to everyone willing to pay a fixed fee F per unit.[17]

At the beginning of period 1, the government decides to liberalize if and only if

$$u_1\Big|_{N_1=\overline{N}} < \underline{u} \text{ and } u_1\Big|_{N_1>\overline{N}} \geq \underline{u}, \quad \underline{u} > 0, \tag{10}$$

where $u_1\Big|_{N_1=\overline{N}}$ is the utility level that the representative household can get in period 1 if the entry into the non-tradable sector is not liberalized, u is the minimum utility level that is deemed socially (and politically) acceptable in this economy, and $u_1\Big|_{N_1>\overline{N}}$ is the utility level that the representative household can get in period 1 if the entry into the non-tradable sector is liberalized.

4 Equilibrium, Expectations and Rationality

4.1 Equilibrium Conditions

Markets for labor and for the non-tradable good are purely domestic. Equilibrium in the labor market implies

$$W_t > \underline{W}, \quad t = 0, 1 \tag{11a}$$

and

$$N_t L_{Nt} + L_{Tt} = H, \quad t = 0, 1, \tag{12a}$$

or, alternatively,[18]

$$W_t = \underline{W}, \quad t = 0, 1 \tag{11b}$$

[17]Notice that in this institutional framework the households can directly appropriate the rent created by the government through the issuance of a limited number of licenses for operating in the non-tradable sector. The same equilibrium configuration would emerge in an institutional framework where the government sells the licenses directly to the firms and redistributes the rents to the households through the fiscal transfers. In this alternative framework, at the beginning of period 0, $\overline{N}$ licenses are sold at auction to the firms by the government, thus determining a market price of Q_0 per unit. Then, the government redistributes the revenues to the households $(T_0 = Q_0\overline{N})$. At the beginning of period 1, the government may again sell $\overline{N}$ licenses at auction to the firms and redistribute its revenues $Q_1\overline{N}$ to the households, or alternatively it can sell a license to any firm willing to pay a fixed price F for it, thus selling N_1 licenses and redistributing its revenues FN_1 to the households.

[18]The corner solution entails $W_t = \underline{W}$ and $N_t L_{Nt} + L_{Tt} = H$, t = 0, 1.

and

$$N_t L_{Nt} + L_{Tt} < H, \quad t = 0, 1. \tag{12b}$$

Equilibrium in the market for the non-tradable good requires:

$$N_t Y_{Nt} = N_t K_{Nt}^{\gamma} L_{Nt}^{\beta} = C_{Nt}, \quad t = 0, 1. \tag{13}$$

The market for the tradable good is internationally integrated. Equilibrium in this market requires:

$$Y_{Tt} = C_{Tt} + K_{t+1} + TA_t, \quad t = 0, 1, \tag{14}$$

where TA_t is the trade account (net exports) in period t.

Equilibrium in the market for productive assets entails

$$K_t = N_t K_{Nt} + K_{Tt}, \quad t = 0, 1, \; K_0 = \overline{K} \text{ given}. \tag{15}$$

The representative firms equalize the value of the marginal productivity of capital to the rental rate of capital and the value of the marginal productivity of labor to the wage:

$$(1 - \alpha) L_{Tt}^{\alpha} = R_t = \gamma P_{Nt} K_{Nt}^{\gamma - 1} L_{Nt}^{\beta}, \quad t = 0, 1, \tag{16}$$

$$\alpha K_{Tt} L_{Tt}^{\alpha - 1} = W_t = \beta P_{Nt} K_{Nt}^{\gamma} L_{Nt}^{\beta - 1}, \quad t = 0, 1. \tag{17}$$

By solving for the output that the representative firm operating in the non-tradable sector produces in equilibrium (see the Appendix), one can obtain from the market-clearing condition (13) that

$$C_{Nt} = N_t Y_{Nt} = \frac{N_t}{W_t^{\beta} R_t^{\gamma}} \left[\frac{(\beta + \gamma) Q_t}{(1 - \beta - \gamma) \Psi} \right]^{\beta + \gamma}, \quad t = 0, 1, \tag{18}$$

where $\Psi \equiv \left(\frac{\beta}{\gamma}\right)^{\frac{\gamma}{\beta+\gamma}} + \left(\frac{\gamma}{\beta}\right)^{\frac{\beta}{\beta+\gamma}}$.

The equilibrium price of the non-tradable good is given by (see the Appendix):

$$P_{Nt} = \frac{W_t^{\beta} R_t^{\gamma} Q_t^{1 - \beta - \gamma}}{(1 - \beta - \gamma)} \left[\frac{(1 - \beta - \gamma) \Psi}{(\beta + \gamma)} \right]^{\beta + \gamma}, \quad t = 0, 1. \tag{19}$$

Solving the optimization problem of the representative household, one obtains that in equilibrium:

$$K_2 = D_2 = 0, \tag{20}$$

$$C_{Tt} = \eta C_{Nt}, \quad t = 0, 1, \tag{21}$$

$$\frac{C_{T0}^{-\xi}}{(\eta + P_{N0})} = \frac{\theta R_1 C_{T1}^{-\xi}}{(\eta + P_{N1})}, \tag{22}$$

$$\frac{C_{T0}^{-\xi}}{(\eta + P_{N0})} = \frac{\theta(1 + r) C_{T1}^{-\xi}}{(\eta + P_{N1})}. \tag{23}$$

Notice that (22)–(23) entails $R_1 = 1 + r$. Moreover, by using (1), (2), (4), (9), (13) and (20), one can derive from the households' budget constraint (8) that in equilibrium

$$K_{T0} L_{T0}^{\alpha} + \frac{K_{T1} L_{T1}^{\alpha}}{1 + r} = C_{T0} + K_1 + \frac{C_{T1}}{1 + r}. \tag{24}$$

4.2 *Number of Firms and Price of Licenses in the Non-tradable Sector*

If in period t the government restricts the issuance of licenses required to operate in the non-tradable sector, the price that firms are willing to pay for using a license increases up to the point where their profits go to zero. Hence, one has:

$$N_t = \overline{N}, \quad t = 0, 1, \tag{25a}$$

thus obtaining from (18)

$$Q_t = \frac{(1 - \beta - \gamma)\Psi}{(\beta + \gamma)} \left(\frac{W_t^{\beta} R_t^{\gamma} C_{Nt}}{\overline{N}} \right)^{\frac{1}{\beta + \gamma}} > F, \quad t = 0, 1. \tag{26a}$$

In contrast, if in period 1 the government grants licenses to everyone willing to pay a unit price F, the number of firms that intend to operate in the non-tradable sector increases up to the point where their profits go to zero. Hence, one has

$$Q_1 = F. \tag{25b}$$

Thus, from (18) one can obtain

$$N_1 = W_1^{\beta} R_1^{\gamma} C_{N1} \left[\frac{(1 - \beta - \gamma)\Psi}{(\beta + \gamma)F} \right]^{\beta + \gamma} > \overline{N}. \tag{26b}$$

4.3 Pessimistic Expectations

If at time 0 the households expect that the government will restrict the issuance of licenses required to operate in the non-tradable sector also in period 1 (and thus believe that $N_0^* = N_1^* = \overline{N}$), one can use (11a, b)–(24) and (25a)–(26a) to solve for what the households consume, work, invest and borrow in the present (i.e., for $C_{T0}^*, C_{N0}^*, L_0^*, K_1^*, D_1^*$) and for what they plan to consume and to work in the future (i.e., for $C_{T1}^*, C_{N1}^*, L_1^*$). Together, one can solve for the associated $Q_0^*, W_0^*, R_0^*, P_{N0}^*, K_{T0}^*, K_{N0}^*, L_{T0}^*, L_{N0}^*, Y_{T0}^*, Y_{N0}^*, Q_1^*, W_1^*, R_1^*, P_{N1}^*, K_{T1}^*, K_{N1}^*, L_{T1}^*, L_{N1}^*, Y_{T1}^*, Y_{N1}^*$.

Two possible cases can occur.

Suppose that when the future arrives the authorities maintain the restriction on the issuance of licenses for producing non-tradables. In this case, the households' pessimistic expectations are fulfilled and the agents actualize at time 1 the optimal plan made in the previous period, thus consume C_{T1}^* units of tradable good and C_{N1}^* units of non-tradable good, and supply L_1^* units of labor. Their associated utility is u_1^*. All the other variables at time 1 take the values predicted at time 0 $(Q_1^*, W_1^*, R_1^*, P_{N1}^*, K_{T1}^*, K_{N1}^*, L_{T1}^*, L_{N1}^*, Y_{T1}^*, Y_{N1}^*)$.

In contrast, suppose that when the future arrives the authorities liberalize firms' entry into the non-tradables sector. In this case, the households' pessimistic expectations are not fulfilled and the agents revise in period 1 the optimal plan made in the previous period on the basis of the pessimistic expectations. One can obtain the values $C_{T1}^{**}, C_{N1}^{**}, L_1^{**}, u_1^{**}, Q_1^{**}, N_1^{**}, W_1^{**}, R_1^{**}, P_{N1}^{**}, K_{T1}^{**}, K_{N1}^{**}, L_{T1}^{**}, L_{N1}^{**}, Y_{T1}^{**}, Y_{N1}^{**}$ which the endogenous variables take in t = 1 when the pessimistic expectations are not fulfilled and agents revise their plans, by using (11a, b)–(21) (where $K_1 = K_1^*$ is given), (25b)–(26b) and the budget constraint (8), which in period t = 1 entails

$$K_{T1}L_{T1}^{\alpha} = C_{T1} + (1 + r)D_1, \qquad D_1 = D_1^* \text{ given.} \tag{27}$$

Typically, $u_1^{**} > u_1^*$ (see the Appendix for a numerical example): by removing in t = 1 the distortion caused by the restriction on the number of firms that may enter the non-tradable sector, the well-being of the representative household at time 1 improves with respect to the case of no liberalization. However, by checking (10) (and noticing that—when households have pessimistic expectations —$u_1\big|_{N_1 > \overline{N}} = u_1^{**}$ and $u_1\big|_{N_1 = \overline{N}} = u_1^*$), one can easily verify that $u_1^{**} > u_1^*$ is a necessary but not a sufficient condition for inducing the government to liberalize the entry into the non-tradable sector at time 1. Indeed, for the authorities to overcome the institutional inertia and trigger a change in the regulatory regime, one needs that both $u_1^* < \underline{u}$ and $u_1^{**} \geq \underline{u}$ hold true.

It follows that, when households' expectations are pessimistic, a necessary and sufficient condition for the liberalization of the non-tradable sector in period 1 is:

$$u_1^{**} \geq \underline{u} > u_1^*. \tag{28}$$

Clearly, if (28) holds, it is irrational for economic agents to have pessimistic expectations at time 0 with regard to the possibility of a future liberalization of the regulatory regime governing the non-tradable sector.

4.4 Optimistic Expectations

If at time 0 the households expect that in period 1 the government will stop restricting the issuance of licenses required to operate in the non-tradable sector (and thus believe that $\mathrm{N}_0^{\circ} = \overline{\mathrm{N}} < \mathrm{N}_1^{\circ}$), one can use (11a, b)–(24) and (25b)–(26b) to solve for what the households consume, work, invest and borrow in the present (i.e., for $\mathrm{C}_{\mathrm{T0}}^{\circ}, \mathrm{C}_{\mathrm{N0}}^{\circ}, \mathrm{L}_0^{\circ}, \mathrm{K}_1^{\circ}, \mathrm{D}_1^{\circ}$) and for what they plan to consume and to work in the future (i.e., for $\mathrm{C}_{\mathrm{T1}}^{\circ}, \mathrm{C}_{\mathrm{N1}}^{\circ}, \mathrm{L}_1^{\circ}$). Together, one can solve for the associated $\mathrm{Q}_0^{\circ}, \mathrm{W}_0^{\circ}, \mathrm{R}_0^{\circ}, \mathrm{P}_{\mathrm{N0}}^{\circ}, \mathrm{K}_{\mathrm{T0}}^{\circ}, \mathrm{K}_{\mathrm{N0}}^{\circ}, \mathrm{L}_{\mathrm{T0}}^{\circ}, \mathrm{L}_{\mathrm{N0}}^{\circ}, \mathrm{Y}_{\mathrm{T0}}^{\circ}, \mathrm{Y}_{\mathrm{N0}}^{\circ}, \mathrm{N}_1^{\circ}, \mathrm{Q}_1^{\circ}, \mathrm{W}_1^{\circ}, \mathrm{R}_1^{\circ}, \mathrm{P}_{\mathrm{N1}}^{\circ}, \mathrm{K}_{\mathrm{T1}}^{\circ}, \mathrm{K}_{\mathrm{N1}}^{\circ}, \mathrm{L}_{\mathrm{T1}}^{\circ}, \mathrm{L}_{\mathrm{N1}}^{\circ}, \mathrm{Y}_{\mathrm{T1}}^{\circ}, \mathrm{Y}_{\mathrm{N1}}^{\circ}$.

Again, two possible cases can occur.

Suppose that when the future arrives the authorities stop restricting the number of firms allowed to produce non-tradables. In this case, the households' optimistic expectations are fulfilled and the agents actualize at time 1 the optimal plan made in the previous period, thus consuming $\mathrm{C}_{\mathrm{T1}}^{\circ}$ units of tradable good and $\mathrm{C}_{\mathrm{N1}}^{\circ}$ units of non-tradable good, and supplying L_1° units of labor. Their associated utility is u_1°. All the other variables take at time 1 the values predicted at time 0 ($\mathrm{N}_1^{\circ}, \mathrm{Q}_1^{\circ}, \mathrm{W}_1^{\circ}, \mathrm{R}_1^{\circ}, \mathrm{P}_{\mathrm{N1}}^{\circ}, \mathrm{K}_{\mathrm{T1}}^{\circ}, \mathrm{K}_{\mathrm{N1}}^{\circ}, \mathrm{L}_{\mathrm{T1}}^{\circ}, \mathrm{L}_{\mathrm{N1}}^{\circ}, \mathrm{Y}_{\mathrm{T1}}^{\circ}, \mathrm{Y}_{\mathrm{N1}}^{\circ}$).

In contrast, suppose that when the future arrives the authorities do not liberalize the entry into the non-tradable sector and continue to restrict the issuance of licenses required to produce non-tradables $\left(\mathrm{N}_1^{\circ\circ} = \overline{\mathrm{N}}\right)$. In this case, the households' optimistic expectations are not fulfilled and the agents revise in period 1 the optimal plan made in the previous period on the basis of these expectations. One can obtain the values $\mathrm{C}_{\mathrm{T1}}^{\circ\circ}, \mathrm{C}_{\mathrm{N1}}^{\circ\circ}, \mathrm{L}_1^{\circ\circ}, \mathrm{u}_1^{\circ\circ}, \mathrm{Q}_1^{\circ\circ}, \mathrm{N}_1^{\circ\circ}, \mathrm{W}_1^{\circ\circ}, \mathrm{R}_1^{\circ\circ}, \mathrm{P}_{\mathrm{N1}}^{\circ\circ}, \mathrm{K}_{\mathrm{T1}}^{\circ\circ}, \mathrm{K}_{\mathrm{N1}}^{\circ\circ}, \mathrm{L}_{\mathrm{T1}}^{\circ\circ}, \mathrm{L}_{\mathrm{N1}}^{\circ\circ}, \mathrm{Y}_{\mathrm{T1}}^{\circ\circ}, \mathrm{Y}_{\mathrm{N1}}^{\circ\circ}$ which the endogenous variables take in $\mathrm{t} = 1$ when the optimistic expectations of the households are not fulfilled and agents revise their plans, by using (11a, b)–(21) (where $\mathrm{K}_1 = \mathrm{K}_1^{\circ}$ is given), (25a)–(26a) and the budget constraint (8), which in period $\mathrm{t} = 1$ entails

$$\mathrm{K}_{\mathrm{T1}}\mathrm{L}_{\mathrm{T1}}^{\alpha} = \mathrm{C}_{\mathrm{T1}} + (1 + \mathrm{r})\mathrm{D}_1, \quad \mathrm{D}_1 = \mathrm{D}_1^{\circ} \text{ given.} \tag{29}$$

Typically, $u_1^{\circ} > u_1^{\circ\circ}$ (see in the Appendix for a numerical example): again, by removing at time 1 the distortion caused by the restriction to the number of firms that can enter the non-tradable sector, the well-being of the representative household improves. However, $u_1^{\circ} > u_1^{\circ\circ}$ is a necessary but not sufficient condition for the government to change the status quo and liberalize the entry into the non-tradable sector. Indeed, for the authorities to overcome the institutional inertia and trigger a change in the regulatory regime, one needs both $\overset{\circ}{u}_1 \geq \underline{u}$ and $u_1^{\circ\circ} < \underline{u}$, since—when households have optimistic expectations—$u_1\Big|_{N_1 > \overline{N}} = \overset{\circ}{u}_1$ and $u_1\Big|_{N_1 = \overline{N}} = u_1^{\circ\circ}$.

A sufficient condition for the government not to liberalize the non-tradable sector in period 1, thus keeping the number of firms operating in this sector restricted to $\overline{N}$ when the households hold optimistic expectations, is given by:

$$u_1^{\circ\circ} \geq \underline{u}. \tag{30}$$

If condition (30) holds, it is irrational for economic agents to have optimistic expectations at time 0 with regard to the possibility of a future liberalization of the regulatory regime governing the non-tradable sector.

4.5 Self-defeating Expectations

Before proceeding, we propose two definitions.

Definition 1 We say that a set of expectations is *self-defeating* if acting on the basis of these expectations creates the condition for their falsification.

In the model presented here, pessimistic (optimistic) expectations about the possibility of a future regulatory reform are self-defeating if (28) [if (30)] holds: acting on the basis of pessimistic (optimistic) expectations, economic agents invest less (more) than otherwise, thereby reducing (increasing) households' future well-being and generating more (less) pressure on the authorities to implement the reform.

Consistently with Definition 1, not all sets of wrong expectations are self-defeating: we may have expectations whose fulfillment (or disappointment) does not depend on the conduct that they activate.

Definition 2 A *self-defeating expectations trap* is a situation where all possible sets of expectations are *self-defeating* because no set of expectations has the potential for self-fulfillment.

It is straightforward that, whenever both (28) and (30) hold, no rational expectations equilibrium can exist and the economy is in a self-defeating expectations trap. What conditions have to be satisfied in the present model for ruling out the existence of a rational expectations equilibrium? One can easily verify that $u_1^{\circ\circ} > u_1^*$ is a necessary condition for the truth of both (28) and (30). Hence, $u_1^{\circ\circ} > u_1^*$ is a necessary condition for the existence of a self-defeating expectations trap.

It is worth pointing out that the condition $u_1^{\circ\circ} > u_1^*$ is very likely to hold: economic agents tend to invest more in productive assets when they expect that reforms augmenting the efficiency of the economy will be implemented $\left(\overset{\circ}{K}_1 > K_1^*\right)$

and households' well-being is higher the larger the investment in productive assets in the past. Hence, even if the reforms will be never implemented, households' well-being is higher if economic agents were optimistic about their implementation $\left(u_1^{\circ\circ} > u_1^*\right)$. Thus, there is a real possibility that both (28) and (30) hold (see the numerical example in the Appendix).

5 Three Realistic Extensions of the Model

To show that the previous results carry over to more complex and realistic environments, we develop and discuss three extensions of the basic model.

5.1 Probability of a Regulatory Change

One could argue that the previous discussion applies to the special case in which the representative household attaches probability one (pessimistic expectations), or alternatively probability zero (optimistic expectations), to the possibility that the status quo will prevail and a regulatory change will not be implemented in the future. We can generalize our results considering the case in which the representative household attaches probability q, with $0 \leq q \leq 1$, to the possibility that the number of firms operating in the non-tradable sector will remain restricted to $\overline{N}$ in period 1. In this case, at time 0 the representative household maximizes its expected lifetime utility $U^e = u_0 + \theta\left[q u_1\big|_{N_1=\overline{N}} + (1-q)u_1\big|_{N_1>\overline{N}}\right]$, and the economy is still governed by (11a, b)–(21) and (24)–(26a, b), while (22)–(23) must be rewritten as

$$\frac{C_{T0}^{-\xi}}{(\eta + P_{N0})} = \theta\left[q\frac{R_1 C_{T1}^{-\xi}}{(\eta + P_{N1})}\Bigg|_{N_1=\overline{N}} + (1-q)\frac{R_1 C_{T1}^{-\xi}}{(\eta + P_{N1})}\Bigg|_{N_1>\overline{N}}\right], \tag{22a}$$

$$\frac{C_{T0}^{-\xi}}{(\eta + P_{N0})} = \theta(1+r)\left[q\frac{C_{T1}^{-\xi}}{(\eta + P_{N1})}\Bigg|_{N_1=\overline{N}} + (1-q)\frac{C_{T1}^{-\xi}}{(\eta + P_{N1})}\Bigg|_{N_1>\overline{N}}\right]. \tag{23a}$$

By solving the model, one can check that the agents tend to invest more in productive assets if they attach a higher probability to the possibility that reforms augmenting the efficiency of the economy will be implemented: $\frac{\partial K_1^{\#}}{\partial q} < 0$ and $K_1^{\circ} \geq K_1^{\#} \geq K_1^*$, where "#" denotes the value of a variable when the households assign probability q to the absence of any liberalization in the non-tradable sector.

Hence, one has $\frac{\partial u_1^{\#}\big|_{N_1=\overline{N}}}{\partial q}<0$ and $u_1^{\circ\circ} \geq u_1^{\#}\big|_{N_1=\overline{N}} \geq u_1^{*}$: even if the liberalization will never be implemented, households' future well-being is higher if economic agents did attach a higher probability to the implementation of the reform.

If both (28) and (30) hold, the fact that $\frac{\partial u_1^{\#}\big|_{N_1=\overline{N}}}{\partial q}<0$ implies that there exists an unique value of q < 1, say $\overline{q}$, such that $u_1^{\#}\big|_{N_1=\overline{N}} = \underline{u}$ if the agents attach probability $\overline{q}$ to the absence of any liberalization. In this case, one has that for $q > \overline{q}$ (i.e., if the households are relatively pessimistic about the possibility that the authorities will liberalize firms' entry into the non-tradable sector), the authorities will implement the liberalization (since $u_1^{\#}\big|_{N_1=\overline{N}} < \underline{u}$). On the contrary, if the households are relatively optimistic (i.e., if $q \leq \overline{q}$), the authorities will not undertake the reform. In other words, if both (28) and (30) hold, a self-defeating expectations trap emerges even if the households attach probability q to the possibility that the number of firms operating in the non-tradable sector will remain restricted to $\overline{N}$ in period 1.

5.2 Distributive Conflict

In the previous section, we invoked a somehow unspecified institutional inertia as the reason why the authorities are reluctant to change a regulatory framework that is clearly Pareto inferior. The existence of a distributive conflict across heterogeneous agents is one of the possible explanations of this inertia (see Footnote 5 for a discussion), but in the basic model we could not capture the redistributive implications of the liberalization of the non-tradable sector because of the simplifying assumption of a unique representative household. Here, we abandon such setup by recognizing that there may be diverging interests among households concerning the removal of restrictions to the number of firms that can operate in the non-tradable sector.

Hence, we assume that at time 0 the population consists of two groups: a fraction λ ($0 < \lambda < 1$) of the households is endowed with the licenses for operating in the non-tradable sector (the "rentiers"), while the remaining fraction $1 - \lambda$ is not (the "non rentiers"). Assuming that all the rest remains the same as in the basic model, the two groups of households differ solely because of their budget constraint, since the rent due to the possession of the licenses is only part of the rentiers' income:

$$\begin{aligned} K_{t+1}^{s} + D_t^{s}(1+r) + P_{Nt}C_{Nt}^{s} + C_{Tt}^{s} &\leq R_t K_t^{s} + D_{t+1}^{s} \\ &+ N_t \pi_{Nt} + \pi_{Tt} + T_t + (N_t L_{Nt} + L_{Tt})W_t \\ &+ N_t(Q_t - F), \quad K_0^{s} = \overline{K}^{s}, D_0^{s} = 0 \text{ and } N_0 = \overline{N} \text{ given}, D_2^{s} \leq 0,\ t = 0, 1, \end{aligned} \tag{8a}$$

$$
\begin{aligned}
K^{n}_{t+1} &+ D^{n}_{t}(1+r) + P_{Nt}C^{n}_{Nt} + C^{n}_{Tt} \leq R_{t}K^{n}_{t} \\
&+ D^{n}_{t+1} + N_{t}\pi_{Nt} + \pi_{Tt} + T_{t} \\
&+ (N_{t}L_{Nt} + L_{Tt})W_{t},\ K^{n}_{0} = \overline{K}^{n}, \\
&D^{n}_{0} = 0 \text{ and } N_{0} = \overline{N} \text{ given}, D^{n}_{2} \leq 0, t = 0, 1,
\end{aligned} \tag{8b}
$$

where the superscript "s" ("n") denotes the value of a variable controlled by the rentiers (non rentiers). Notice also that total capital stock K_t, net foreign debt D_t, consumption of tradables C_{Tt} and consumption of non-tradables C_{Nt} are now given by $K_t = \lambda K^s_t + (1-\lambda)K^n_t$, $D_t = \lambda D^s_t + (1-\lambda)D^n_t$, $C_{Tt} = \lambda C^s_{Tt} + (1-\lambda)C^n_{Tt}$ and $C_{Nt} = \lambda C^s_{Nt} + (1-\lambda)C^n_{Nt}$, t = 0, 1.

It is straightforward to notice that the rentiers do not like the removal of the restriction to the number of firms operating in the non-tradable sector, since this reform will eliminate the rent that they enjoy as holders of the licenses. The government is realistically assumed to preserve the regulatory regime favoring the rentiers (possibly as a result of some rent-seeking activities by the latter): if and only if the utility of the non rentiers falls below that minimum level which is deemed socially acceptable, the government will accept to lift the barrier to entry into the non-tradable sector. More formally, at the beginning of period 1, the government decides to liberalize if and only if

$$
u^{n}_{1}\Big|_{N_1=\overline{N}} < \underline{u} \quad \text{and} \quad u^{n}_{1}\Big|_{N_1>\overline{N}} \geq \underline{u}. \tag{10a}
$$

As in the previous section, a necessary and sufficient condition for liberalizing the non-tradable sector in period 1 when the households expected at time 0 that the government will not liberalize it is:

$$
u^{n**}_{1} \geq \underline{u} > u^{n*}_{1}, \tag{28a}
$$

where u^{n**}_{1} is the utility level that the non rentiers can achieve in period 1 if the households erroneously believed that the government would not liberalize the entry into the non-tradable sector, and u^{n*}_{1} is the utility level that the non rentiers can achieve in period 1 if the households correctly believed that the government would not liberalize.

As in the previous section, a sufficient condition for the authorities not to liberalize the entry in the non-tradable sector in period 1 (thus, keeping the number of operating firms restricted to $\overline{N}$), when the households believed at time 0 that liberalization would instead occur, is given by:

$$
u^{noo}_{1} \geq \underline{u}, \tag{30a}
$$

where u^{noo}_{1} is the utility level that the non rentiers can achieve in period 1 if the households erroneously believed that the government would liberalize the entry into the non-tradable sector.

Again, there is a realistic possibility that both (28a) and (30a) hold, thus realizing a self-defeating expectations trap in a framework of heterogeneous agents with distributive conflicts.

5.3 *Possibility of Default*

In Sect. 4, we implicitly ruled out the possibility that the households can default on their foreign debt, namely we assumed that $K_{T1}L_{T1}^{\alpha} \geq C_{T1} + D_1(1+r)$ must necessarily hold. Here, we relax this assumption by admitting that the households will honor their entire debt service if and only if this will not prevent them from reaching in period 1 the minimum acceptable level of consumption $\underline{C}$, where $\underline{C}$ is such that $\underline{u} = \frac{\underline{C}^{1-\xi}}{1-\xi}$.

This possibility of partial or total repudiation of the debt on the part of the households can be simply modeled by reformulating u_1 as

$$u_1 = \begin{cases} \frac{C_1^{1-\xi}}{1-\xi} - \zeta Z_1 & \text{if } C_1 \geq \underline{C}, \\ -\zeta Z_1 & \text{otherwise, } \zeta \geq \underline{C}^{-\xi}, \end{cases} \tag{31}$$

where $Z_1, 0 \leq Z_1 \leq D_1(1+\hat{r})$, is the amount of the outstanding debt service repudiated by the households, ζ is a parameter measuring the households' sensitivity to the reputational loss due to the repudiation of Z_1, and $\hat{r}$ (with $\hat{r} \geq r$) is the interest rate at which the representative household can go into debt. It derives from (31) that in period 1 the representative household sets

$$Z_1 = \begin{cases} 0 & \text{if } D_1(1+\hat{r}) \leq K_{T1}L_{T1}^{\alpha} - \underline{C}, \\ \underline{C} + D_1(1+\hat{r}) - K_{T1}L_{T1}^{\alpha} & \text{otherwise,} \end{cases} \tag{32}$$

where it is assumed that $K_{T1}L_{T1}^{\alpha} - \underline{C} \geq 0$ (the households, by repudiating entirely their outstanding debt service, can **at least** reach the minimum acceptable level of consumption) and $\frac{\underline{C}^{1-\xi}}{1-\xi} - \zeta\left[\underline{C} + D_1(1+\hat{r}) - K_{T1}L_{T1}^{\alpha}\right] > 0$ [if the households cannot reach $\underline{C}$ by honoring entirely their debt service, they are strictly better off by repudiating that amount of debt service which is necessary to reach $\underline{C}$ than by paying off entirely $D_1(1+\hat{r})$]. Together with $\zeta \geq \underline{C}^{-\xi}$, this implies that whenever their debt service is excessive (i.e., whenever $D_1(1+\hat{r}) > K_{T1}L_{T1}^{\alpha} - \underline{C}$), it is optimal for the households to repudiate **exactly** that amount of debt service which is necessary to reach $\underline{C}$.

International investors are aware of the possibility that their credits will not be entirely repaid. Hence, the interest rate at which they are willing to lend to the domestic households ($\hat{r}$) may be higher than the world (risk-free) interest rate:

$$\hat{r} = r + \frac{Z_1}{D_1}. \tag{33}$$

In a self-defeating expectations trap, that is when both conditions (28) and (30) hold, the possibility for the households to default on their debt is particularly relevant for the case in which the households' pessimistic expectations about reform implementation in period 1 will be validated. When the households' pessimistic expectations are validated and agents do not have the possibility to default, one has that $C_1^* < \underline{C}$ (see the previous section). Instead, when the households' pessimistic expectations are validated and agents have the possibility of repudiating (partially or entirely) the debt, agents would choose to default whenever it is convenient for them to go excessively into debt in period 0 in the anticipation that they will not repay (partially or entirely) it. More formally, the households will honor entirely their debt service if, in the situation in which at time 1 no debt repudiation will occur and they will consume exactly $\underline{C}$, the marginal increase in utility brought about by the increment in consumption at time 0 obtainable by one additional unit of debt is lower than the future discounted disutility of repudiating that unit of debt (and the interest payment on it), i.e., if and only if[19]

$$\left.(C_0^*)^{-\xi}\right|_{\substack{Z_1 = 0 \\ C_1 = \underline{C}}} \leq \theta(1+r)\zeta. \tag{34}$$

Condition (34) is necessary for avoiding a default on the households' debt when the households' expectations are pessimistic and the authorities do not liberalize the firms' entry into the non-tradable sector. It is straightforward that (34) holds when the cost of default is relatively large and the households do not discount the future too heavily: under these circumstances, if the households' pessimistic expectations will be validated by the government, they will not default in $t = 1$ and their utility will be $u_1^* = \underline{u}$. Hence, condition (28) does not hold and there is no self-defeating expectations trap: recalling (10), it is rational to expect that the households' pessimistic expectations will be validated.

In contrast, if (34) does not hold, the households' pessimistic expectations cannot be validated, since—in the absence of the liberalization of the non-tradable sector—the households would default on their debt and their utility in period 1 would be $u_1^* = \frac{\underline{C}^{1-\xi}}{1-\xi} - \zeta Z_1^* < \underline{u}$, where $Z_1^* > 0$. Being aware that—without the

[19]Notice that C_0^* can be obtained by solving (11a, b)–(21), (23)–(24), (25a)–(26a) and $C_1 = \underline{C}$ in the case in which the households have pessimistic expectations, and by solving (11a, b)–(21), (23)–(24), (25b)–(26b) and $C_1 = \underline{C}$ in the case in which they have optimistic expectations.

removal of the barriers limiting firms' entry into the non-tradable sector—households' utility in period 1 would fall below $\underline{u}$, the government is induced in this period to liberalize the non-tradable sector. In other words, if the cost of default is relatively small and the households discount the future heavily, they tend to augment their consumption in period 0 by increasing excessively their debt, thus going into default and reducing their well-being in period 1 in the absence of a regulatory reform on the part of the government. This will lead the government to implement this reform, thus falsifying the households' pessimistic expectations: again, a self-defeating expectations trap is at work.

6 Closing Remarks

This work addresses the underexplored implications of agents' expectations about structural reforms in a context characterized by institutional inertia, whereby the authorities do not implement reforms unless social welfare falls below a critical (politically and socially sustainable) level. By means of a stylized small open economy with tradable and non-tradable sectors and encompassing policy-induced barriers to entry in the non-tradable sector, this work shows that optimistic (pessimistic) expectations about reforms may boost (weaken) the economic performance of the economy and thus reduce (increase) the incentives for the authorities to implement the reform. In addition, the model reveals that there might be circumstances in which no set of expectations has the potential for self-fulfillment, leaving agents to face a high degree of indeterminacy.

Notwithstanding the stylized nature of the analytical set-up, the focus on the interplay between structural reforms and agents' expectations allows to shed some light on the recent Eurozone problems. To start, the model suggests that, if the authorities exhibit a status quo bias against reforms, expectations about the realization of the reforms may be self-defeating and the disciplining effects of the monetary union may fail to materialize. This seems to be consistent with what observed in a number of Eurozone periphery countries. Furthermore, by identifying the case of self-defeating expectations traps, the model reveals a new kind of problem that may possibly emerge in a monetary union among highly heterogeneous members, that is the risk of not having a rational expectations equilibrium and no obvious criterion for the agents to form their expectations.

Thus, while the literature on the European sovereign debt crisis has explained the turmoil in terms of self-fulfilling prophecies and multiple equilibria in the sovereign debt markets, this work suggests that the limited real economic convergence negatively affecting the prospects of the Eurozone may in fact represent a case of self-defeating expectations about structural reforms. This raises a number of questions that the work does not tackle and could be a venue of further research: did the economic agents miscalculate the reaction functions of the governments in the Eurozone periphery? could they do better, had they taken in due account the status quo bias of the authorities? did the EMU experience a self-defeating expectations trap? In such a case, how should rational agents have behaved and is there any positive role for the authorities of the European Union? Can international arrangements and numerical rules, such as those contained in the reformed Stability and Growth Pact, reduce the likelihood of self-defeating expectations? Could domestic commitment devices, such as the establishment of independent committees of technicians, work equally well?

Appendix

Derivation of the Equilibrium Output of the Representative Firm Operating in the Non-tradable Sector and of the Equilibrium Price of its Output

We find the cost-minimizing demand functions for L_{Nt} and K_{Nt} by solving

$$\min_{L_{Nt},K_{Nt}} W_t L_{Nt} + R_t K_{Nt} + Q_t \quad \text{subject to} \quad L_{Nt}^{\beta} K_{Nt}^{\gamma} \geq Y_{Nt}. \tag{A.1}$$

From the solution to (A.1), one can derive the cost function of the representative firm producing the non-tradable good:

$$C(W_t, R_t, Q_t, Y_{Nt}) = \begin{cases} \Psi(Y_{Nt} W_t^{\beta} R_t^{\gamma})^{\frac{1}{\beta+\gamma}} + Q_t & \text{if } Y_{Nt} > 0 \\ 0 & \text{otherwise}, \Psi \equiv \left(\frac{\beta}{\gamma}\right)^{\frac{\gamma}{\beta+\gamma}} + \left(\frac{\gamma}{\beta}\right)^{\frac{\beta}{\beta+\gamma}}. \end{cases} \tag{A.2}$$

By solving

$$\max_{Y_{Nt}} P_{Nt} Y_{Nt} - C(W_t, R_t, Q_t, Y_{Nt}). \tag{A.3}$$

One can find the supply function of the representative firm producing the non-tradable good:

$$Y_{Nt} = \begin{cases} \left\{ \frac{P_{Nt}(\beta+\gamma)(W_t^{\beta} R_t^{\gamma})^{\frac{-1}{\beta+\gamma}}}{\Psi} \right\}^{\frac{\beta+\gamma}{1-\beta-\gamma}} & \text{if } P_{Nt} \geq \text{Min } AC(W_t, R_t, Q_t, Y_{Nt}) \\ 0 & \text{otherwise.} \end{cases} \tag{A.4}$$

Notice that $AC(W_t, R_t, Q_t, Y_{Nt})$ is the average cost function of the representative firm operating in the non-tradable sector:

$$AC(\mathrm{W_t, R_t, Q_t, Y_{Nt}}) = \begin{cases} \Psi(\mathrm{Y_{Nt}^{1-\beta-\gamma} W_t^{\beta} R_t^{\gamma}})^{\frac{1}{\beta+\gamma}} + \frac{\mathrm{Q_t}}{\mathrm{Y_{Nt}}} & \text{if } \mathrm{Y_{Nt}} > 0 \\ 0 & \text{otherwise.} \end{cases} \tag{A.5}$$

Knowing that in equilibrium the representative firm produces the quantity which minimizes its average cost, one can solve

$$\min_{\mathrm{Y_{Nt}}} AC(\mathrm{W_t, R_t, Q_t, Y_{Nt}}), \tag{A.6}$$

thus obtaining the equilibrium output of the representative firm producing the non-tradable good:

$$\mathrm{Y_{Nt}} = \mathrm{W_t^{-\beta} R_t^{-\gamma}} \left[\frac{(\beta+\gamma)\mathrm{Q_t}}{(1-\beta-\gamma)\Psi} \right]^{\beta+\gamma}. \tag{A.7}$$

Moreover, knowing that in equilibrium the price of the non-tradable good equalizes the minimum of the average cost function, one can use (A.7) to substitute for $\mathrm{Y_{Nt}}$ in (A.5), thus obtaining (19).

Numerical Example

Let us assume that $\alpha = 0.7$; $\beta = 0.6$; $\gamma = 0.2$; $\eta = 0.3615336$; $\theta = 0.7986$; $\xi = 0.8636241$; $r = 0.0898415$; $F = 8.3777348$; $H = 42.314599$; $\overline{K} = 49.0208565$; $\overline{N} = 4$; $\underline{u} = 9.784406$, and $\underline{W} = 3.1350538$.

Pessimistic Expectations

Taking the parameter values and initial conditions given above, one can solve for the case in which agents' expectations are pessimistic, thus obtaining: $C^*_{T0} = 8.574346$; $C^*_{N0} = 23.716595$; $L^*_0 = H$; $W^*_0 = 3.616183$; $R^*_0 = 1.084547$; $N^*_0 = \overline{N}$; $Q^*_0 = 10.861741$; $P^*_{N0} = 9.159613$; $K^*_{T0} = 8.960856$; $K^*_{N0} = 10.015$; $L^*_{T0} = 6.270824$; $L^*_{N0} = 9.010944$; $Y^*_{T0} = 32.39491$; $Y^*_{N0} = 5.929149$; $K^*_1 = 42.16378$; $D^*_1 = 18.343216$; $C^*_{T1} = 8.28969$; $C^{**}_{T1} = 8.497391$; $C^*_{N1} = 22.929234$; $C^{**}_{N1} = 23.503738$; $N^*_1 = \overline{N}$; $N^{**}_1 = 4.489750$; $Q^*_1 = 9.36689$; $Q^{**}_1 = F$; $L^*_1 = H = L^{**}_1$; $W^*_1 = \underline{W}$; $W^{**}_1 = 3.138048$; $R^*_1 = 1 + r$; $R^{**}_1 = 1.094759$; $P^*_{N1} = 8.17026$ $P^{**}_{N1} = 8.001695$; $K^*_{T1} = 7.7848581$; $K^{**}_{T1} = 7.807343$; $K^*_{N1} = 8.59473$; $K^{**}_{N1} = 7.652585$; $L^*_{T1} = 6.3145995$; $L^{**}_{T1} = 6.3553444$; $L^*_{N1} = 8.96338$; $L^{**}_{N1} = 8.0091889$; $Y^*_{T1} = 28.28087$; $Y^{**}_{T1} = 28.490536$; $Y^*_{N1} = 5.732308$; $Y^{**}_{N1} = 5.2349767$; $u^*_1 = 9.78428$; $u^{**}_1 = 9.8173558$. It is worth to notice that condition (28) is satisfied $\left(u^{**}_1 = 9.8173558 \geq \underline{u} = 9.784406 > u^*_1 = 9.78428\right)$.

Optimistic Expectations

Taking again the parameter values and initial conditions given above, one can solve for the case in which agents' expectations are optimistic, thus obtaining: $C^{\circ}_{T0} = 8.5655285$; $C^{\circ}_{N0} = 23.692206$; $L^{\circ}_{0} = H$; $W^{\circ}_{0} = 3.6328049$; $R^{\circ}_{0} = 1.0898415$; $N^{\circ}_{0} = \overline{N}$; $Q^{\circ}_{0} = 10.898415$; $P^{\circ}_{N0} = 9.2$; $K^{\circ}_{T0} = 9.0208565$; $K^{\circ}_{N0} = 10$; $L^{\circ}_{T0} = 6.3145994$; $L^{\circ}_{N0} = 9$; $Y^{\circ}_{T0} = 32.771011$; $Y^{\circ}_{N0} = 5.9230515$; $K^{\circ}_{1} = 42.39325$; $D^{\circ}_{1} = 18.187768$; $C^{\circ}_{T1} = 8.5185921$; $C^{\circ\circ}_{T1} = 8.3187641$; $C^{\circ}_{N1} = 23.56238$; $C^{\circ\circ}_{N1} = 23.009657$; $N^{\circ}_{1} = 4.5$; $N^{\circ\circ}_{1} = \overline{N}$; $Q^{\circ}_{1} = F$; $Q^{\circ\circ}_{1} = 9.3997928$; $L^{\circ}_{1} = H = L^{\circ\circ}_{1}$; $W^{\circ}_{1} = 3.1416507$; $W^{\circ\circ}_{1} = \underline{W}$; $R^{\circ}_{1} = 1 + r$; $R^{\circ\circ}_{1} = 1.0860535$; $P^{\circ}_{N1} = 8$; $P^{\circ\circ}_{N1} = 8.1703028$; $K^{\circ}_{T1} = 7.8012393$; $K^{\circ\circ}_{T1} = 7.77325$; $K^{\circ}_{N1} = 7.6871134$; $K^{\circ\circ}_{N1} = 8.655$; $L^{\circ}_{T1} = 6.3145994$; $L^{\circ\circ}_{T1} = 6.2832683$; $L^{\circ}_{N1} = 8$; $L^{\circ\circ}_{N1} = 8.9948630$; $Y^{\circ}_{T1} = 28.34038$; $Y^{\circ\circ}_{T1} = 28.1405485$; $Y^{\circ}_{N1} = 5.2360845$; $Y^{\circ\circ}_{N1} = 5.7524142$; $u^{\circ}_{1} = 9.8206926$; $u^{\circ\circ}_{1} = 9.7889524$. It is worth to notice that condition (30) is satisfied $\left(u^{\circ\circ}_{1} = 9.7889524 \geq \underline{u} = 9.784406\right)$.

Since both conditions (28) and (30) are satisfied, this numerical example is consistent with the existence of a self-defeating expectations trap: given the parameter values and initial conditions specified above, no rational-expectations equilibrium can exist.

References

Abiad, A., and A. Mody. 2005. Financial reform: what shakes it? What shapes it? *American Economic Review* 95(1): 66–88.

Acemoglu, D., J.A. Robinson, and T. Verdier. 2012. Can't we all be more like scandinavians? Asymmetric growth and institutions in an interdependent world. CEPR Discussion Paper 9113.

Aizenman, J., M. Hutchison, and Y. Jinjarak. 2013. What is the risk of European sovereign debt defaults? Fiscal space, CDS spreads and market pricing of risk. *Journal of International Money and Finance* 34(C): 37–59.

Aizenman, J., and S.-S. Yi. 1998. Regret theory and policy reform. *Journal of Policy Reform* 2: 269–280.

Alesina, A., S. Ardagna, and V. Galasso. 2011. The euro and structural reforms. *Review of Economics and Institutions* 2(1).

Alesina, A., and A. Drazen. 1991. Why are stabilizations delayed? *American Economic Review* 81 (5): 1170–1188.

Angeletos, G.-M., and J. La'O. 2013. Sentiments. *Econometrica* 81(2): 739–779.

Arnold, J., G. Nicoletti, and S. Scarpetta. 2010. Much Ado about something? Regulation, resource allocation and firm-level productivity in a panel of countries. Paper presented at the Ifo/CESifo and OECD conference on regulation, Munich, 29–20 Jan 2010.

Barone, G., and F. Cingano. 2011. Service regulation and growth: evidence from OECD countries. *Economic Journal* 121(555): 931–957.

Barro, R.J., and X. Sala-i-Martin. 1995. *Economic growth*. New York: McGraw-Hill.

Bartelsman, E., J. Haltiwanger, and S. Scarpetta. 2013. Cross-country differences in productivity: the role of allocation and selection. *American Economic Review* 103(1): 305–334.

Bateman, I., A. Munro, B. Rhodes, C. Starner, and R. Sugden. 1997. A test of the theory of reference-dependent preferences. *Quarterly Journal of Economics* 62: 479–505.
Bean, C. 1998a. Monetary policy under EMU. *Oxford Review of Economic Policy* 14: 41–53.
Bean, C. 1998b. The interaction of aggregate demand policies and labor market reform. *Swedish Economic Policy Review* 5: 353–382.
Belke, A., B. Herz, and L. Vogel. 2005. Structural reforms and the exchange rate regime: a panel analysis for the world versus OECD countries. IZA Discussion Papers 1798.
Bems, R. 2008. Aggregate investment expenditures on tradable and nontradable goods. *Review of Economic Dynamics* 11: 852–883.
Bentolila, S. and G. Saint-Paul. 2000. Will EMU increase eurosclerosis? CEPR Discussion Papers 2423.
Bertola, G., and L. Mola. 2010. Services provision and temporary mobility: freedoms and regulation in the EU. *World Economy* 33(4): 633–653.
Bianchi, F. 2013. Regime switches, agents' beliefs, and post-world war II U.S. Macroeconomic Dynamics. *Review of Economic Studies* 80(2): 463–490.
Bonatti, L., and A. Fracasso. 2014. The German model and the euro crisis. *Journal of Common Market Studies* 51(6): 1023–1039.
Borchert, I., B. Gootiiz, and A. Mattoo. 2013. Policy barriers to international trade in services: evidence from a new database. *World Bank Economic Review* (forthcoming).
Bouis, R., O. Causa, L. Demmou, R. Duval, and A. Zdzienicka. 2012. The short-term effects of structural reforms: an empirical analysis. OECD Economics Department Working Papers, No. 949.
Bourguignon, F. 2011. Status quo in the welfare analysis of tax reforms. *Review of Income and Wealth* 57(4): 603–621.
Brou, D., and M. Ruta. 2013. Rent-seeking, market structure, and growth. *Scandinavian Journal of Economics* 115(3): 878–901.
Cacciatore, M., R. Duval, and G. Fiori. 2012. Short-term gain or pain? A DSGE model-based analysis of the short-term effects of structural reforms in labour and product markets. OECD Economics Department Working Papers, No. 948.
Cason, T.N., and V.-L. Mui. 2005. Uncertainty and resistance to reform in laboratory participation games. *European Journal of Political Economy* 21(3): 708–737.
Conway, P., and G. Nicoletti. 2006. Product market regulation in the non-manufacturing sectors of OECD countries: measurement and highlights. OECD Economics Department Working Papers 530.
Coudert, V., C. Couharde, and V. Mignon. 2013. On currency misalignments within the euro area. *Review of International Economics* 21(1): 35–48.
De Grauwe, P., and Y. Ji. 2012. Mispricing of sovereign risk and macroeconomic stability in the Eurozone. *Journal of Common Market Studies* 50: 866–880.
De Grauwe, P., and Y. Ji. 2013. Self-fulfilling crises in the Eurozone: an empirical test. *Journal of International Money and Finance* 34: 15–36.
Dewatripont, M., and G. Roland. 1992a. Economic reform and dynamic political constraints. *Review of Economic Studies* 59: 703–730.
Dewatripont, M., and G. Roland. 1992b. The virtues of legitimacy and gradualism in the transition to a market economy. *Economic Journal* 102: 291–300.
Di Cesare A., G. Grande, M. Manna, and M. Taboga. 2012. Recent estimates of sovereign risk premia for euro-area countries. Bank of Italy Questioni di Economia e Finanza (Occasional Papers) 128.
Djankov, S. 2009. The regulation of entry: a survey. *World Bank Research Observer* 24(2): 183–203.
Drazen, A. 2000. *Political economy in macroeconomics*. Princeton: Princeton University Press.
Duval, R., and J. Elmeskov. 2006. The effects of EMU on structural reforms in labour and product markets. European Central Bank, Working Paper Series 596.
Eterovic, D.S. 2011. Institutional bias towards the status quo. *Journal of Institutional and Theoretical Economics* 167(3): 489–514.

Fernandez, R., and D. Rodrik. 1991. Resistance to reform: status quo bias in the presence of individual-specific uncertainty. *American Economic Review* 81(5): 1146–1155.

Fernández-Villaverde, J., L. Garicano, and T. Santos. 2013. Political credit cycles: the case of the Eurozone. *Journal of Economic Perspectives* 27(3): 145–166.

Forni, L., A. Gerali, and M. Pisani. 2010. Macroeconomic effects of greater competition in the service sector: the case of Italy. *Macroeconomic Dynamics* 14(05): 677–708.

Frankel, M. 1962. The production function in allocation and growth: a synthesis. *American Economic Review* 52: 995–1022.

Giavazzi, F., and L. Spaventa. 2010. Why the current account may matter in a monetary union: lessons from the financial crisis in the Euro area. CEPR Discussion Papers 8008.

Grossman, G., and E. Helpman. 2001. *Special interest politics*. Cambridge: MIT Press.

Hoj, J., V. Galasso, G. Nicoletti, and D. Thai-Thanh. 2006. The political economy of structural reform. OECD Economics Department, Working Paper 501.

Jain, S., and S.W. Mukand. 2003. Redistributive promises and the adoption of economic reform. *American Economic Review* 93(1): 256–264.

Katsimi, M., and T. Moutos. 2010. EMU and the Greek crisis: the political economy perspective. *European Journal of Political Economy* 26: 568–576.

Krueger, A.O. 1974. The political economy of the rent-seeking society. *American Economic Review* 64: 752–769.

Krusell, P., and J.-V. Rios-Rull. 1996. Vested interests in a positive theory of stagnation and growth. *Review of Economic Studies* 63(2): 301–329.

Lusinyan, L., and D. Muir. 2013. Assessing the macroeconomic impact of structural reforms the case of Italy. IMF Working Papers 13/22.

Miller, M., and A. Stuherland. 1991. The 'Walters critique' of the EMS—a case of inconsistent expectations? *Manchester School* LIX(S1): 23–37.

Moutos, T. and L. Pechlivanos. 2013. The democratization of rent seeking in Greece. CESifo Working Paper 4331.

OECD. 2010. *Making reform happen lessons from OECD countries: lessons from OECD countries*. Paris: OECD Publishing.

Olson, M. 1965. The logic of collective action: public goods and the theory of groups. Cambridge, MA: Harvard University Press.

Perotti, R., and Y. Kontopoulos. 2002. Fragmented fiscal policy. *Journal of Public Economics* 86 (2): 191–222.

Persson, T., and G. Tabellini. 2000. *Political economics: explaining economic policy*. Cambridge: MIT Press.

Reis, R. 2013. The Portuguese slump-crash and the euro crisis. Paper presented at the Brookings panel on economic activity. Brookings Institution, March, 21–22.

Rodrik, D. 1996. Understanding economic policy reform. *Journal of Economic Literature* XXXIV:9–41.

Rodrik, D. 2005. Growth strategies. In *Handbook of economic growth*, vol. 1, ed. P. Aghion, and S.N. Durlauf, 967–1014. Amsterdam: Elsevier. (Ch. 14).

Rodrik, D. 2008. The real exchange rate and economic growth. *Brookings Papers on Economic Activity* 2: 365–412.

Roland, G. 2002. The political economy of transition. *Journal of Economic Perspectives* 16(1): 29–50.

Samuelson, W., and R. Zeckhauser. 1988. Status quo bias in decision making. *Journal of Risk and Uncertainty* 1: 7–59.

Tompson, W. 2009. *The political economy of reform. Lessons from pensions, product markets and labour markets in ten OECD countries*. Paris: OECD Publishing.

Turnovsky, S.J. 1997. *International macroeconomic dynamics*. Cambridge: MIT Press.

Tversky, A., and D. Kahneman. 1991. Loss aversion in riskless choice: a reference-dependent model. *Quarterly Journal of Economics* 106(4): 1039–1061.

Valderrama, L. 2009. Political risk aversion. IMF Working Paper 09/194.

Transatlantic Austerity 2010–13. A Comparative Assessment

Roberto Tamborini

Abstract Drawing on a large data collection, this paper offers a comprehensive assessment of fiscal austerity in twenty-nine major countries in the Transatlantic area in the aftermath of the Great Recession of 2008–09. Countries include the seventeen Euro members as of 2013, and twelve non-Euro countries, the ten other members of the European Union, United States and Canada. The paper is organized in two parts. First, an index of austerity is proposed based on the contraction of the public sector's net contribution to the economy. Then, there follows an assessment of austerity under the two dimensions of the improvement of public finances and interest rates, and of the collateral effects on economic activity and employment. The assessment is accompanied by reasoned discussion of the theoretical motivations and underpinnings of fiscal austerity and relevant criticisms. The main conclusion is that austerity in general has so far missed its promised goals, for (1) except budget deficits, public finances have further deteriorated, (2) countries under stronger austerity have achieved neither consolidation nor faster recovery but rather lower shock absorption, worse recovery performances, and higher unemployment. Claims that austerity failures are due to country-specific factors, such as mistakes in implementation and pre-crisis structural weaknesses, are not supported by robust evidence.

1 Introduction

'Austerity' was the 2010 word of the year according to the *Merriam-Webster Dictionary*, with more than 250,000 clicks on the online edition. Austerity is today a notorious word that stands for what economists call "fiscal consolidation policies", recommended, and largely activated, all across the developed countries after the remarkable deployment of various fiscal supports to countervail the global

---

R. Tamborini (✉)
Department of Economics and Management, University of Trento, Trento, Italy
e-mail: roberto.tamborini@unitn.it

L. Paganetto (ed.), *Achieving Dynamism in an Anaemic Europe*,
DOI 10.1007/978-3-319-14099-5_7

financial and economic crisis exploded in 2008–09.[1] Austerity thus encompasses fiscal policies variably intended to keep the public budget in balance, or abstain from excess expenditure, or actively pursue budget restrictions, even though the economy may be suffering from low production and high unemployment. In this sense, austerity stands in opposition to the so-called "Keynesian fiscal policies" which recommend deficit spending as a means to overcome economic depressions. "The boom, not the slump, is the right time for austerity at the Treasury" Keynes said in 1937 in one of his famous radio broadcasts.

The motivations put forward for austerity vary according to the circumstances. For countries on the brink of a sovereign debt crisis, as it has been the case in the Euro Zone (EZ), austerity may appear to be an obvious necessity. However, since all countries activated fiscal stimuli in 2008–09 leading to substantial budget deficits, the overarching motivation for austerity has been fiscal consolidation, with variable force and urgency from country to country.

If not dictated by immediate threats, austerity has also been prescribed as a requisite for reinstating sound growth conditions before prolonged fiscal stimuli to the economy become self-defeating as public debt grows too high.

> There should be little question that European economies share the need to reduce public deficits and debts from levels that, as confirmed by a growing strand of empirical literature [...] are likely to be harmful for growth in the medium term [...] (Buti and Pench 2012, p. 1)

In this perspective, the true issue at stake is whether austerity is a means to achieve fiscal consolidation with little or no output and employment losses, or as a means to restore growth, in the course of a recession.

> Some argue that budget consolidation and fostering growth appear contradictory to one another [...] As consolidated public finances enhance the trust of financial markets in each respective country, budget discipline is a key prerequisite for economic success and should not be perceived as a hurdle to growth (OECD 2012, p. 5)

In the face of the persistence of slumps in the EZ, the policy strategy has been rephrased as a matter of trading off some economic losses immediately with more austerity and economic losses in the future, while the policy assessment has progressively been shifted from short to longer time horizons, albeit undetermined.

> It is undeniable that the front-loaded fiscal consolidation had a negative impact on Eurozone growth, and the factors that have aggravated the impact of consolidation on growth are well known [...] The jury is still out on the relative merits of a more front loaded consolidation, allowing a smaller adjustment later on, and a delayed consolidation (US), requiring a more drastic effort when the recovery is still fragile (Buti and Padoan 2013, p. 1)

---

[1]Indeed, austerity is a word with a long history which, to remain within contemporary history, may be traced back to the inter-war years of the Great Depression. See Blyth (2013) for a thorough historical reconstruction.

As a matter of fact, today austerity not only is widely unpopular, but it is also highly controversial and increasingly criticized from various academic camps.[2] Inevitably, the debate has so far grown out of contingent events in a short-run perspective. Completing the fifth year after the crisis, and hence in a medium-run retrospective, this paper aims to offer a first systematic quantitative assessment of austerity since the outbreak of the crisis. The time span has been selected to encompass the first year of generalized recession, 2009,[3] up to 2013, the last year of available official data of public finances.

The first aim is to widen the view to a comparative spectrum of different countries across the Transatlantic area. Indeed, the crisis has invested the whole Western world, and austerity is not an exclusive policy of the EZ countries. On the other hand, it is well known that policy design as well as policy results are also dependent on country-specific characteristics and institutions; as will be seen, austerity is no exception. The choice of countries has been made using EZ membership as institutional criterion in the first place, and then along other dimensions. The EZ is regarded as the epicentre of austerity mainly in force of the fiscal rules contained in the constitutive treaties and subsequent modifications. Accordingly, some scholars find that the "Euro dummy" may explain (adverse) phenomena that are peculiar to EZ countries with respect to other similar "stand-alone" countries (e.g. De Grauwe 2011; De Grauwe and Ji 2012).[4] Therefore, the seventeen EZ members present in 2013 have been selected first. This group has been split in two: the twelve early members (EEZ),[5] and the five late members (LEZ).[6] The latter have a shorter track of membership and they overall represent a thin fraction of the aggregate economy of the EZ. Nonetheless this group may provide useful information as a control group with respect to the early members. Further, in consideration of the features of the sovereign debt crisis of 2010–12, EEZ has been disaggregated into two subgroups: EEZ5, the group of the most fiscally distressed

[2]As examples in the flood of materials available, especially via internet, see the interventions collected by Corsetti (ed., 2012) representative of perplexities from more orthodox scholars, the papers in the special issue of the *Cambridge Journal of Economics* reviewed by King et al. (2012) for more radical Keynesian views, and Blyth (2013) for a discussion of the various positions pro and against austerity.

[3]Only the following countries were in recession in 2008: France, Greece, Ireland, Italy, Estonia, Latvia, Denmark, Sweden, UK, US.

[4]De Grauwe highlights that EZ members have suffered higher risk premia than non-Euro countries with similar (deteriorating) public finance indicators. He argues that Euro-membership (lack of independent monetary policy) is an institutional variable that per se has been penalized by financial investors. More severe austerity can then be seen as the policy response emerged within the Euro Zone context.

[5]Austria, Belgium, Finland, France, Germany, Greece, Ireland, Italy, Luxembourg, Netherlands, Portugal, Spain.

[6]Slovenia, Cyprus, Malta, Slovakia, Estonia.

members (combining high public deficit, debt, and interest rate),[7] and the remaining EEZ7. Then, twelve non-EZ countries (NoEZ) have been added, namely ten other EU countries (OEU)[8]—which are comparable with EZ in terms of development, average size, and other institutional features except the common currency—and the two larger North-American (NA) countries, Canada and United States, dimensionally comparable with EZ as a whole. In total, twenty-nine countries highly representative of the Transatlantic area.

The second aim is to set the stage for reasoned assessment of austerity by means of a wide data set covering the most relevant phenomena. To this end, as far as possible data have been collected from a single official source, Eurostat (online database AMECO[9]) unless otherwise stated.

The paper is organized in two parts. The first (Sect. 2) introduces a measure of austerity. Various measures are available and used in the debate, depending on the specific aspect of interest. For reasons that will be seen, a suitable measure of austerity for our purposes is the year change in the public sector net contribution to income formation (i.e. the primary deficit) as a ratio to current GDP. Transatlantic austerity is then gauged under three dimensions that are regarded as relevant to achieve successful austerity: *timing and intensity* ("front-loaded"/large vs. "back-loaded"/progressive), and *composition* (cutting expenditure vs. raising taxes) (e.g. OECD 2012; Buti and Padoan 2012; Buti and Pench 2012; EU Commission 2013).

The second part (Sect. 3) is devoted to the assessment of the results of austerity. This is not an easy task, with several areas of controversy, because austerity is a multifaceted medium-run policy strategy, so that results may be better in some aspects and worse in others, and a sufficiently long gestation may be invoked. However, it seems fair to focus on two main areas, under the guidance of the austerity literature. One is obviously public finances, that is deficits, debts and interest rates, where results were expected to be tangible in the short run. The other is the real economy, namely economic activity, growth and employment, where the side effects of successful austerity ought to be transitory if negative, and conducive to faster recovery to growth in the medium run.

Given the objective intricacy of arguments and phenomena, and the relative scarcity of observations, it seems hard to provide a definite assessment of austerity in one single, integrated, all-encompassing empirical model. Rather, the paper will offer the reader a detailed analysis of country data and responses for each major issue of the austerity experience mostly by means of partial correlation analysis. The basic correlation indicators will be provided, together with, where useful, the best OLS interpolation function in terms of determination coefficient. Since correlation is not

---

[7]Greece, Ireland, Italy, Portugal and Spain. For statistical and econometric analyses identifying this cluster of countries as the eye of the debt storm see e.g. De Grauwe and Ji (2013a, b), Favero and Missale (2011).

[8]Bulgaria, Czech Republic, Denmark, Hungary, Latvia, Lithuania, Poland, Romania, Sweden, United Kingdom. Croatia is not included because it has joined the EU later.

[9]http://ec.europa.eu/economy_finance/db_indicators/ameco/index_en.htm.

causation, no strong causal inferences will be drawn,[10] and yet a statistically qualified characterization will emerge of the role of austerity *vis-à-vis* the above mentioned set of variables across the Transatlantic area.

It will be seen that austerity in general has so far missed its promised goals, in particular in the EZ, for (1) except budget deficits, public finances have further deteriorated, (2) countries under stronger austerity (e.g. EEZ5) have achieved neither consolidation nor faster recovery; rather, they present lower shock absorption, worse recovery performance, and higher unemployment. Claims that austerity failures are due to country-specific factors, such as mistakes in implementation and pre-crisis structural weaknesses, are not supported by robust evidence. Summary of results and conclusions will follow in Sect. 4.

2 Gauging Austerity

A basic problem in the empirical analysis of austerity is its correct and appropriate measurement. Indeed, a number of different measures are possible and available in the literature depending on the purpose of analysis. To begin with, four different actors are involved with different viewpoints and stakes: the government, the recipients of fiscal decisions, the investors in public debt, and external agencies. Each actor may assess, or perceive, whether or not fiscal policy is austere in different ways, and it is not difficult to imagine situations in which assessments are even of different sign. A simple example may clarify the issues involved and the rationale of the austerity indicator proposed here.

Suppose that the economy is in a downturn and the government cuts some current expenditure. This is intended to be an austerity policy "ex ante". But how this ex-ante austerity policy affects the economy depends on how the recipients of current expenditure are actually affected. Suppose that some automatic stabilizers are in place such that other components of current expenditure increase: overall, total expenditure indicates little or no change and, consequently, "ex-post" austerity results smaller than it is ex ante, probably with a negligible effect on the economy. At the same time, investors in public debt, possibly in line with external agencies like rating agencies, the IMF, or the EU Commission, are concerned with financial stability and focus on the evolution of indicators like the deficit/GDP ratio or the debt/GDP ratio. Since the economy is in a downturn, and the ex-ante austerity policy is ex-post-neutral on current public expenditure, the business cycle will probably follow its own course so that current GDP will be lower than the previous year, thus pulling tax revenues down: overall, the deficit/GDP ratio, and hence the debt/GDP ratio, will be worse than in the previous year, turning the ex-ante austere

[10] Hence the significance of coefficients of interpolation functions is not an issue.

government into an ex-post profligate one. The "denominator bias" due to the use of GDP ratios is usually corrected by taking the primary budget net of interest and with "cyclical adjustment" (CA) techniques (for a recent assessment of this issue see EU Commission 2013). Hence the CA primary budget can be regarded as a good approximation of the "true" ex-ante policy stance of the government. Yet, apart from various and unresolved technical problems, consider again the previous example. With a correct CA technique an observer might identify the ex-ante austerity policy of the government, but this fact is not particularly relevant to the economic impact of fiscal policy. What is relevant in this perspective is the actual evolution of fiscal balances for their terminals in the economy, which include the working of automatic stabilizers. Who is right, and what should the external observer look at?

2.1 An Austerity Indicator

The ideal indicator should be simple and transparent, and seek to comply with two criteria, at least for the purposes of the present study. (1) *Governments are responsible for what they can control directly*; hence the indicator should be "ex ante" as much as possible. (2) *The assessment of fiscal policy should necessarily go through its effects on the economy*, which largely depend on the actual evolution of relevant fiscal variables.

My proposed fiscal austerity indicator is the following. Let F_t be the public sector net contribution to income formation in year t, given by public expenditure net of interest payments and total fiscal revenue (i.e. the primary deficit), and let Y_t denote the nominal GDP. Then fiscal adjustment, as the change in the public sector net contribution in year t, is measured by $F_t - F_{t-1}$, and its impact on the economy by

$$FA_t \equiv (F_t - F_{t-1})/Y_t \tag{1}$$

where $FA_t < 0$ indicates austerity.

Overall, this austerity indicator seems to strike a reasonable balance between the two criteria mentioned above, and to provide a comparable measure of the impact of actual changes in the public sector net contribution while avoiding the bias inherent in taking GDP ratios as primitives.[11] Following the literature on austerity, three dimensions stand out as critical: timing, intensity and composition.

[11]Note that, generally, $(F_t - F_{t-1})/Y_t \neq F_t/Y_t - F_{t-1}/Y_{t-1}$ unless GDP is constant or $F_{t-1} = 0$. Otherwise, consider the case $F_{t-1} > 0$, $FA_t < 0$. If we use the GDP ratios instead, positive growth adds a negative bias (austerity is overvalued), whereas negative growth adds a positive bias (austerity is undervalued).

2.2 Timing and Intensity

The first key ingredient in the recipe for successful austerity is an "ambitious", front-loaded restoration of sustainable public finances that stops speculative attacks, regenerates investors' confidence, and regains access to the debt market at lower interest rates.[12] Table 1 provides the summary statistics of *FA* indicators for all countries from 2009 to 2013. Our data allow for the following considerations. As to timing, after the generalized anti-crisis fiscal stimuli of 2009, the large majority of countries (20/29) moved into austerity in 2010, reaching a global average of almost −1 % of national GDP. All countries, with no exceptions, were in the austerity regime by 2011, the peak austerity year with a global average of −1.4 %. Hence data identify a generalized "austerity period" spanning from 2010 to 2013. As quantitative hint, over this period 74 % of *FA* observations are negative (86/116).

Figure 1 provides a snapshot of the *FA*s since 2010 for the groups of countries. There is some evidence that on average all groups of countries followed the front-loading strategy prescribed by the austerity agencies: the bulk of restriction was realized in 2010–11. Notable exceptions to the front-loading strategy are UK, US and Italy, which postponed major restrictions until the debt attack of the second half of 2011. The time and intensity profile of austerity is similar for EZ and no-EZ as whole, so that the "euro dummy" does not seem important. However, the no-EZ is the result of two different patterns: OEU tracked EZ quite closely while NA followed a more moderate path: the "*Europe* dummy" seems more to the point.

It is also clear that in EZ the austerity turn was largely driven by the EEZ5 group of the most financially distressed countries (primarily Greece, Ireland, Spain) averaging around −3 % of GDP in 2010 and −2.4 % in 2011. The EEZ7 countries remained almost neutral or slightly expansionary in 2010 (except Belgium, which was in fact a high debt country), and yet they were also driven into austerity in 2011 (−1.4 % on average) led by Germany with a remarkable −3.4 %.

From this initial overview, austerity appears as a medium-term policy. Hence, whether front- or back-loaded it is informative to have a measure of its overall intensity. To this end, Table 1 displays two additional indicators (see Fig. 2 for the groups of countries) of the *cumulated fiscal adjustment* (*CFA*), that is the sum of *FA*s over time. One indicator measures the overall injection of austerity from 2010 to 2013. The other includes the fiscal stimulus of 2009; hence it tells us whether austerity has more or less than reversed the initial fiscal stimulus. This adds important information with regard to the "shock absorption" and "budget smoothing" functions of public finance. According to the budget smoothing principle, this second indicator should point to zero as GDP returns to normality.

[12]According to the evidence analysed by Buti and Pench (2012), gradual consolidations seem more likely to be successful, but gradualism may be harmful for countries starting with high debt levels and major financial distress.

Table 1 *FA* indicators, 2009–2013, (% of GDP)

	FA					CFA	
	2009	2010	2011	2012	2013	2009–13	2010–13
AUS	3.04	0.55	−1.72	−0.06	−0.99	0.82	−2.22
BEL	4.84	−1.43	−0.02	0.26	−1.22	2.43	−2.41
FIN	7.48	0.19	−1.94	1.29	0.39	7.41	−0.07
FRA	4.70	−0.34	−1.94	−0.25	−0.27	2.27	−2.80
GER	3.34	1.29	−3.36	−0.90	0.24	0.60	−2.74
LUX	3.94	0.04	−0.32	−0.60	−0.07	2.99	−0.95
NET	6.20	−0.19	−0.39	−0.47	−1.43	3.71	−2.48
EEZ7	**4.79**	**0.01**	**−1.38**	**−0.11**	**−0.48**	**2.84**	**−1.95**
GRE	5.58	−5.92	−2.79	−0.99[a]	−0.15[a]	−1.36	−9.86
IRE	5.29	−5.93[a]	−0.23[a]	−1.45	−1.96	2.83	−9.57
ITA	3.32	−0.74	−1.01	−1.50	0.28	1.21	−2.97
POR	6.69	−0.18	−6.65	−0.57[a]	0.83	0.12	−6.57
SPA	6.40	−1.95	−1.17	−2.91[a]	−0.22[a]	0.16	−6.24
EEZ5	**5.46**	**−2.94**	**−2.37**	**−1.48**	**−0.24**	**0.59**	**−7.04**
CYP	7.39	−0.40	0.99	−0.74	0.63	7.88	0.49
EST	−1.43	−2.03	−0.97	1.24	0.13	−3.05	−1.62
MAL	−0.84	0.04	−0.86	0.43	0.12	−1.11	−0.27
SLK	5.69	0.04	−2.53	−0.71	−1.47	1.01	−4.68
SLO	4.19	−0.76	0.26	−2.83	1.33	2.18	−2.00
LEZ	**2.45**	**3.00**	**−0.62**	**−0.62**	**−0.52**	**1.59**	**−1.62**
EZ	**1.92**	**4.46**	**−1.04**	**−1.45**	**−0.63**	**1.11**	**−3.35**
BUL	6.16	−1.06	−1.00	−1.31	1.26	4.04	−2.11
CZE	3.31	−1.16	−1.48	1.14	−1.60	0.22	−3.10
DEN	5.83	−0.02	−0.75	2.39	−2.36	5.09	−0.74
HUN	0.40	0.26	−1.28[a]	−1.28[a]	0.91	−1.00	−1.39
LAT	3.77	−1.71	−3.94	−1.94	−0.05	−3.87	−7.64
LIT	4.99	−2.45	−1.12	−2.07	−0.18	−0.84	−5.82
POL	3.44	0.62	−2.51	−1.14	1.13	1.55	−1.90
ROM	2.40	−1.92	−1.03	−2.52	−0.43	−3.50	−5.90
SWE	3.69	−0.88	−0.12	0.62	0.54	3.86	0.17
UK	7.34	−1.91	−0.90	−1.89	−2.26	0.39	−6.95
OEU	**1.59**	**4.13**	**−1.02**	**−1.41**	**−0.80**	**0.59**	**−3.54**
CAN	0.26	3.4	0.9	−0.7	−0.4	3.00	−0.39
USA	3.97	5.50	−0.70	−1.05	−1.14	1.39	−4.12
NA	**2.12**	**4.44**	**0.08**	**−0.86**	**−0.76**	**2.19**	**−2.25**
NoEZ	**1.68**	**4.18**	**−0.84**	**−1.32**	**−0.79**	**0.86**	**−3.32**
Global	**4.35**	**−0.96**	**−1.40**	**−0.70**	**−0.29**	**1.01**	**−3.34**

Group data are unweighed averages

[a]Data corrected for bank bailouts and other extraordinary operations with the private sector that these countries have recorded in the current budget

Source EUROSTAT, Database AMECO

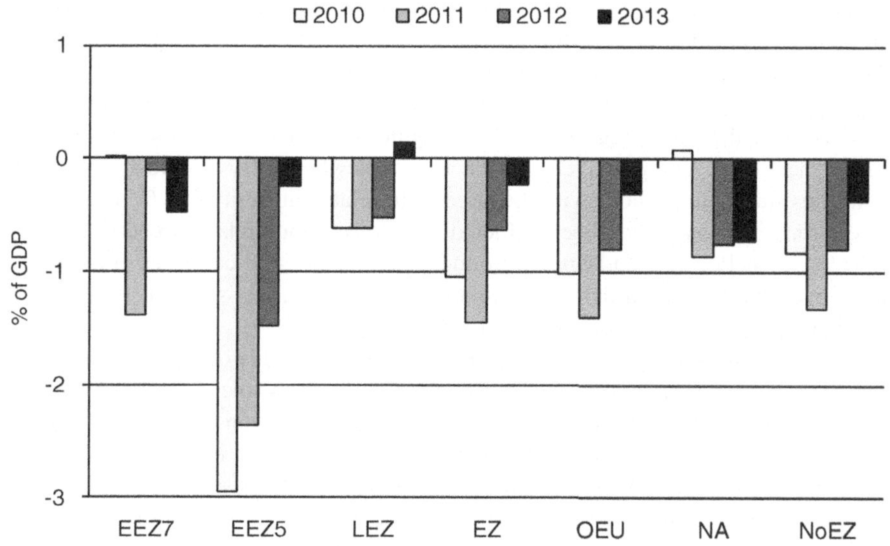

Fig. 1 *FA* indicators, groups of countries, 2010–13. *Source* see Table 1

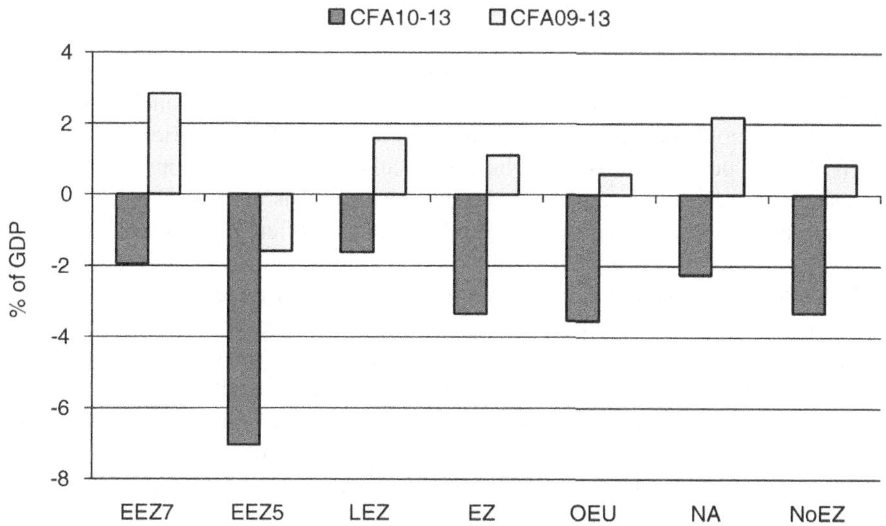

Fig. 2 *CFA* indicators, groups of countries. *Source* see Table 1

Since the first year of generalized austerity (2010) almost all countries (with the exceptions of Sweden and Cyprus) have cumulated sizeable restrictive *CFA*s, reaching a global average of −3.4 % of GDP. This is equivalent to say that the representative Transatlantic country has cut the public sector net contribution to the economy at a year pace of about 0.8 % of GDP for four years. To confirm the comparative patterns of year-by-year austerity pointed out above, the overall austerity effort in EZ has been in line with NoEZ, but both EZ and OEU, that is *Europe as a whole*, are notably more severe than NA (−3.6 and −2.3 % respectively).

However, the disaggregation of EZ is quite instructive. The austerity effort of EEZ7 has been comparatively lower than elsewhere. By contrast, the EEZ5 countries stand out as those with the largest cumulated austerity (−7 % on average). The strongest dosage has been inflicted on Greece and Ireland (reaching almost −10 %), then Portugal and Spain (around −6 %), that is all countries embarked in bank bailouts, sovereign debt crisis and external conditional support. Italy (−3 %) lies between these countries and the EEZ7 group.

Table 1 also displays the *CFA*s from the fiscal stimulus of 2009–2013. In the majority of countries, and in the Transatlantic area as a whole, cumulated austerity fell short of the initial stimulus, leaving a net fiscal expansion of about 1 %. In this respect, EZ (1.1 %) results slightly more expansionary than NoEZ (0.9 %). From the point of view of budget smoothing, it may be argued that austerity has not (yet) been too much, but the critical point is that budget smoothing ought to take place in tandem with the return of economic activity to normality—we will address this point later.

There are however important differences within groups. NoEZ reveals a sharp difference between OEU (0.6 %) and NA (2.2).[13] EZ also hides quite different situations. EEZ7 realized the largest net expansion (2.8 %) whereas the "uniqueness" of EEZ5 re-emerges: except for Ireland's positive residual, this is the single group of countries where austerity completely nullified, or reversed, the initial fiscal stimulus.

In light of this first overview of the data, we may draw two conclusions. First, austerity has not been an exclusive policy imposed onto EZ countries; rather, it has been "freely" pursued across the whole Transatlantic area as the consensus mindset to manage the fiscal consequences of the financial crisis and the Great Recession. Second, austerity has however been implemented in different ways as to its timing and overall intensity. If a Transatlantic divide exists, it is not along the borders of EZ, but between NA and Europe as a whole. Under all dimensions, austerity has been most severely enacted in the EEZ5 countries under worst public finance conditions. It is the joint presence of *two* features, EZ membership *and* public finance distress, that makes the difference and identifies the real epicentre of austerity in the Transatlantic area. As argued by EU Commission officials, diversification and flexibility have in fact been actively pursued in application of the more recent modifications of the EZ fiscal rules (Buti and Carnot 2013, p. 3). On the other hand, the dosage of austerity cumulated in the rest of the EZ *and OEU* countries has been nontrivial, and it appears less justified on the grounds of public

[13]The fact is that four OEU countries ended up with a net *restriction* (Hungary, Latvia, Lithuania, Romania).

finance emergency in comparison with other No-EZ countries. Drawing on De Grauwe's (2011) argument, why should the overall post-crisis fiscal adjustment of the EZ, and Europe, as a whole be more severe than in NA? Thus, I would qualify the European experience as one of "uncoordinated austerity", which may have created unfavourable conditions for the countries facing stronger pressure for fiscal consolidation.[14]

2.3 Composition

The most common austerity prescription is that expenditure cuts have less negative impact (or even a positive one) on the economy and more lasting effect on public finances (see Carnot 2013, for an overview).[15] In this perspective, Table 2 provides the composition of the *CFA*s, respectively. Note that *CFA*s result from the difference between the cumulated (primary) expenditure adjustment (*CEA*) and the cumulated tax adjustment (*CTA*)[16]:

$$FA_t = (G_t - G_{t-1})/Y_t - (T_t - T_{t-1})/Y_t \qquad (2)$$

$$CFA = \sum\nolimits_t \Delta G_t/Y_t - \sum\nolimits_t \Delta T_t/Y_t = CEA - CTA \qquad (3)$$

Figure 3 shows the composition of *CFA*s for the groups of countries in the austerity period 2010–13. Positive histograms indicate increases. We can see that the recommended composition has not enjoyed large audience: the majority of countries, within and outside EZ have implemented cumulated austerity by *increasing tax revenue more than expenditure.* The larger increase in tax revenue may partly be due to the income effect, but some countries traditionally regarded as fiscally virtuous in the EEZ7 and NA groups have let expenditure grow to a remarkable extent over the austerity period. It may come as a surprise that the most aggressive restrictions on the expenditure side have been accomplished within the EEZ5 group, with an average cut of 4.2 %: in the case of Greece, Portugal and Ireland this may be the result of specific Troika interventions; yet Spain has managed a net cut by itself, while Italy has kept cumulated expenditure well below the average (1.4 %).

[14]On the problem of uncoordinated fiscal adjustment plans in the EZ see Tamborini (2013), Berti et al. (2013), in't Veld (2013).

[15]It is sometimes added that the expenditure to be cut is the "unproductive" one. Yet this is a category difficult to identify, hence, in practice, expenditure at large is considered.

[16]Total revenue of the central government.

Table 2 *CFA* indicators and their composition, 2010–13

	CFA	CEA	CTA
AUS	−2.22	4.62	6.85
BEL	−2.41	5.24	7.65
FIN	−0.07	10.38	10.45
FRA	−2.80	4.79	7.59
GER	−2.74	2.29	5.02
LUX	−0.95	8.49	9.44
NET	−2.48	3.99	6.47
EEZ7	**−1.95**	**5.69**	**7.64**
GRE	−9.86	−9.46	0.40
IRE	−9.57	−8.24	1.33
ITA	−2.97	1.39	4.37
POR	−6.57	−3.47	3.10
SPA	−6.24	−2.35	3.89
EEZ5	**−7.04**	**−4.42**	**2.62**
CYP	0.49	2.30	1.81
EST	−1.62	3.58	5.20
MAL	−0.27	8.03	8.30
SLK	−4.68	3.62	8.30
SLO	−2.00	1.70	3.70
LEZ	**−1.62**	**3.85**	**5.46**
EZ	**−3.35**	**2.17**	**5.52**
BUL	−2.11	4.49	6.60
CZE	−3.10	1.77	4.87
DEN	−0.74	9.34	10.08
HUN	−1.39	4.91	6.30
LAT	−7.64	−4.44	3.20
LIT	−5.82	−1.72	4.10
POL	−1.90	7.67	9.57
ROM	−5.90	4.80	10.70
SWE	0.17	7.84	7.67
UK	−6.95	−0.47	6.49
OEU	**−3.54**	**3.42**	**6.96**
CAN	−0.39	6.81	7.20
USA	−4.12	4.65	8.76
NA	**−2.25**	**5.73**	**7.98**
NoEZ	**−3.32**	**3.80**	**7.13**
Global	**−3.34**	**2.85**	**6.19**

CEA Cumulated (primary) expenditure adjustment
CTA Cumulated tax revenue adjustment
CFA = CEA − CTA
Source EUROSTAT, Database AMECO

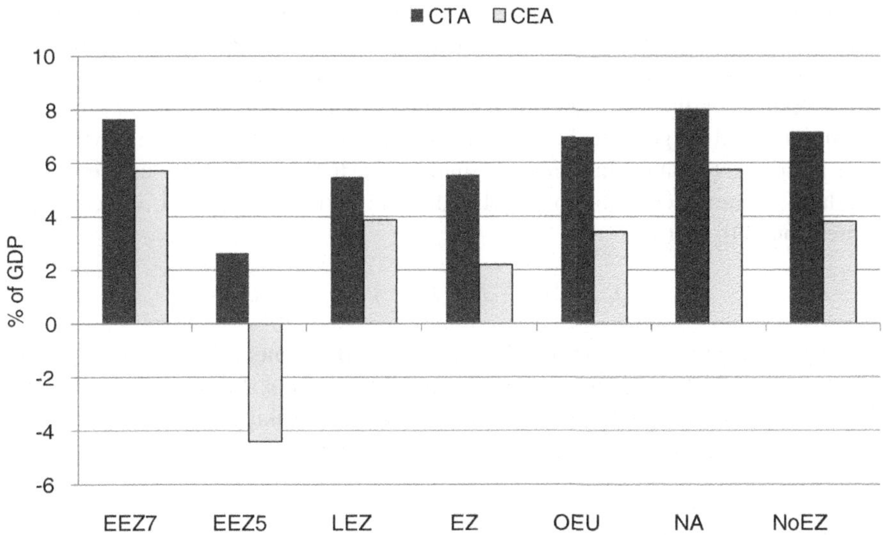

Fig. 3 Composition of *CFA* indicators 2010–13, groups of countries. *Source* see Table 2

3 Assessing Austerity

Assessing austerity is not an easy task. For two main reasons. The first is that austerity is a complex policy recipe with multidimensional implications; it may well happen that some results are negative while others are positive. The second reason relates more to the rhetoric of the economic discourse: pro-austerity arguments, even at the official levels, are remarkably devoid of any clear quantification of the expected results, including their time horizon, against which actual results can be assessed. Hence, we lack a clear and well identified framework for assessment in the first place.

3.1 An Assessment Framework

Strictly speaking, the purpose of austerity is to regain control over, and the sustainability of, public debt. As a matter of fact, however, implementation of orthodox sustainability analysis, based on fiscal fundamentals and the intertemporal budget constraint, encounters a number of non-trivial difficulties (e.g. the choice of the appropriate discount rate, time horizon, and budget items) paving the way to controversial if not inconclusive judgements (e.g. Bohn 1995; Kanda 2011; IMF 2012).

Bearing this premise in mind, public finance assessment in the Maastricht rule framework is mostly driven by two simple indicators: the total deficit/GDP ratio and the gross debt/GDP ratio. Therefore, let us think of austerity in the classical policy framework of *instruments*, *intermediate targets*, and *final targets*. Let the debt/GDP ratio be the final target, whose quantification may vary from, say, stabilization to the reduction plans prescribed by the Fiscal Compact. Given this final target, the government has to choose an instrument. We have already examined this issue, opting for the *FA* indicator (of course, others may well be chosen). This instrument (and in general the instruments fully controllable by the government) have an indirect relationship with the final target. In this regard, we can rewrite the standard dynamic equation of public debt in terms of our *FA* indicator [see expression (1)], that is:

$$D_t = D_{t-1} + I_t + F_{t-1} + FA_t Y_t + X_t \tag{4}$$

where D is the nominal value of debt, I is interest payments, F is the primary deficit and X is other extraordinary operations and adjustments. Let $I_t = i_t D_{t-1}$, where i_t denotes the nominal interest rate on outstanding debt. Taking ratios to current GDP Y_t, and denoting them with small-case letters we obtain

$$\Delta d_t \equiv d_t - d_{t-1} \approx (i_t - n_t)d_{t-1} + f_{t-1} + FA_t + x_t \tag{5}$$

where n_t is the nominal growth rate of GDP, and the usual approximation $(1 + n_t) \approx 1$ is used.

This relationship provides a first benchmark for the *effectiveness* of austerity. If a government follows a consistent path of fiscal restrictions $FA_t < 0$, it may expect d to remain on a non-increasing path $\Delta d_t \leq 0$ (Bohn 1995). If this does not happen, the causes may be: (1) austerity is *insufficient*, given initial conditions and the paths of i and n, (2) adverse evolutions of i and n.

The most critical issue in austerity assessment, being a source of confusion and disagreement, is that the two sets of causes are in fact interconnected and cannot be easily disentangled. To put it in analytical terms, i and n are, in part at least, endogenous to *FA*. Moreover, these collateral effects of austerity are another area of large disagreement. In the pro-austerity view, its effectiveness hinges on driving i down and being neutral or positive on n (OECD 2012; Buti and Padoan 2012; Buti and Pench 2012; EU Commission 2013). The typical anti-austerity argument is that it can easily be *excessive*, driving n downwards and i upwards (e.g. De Grauwe and Ji 2013a; Tamborini 2013). If this happens, the pro-austerity counterargument is that the problem is not austerity in itself, but that it has probably been implemented in the wrong way (see above Sects. 2.2 and 2.3). Another line of defence is that low growth and high unemployment in some countries are unrelated to austerity since they come from long-lasting structural weaknesses (e.g. Bini Smaghi 2013; Manasse and Rota Baldini 2013). Also, there has been a recent reformulation of austerity assessment according to which possible economic losses of immediate austerity should be assessed against possibly larger losses due to delayed austerity when recovery comes (e.g. Buti and Padoan 2013). On the other hand, this style of reasoning leaves the time dimension of assessment undetermined, and it seems to presume that there is no connection between the present course of policy and how much time the recovery takes to come.

Therefore, public finances and interest rates will be examined in the first place, and subsequently the side effects on economic activity and employment.

3.2 Public Finances

In Sect. 2 we saw that between 2010 and 2013 almost all countries engaged in cumulated fiscal restrictions; those in the epicentre of the EZ sovereign debt crisis by and large followed orthodox recommendations as to timing and composition. Did austerity deliver the promised results in terms of financial consolidation? Let us first examine whether austerity has been effective on the basic indicators of "sound" public finances.

Table 3 provides the relevant data. As austerity has been a generalized policy, so all countries progressively brought their deficit/GDP ratio under control. In the EZ, the average ratio fell from 6.3 % in 2009 to 3.8 % in 2013. In 2009 all countries (except Finland and Luxembourg) were above the 3 % ceiling, in 2013 only seven (France, Greece, Ireland, Portugal, Spain, Cyprus, Slovenia), some of which by virtue of special arrangements with the EU Commission and other official agencies. Interestingly, also countries with no formal deficit/GDP target moved in tandem with the EZ: the average NoEZ deficit was cut from 6.8 % in 2009 to 2.6 % in 2013 (but note that UK and US still have deficits twice larger than the global average).

As regards public debt, the outcome of austerity has been much poorer. In Fig. 4, the time profile of the debt/GDP ratio from 2008 to 2013 has been quite similar across countries. The first spike occurred in 2009 as a consequence of the post-shock fiscal stimuli; thereafter, however, debt to GDP went on rising. All countries (except Sweden) ended 2013 with a ratio greater than in 2009: 22.9 points on average in EZ, 7.8 points in NoEZ. The EZ worse performance is due to the fact that the faster debt accumulators reside in the EEZ5 group (41.4 point on average). Yet the club of countries recording a two-digit increase in their debt/GDP ratio includes traditionally fiscally sound and strong economies like UK (20.9), Germany (14.3), US (14.2), France (13.5), Netherlands (12.7). Now the Transatlantic area is split *across* the ideal border of the EZ between a higher debt group above 90 % of GDP (Belgium, France, Greece, Ireland, Italy, Portugal, Spain, Cyprus, UK, Canada and US) and a lower debt group.

These data indicate that cumulated austerity subsequent to the 2009 debt creation generally failed to curb the growth of debt relative to GDP. As a matter of fact, if a relationship exists between *CFA*s and debt/GDP ratios, this is perverse, as shown by Fig. 5 where stronger cumulated austerity is associated with higher debt/GDP growth. The correlation coefficient is 0.66. Interestingly, the best interpolation function is quadratic, which captures *accelerating* debt-growth/*CFA* relationships. Paradoxically, the EEZ5 countries, which underwent the most severe austerity motivated by their debt emergency, are also the countries with the worst debt/GDP performance. According to the R^2 indicator, differences in *CFA*s account for 50 %

Table 3 Central government's total deficit and gross debt as % of GDP, 2009–13

	2009		2010		2011		2012		2013	
	DEF	DEB	DEF	DEB	DEF	DEB	DEF	DEB	DEF	DEB
AUS	4.1	69.5	4.5	71.9	2.6	72.2	2.6	74.2	1.5	74.5
BEL	5.7	95.8	3.9	96.0	3.9	98.0	4.1	100.5	2.6	101.5
FIN	2.7	43.5	2.8	48.4	0.9	48.6	1.8	50.5	2.1	57.0
FRA	7.6	79.2	7.1	82.3	5.2	85.8	4.9	90.5	4.3	93.5
GER	3.2	74.4	4.3	83.0	1.0	81.2	−0.1	82.2	0.0	78.4
LUX	0.8	14.8	0.9	19.1	0.6	18.2	0.0	20.3	−0.1	23.1
NET	5.6	60.8	5.0	62.9	4.6	65.2	4.1	70.1	2.5	73.5
EEZ7	**4.2**	**62.6**	**4.1**	**66.2**	**2.7**	**67.0**	**2.5**	**69.7**	**1.8**	**71.6**
GRE	15.6	129.4	10.5	145.0	9.2	165.3	8.9	160.6	12.7	175.1
IRE	14.0	65.1	9.5	92.5	9.7	108.2	8.2	116.1	7.2	123.7
ITA	5.4	116.0	4.5	119.3	3.8	120.8	3.0	127.0	3.0	132.6
POR	5.6	83.1	9.8	93.3	4.2	107.8	6.4	113.9	4.9	129.0
SPA	10.2	53.9	9.3	61.2	8.5	68.5	10.6	80.9	7.1	93.9
EEZ5	**10.1**	**89.5**	**8.7**	**102.2**	**7.1**	**114.1**	**7.4**	**119.7**	**7.0**	**130.9**
CYP	6.1	58.5	5.3	61.3	6.3	71.5	6.4	86.6	6.4	111.7
EST	2.0	7.1	−0.2	6.7	−1.1	6.1	0.2	9.8	0.2	10.0
MAL	3.7	66.5	3.5	66.8	2.8	69.5	3.3	71.3	3.3	73.0
SLK	8.0	35.6	7.7	41.0	5.1	43.4	4.5	52.4	4.5	55.4
SLO	6.3	35.2	5.9	38.7	6.3	47.1	4.0	54.4	4.0	71.7
LEZ	**5.2**	**40.6**	**4.4**	**42.9**	**3.9**	**47.5**	**3.7**	**54.9**	**3.7**	**64.4**
EZ	**6.3**	**62.7**	**5.5**	**68.5**	**4.3**	**73.6**	**4.3**	**78.7**	**4.3**	**85.7**
BUL	4.3	14.6	3.1	16.2	2.0	16.3	0.8	18.5	0.8	18.9
CZE	5.8	34.6	4.7	38.4	3.2	41.4	4.2	46.2	4.2	46.0
DEN	2.7	40.7	2.5	42.7	1.8	46.4	3.8	45.4	3.8	44.5
HUN	9.4	79.8	7.2	82.2	5.5	82.1	2.1	79.8	2.1	79.2
LAT	9.8	36.9	8.1	44.4	3.6	41.9	1.3	40.6	1.3	38.1
LIT	4.6	29.3	4.3	37.8	−4.3	38.3	3.2	40.5	3.2	39.4
POL	7.5	50.9	7.9	54.9	5.0	56.2	3.9	55.6	3.9	57.0
ROM	9.0	23.6	6.8	30.5	5.6	34.7	3.0	37.9	3.0	38.4
SWE	0.7	42.6	−0.3	39.4	−0.2	38.6	0.6	38.2	0.6	40.6
UK	11.4	69.6	10.1	79.6	7.7	85.7	6.1	89.1	6.1	90.6
OEU	**6.5**	**42.3**	**5.4**	**46.6**	**3.0**	**48.2**	**2.9**	**49.2**	**2.9**	**49.3**
CAN	4.5	87.4	4.9	89.5	3.7	93.6	3.4	96.1	3.4	97.0
USA	11.4	90.4	10.9	99.1	9.8	103.5	9.2	102.9	9.2	104.5
NA	**8.0**	**88.9**	**7.9**	**94.3**	**6.7**	**98.6**	**6.3**	**99.5**	**6.3**	**100.8**
NoEZ	**6.8**	**50.0**	**5.9**	**54.6**	**3.6**	**56.6**	**3.5**	**57.6**	**3.5**	**57.8**
Global	**6.5**	**58.24**	**5.7**	**63.6**	**4.0**	**67.5**	**3.9**	**70.8**	**3.9**	**74.9**

Source EUROSTAT, Database AMECO

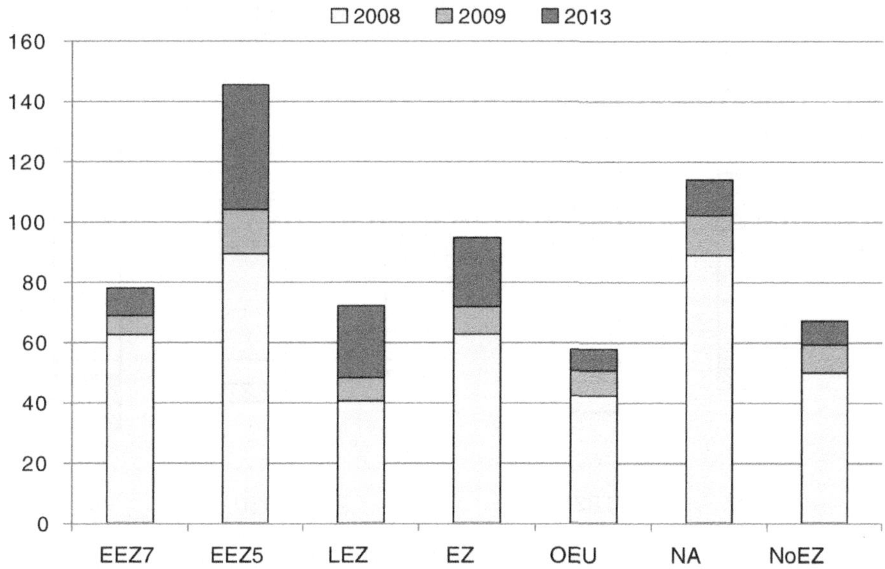

Fig. 4 Debt/GDP ratios from 2008 to 2013, groups of countries. *Source* see Table 3

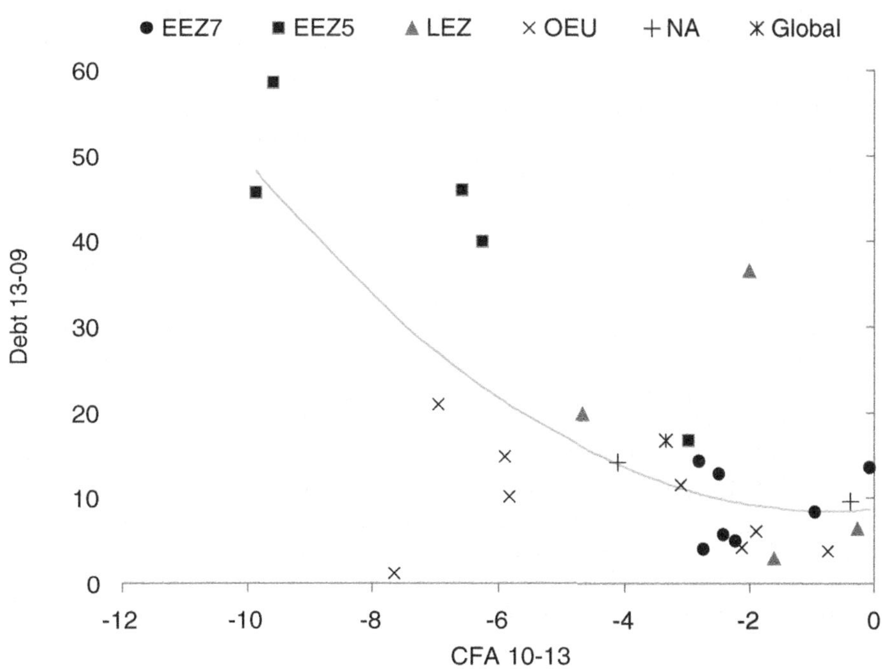

Fig. 5 Increase in the debt/GDP ratio 2009–13 and *CFA* 2010–13, all countries with *CFA* < 0. Correlation coefficient 0.66. OLS interpolation function: $y = 9.2 + 0.7x + 0.48x^2$, $R^2 = 0.50$. *Source* see Tables 2 and 3

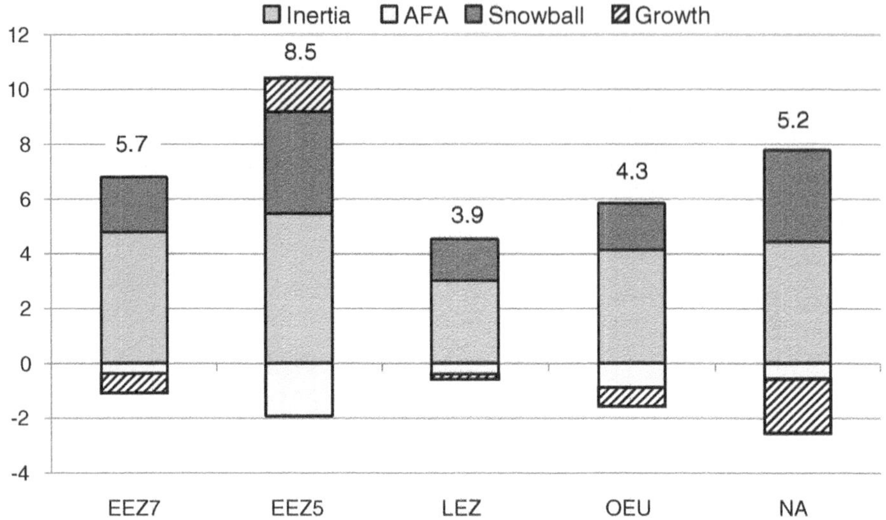

Fig. 6 Decomposition of the growth of the debt/GDP ratio 2009–13, groups of countries. *Source* Author's elaborations

of differences in debt growth. There are, in fact, some large outliers across the group. Considering the EEZ countries alone, the group most consistently exposed to austerity policy, we obtain an analogous accelerating interpolation function, but the explanatory power of *CFA*s rises to 85 %, which indicates that other country-specific factors (e.g. the initial debt level) have played a minor role.

Austerity defenders may argue that this is evidence that austerity has been *insufficient*, and that without austerity debt growth would have been much worse. Yet this argument is not so obvious as it appears. As is well known, the debt to GDP dynamics depends not only on the control of the primary budget but also on the gap between the interest rate paid on debt and on the growth rate of GDP. Equation (5) provides guidance in decomposing the drivers of the debt/GDP ratio. Apart from extraordinary operations and adjustments x_t, and given the government's fiscal impulse FA_t, three other factors can be identified: "fiscal inertia", given by the previous year's primary deficit/GDP ratio f_{t-1}, "growth effect" $-n_t d_{t-1}$, and "snowball effect" given by the evolution of interest payments $i_t d_{t-1}$. Figure 6 presents the decomposition of the growth of debt/GDP ratios for the groups of countries (figures above the histograms indicate the total impulse to debt/GDP growth). To capture the medium-term evolution of debt, $t - 1$ is 2009, and t is the "average year" 2010–13.[17] Differences, and hints about whence the ineffectiveness of austerity derives, appear quite clearly.

[17]Since "the" interest rate actually paid on the outstanding debt is in fact a complex composition of different rates and maturities, for these empirical calculations i_t has obtained as the ratio of actual interest payments on debt.

Let us compare the average EEZ7 country with the average EEZ5 country. The initial impulse in 2009 ("inertia") is quite similar, while the subsequent fiscal adjustment ("average *FA*") is consistently larger for EEZ5. Why does the latter end up with such a stronger impulse to debt/GDP growth? Clearly for two factors: the snowball effect, that is higher unit cost of debt, and the growth effect, such that *negative* growth pushes the debt/GDP ratio up for EEZ5 whereas *positive* growth pulls it down for EEZ7. Indeed, EEZ5 is the single group where high interest rates and low growth jointly plaid the most perverse effect on the debt/GDP ratio. As said, the critics of austerity point out that it may in itself be partly responsible for worsening debt/GDP ratios by depressing growth, and possibly increasing risk premia. But of course, it should be proved that austerity is responsible for both perverse effects. Hence, let us now turn to the evolution of interest rates.

3.3 Interest Rates

The interest rate on public debt is a key variable in the austerity strategy. Strong and fast fiscal consolidation is expected to reduce the interest rate quickly, which helps fiscal consolidation on the one hand, and fosters private expenditure on the other. Hence the evolution of interest rates after the outbreak of the crisis and throughout the austerity period has seized the greatest concern of governments and analysts. Especially so in the EZ, where a sequence of sovereign debt crises, mostly in the EEZ5 group, erupted from 2010 to 2012. Thus analyses have concentrated on the key symptom of the EZ sovereign debt crises, namely the spread between interest rates on long-term State bonds *vis-à-vis* Germany. In our Transatlantic perspective this approach is not entirely appropriate, because No-EZ countries have freely floating exchange rates against Germany (hence the relative interest-rate spread may reflect not only the pure default risk), and because outside Europe there exists another safe asset *par excellence*, namely the US Federal bonds. It is therefore more correct to look first at the *level* of interest rates, and indeed it is the level of the interest rate that matters for public finances.

Figure 7 highlights an important fact that is often disregarded: from 2008 onwards interest rates in the Transatlantic area have been on a *downward* trend, except for the EEZ5 escalation between 2010 and 2012 the bulk of which is due to Greece. The general trend was mainly due to the large and persistent easing of monetary policies by the major central banks. Higher spreads against Germany (or the US) arose owing to the faster fall of the interest rate on safe assets.[18] As a matter of fact, EEZ5 (in particular Greece, Ireland and Portugal) is the only group of countries which suffered from *both* high spread against Germany *and* high level of the interest rate.

---

[18]For Germany, the "flight to quality" effect has been documented by e.g. Favero and Missale (2011), Tamborini (2014b).

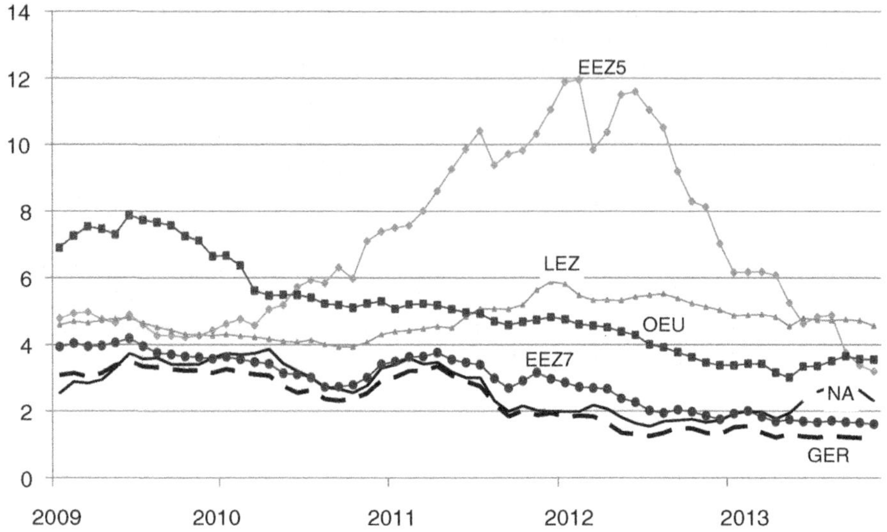

Fig. 7 Year average of montly values of interest rates on long-term State bonds, 2009–13. Groups of countries and Germany. *Source* ECB, Statistical Warehouse, Interest rates statistics

As said above, the relationship between austerity and the evolution of spreads against Germany as a measure of default risk is a specific EZ issue. Empirical research on risk premia in the EZ sovereign debt crises is burgeoning.[19] Challenging technical problems aside, some convergence in conclusions can be detected. Overall, the EZ turmoil has shaken the reliance on financial market efficiency in providing the right stick-and-carrot mix that should drive fiscal consolidation. However, the same studies widely agree that, among the fundamentals, the evolution of debt/GDP ratios maintains a significant influence on spreads. Hence, having seen austerity's scant success in harnessing debt/GDP growth, it is not so surprising that spreads have failed to fall as well. This can be seen by means of Fig. 8. Taking a medium-term perspective, it plots the year average of monthly values of spreads against the year *CFA*s, that is the sum of *FA*s year after year, over the austerity period.

Figure 8 in fact highlights a positive correlation between increasing doses of austerity and spreads (correlation coefficient 0.74). Also in this case, the best interpolation function is quadratic and denotes an *accelerating* relationship between austerity doses and spreads. Differences in the former account for 64 % of differences in spreads.

[19]To mention only a few recent comprehensive contributions: Attinasi et al. (2009), Caceres et al. (2010), Favero and Missale (2011), De Grauwe and Ji (2012).

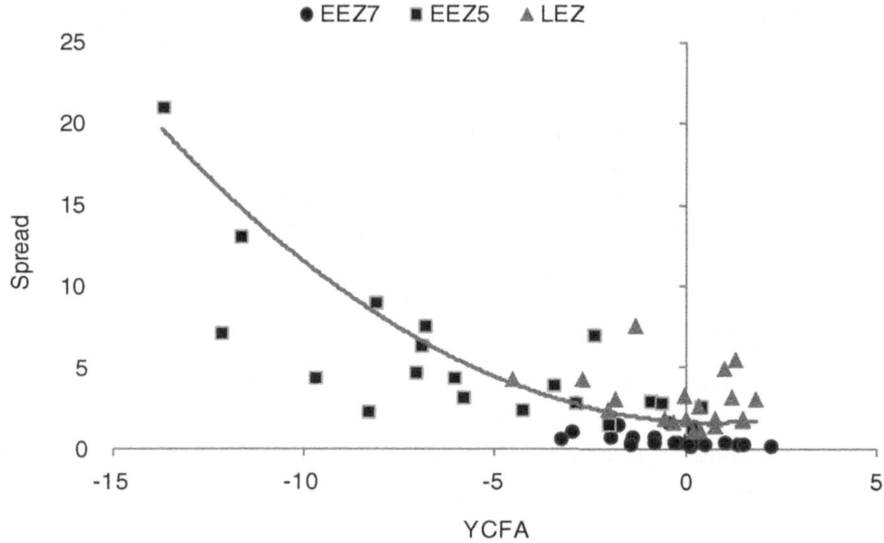

Fig. 8 Year average of monthly values of spreads of long-term interest rates over German bonds and year *CFA*s, EZ countries, 2010–2013.Correlation coefficient 0.74. OLS interpolation function: $y = 1.6 + 0.01x + 0.08x^2$, $R^2 = 0.64$

This evidence can be interpreted in two ways, however. The first is that in financially distressed countries, spreads have been strong drivers of austerity, as they should be, to the point that governments have been chasing their spreads with repeated doses of austerity. However, reverse causality is also possible. Reverse causality, or the "positive feedback" mechanism going from austerity to higher spreads to more austerity and so on, is embedded in the growing literature on "self-fulfilling expectations" of sovereign-debt crises, which challenges both the efficient market hypothesis and the austerity doctrine (e.g. Corsetti and Dedola 2011; De Grauwe 2011; Gros 2012; Cooper 2012; Ghosh et al. 2013; Tamborini 2014a). In this literature, the dimension and timing of consolidation plans is a double-edged blade: if small and progressive, the plan may strain *credibility*, if large and immediate it may be judged *unsustainable*. As stressed in particular by Gros (2012) and Tamborini (2014a), an essential factor from the investors' viewpoint is the difficulty of assessing unsustainability due to the large and blurred set of factors, many of which extra-economic, that may impinge on the government's decision. This adds a source of peculiar uncertainty not amenable to "objective" analysis of the so-called "fundamentals". Unsustainability of consolidation plans is thus embodied in sovereign risk premia. Contrary to the credibility approach, sustainability indeed predicts that governments engaged in larger and larger fiscal adjustments will pay a *higher* interest rate. This happens because, as the fiscal adjustment increases, the probability attributed to the government's option for default increases, and so does the risk premium.

Causality is an issue that can hardly be settled once and for all by pure statistics, especially in a context of limited availability of data and in times of exceptional events. De Grauwe and Ji (2013b) provide an econometric test that supports the reverse causality hypothesis. At any rate, what seems indisputable in the data is that, over time, austerity has failed to deliver lower spreads. At the beginning of 2012 the spreads of all EEZ5 countries were still high or rising. The true turning point occurred in the second half of 2012, and to many observers it was only due to the credible launch of the ECB Outright Monetary Transactions programme (the safety net for sovereign debt prices and spreads) and to President Draghi's celebrated commitment that "the ECB will do whatever it takes" (for pleas to adopt this new approach, and predictions of its outcome, see e.g. De Grauwe 2010; Wyplosz 2011). Thereafter, spreads fell though debt/GDP ratios went on rising as seen above. It may be argued that austerity paved the way, both financially and politically, to the ECB intervention (Buti and Carnot 2013). However, the ECB intervention mechanism is heterodox, not complementary, with respect to the austerity doctrine, and it was in fact fiercely opposed by integral supporters of the doctrine. So in the end the question remains: Why was austerity by itself ineffective on spreads? Was austerity too little, or too much?

3.4 Output and Growth: Where Do We Stand, and Why?

The impact of austerity on economic activity is ostensibly the most controversial issue. It revolves around the time-honoured issue of "crowding out" and "crowding in": that is, the relationship between changes in fiscal variables and in private expenditures (e.g. Bernheim 1989). The counterparty, at the aggregate level, is the never settled issue of the extent of "fiscal multipliers", that is, the relationship between a unit change in a fiscal variable and the change in GDP. Net of differences in the specific treatments, the essential pro-austerity argument remains that, if not immediately, in the medium term the "crowding out" effect of fiscal expansions and the "crowding in" effect of fiscal restrictions are both large and symmetric (or fiscal multipliers are small). Which means that fiscal restrictions may be neutral (as in the Barro-Ricardo framework; Barro 1974, 1989), negative in the short run but positive in the long run (which is more typical of New Keynesian models; e.g. Corsetti et al. 2010, 2012; Roeger and in't Veld 2013) or altogether positive according to the so-called "non-Keynesian effects of fiscal policy" or "expansionary fiscal restrictions" (popularized by Giavazzi and Pagano 1996; Alesina and Perotti 1997; Alesina and Ardagna 2010) for which the right timing and composition are critical (see Sects. 2.2 and 2.3).

In the course of the crisis, a marked shift of consensus has occurred from small, non-Keynesian, back to large, Keynesian, fiscal multipliers. These now seem prevalent, though their magnitude varies considerably, according to systematic studies especially at the IMF (e.g. Coenen et al. 2010). Particularly remarkable has sounded the *mea culpa* of IMF chief economists Blanchard and Leigh (2013) with regard to underestimation of the recessionary effects of austerity. Perotti (2011) has revised critically the evidence supporting the chances of "expansionary fiscal restrictions". Here I will not enter into this controversy in detail. In light of the previous data about fiscal consolidation, I will examine the evolution of output, growth and unemployment in the four years of austerity.

To begin with output and growth, Table 4 displays the relevant data for all countries. Looking at post-shock data, the first patent fact is their high correlation. Evidence collected prior to the crisis showed increasing synchronization of business cycles in the EZ—an expected result of integration (e.g. De Haan 2008). As already observed, all countries fell into recession in the same year, 2009. Over the whole period under consideration, the correlation coefficient of each EZ country's GDP with that of EZ as a whole exceeds 0.9, with three interesting exception: Ireland (0.73), Portugal (0.69) and Greece (−0.47), the only country with a full sequence of negative growth rates. This statistical evidence should call into question the entrenched belief that low cyclical correlation is one of the reasons for the EZ not being an optimal currency area, and that asymmetric shocks should be the overarching concern. Not only. Post-shock GDP correlation is also above 0.9 across EZ, OEU and NA. Therefore, if anything the Great Recession has been a *macro symmetric shock*, with GDP fluctuations being largely driven by common factors across the whole Transatlantic area.

This of course does not mean that the *magnitude* of fluctuations has been the same in all countries (see Fig. 9a). Indeed, the EEZ5 group stands out for being unable to recover positive growth in the austerity period (mainly owing to Greece and Portugal, but also to anaemic and intermittent growth in the other three). Note that after the short-lived 2010 recovery, the other EZ groups too have lost contact with the No-EZ groups, with the EZ as a whole falling back into negative territory in 2013.

Regaining the pre-crisis growth rate would be important, but the *level* of GDP is equally so. Hence a better gauge of the overall post-recession performance is the compound growth rate (*CGR*) reported in Table 4 and Fig. 9b from the first year of recession to 2013: if negative, it indicates a net output loss, if positive a net output gain, with respect to the last year of positive growth.[20] Almost two thirds of countries in the Transatlantic area ended 2013 still suffering a net output loss. They are all European: 12 in the EZ, of which all the EEZ5 with the dramatic −22.9 % of Greece, and 6 in OEU. The remaining 6 EZ countries belong to the group which have gained a net output growth, which is however of relatively modest entity if distributed over five-six years. We can clearly see a cleavage between European and Non-European countries, making of Europe as a whole the income-loss area of the Western world. Declaration of the end of the Recession War seems premature.

[20]A more severe, and perhaps correct, measure of output loss would take into account that, in the absence of the crisis, GDP would have probably grown. Here the problem is the choice of the trend growth rate, which is obviously arbitrary.

Table 4 GDP growth rates at constant 2005 prices (% values)

	2008	2009	2010	2011	2012	2013	CGR 08 (09)–13	CGR 10–13
AUS	1.4	−3.8	2.3	3.1	0.2	0.3	2.0	7.7
BEL	1.0	−2.8	2.3	1.9	−0.1	0.1	1.2	5.4
FIN	0.3	−8.4	3.7	2.9	−0.6	−1.5	−4.3	5.0
FRA	−0.1	−2.7	1.5	1.7	0.0	0.4	0.7	4.5
GER	1.1	−5.1	3.7	3.0	1.3	0.5	3.1	10.6
LUX	0.8	−5.3	2.7	0.6	1.3	0.2	−0.7	6.7
NET	1.8	−3.5	1.7	1.2	−0.7	−2.1	−3.5	0.3
EEZ7	**0.9**	**−4.5**	**2.5**	**2.0**	**0.2**	**−0.3**	**−0.2**	**5.8**
GRE	−0.2	−3.3	−3.5	−6.9	−7.1	−4.3	−22.9	−19.7
IRE	−3.0	−7.0	−0.4	0.7	3.5	−1.0	−7.3	4.4
ITA	−1.2	−5.5	1.7	0.3	−2.3	−1.9	−8.6	−1.5
POR	0.0	−2.9	1.4	−1.6	−3.0	−1.1	−7.1	−3.6
SPA	0.9	−3.7	−0.1	0.7	−2.0	−1.8	−6.8	−2.6
EEZ5	**−0.7**	**−4.5**	**−0.2**	**−1.4**	**−2.2**	**−2.0**	**−10.6**	**−4.6**
CYP	3.6	−1.9	1.3	0.4	−2.4	−8.7	−11.1	−9.4
EST	−4.2	−14.1	2.6	9.6	3.9	1.3	−2.6	18.3
MAL	3.9	−2.8	4.0	1.6	0.8	1.8	5.4	8.4
SLK	5.8	−4.9	4.4	3.0	1.8	0.9	5.0	10.5
SLO	3.4	−7.9	1.3	0.7	−2.5	−2.7	−11.0	−3.3
LEZ	**2.5**	**−6.3**	**2.7**	**3.1**	**0.3**	**−1.5**	**−2.9**	**4.9**
EZ	**0.9**	**−5.0**	**1.8**	**1.3**	**−0.5**	**−1.2**	**−4.0**	**1.7**
BUL	6.2	−5.5	0.4	1.8	0.8	0.5	−2.1	3.5
CZE	3.1	−4.5	2.5	1.8	−1.0	−1.0	−2.4	2.2
DEN	−0.8	−5.7	1.6	1.1	−0.4	0.3	−4.0	2.6
HUN	0.9	−6.8	1.1	1.6	−1.7	0.7	−5.2	1.7
LAT	−2.8	−17.7	−1.3	5.3	5.0	4.0	−9.2	13.5
LIT	2.9	−14.8	1.6	6.0	3.7	3.4	−1.6	15.5
POL	5.1	1.6	3.9	4.5	1.9	1.3	13.9	12.1
ROM	7.3	−6.6	−1.1	2.2	0.7	2.2	−2.9	3.9
SWE	−0.6	−5.0	6.6	2.9	1.0	1.1	5.7	12.0
UK	−0.8	−5.2	1.7	1.1	0.1	1.3	−1.8	4.3
OEU	**2.1**	**−7.0**	**1.7**	**2.8**	**1.0**	**1.4**	**−1.0**	**7.1**
CAN	0.7	−2.8	3.2	2.4	1.8	1.8	6.5	9.5
USA	−0.3	−2.8	2.5	1.8	2.8	1.6	5.6	9.0
NA	**0.2**	**−2.8**	**2.9**	**2.1**	**2.3**	**1.7**	**6.0**	**9.2**
NoEZ	**1.8**	**−6.3**	**1.9**	**2.7**	**1.2**	**1.4**	**0.2**	**7.5**
Global	**1.3**	**−5.6**	**1.8**	**1.9**	**0.2**	**−0.1**	**−2.3**	**4.1**

Ave. 2000–07(08): average growth rate from 2000 to the last year of positive growth
CGR 08(09)–13: compound growth rate from the first year of recession to 2013
Source EUROSTAT, Database AMECO

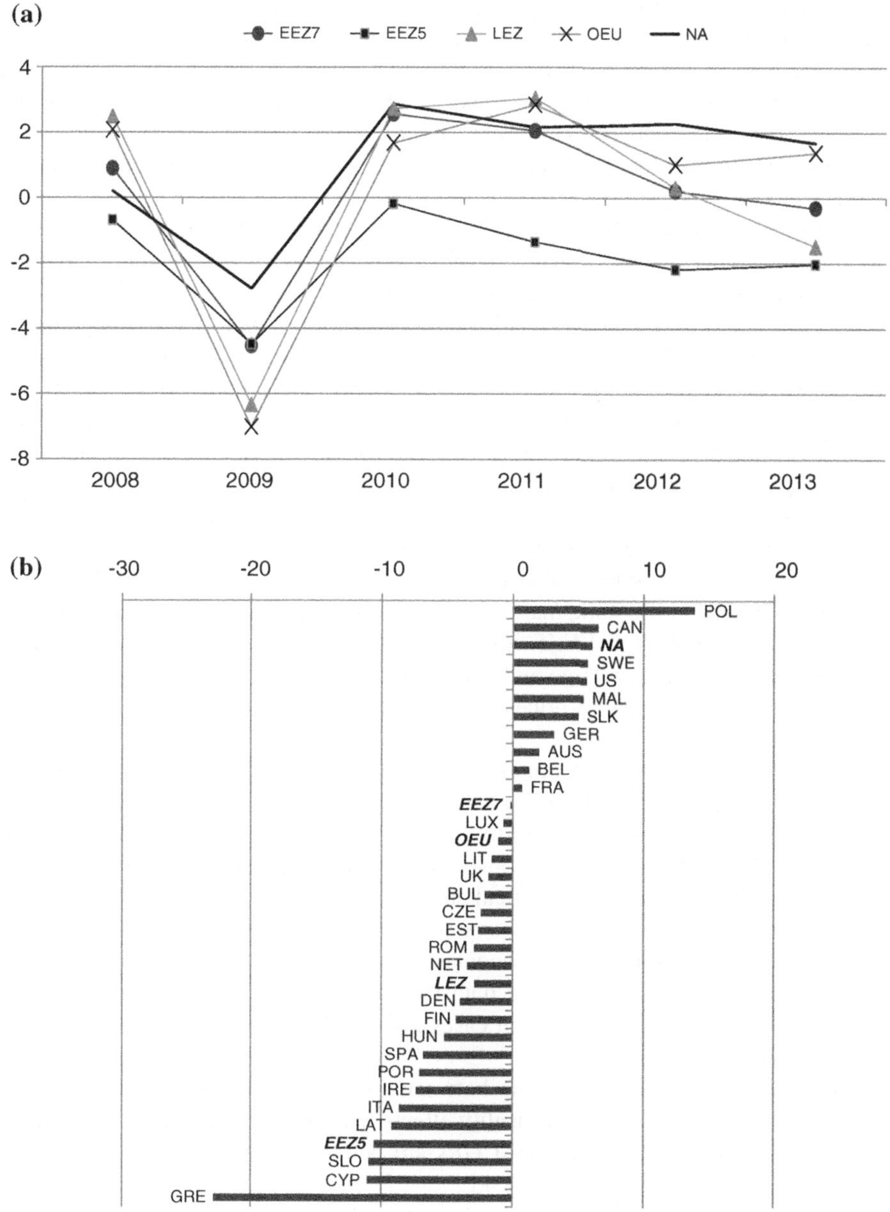

Fig. 9 **a** GDP growth rate 2008–13, groups of countries. **b** Compound growth rate, 2008 (09)–13, all countries. *Source* see Table 4

These figures vividly depict the unprecedented width and depth of the crisis, as well as the slow and scant recovery of most countries. Indeed, this gloomy picture is in line with recent research on the abnormal effects of "financial cycles" with respect to more "usual" business cycles, which focuses on the peculiar role of the financial sector in modern economies (Borio 2012; Hall 2010). How do fiscal policies, and their differences, relate to these facts? And, does the "euro dummy" matter?

These questions can be approached from two sides. The first is the cyclical timing of austerity. The second is the effect of austerity on the economy's performance over the whole period under consideration.

The cyclical position of the economy can be measured in different ways none of which is free from drawbacks. For our purposes, it is convenient to accept one of the measures elaborated by official agencies, namely the *output gap*, that is the percent difference between actual and potential output at constant prices[21]: see Table 5. A negative output gap indicates a cyclical downturn and, concomitantly, a lack of aggregate demand driving actual output below potential aggregate supply. According to the New Keynesian brand of orthodoxy, output gaps also indicate the room for demand stimulus, once account is taken for the concomitant inflation trend. There is clear evidence that the 2009 recession was associated with a large output gap of almost the same magnitude in all countries. The subsequent evolution has been diversified, with EEZ5 countries lagging behind in closing their output gaps, but it is striking how large and persistent output gaps have remained all across the Transatlantic area, while prices have nowhere shown upward tensions, if not signs of deflation.

I now simply wish to give a quantitative representation of the cyclical timing of austerity. To this end, Fig. 10 plots all the 116 joint observations of output gaps and *FA*s for the 29 countries from 2010 to 2013. Recall that austerity episodes ($FA < 0$) account for 74 % (86/116) of total observations. Anticyclical austerity falls into the first (north–west) quadrant; procyclical austerity falls into the fourth quadrant. It can be seen that 92 % of austerity episodes (81/86) have been procyclical, with a tendency for large *FA*s to be associated with large output gaps. This mostly occurred in EEZ5 and LEZ. These data indicate that austerity has been activated procyclically in the large majority of cases and countries beyond those under worst public finance conditions.

Considering now the relationship between austerity and GDP, in order to avoid short-run noise factors, reverse causality effects, etc., it seems sensible to maintain a medium-term perspective whereby *CGR*s are better compared against *CFA*s over the whole austerity period: see Fig. 11.

The correlation between *CGR*s and *CFA*s is positive (0.25), with a nonlinear interpolation suggesting that the effect of austerity on growth in this set of countries has accelerated beyond −4 % of *CFA*. However the relationship is rather loose,

[21]The source is Eurostat for all countries except Canada and United States for which the source is OECD.

Table 5 Output gap between actual GDP and potential GDP at constant 2005 prices, 2008–13 (% values)

	2008	2009	2010	2011	2012	2013
AUS	1.9	−2.9	−1.8	−0.1	−0.6	−0.3
BEL	1.6	−2.3	−1.2	−0.4	−1.4	−1.0
FIN	3.2	−6.3	−3.8	−2.1	−2.1	−1.6
FRA	1.1	−2.8	−2.5	−2.1	−2.8	−2.4
GER	2.1	−3.8	−1.4	0.0	−0.9	−0.7
LUX	2.6	−4.2	−2.7	−2.2	−2.4	−1.4
NET	2.2	−2.7	−2.1	−2.1	−3.7	−2.2
EEZ7	**2.1**	**−3.6**	**−2.2**	**−1.3**	**−2.0**	**−1.4**
GRE	2.0	−1.4	−3.7	−8.4	−10.7	−7.9
IRE	−0.1	−5.9	−4.9	−2.7	0.6	−1.2
ITA	1.1	−4.3	−2.5	−2.0	−2.9	−1.6
POR	0.0	−2.8	−1.5	−2.7	−4.6	−1.4
SPA	0.2	−4.4	−4.6	−3.8	−4.4	−2.5
EEZ5	**0.6**	**−3.8**	**−3.4**	**−3.9**	**−4.4**	**−2.9**
CYP	3.9	0.7	0.8	1.0	0.0	−5.8
EST	4.4	−9.4	−6.5	1.0	2.9	1.2
MAL	3.0	−1.7	0.1	−0.1	−0.9	−0.5
SLK	7.0	−1.9	−0.7	−1.3	−2.1	−3.3
SLO	5.7	−3.9	−2.5	−0.8	−2.3	−3.1
LEZ	**4.8**	**−3.2**	**−1.7**	**−0.1**	**−0.5**	**−2.3**
EZ	**1.4**	**−3.6**	**−2.4**	**−1.7**	**−2.6**	**−2.2**
BUL	6.2	−2.2	−2.4	−0.9	−1.0	−1.7
CZE	5.3	−1.8	−1.0	−0.2	−1.8	−3.4
DEN	2.2	−4.4	−3.6	−3.1	−4.1	−4.7
HUN	2.8	−4.5	−3.6	−2.2	−3.9	−3.5
LAT	4.9	−12.3	−11.6	−6.2	−1.9	0.2
LIT	6.9	−10.5	−8.1	−2.1	−0.7	0.0
POL	3.2	1.0	0.8	0.8	−0.7	−2.1
ROM	7.8	−0.2	−2.2	−1.4	−2.3	−1.8
SWE	0.6	−5.7	−1.4	−0.5	−1.6	−2.3
UK	1.5	−4.1	−2.9	−2.4	−2.8	−2.2
OEU	**4.1**	**−4.5**	**−3.6**	**−1.8**	**−2.1**	**−2.2**
CAN	1.3	−2.9	−1.2	−0.4	−0.5	−0.8
USA	0.4	−3.4	−2.1	−1.7	−0.7	−1.2
NA	**0.8**	**−3.2**	**−1.7**	**−1.0**	**−0.6**	**−1.0**
NoEZ	**3.4**	**−4.4**	**−3.3**	**−1.8**	**−1.9**	**−2.0**

Source EUROSTAT, Database AMECO

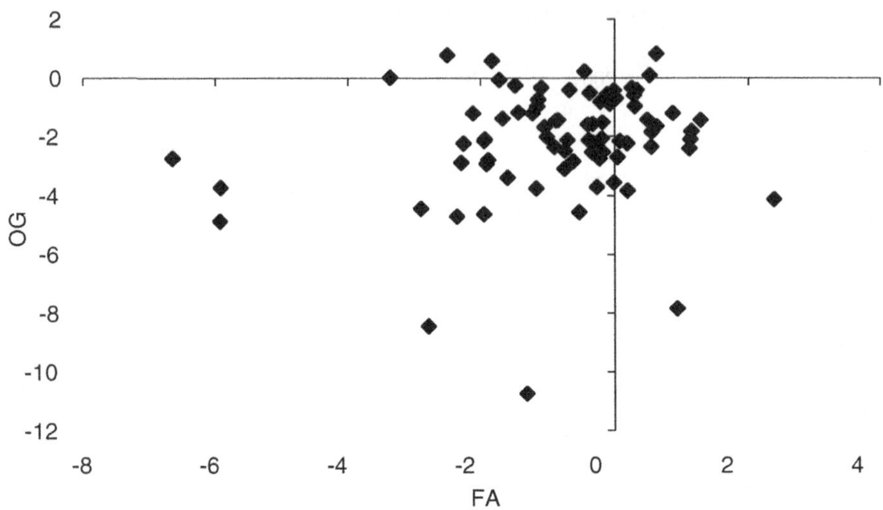

Fig. 10 Output gaps and *FA* 2010–13, all countries. *Source* see Table 5

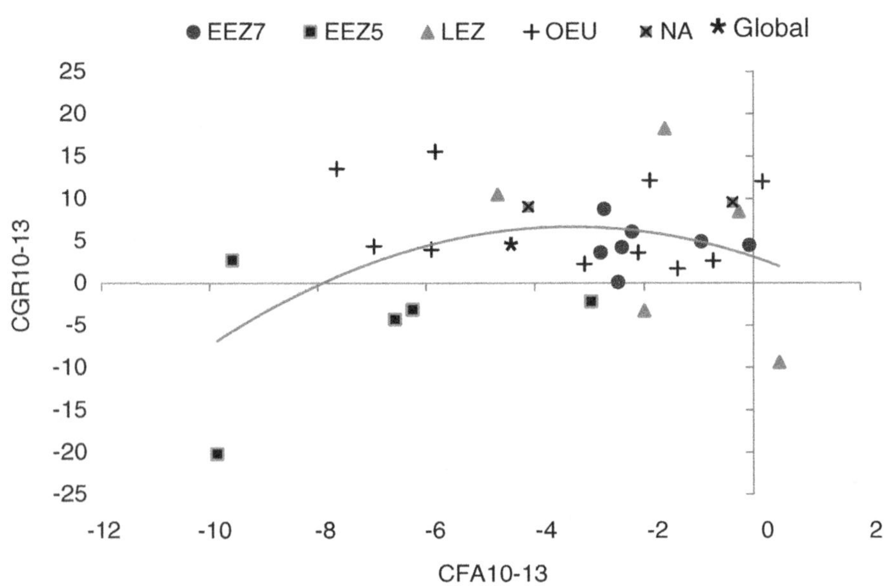

Fig. 11 *CGR* and *CFA* 2010–13, all countries Correlation coefficient 0.25. OLS interpolation function: $y = 3.1 - 2.1x - 0.3x^2$, $R^2 = 0.18$. *Source* Author's elaboration

pointing to the presence of other factors than austerity at work. If the "euro dummy" matters, that is if independent monetary and fiscal policies and flexible exchange rate matter, we may expect *CFA*s to be more informative about *CGR*s as we restrict

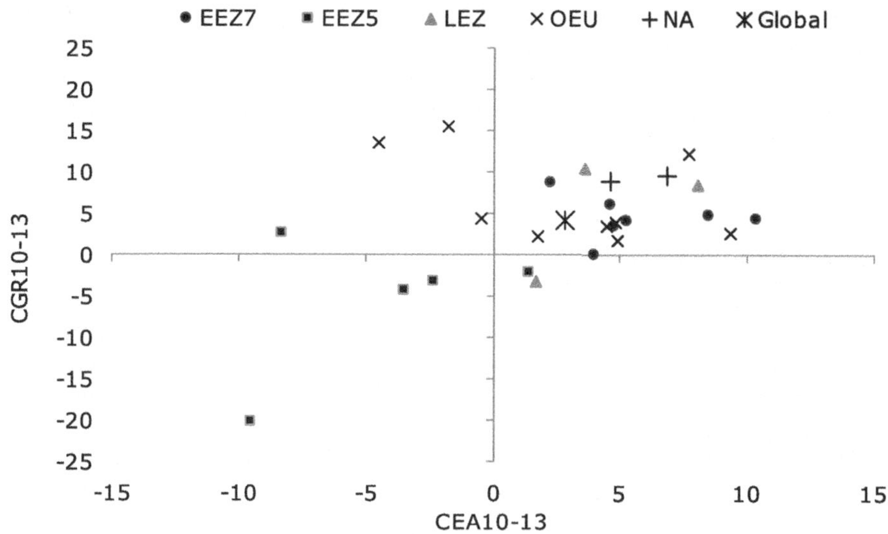

Fig. 12 *CGR* and *CEA* 2010–11, all countries with *CFA* < 0 *Source* Author's elaboration

to the more similar, integrated and long-run members of the EEZ group. This is indeed the case. The plot reveals a cluster of milder-*CFA*/better-*CGR* (EEZ7) against a cluster of stronger-*CFA*/worse-*CGR* (EEZ5), so that correlation is tighter (coefficient 0.69), and the nonlinear interpolation function has an explanatory power of 48 %. In other words, about a half of the differences in post-crisis growth across these countries may be accounted for by differences in cumulated austerity.

As said in Sect. 2.3, in the pro-austerity literature "composition matters" in order to account for other factors. Accordingly, the recessionary effects of austerity are attributed to a composition unbalanced towards higher taxation instead of lower expenditure. Lower expenditure is instrumental to cut tax rates, which eventually generate larger tax revenue via income effect. Correlation analysis of *CGR*s and composition of *CFA*s in the austerity period does not lend support to this view. Table 2 reported the decomposition of *CFA*s between tax (*CTA*) and expenditure (*CEA*) adjustment. We saw that most countries engineered austerity by getting the tax revenue grow more than expenditure. Figure 12 shows the correlation between *CEA* and *CGR* of each country with *CFA* < 0.

The composition of austerity is little informative about differences in growth performance, both statistically and economically. The majority of countries lies in the north-east quadrant: better *CGR* is associated with *higher CEA* with correlation coefficient of 0.41. These countries also obtained larger *CTA* exceeding *CEA*. This may partly be due to a positive income effect, but the concomitant increase in expenditure indicates that the income effect cannot be due to the "expansionary fiscal contraction" recipe, which should manifest itself in the north-west quadrant. There we see only three No-EZ cases (UK, Latvia and Lithuania) and one EZ case (Ireland). These cases are however quite different: Latvia and Ireland had more expenditure cut than tax increase, UK and Lithuania more tax increase than expenditure cut. On the other hand, Latvia and Lithuania had much better growth than UK and Ireland, which were also outperformed by most of the countries in the north-east quadrant. As already stressed, the most aggressive austerity on the expenditure side was realized in the EEZ5 group, which has however suffered the largest output losses.

3.5 Unemployment

Since 2007 unemployment has soared significantly in all countries apart from Germany and few others. Table 6 and Fig. 13 highlight that the crisis has created a clear break in the previous trends, which were either stable at relatively low levels or gradually decreasing.

However there are significant differences across groups. At first sight EZ did worse than NoEZ, with unemployment increasing 5.6 points *vis-à-vis* 2.8. Yet this is the result of three sharply different groups. The most dramatic unemployment peaks have occurred in EEZ5, where average unemployment in 2013 was 12.4 points higher than in 2007 (mostly concentrated in Greece and Spain). By contrast, EEZ7 has obtained the least increase (less than 1 %, and 1.5 % net of the unique German performance, the single country will less unemployment than in 2007). LEZ lies in the middle. Hence the "euro dummy" does not seem uniformly critical in this case. However, note that, as in the case of GDP growth (see Fig. 9), since 2011 unemployment in *all* three EZ groups has started to diverge upwards with respect to the two NoEZ groups.

What does seem critical fro unemployment performance is medium-term growth. Figure 14a presents the change in unemployment from 2007 to 2013 against the *CGR* over the same period for all countries. A negative correlation appears fairly tight (coefficient −0.72). Along the best fitting function, differences in *CGR*s account for almost 60 % of differences in unemployment performance. The curvature of the function suggests that the growth component of unemployment displays an increasing marginal impact.

Since we found above a non-trivial statistical correlation between *CGR*s and *CFA*s, it may be expected that differences in *CFA*s, too, have some bearing upon unemployment performances. The effects of austerity on the labour market are a contentious and intricate issue that cannot be fully developed here, but our data do offer some evidence for further consideration. In the first place (see Fig. 14b) in the austerity period 2010–13 the substantial majority of countries had unemployment further deteriorating or unchanged. At group level, NA is the single one which (slightly) improved. The correlation between changes in unemployment and *CFA* is negative (coefficient −0.24) but not very tight. Yet the countries with largest rise in unemployment (EEZ5) have also the worst *CFA*s while better performers have more moderate *CFA*s (less than 4 %). Note, also, that the countries whose labour market better absorbed more than 4 % of cumulated austerity are all small countries outside the EZ (Latvia, Lithuania, Czech Republic, Romania), except Ireland.

Table 6 Unemployment rate 2000–13, all countries

	Ave. 2000–07	2008	2009	2010	2011	2012	2013
AUS	4.4	3.8	4.8	4.4	4.2	4.3	4.7
BEL	7.7	7.0	7.9	8.3	7.2	7.6	8.0
FIN	8.6	6.4	8.2	8.4	7.8	7.7	8.1
FRA	8.8	7.8	9.5	9.7	9.6	10.2	10.6
GER	9.4	7.5	7.8	7.1	5.9	5.5	5.4
LUX	3.6	4.9	5.1	4.6	4.8	5.1	5.5
NET	3.9	3.1	3.7	4.5	4.4	5.3	6.9
EEZ7	**6.6**	**5.8**	**6.7**	**6.7**	**6.3**	**6.5**	**7.0**
GRE	9.9	7.7	9.5	12.6	17.7	24.3	27.0
IRE	4.4	6.4	12	13.9	14.7	14.7	14.2
ITA	8.1	6.7	7.8	8.4	8.4	10.7	11.8
POR	6.9	8.5	10.6	12	12.9	15.9	18.2
SPA	10.2	11.3	18	20.1	21.7	25	27.0
EEZ5	**7.9**	**8.1**	**11.6**	**13.4**	**15.1**	**18.1**	**19.6**
CYP	4.3	3.7	5.4	6.3	7.9	11.9	16.7
EST	9.3	5.5	13.8	16.9	12.5	10.2	9.3
MAL	7.2	6.0	6.9	6.9	6.5	6.4	6.4
SLK	16.8	9.6	12.1	14.5	13.7	14.0	13.9
SLO	6.2	4.4	5.9	7.3	8.2	8.9	11.1
LEZ	**8.8**	**5.8**	**8.8**	**10.4**	**9.8**	**10.3**	**11.5**
EZ	**7.6**	**6.5**	**8.8**	**9.8**	**9.9**	**11.0**	**12.0**
BUL	13.2	5.6	6.8	10.3	11.3	12.3	12.9
CZE	7.6	4.4	6.7	7.3	6.7	7.0	7.1
DEN	4.6	3.4	6.0	7.5	7.6	7.5	7.3
HUN	6.4	7.8	10.0	11.2	10.9	10.9	11.0
LAT	10.7	8.0	18.2	19.8	16.2	15.0	11.7
LIT	11.0	5.3	13.6	18.0	15.4	13.4	11.7
POL	16.8	7.1	8.1	9.7	9.7	10.1	10.7
ROM	7.1	5.8	6.9	7.3	7.4	7.0	7.3
SWE	6.5	6.2	8.3	8.6	7.8	8.0	8.1
UK	5.1	5.6	7.6	7.8	8	7.9	8.0
OEU	**8.9**	**5.9**	**9.2**	**10.8**	**10.1**	**9.9**	**9.6**
CAN	7.0	6.1	8.3	8.0	7.4	7.3	7.2
USA	5.1	5.8	9.3	9.6	8.9	8.1	7.7
NA	**6.0**	**6.0**	**8.8**	**8.8**	**8.2**	**7.7**	**7.4**
NoEZ	**8.0**	**6.0**	**9.4**	**10.4**	**9.6**	**9.3**	**8.9**
Global	**7.6**	**6.4**	**9.0**	**9.9**	**9.8**	**10.4**	**10.7**

Source EUROSTAT, Database AMECO

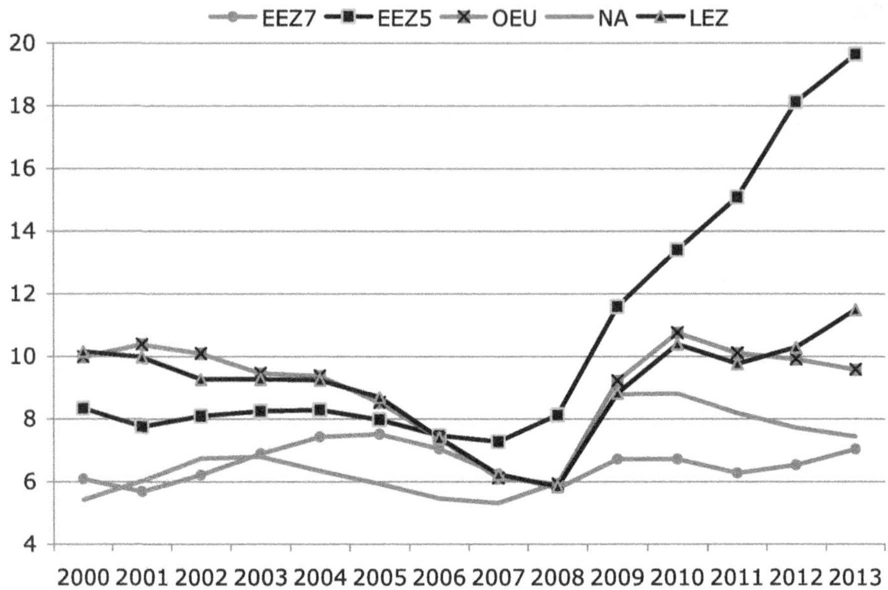

Fig. 13 Unemployment rate 2000–13, groups of countries. *Source* see Table 6

Hence, if we concentrate on the more homogeneous EEZ group, once again we find a stricter correlation, with differences in *CFA* explaining 54 % of differences in the unemployment performance.

It is well-known that orthodox macroeconomic schools share the view that large cyclical effects of GDP on unemployment should be traced back to labour-market rigidities, whether "nominal" or "real". Parallelly, one standard ingredient in the recipe for growth-friendly austerity is that there should be concomitant "structural"—i.e. labour market—reforms injecting more flexibility into wage changes as well as job relocations. This conveys the idea that austerity may have undesirable effects on unemployment owing to labour market rigidity, and also the idea that if large losses of employment are observed, these are more the result of rigidities than of austerity per se. These propositions, which are very popular in the pro-austerity narratives, are hard to test because they usually come with no indication about what the ideal response of unemployment should be for the given rate of austerity (perhaps zero, or less than zero?).

Inspection of standard labour market statistics does not lend much support to these narratives in two respects. The first is that there is not much evidence that labour markets have remained rigid in the face of falling output and rising unemployment. The second is that differences in rigidity across countries amount to a thin explanation of differences in unemployment performances.

Rigidity is a difficult concept to render operational. It combines institutional factors with other factors that condition the functioning of the labour market in specific economic circumstances. From the former point of view, the OECD offers a

(a)

(b)

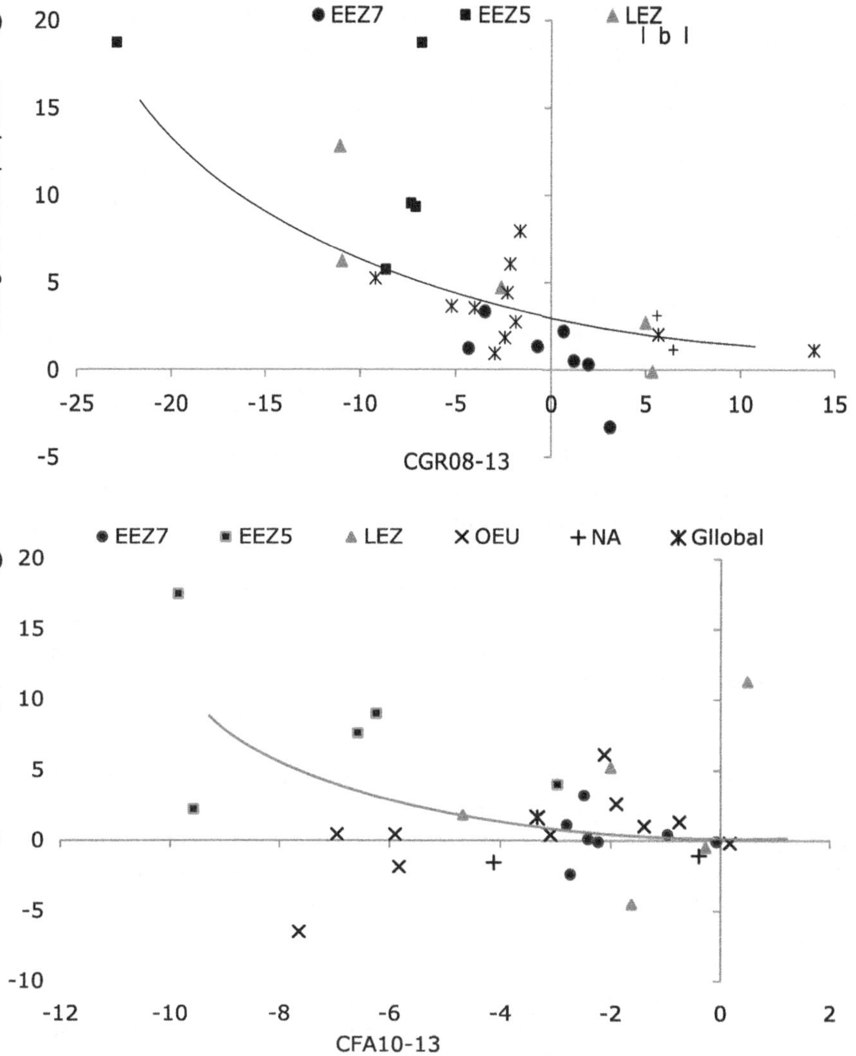

Fig. 14 **a** Change in the unemployment rate 2007–13 and *CGR* 2008 (09)–13, all countries. Correlation coefficient −0.72. OLS interpolation function: $y = 2.8 - 0.4x + 0.1x^2$, $R^2 = 0.58$. **b** Change in the unemployment rate 2009–13 and *CFA* 2010–13, all countries. Correlation coefficient −0.22. OLS interpolation function: $y = 2.7 - 1.4x + 0.2x^2$, $R^2 = 0.18$. *Source* Elaborations on Tables 1 and 6

well-known set of indicators, the Employment Protection Indicators (EPI),[22] which are widely used by labour researchers for comparative analyses. A high value of the indicator provides a measure of rigidity in terms of legislations and regulations that may hamper wage changes and/or workers mobility across jobs and sectors.

[22] http://www.oecd.org/employment/emp/oecdindicatorsofemploymentprotection.htm.

To gauge how this dimension of labour market rigidity may relate to differences in unemployment performance across countries during the crisis, I have elaborated a synthetic index for each applicable country based on two EPI: "Strictness of employment protection; Individual and collective dismissal (regular contracts)" (version 3), and "Temporary employment" (version 3).[23] My index is the average of the average value of the two EPI from 2008 to 2013 (actually, EPI have remained constant or have changed very little in this period of time). The relationship between this rigidity index and the change of unemployment is shown in Fig. 15.

If *some* countries with higher index display a greater increase in unemployment than do *some* countries with lower index, this pattern is far from providing an exhaustive explanation of the differences in unemployment performance. True, the more flexible NA economies have suffered relatively smaller increases in unemployment, but the majority of the European economies, with much higher indices, have done no worse, or even better. Germany's celebrated Hartz reforms have changed little its mid-EPI ranking, and yet its employment resilience has been extraordinary. The much worse unemployment performance of the EEZ5 countries seems unrelated to significant differences in rigidity with respect to the other Euro partners.

The EPI provides a "static snapshot" of the institutional arrangements governing labour relations. However, the actual response of labour markets to economy-wide shocks may be more or less rigid also depending on specific circumstances that cannot be accounted for *ex ante*. It is therefore useful to extend our analysis to some economic indicators. I propose here the most classic labour market indicator, the Phillips Curve, or better the "real" Phillips curve, that is the relationship between the change in unemployment and in the real unit labour cost (RULC). The latter results from two components: the real compensation per employee and the productivity per employee. As recalled above, one traditional explanation of unemployment is that *real* wage deflation, if any, may be insufficient relative to productivity, so that the RULC actually rises triggering layoffs—the so-called "real rigidity" problem. Figure 16 summarizes the dynamics of the RULC before and after the crisis taking 2007 as base year (a positive value indicates increase or efficiency loss). As is well known, the groups with larger efficiency gains before the crisis were EEZ7 (first and foremost Germany) and OEU (especially the emerging Eastern Europe), while EEZ5 lagged behind. However, as seen above, those were also year of *convergence* in unemployment rates. By contrast, the sharpest RULC adjustment after the crisis took place in EEZ5 (except Italy), while EEZ7 let real wages recover above productivity, but the result was *divergence* in unemployment rates.

Overall, a Transatlantic Phillips Curve emerges which is downward sloping as it should be (correlation coefficient −0.58), with larger increases in unemployment associated with larger cuts in the RULC. This is particularly evident for EEZ5

[23]Considering both segments of the labour market is important since temporary jobs are becoming increasingly common and typically less regulated than open-ended contracts. Both versions 3 encompass a larger number of indicators, and are available from 2008 to 2013.

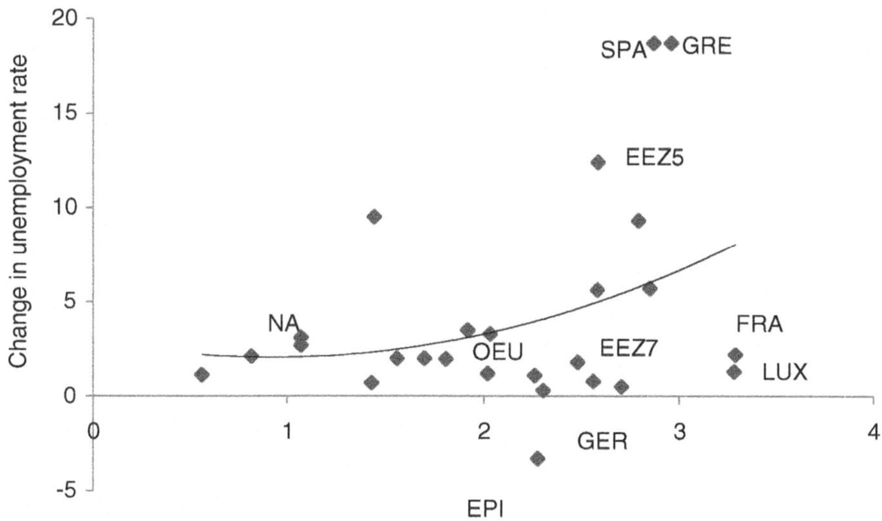

Fig. 15 Employment protection index and unemployment change 2007–13, selected countries. Correlation coefficient 0.27. OLS interpolation function: $y = 3.5 + 2.2x + 1.1x^2$, $R^2 = 0.08$. *Source* Elaborations on OECD Employment Protection Indicators

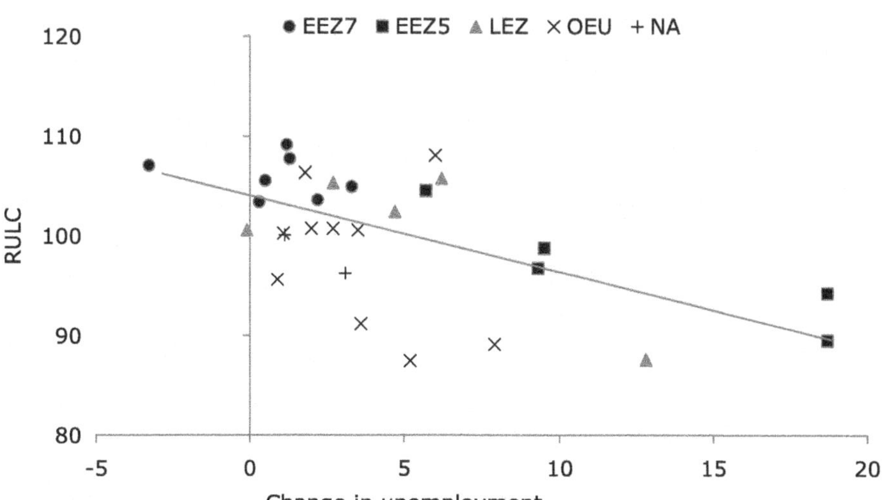

Fig. 16 Change in RULC from 2007 = 100 and change in the unemployment rate 2007–13. Correlation coefficient −0.58. OLS interpolation function: $y = 103.4 - 0.7x$, $R^2 = 0.34$. *Source* Elaborations on Table 6 and Eurostat, Database AMECO

countries and the small Eastern European countries. In conclusion, there is no overwhelming evidence of "real rigidity" in the labour market of high unemployment countries. Labour market flexibility may be a precondition for achieving "smart" austerity, but there is little support for the argument that the "nasty" austerity now being experienced in some EZ countries can be entirely traced back to labour market institutions.

4 Conclusions

Assessment of austerity is matter of lively and unresolved dispute. As stressed in this chapter, an additional difficulty is that the advocates of austerity usually fail to clearly specify the criteria against which this policy should be assessed. This enhances, rather than dispelling, the suspicion that austerity is a *must* without alternatives also for extra-economic reasons.

In this paper I have sought to present the reader with a wide set of data and "stylized facts", in order to assess and characterize the 2010–13 four years of austerity on both sides of the Atlantic. The first fact to be stressed is that austerity has not been confined within the EZ; rather, it appears a generalized "consensus policy" throughout the Transatlantic area to manage the fiscal consequences of the global crisis. However, austerity has been enacted with different timing and intensity. From this point of view, the perception of the EZ as being particularly austere is correct, but this is true of *Europe as a whole* with respect to North America. Also, the epicentre of austerity has not been Europe in its entirety, but the group of five EZ countries under worst public finance conditions and sovereign debt attack. On the other hand, the intensity of austerity in the rest of Europe has been nontrivial and, in most cases, procyclical, though less justified on the grounds of fiscal emergency. Hence, a picture of "uncoordinated austerity" emerges, which may have impinged upon the chances of success of the countries under necessity of stronger fiscal adjustment.

Data analysis has been organized around two assessment criteria: the primary goal of improving public finances and lowering interest rates, and the collateral effects on economic activity and unemployment. The results provide a first comprehensive view of the role of austerity *vis-à-vis* the criteria of interest, and pave the way for further and deeper statistical analyses.

According, for instance, to Buti and Carnot (2013), austerity has been on the main target, since "on average the euro area structural balance has been cut from 4.5 to 1.25 % between 2009 and 13 (…). There has also been visible progress in improving external and relative competitiveness positions" (p. 2). These are indeed two facts that we have found in the data. However, that strong fiscal adjustments coupled with domestic deflation can eventually produce such results is not surprising. The key test of the ex-ante austerity prescriptions and narratives is that *such results should come at low or negligible real and welfare costs followed by fast recovery*, since front-loaded fiscal consolidation produces an immediate fall in interest rates and a rise in confidence that foster long-term private expenditure. The main accusation brought against austerity is that this prediction, or promise, has not materialized, particularly in the group of countries under the most severe austerity therapy. Debts have increased further, spreads have remained high until the ECB has stepped in, recessionary effects have been much longer and deeper than expected, and the political and social costs have been impressive.

While respecting the principle that correlation is not causation, partial correlation analyses presented in this chapter indicate that differences in cumulated austerity 2010–13 in the EZ account for 73 % of differences in debt/GDP growth, and for 65 % of higher spreads. As to the excess austerity hypothesis (austerity is itself responsible for higher debt/GDP ratios by depressing the denominator), we saw that cumulated austerity is positively correlated with worse post-shock growth, and that it accounts for 31 % of differences in the latter. If we restrict analysis to the more homogenous group of the early twelve EZ members, correlation results tighter and the explanatory power of austerity climbs to 48 %. Since the rise of unemployment across countries results highly correlated with compound growth rates, and the latter have a larger explanatory power (58 %) than labour market rigidity variables, the excess austerity hypothesis may also be extended to the labour market.

Against these "collateral damages", the usual line of defence consists of a number of side-arguments that methodologists call the "protective belt". Arguments of this sort usually exploit the fact that articulated theories, or policy prescriptions in our case, do depend on a number of side-conditions. Hence, if some facts do not fit the theory, the core is preserved, while the problem is shifted onto the side conditions. Here we have examined those which are more frequently invoked: too little, too late, too much taxes, too much labour rigidity. Again, assessment is questionable as long as we are not given a benchmark. At any rate, the data lend little support to the argument that austerity failures are essentially due to these concomitant factors. Quite the contrary: the countries which have benefited the least and suffered the most from austerity—in particular Greece, Ireland, Spain and Portugal—are also those where the right precepts have been followed, or imposed, more faithfully.

Elusive deadlines for policy assessment are another typical protective strategy. As the Euro-crisis progressed, delivery of promised austerity rewards has been shifted into a farther future. This style of argumentation is purely rhetorical since there is no clear ex-ante commitment stating (1) *how much* recession is compatible with the given policy, (2) *how long* the long run is.

> In the long run we are all dead. Economists set themselves too easy, too useless a task if in a tempestuous season they can only tell us that when the storm is long past the ocean is flat again (Keynes 1923).

Appendix

See Tables 1, 2, 3, 4, 5 and 6.

References

Alesina A., and S. Ardagna. 2010. Large changes in fiscal policy: Taxes versus spending, NBER Working Paper, n. 15438.

Alesina A., and R. Perotti. 1997. Fiscal adjustment in OECD Countries: Composition and macroeconomic effects. IMF Staff Papers, n. 42.

Attinasi M.G., C. Checherita., and C. Nickel. 2009. What explains the surge in Euro area sovereign spreads during the financial crisis of 2007–09? ECB working paper, n. 1131.

Barro, R.J. 1974. Are government bonds net wealth? *Journal of Political Economy* 82: 723–748.

Barro, R.J. 1989. The neoclassical approach to fiscal policy. In *Modern business cycle theory*, ed. R.J. Barro. Cambridge: Harvard University Press.

Bernheim, D.G. 1989. A neoclassical perspective on budget deficits. *Journal of Economic Perspectives* 3: 55–72.

Berti K., F. De Castro., and M. De Salto. 2013. Effects of fiscal consolidation envisaged in the 2013 stability and convergence programmes on public debt dynamics in EU member states. *European Economy*, Economic Papers, n. 504.

Bini Smaghi L. 2013. Austerity and stupidity. *Vox-EU*, November.

Blanchard O.J., and D. Leigh. 2013. Growth forecast errors and fiscal multipliers. IMF Working Paper, n. 1.

Blyth M. 2013. Austerity. History of a Dangerous Idea.

Bohn, H. 1995. The sustainability of budget deficits in a stochastic economy. *Journal of Money Credit and Banking* 27: 257–271.

Borio C. 2012. The financial cycle and macroeconomics: What Have We Learnt? BIS Working Paper, n. 395.

Buti M., and N. Carnot. 2013. The debate on fiscal policy in Europe: Beyond the austerity myth. ECFIN *Economic Brief*, n. 20.

Buti M., and P. Padoan. 2012. From vicious to virtuous: A five-point plan for Eurozone restoration. CEPR *Policy Insight*, n. 61.

Buti M., and P.C. Padoan. 2013. How to make Europe's incipient recovery durable. A rejoinder. *Vox EU*, October.

Buti M., and L. Pench. 2012. Fiscal austerity and policy credibility. *Vox EU*, Apr 20.

Caceres C., V. Guzzo., and M. Segoviano. 2010. Sovereign spreads: Global risk aversion, contagion or fundamentals? IMF Working Paper, n. 120.

Carnot N. 2013. The composition of fiscal adjustments: Some principles. ECFIN *Economic Brief*, n. 23.

Coenen G., C. Erceg., C. Freedman., D. Furceri., M. Kumhof., R. Lalonde., D. Laxton., J. Lindé., A. Mourougane., D. Muir., S. Mursula., C. de Resende., J. Roberts., W. Roeger., S. Snudden., M. Trabandt., and J. in 't Veld. 2010. Effects of fiscal stimulus in structural models. IMF working paper, n. 73.

Cooper R. 2012. Fragile debt and the credible sharing of strategic uncertainty. NBER Working Paper, n. 18377.

Corsetti, G. (ed.). 2012. *Austerity: Too much of a good thing?*. London: CEPR.

Corsetti G., and L. Dedola. 2011. Fiscal crises, confidence and default. A bare-bones model with lessons for the Euro Area. mimeo.

Corsetti, G., K. Kuester, A. Meier, and G. Mueller. 2010. Debt consolidation and fiscal stabilization in deep recessions. *American Economic Review* 100: 41–45.

Corsetti G., K. Kuester., A. Meier., and G. Mueller. 2012. Sovereign risk, fiscal policy, and macroeconomic stability. CEPR Discussion Paper, n. 8779.

De Grauwe P. 2010. Fighting the wrong enemy, *Vox EU*, May 19.

De Grauwe P. 2011. The governance of a fragile Eurozone. CEPS Working Document, n. 346.

De Grauwe P., and Y. Ji. 2012. Mispricing of sovereign risk and multiple equilibria in sovereign risk. CEPS Working Document, n. 361.

De Grauwe P., and Y. Ji. 2013a. More evidence that financial markets imposed excessive austerity in the eurozone. CEPS Commentary, February.
De Grauwe, P., and Y. Ji. 2013. Self-fulfilling crises in the eurozone. An empirical test. *Journal of International Money and Finance* 34: 15–36.
De Haan, J. 2008. Will business cycles in the euro area converge? A critical survey on empirical research. *Journal of Economic Surveys* 22: 234–273.
EU Commission. 2013. Report on public finances 2013. *European Economy*, n. 4.
Favero C.A., and A. Missale. 2011. Sovereign spreads in the Euro area: Which prospects for a eurobond? CEPR Discussion Paper, n. 8637.
Ghosh, A.R., J.I. Kim, E.G. Mendoza, J.D. Ostry, and M.S. Qureshi. 2013. Fiscal fatigue, fiscal space and debt sustainability in advanced economics. *Economic Journal* 123: F4–F30.
Giavazzi, F., and M. Pagano. 1996. Non Keynesian effects of fiscal policy changes: International evidence and Swedish experience. *Swedish Economic Policy Review* 3: 67–103.
Gros D. 2012. A Simple model of multiple equilibria and default. CEPS Working Document, n. 366.
Hall, R.E. 2010. Why does the economy fall to pieces after a financial crisis? *Journal of Economic Perspectives* 24: 3–20.
IMF. 2012. A Toolkit to assessing fiscal vulnerabilities and risks in advanced economies, Working Paper, n. 11.
in't Veld J. 2013 Fiscal consolidations and spillovers in the Euro area periphery and core. European Economy, Economic Papers. n. 506.
Kanda D. 2011. Modeling optimal fiscal consolidation paths in a selection of European countries. IMF Working Paper, n. 164.
Keynes J.M. 1923. A tract on monetary reform, London, Macmillan. In *The Collected Writings of John Maynard Keynes,* vol. IV, ed. Moggridge E., London, Macmillan, 1973.
King L., Kitson M., Konzelmann S., Wilkinson F. 2012. Making the Same Mistake Again—Or Is This Time Different?. *Cambridge Journal of Economics*, 36: 1–15.
Manasse P., and I. Rota Baldini. 2013. What's wrong with Europe? CEPR *Policy Insight*, n. 67.
OECD. 2012. *Restoring Public Finances. 2012 Update*, Public Governance Committee.
Perotti R. 2011. The austerity myth. Gain without pain? NBER Working Paper n. 17571.
Roeger W., and J. in't Veld 2013. Expected sovereign defaults and fiscal consolidations, *European Economy*, Economic Papers, n. 479.
Tamborini, R. 2013. The new fiscal rules for the EMU. Threats from heterogeneity and interdependence. *The European Journal of Comparative Economics* 10: 315–336.
Tamborini R. 2014a. Market beliefs, fundamentals, and the sovereign debt crisis in the Euro Zone. LUISS Guido Carli, SEP Working Paper, n. 5.
Tamborini, R. 2014b. Interest-Rate spread and public-debt dynamics in a two-country monetary-union portfolio model. *Open Economies Review* 25: 243–261.
Wyplosz C. 2011. A Failsafe way to end the Eurozone crisis. *VoxEU*, October.

What Went Wrong with Western Europe? An Essay on the Causes of Its Economic Decline and on Possible Remedies

Giuseppe Tullio

Abstract This paper deals with the causes of the economic crisis of Western Europe (WE) by taking a very long run`and classical approach to the slow build up of structural imbalances. It maintains that the growth beyond acceptable levels of the state sectors and labour costs and the fact that the BRIC have learned how to produce industrial goods are among the main causes. The collapse of communism, the market oriented policies of China and a very high degree of forward shifting of taxation onto wages in WE have also played an important role. The long run growth of government expenditures and taxation and their effects on wages, employment, investment and economic growth are analyzed. The crisis has also a cyclical component linked to successive waves of tax increases and to high real interest rates. Only a drastic rethinking of the role and functions of the state sectors can bring back prosperity and freedom in WE.

1 Introduction

In the period 2008–12 Western Europe (WE) recorded an unprecedented and unusually long slowdown in economic activity, while Brazil, Russia, India and China (BRIC) and other developing countries continued to grow at high rates. For instance in 2013 real GDP in Brazil was 23.4 % above its level in 2007, while in Italy it was 8.4 % below. The crisis in WE has a cyclical component aggravated by successive waves of tax increases which were implemented in order to keep government budgets within the 3 % limit imposed by the Monetary Union (MU) and, especially in Southern Europe, to keep the countries in the Euro area. In addition the risk of abandoning MU led to very high real interest rates in some member countries. However, the main causes of the crisis of WE are first that in the last decades labour costs have grown too much, except in Germany, and that the overall

G. Tullio (✉)
University of Brescia, Brescia, Italy
e-mail: gt@giuseppetullio.com

L. Paganetto (ed.), *Achieving Dynamism in an Anaemic Europe*,
DOI 10.1007/978-3-319-14099-5_8

investment environment is not as favourable as it used to be. Second the BRIC countries have finally learned how to produce industrial goods which before only the West could produce and their macroeconomic policies have become more reasonable than in the first decades of the post World War II period. The end of communism in several developing countries and the fact that since the 1980s China's economic policies have become much more market oriented also played an important role. This "awakening" of many countries occurred while in WE the size of governments and taxation grew beyond acceptable levels, thus contributing significantly to the excessive increase in labour costs and to the worsening of the investment environment. WE wages are today more than 10 times higher than in China and more than 5 times higher than in Brazil. These enormous differences undermine the industrial sectors of WE, where labour markets are much more rigid than in the US. The financial crisis, which started in the US in 2007 and the crisis of the Euro are often also listed as causes. However, they are merely aggravating factors.[1] To guarantee a return to acceptable rates of economic growth, drastic measures would have to be taken to correct the accumulated structural imbalances. Excluding autarky, which would damage the whole world and which completely contradicts the economic principles which the West has stood for since the end of World War II, the only possible strategy consists in reducing significantly the cost of labour, in making WE a much more hospitable place for investment, in reducing in a drastic way the role and functions of the State and allowing thereby a massive reallocation of resources towards sectors in which WE has a high comparative advantage. This is admittedly extremely difficult to do, because of the many powerful vested interests which are against it.

2 The Growth of Government Expenditures and Real GDP in Western Europe Since the 1950s

Table 1 shows from 1952 to 2012 the individual growth rates of 17 countries, 8 industrial and 9 developing ones, and the average growth rates for 3 groups of countries: WE, BRIC and 5 smaller developing ones. The data show that in the 2008–12 period the recession in WE was very severe, especially if one compares it with economic growth elsewhere, and that the slowdown has been steady since the 1950s, especially in Italy, Germany and France, although their high growth rate in 1952–1959 is distorted by post-war reconstruction. In the period 2008–12 real GDP per capita fell in WE by 0.68 % per year on average, much more than real GDP.

Table 2 shows General Government Total Expenditures from 1870 to 2012 for 6 EU countries, the US and Japan. In 1870 in the 5 WE countries for which the data is available Government Expenditure (GE) was between 9.1 % of GDP in the Netherlands and 13.7 % in Italy, the simple average being 11 %. For the 5 countries

[1]There is no record in history of a great economic crisis not accompanied also by a financial crisis.

Table 1 Real GDP/GNP growth by country and groups of countries, 1952–2012

	1952–69	1970–89	1990–99	2000–07	2008–12
Germany	6.1	2.5	2.3	1.4	0.8
France	5.1	3.1	1.9	2.0	0.3
Italy	5.9	2.8	1.5	1.4	−1.4
Spain	6.0[a]	3.2	2.8	3.6	−0.8
Netherlands	5.2	2.5	3.1	2.1	−0.1
UK	2.7	2.2	2.2	2.7	−0.3
US	3.5	3.0	3.1	2.5	1.0
Japan	8.8	5.5	1.5	1.7	−0.3
Brazil	6.6[b]	5.8	1.7	3.4	3.1
Russia	–	–	0.7[c]	7.1	1.8
India	3.6[d]	4.2	5.6	7.1	6.5
China	–	9.2[e]	9.9	8.1	10.7
Colombia	4.8	4.6	2.8	4.2	3.5
Philippines	5.5	4.0	2.7	3.4	4.9
Thailand	6.3	7.1	4.9	4.9	3.0
Turkey	5.6	4.8	3.7	5.0	2.7
Vietnam	–	–	7.1	7.4	5.9
Western Europe[f]	5.2	2.9	2.3	2.2	−0.2
BRIC	–	–	4.5[g]	6.4	5.6
Other developing[f]	5.6[h]	5.1[h]	4.2	5.0	4.0

Yearly averages; *Source* IMF, IFS, various issues and www.economywatch.com
[a]1955–69
[b]1950–69
[c]1996–2007
[d]1960–69
[e]1980–89
[f]Simple average
[g]Russia included only starting in 1996
[h]Excluding Vietnam

plus Spain the simple average increased to 13.6 % in 1913, 21.9 % in 1920, 30.3 % in 1960 and 48.9 % in 2012. During these 142 years real GDP grew by a factor of about 20 but GE grew a lot more. Only between 1960 and 2012 the ratio increased by a remarkable 18.6 percentage points.

In 1870 all 6 Western European countries had a public administration, a parliament, a judicial system, a police force and an army. Except for France they also had kings or emperors the costs of whose courts fell largely on the government budget. Two countries, Germany and France, were even at war with each other.[2] In 1960 social security and a public health systems were already in place in most of

[2]In 1937 also Italy and Japan were at war, yet in that year the ratio was 31.1 and 25.4 % respectively.

Table 2 General government total expenditures as percent of GDP in industrial countries

	Around 1870	Around 1913	1920	1937	1960	1980	2007	2012
Germany	10.0	14.8	25.0	34.1	32.4	49.5	43.5	45.5
France	12.6	17.0	27.6	29.0	34.6	46.0	52.6	56.6
Italy	13.7	17.1	30.1	31.1	30.1	42.1	47.6	50.7
Spain	–	11.0	8.3	18.4	18.8	30.5	39.2	46.7
Netherlands	9.1	9.0	13.5	19.0	33.7	54.0	45.3	50.1
UK	9.4	12.7	26.6	30.0	32.2	42.7	40.2	43.5
US	7.3	7.5	12.1	19.7	27.0	34.0	36.7	40.3
Japan	8.8	8.3	14.8	25.4	7.5	32.1	33.3	41.3
Average for WE[a]	11.0	13.6	21.9	26.9	30.3	44.1	44.7	48.9

Sources Ministry of Economics, MEF (2011), Rome, www.rgs.mef.gov.it and www.economywatch.com, www.ecb.europa.eu
[a]Simple average

the 6 countries. It follows that the comparison between GE today and in 1960 is probably more relevant. An important question is then if there are solid theoretical reasons to believe that the observed enormous growth of this ratio from 1960 to 2012 had very negative effects on employment, economic growth, the well-being of citizens and individual freedom.

Table 3 shows the same ratio from the 1990s to 2012 for the same 9 developing countries of Table 1. In 2007 the average ratio was 27.8 %, with the highest recorded in Brazil (38.4 %) and the lowest in China (18.9 %). In 2012 the average ratio was 29.6 %, only moderately higher than in 2007. Thus by 2012 the ratio reached in developing countries the level recorded in WE in 1960.

Table 3 General government total expenditures as percent of GDP in developing countries

	1990	2007	2012
Brazil	38.9 (1996)	38.4	40.0
Russia	32.8 (2000)	33.1	36.6
India	20.1	26.5	27.5
China	21.0	18.9	24.8
Colombia	17.5	28.0	28.2
Philippines	20.3 (1994)	19.0	18.8
Thailand	17.3 (1995)	21.3	24.1
Turkey	42.7 (2002)	33.3	36.1
Vietnam	20.3 (1998)	30.6	30.5
Simple average	25.9	27.8	29.6

Source www.economywatch.com, www.ecb.europa.eu. The numbers in parenthesis are the years for which sufficiently reliable data became available

3 The Effects According to Classical Economic Theory of an Increase in Government Expenditures on the Cost of Labour

From 2000 to 2011 real wages grew by a moderate 5 % in the developed world, while they grew by 15.1 % in Latin America and the Caribbean, 17.8 % in Africa, 94.9 % in Asia and 171.3 % in Eastern Europe and Central Asia.[3] Thus in the last 12 years there was a certain wage moderation in the West and a significant degree of catching up of wages elsewhere. However, the wage gap remains huge. Today real wages in WE are at least 5 times higher than in Brazil and 10 times higher than in China. Table 4 compares absolute wages in a number of countries.

A crucial issue in this paper is how the huge increase in GE and taxes in WE influenced the cost of labour and international competitiveness. The components of the cost of labour are three: the after tax wage, taxes and social security contributions and the productivity of labour. A crucial link between taxes and the cost of labour is the degree of shifting forward of taxation onto wages, which can in principle be anything between zero and 100 %. In lectures of economics it is in general maintained that for Adam Smith and David Ricardo the after tax wage cannot fall below the subsistence wage, since workers cannot otherwise live and reproduce themselves. Hence the degree of forward shifting is supposed to be 100 %. However, upon a closer analysis of classical economic theory, the subsistence wage is a long run concept influenced also by cultural determinants (Tullio 1989). Smith for instance argued that:

> "The labouring poor will not now be contented with the same food, clothing and lodging which satisfied them in former times" (Smith 1776, 1976, p. 96) and that necessities include "not only the commodities which are indispensably necessary for the support of life, but whatever the custom of the country renders it indecent for creditable people, even of the lowest order, to be without" (Smith 1776, p. 870). And according to Ricardo the subsistence wage "varies at different times in the same country and very materially differs in different countries" (Ricardo 1817, 1976, p. 54–55).

Thus for both authors the positive effect of taxes on labour and necessities on wages "does not in fact stand or fall with the subsistence assumption" (Hollander 1979, p. 387). The above considerations are very important to understand why in WE the increase in taxes did not lead to a proportionate reduction in the after tax wage and why the growth of government has increased labour costs. Another crucial question is what value workers and labour unions attribute to GE. The less they value them, the higher is the degree of shifting forward of taxation. In classical economic theory all GE was wasted on wars or on lavish expenditures of the ruling class. This is clearly not the case in WE, where in the early post war period the size of government may have been below the social optimum and as a result the marginal benefit of public expenditures may have been above their marginal cost. However, in many Western European countries, sometime in the early post war

---

[3] International Labor Office, Geneva.

Table 4 Nominal salaries in US dollars, 2010, international comparisons

Brazil	5.41	France	21.06
Portugal	7.16	UK	21.16
Argentina	8.68	US	23.32
Greece	13.01	Netherlands	23.49
Spain	14.53	Germany	25.05
Japan	18.32	Switzerland	34.29
Italy	18.96	Denmark	34.78

Source International Labour Office, Geneva

period, the marginal cost started exceeding the marginal benefit and the difference between them grew further with the size of government. Thus sometime after 1950 the degree of shifting forward of taxation onto wages must have increased significantly in all countries and probably approached 100 % in some, along the lines predicted by Smith and Ricardo, despite the fact that wages were well above the level of subsistence. It is therefore not a coincidence that the rates of economic growth started tapering off in WE. The degree of forward shifting is positively influenced not only by the level of GE, but also by the inefficiencies of government, waste, corruption and the usefulness of public goods offered, such as perceived by workers. Smith for instance compared the acceptance of taxes by the population in a small Republic like Hamburg with the reluctance to pay them in a large country:

> This tax is generally supposed to be paid with great fidelity. In a small republick, where the people have entire confidence in their magistrates, are convinced of the necessity of the tax for the support of the state, and believe that it will be faithfully applied to that purpose, such conscientious and voluntary payment may sometimes be expected. It is not peculiar to the people of Hamburgh (Smith 1776, p. 850).

Evidence about the degree of forward shifting of taxation in WE can be obtained by estimating wage equations which include taxes as independent variables. The degree of forward shifting has been found to be high and significant (Knoester and van der Windt 1987; Gordon 1971) and it is generally higher for taxes on wages, followed by indirect or sales taxes, with social security contributions coming last.[4] The degree of forward shifting is also in general found to be higher in WE than in the US. An additional channel through which the growth of government influences positively the cost of labour is the competition for labour between the private and the public sector:

> … the fund raised by the tax is employed by the government in maintaining labourers, unproductive indeed, but still labourers. If the price of labour were not to raise when wages are taxed, there would be a great increase in the competition for labour, because the owners of capital … would have the same funds for employing labour, whilst the government who received the tax would have an additional fund for the same purpose. Government and people thus become competitors and the consequence of their competition is a rise in the price of labour (Ricardo 1976, p. 144).

[4]Social security contributions have a smaller effect because workers associate them with specific benefits.

4 Taxes on Wages are Taxes on Profits: Their Effects on Capital Accumulation, Foreign Direct Investment, Private Employment and Economic Growth According to Classical Economic Theory

For the classical economists taxes on wages are taxes on profits, because the after tax wage cannot fall below the level of subsistence. Ricardo argued that the burden of the tax on wages falls on stockholders (profits):

> "Taxes on wages will raise wages and therefore will diminish the rate of the profit of stock (capital) …. A tax on wages is wholly a tax on profits; a tax on necessaries is partly a tax on profits and partly a tax on rich consumers." (Ricardo 1976, p. 140) and elsewhere he states: "Taxes are not necessarily taxes on capital because they are laid on capital" (Ricardo 1976, p. 95).

In an integrated world in which capital is mobile the after tax profit rate tends to be equalized across countries in the very long run because of the movement of capital and labour between countries. The world today is very open and globalized, probably more than the British Empire was in the 18th and 19th centuries. Since the after tax profit rates are now so much lower in WE than in developing countries investment in the production of industrial goods and of internationally tradable services increases in developing countries and falls in developed ones, other things being equal, until the adjustment of after tax profits will be completed. In Ricardo's words:

> "Notwithstanding the immense expenditure of the English government during the last 20 years, there can be little doubt that the increased production on the part of the people has more than compensated for it …. Still, however, it is certain that, but for taxation, this increase of capital would have been much greater. There are no taxes which have not a tendency to lessen the power to accumulate" (Ricardo 1976, p. 95). According to Ricardo, in open economies taxes on wages also affect capital accumulation negatively via the loss in competitiveness which they cause: " … it may be objected against such a tax[5] … that raising wages and lowering profits is a discouragement to accumulation, and acts in the same way as the natural poverty of the soil … that by raising the prices of raw produce the prices of all commodities into which the raw produce enters would be raised, and that therefore we should not meet the foreign manufacturer on equal terms in the general market" (Ricardo 1976, p. 865).

Some WE governments complain that firms close factories at home and open them elsewhere.[6] However, governments have no right to interfere with the profit-maximizing behaviour of firms, which is one of the fundamental building-blocks of the wealth of nations. Smith and Ricardo also analyzed the effect of higher wage costs (product wage) on the demand for labour by firms and on employment. Smith held that:

---

[5]Ricardo refers here to a tax on "raw produce" by which he means a tax on raw materials, food or necessities.

[6]For instance Fiat, which recently bought Chrysler in the US, is rightly threatening to close more factories in Italy.

"If direct taxes upon the wages of labour have not always occasioned a proportionable rise in those wages, it is because they have generally occasioned a considerable fall in the demand for labour" (Smith 1776, p. 865) and Ricardo distinguished between a direct effect of a higher product wage on the demand for labour from an indirect effect via lower capital accumulation: "Taxes, then, generally as far as they impair the real capital of the country, diminish the demand for labour and therefore it is probable, but not a necessary nor a peculiar consequence of the tax on wages, that though wages would rise, they would not rise by a sum precisely equal to the tax" (Ricardo 1976, p. 145).

Reliable estimates of the elasticity of the private demand for labour with respect to the real wage show that in the long run it is very high in WE, between 0.8 and 1. However, the speed of adjustment of the labor market is generally quite low, up to 4 years, and as a result the short run elasticity is much smaller (Sommariva and Tullio 1987). To sum up, high GE and taxation reduce employment because labour demand depends negatively on real wages and because of their negative effect on capital accumulation. There is strong empirical evidence that already in the period 1955–85, when the ratio of GE to GDP was below its current levels, its growth was reducing the rate of economic growth in industrial countries (Tullio 1987). For the deindustrialization and the economic decay of a country caused by high levels of taxation Smith uses the interesting expression of "declension of industry":

> … the declension of industry, the decrease in employment for the poor, the diminution of the annual produce of the land and labour of the country, have generally been the effects of such taxes (Smith 1776, p. 865).

Table 5 shows net Foreign Direct Investment (FDI) to developing countries in billions of US dollars. It sheds some light on the movement of physical capital from developed to developing countries. Net FDI grew from 167.00 billion in 2002–04 (55.7 billion per year) to 440.62 billion in 2008–12 (110.2 billion per year). These are very large numbers indeed. It is particularly worth noting that FDI to developing countries was not at all affected by the crisis of 2008–12.

Table 6 shows data on net FDI as percent of GDP from 1980 to 2012 for the same countries of Tables 1, 2, and 3 with the exclusion of Germany, the UK, Spain and Russia. The first two have attracted FDI from abroad much more than other EU countries because in these countries the business environment is much friendlier

Table 5 Net foreign direct investment to developing countries by major areas, 2002–2012, in billions of US dollars

	To developing Asia	To Latina America[a]	To Europe[b]	Total[c]
2002–04	64.50	47.40	19.00	167.00
2005–07	138.27	61.70	58.67	340.87
2008–12[d]	202.18	102.58	37.26	440.62

Source IMF, World Economic Outlook, October 2013
[a]Includes Caribbean Islands
[b]To developing Central and Eastern Europe
[c]Includes also net FDI to Africa
[d]Notice that this period includes 4 years while the previous ones only 3

Table 6 Net foreign direct investment as percent of GDP, 1980–2012

	1980–89	1990–99	2000–07	2008–12
France	−0.28	−1.18	−2.56	−2.00
Italy	−0.08	−0.37	−0.53	−1.22
Netherlands	−1.79	−2.25	−2.79	−3.68
US	0.33	−0.11	−0.13	−0.82
Japan	−0.64	−0.57	−0.79	−1.66
Brazil	0.60	0.25	0.22	2.06
India	–	0.40[a]	0.64	1.26
China	0.40[b]	3.35	2.60	2.20
Colombia	1.18	1.86	2.94	2.16
Philippines	0.58	1.55	1.09	0.60
Thailand	0.93	2.30	3.48	0.48
Turkey	0.39[c]	0.36	1.14	1.82
Vietnam	–	7.26[d]	4.50	7.00
3 countries of WE[e]	−0.70	−1.27	−1.96	−2.30
3 BRIC (e)	–	1.33	1.15	1.84
8 developing countries[e]	–	2.17	2.08	2.20
6 d.c. excl. Ph. and Th.	–	2.25	2.01	2.75

Source IFS and OECD, various publications; a *minus sign* indicates a net outflow of capital
[a]1991–99
[b]1982–89
[c]1987–89
[d]1996–99
[e]Simple average

than elsewhere in WE and the share of GE to GDP is significantly lower. Spain and Russia are special cases and have been kept out for this reason.

The simple averages for the 3 groups of countries are reported at the bottom of Table 6. For the 3 WE countries considered net FDI grew steadily over time and in 2008–12 there was no interruption of the trend. Among the developing countries considered the stars are Vietnam, China, Brazil and Colombia, while in the years 2008–12 Thailand and the Philippines suffered from domestic problems, political instability in the first and guerrilla warfare in the second. The numbers reported may seem small, but 2.1 % for Brazil and 2.2 % for China are huge numbers, especially if one considers that they are period averages and that the figures on capital inflows by foreign residents are net of outflows by domestic residents. Overall the data reported in these tables fully confirm Smith and Ricardo's predictions on the direction of international capital flows under the circumstances described.

The channels through which high GE and high taxes affect economic growth discussed so far are by no means exhaustive. Laws on firing workers are too rigid in many WE countries, and it takes too much time and too much money to obtain new licences and to comply with many bureaucratic encumbrances. The laws and regulations are often too complicated and contradictory and the fines in the case of even small errors are often absurdly high. In some countries, certainly in Italy, the officers of the tax police are often under-qualified and/or corrupt. In several WE countries there are very powerful vested interests operating against the public interest and governments listen more to them than to the public interest. In some countries, again certainly in Italy, crony capitalism has become too widespread. Welfare programs tend to have pernicious side effects on the economy and on individuals. People never spend someone else's money as carefully as they spend their own and as a result inefficiency, waste, abuse, theft, and corruption are inevitable. Furthermore these problems tend to be self-perpetuating because they destroy work incentives. Finally these hindrances reduce individual independence and dignity because bureaucrats, who are placed in positions of tremendous power, exercise a great influence over the lives of welfare recipients (von Hayek 1944; Friedman 1980). The progressive growth of welfare programs and of GE in WE has tended over time to shift economic policy towards an atmosphere of central planning and control. It is a sad irony of destiny that all this is happening after many communist regimes collapsed in the early 1990's. Be that as it may, all the factors mentioned in this paragraph further reduce after-tax profits, capital accumulation and economic growth. They also increase the incentives to invest abroad and even to move abroad.

5 Tensions in the Euro Area and Important Differences in EU Countries

The previous sections suggest that the variables on which the WE governments should concentrate if they want to bring WE out of the present crisis are four: the ratio of GE to GDP, wage costs, the reallocation of resources towards competitive sectors and the productivity of labour at the national and the firm's level. On all these fronts there is a very sharp contrast between what has been done in the last 20 years or so by Germany and by Southern Europe. In Germany wages have been very successfully kept under control and firms and labour unions have actively collaborated to increase productivity at the level of the firm. In addition Germany has successfully further specialized in those sectors and markets in which it has a considerable comparative advantage, like high quality capital goods and luxury cars. The main actors in Germany have understood very well, and well in advance with respect to other EU members, the big challenges posed by the awakening of the developing countries and by the exchange rate constraint of the Euro. This asymmetric behaviour has led to problems and tensions within the MU. However, it is wrong to consider the tensions within the Euro as an important cause of the crisis in WE. Since the real causes are much deeper, the decline of WE would continue even if the tensions within MU were to disappear overnight, although there is no doubt that, especially in the last years, the severe exchange rate and the fiscal constraints of the MU have made the management of the business cycle by member governments more difficult. It follows that Germany is not immune to the economic decline discussed in this paper, although it is in a more favourable position than Southern Europe and France. Also the UK is in a more favourable position because it has a more flexible labour market, a less invasive government, more market oriented economic policies, a flexible exchange rate, an independent monetary policy, a high degree of competitiveness in some sectors like banking, a language which is spoken worldwide and the Commonwealth. In Italy virtually nothing has been done in the last two decades on the 4 fronts discussed in this paper. Yet Italy has an immense potential. It has a huge number of citizens with high levels of inventiveness and initiative. It has sectors with a very high comparative advantage, like luxury goods (cars, furniture, fashion), top quality agricultural products (wine, oil, cheese), cuisine, as well as cultural tourism and hospitality in superb listed historical buildings. In the last 20 years Italian governments have devoted their efforts mainly in suffocating the "animal spirits" of the Italians. This criticism fully holds also for all Italian governments which have followed Mr. Berlusconi in 2011. To satisfy the Maastricht criteria they have all dramatically increased taxes in the midst of a severe recession and hardly cut GE.

6 A 10-year Plan of Reductions in Government Expenditures; Keynes Versus the Proponents of Austerity and Concluding Comments

Keynes predicted a negative effect of reduced GE or increased taxes on aggregate demand. In the short run and within a "normal context" the Keynesian negative effect clearly dominates over any positive one caused by a lower budget deficit, a lower debt and lower interest rates. By a "normal context" the author means here a situation in which long run market expectations about future growth and employment are not changed by the fiscal restrictions implemented. However, in the current circumstances a drastic and credible 10 year-program of reductions in GE aiming at bringing the ratio of GE to GDP back to its 1960 level will change instantly and significantly the long run expectations about future growth and about the business and investment environment in such a way that its effects are likely to be very positive even in the short run. Long run expectations of foreign residents are also crucial for the final outcome of the 10-year plan proposed, because they have a strong influence on FDI and capital inflows. Thus in the short run both Keynes and the proponents of austerity can be right, the effect of the reduction of the GE to GDP ratio depending on the magnitude and the credibility of the 10-year plan, on the type of fiscal measures taken and on the planned changes in the role and functions of the State. The signature of a "letters of intent" with the IMF, the EU and the ECB would bind future governments and make the 10-year plan more credible. The sharp reduction in GE and in the role and functions of the State proposed in this paper will likely contribute *per se* to an increased efficiency of government because it is easier to manage something which is small than something which is big. Countries like

Italy could and should implement such a plan on its own initiative, without waiting for the pressure of the EU and Germany to mount to unacceptable levels.

WE governments and EU institutions focus their attention principally on government deficits and debts, which have not been addressed in this paper, simply because they are not as important for long term growth as are the ratio of GE to GDP, the distortions caused by high taxes and the overall business climate. If the main message of this paper is correct, the whole of WE is on the wrong track. Economic policy in WE has been devised and implemented without sufficient understanding of economic theory. The 3 % Maasterricht criteria for the deficit to GDP ratio and the 60 % limit for the debt to GDP ratio, which are both so crucial for Euro members, do not make much economic sense and have brought the whole of WE on a completely wrong track. The government debt is over 200 % of GDP in Japan and the deficit of the US government was 11.6 % in 2009, 9.3 % in 2010 and 7.9 % in 2011, yet in terms of financial stability and prospects of growth the US and Japan are today better off than WE.

One interesting question is why the crisis in WE broke out only in 2008 and not before, given that the structural imbalances discussed in this paper have been present for a long time. There are two reasons for this delay. First the introduction of the Euro in 1999 exerted initially a positive effect on the economies of the EU[7] and second, as a result of the US slowdown in 2001, the technology crash and the September 11 attacks, the FED's monetary policy was very expansionary until 2006. The world was flooded with US dollars and world economic activity was kept high. These factors retarded the outbreak of the crisis in WE.

The gains from international trade and the specialization of countries in the production of goods and services in which they have a high comparative advantage can be enormous, as demonstrated in the 19th century by David Ricardo. The introduction of the Euro in 1999 and the very large increase in international trade among developing countries in the last decades played a very positive role. A similar large gain could come in the next decades from increased trade between the northern shores of the Mediterranean and Black seas and their Southern and Eastern shores. These potentially huge gains would accrue also to the Russian Federation and to the Northern EU countries. For these gains from trade to become a reality the EU, the Russian Federation and the US should strengthen their collaboration to establish a durable peace and stable and moderate governments in North Africa and the Middle East. They also should increase their efforts to eliminate religious sectarism and terrorism in the area and to help moderate governments in North Africa and in the Middle East to eradicate poverty. It is also necessary to invest a lot more in achieving a durable peace between Israel and Palestina. Poverty in the above mentioned areas of the world and constant tensions between Israel and Palestina are two major sources of Islamic terrorism. On these two accounts the foreign policy of the West has completely failed with possible dangerous and unpredictable long run consequences for the whole world.

[7]See for instance in Table 1 the average growth rate of Spain in the period 2000–2007.

References

Friedman, M. 1980. *Free to choose*. San Diego: Harcourt.

Gordon, R. 1971. Inflation in recession and recovery. *Brookings Papers on Economic Activity* 1: 101–166.

Hollander, S. 1979. *The economics of David Ricardo*. London: Heinemann Educational Books.

Knoester, A., and N. Van der Windt. 1987. Real wages and taxation in 10 OECD countries. *Oxford Bulletin of Economics and Statistics* 49: 151–169.

Ministy of Economics and Finance. 2011. La spesa dello Stato dall'Unità d'Italia-Anni 1862–2009, Rome, also available in www.rgs.mef.gov.it.

Ricardo, D. 1976. *The principles of political economy and taxation*. London: Dent. First published in London in 1817.

Smith, A. 1776. *The wealth of nations*, ed. Campbell, H., Skinner, A.S. and W.B. Todd, Vol. 2. Oxford: Clarendon Press, 1976.

Sommariva, A. and G. Tullio. 1987. *German macro-economic history: 1880–1979—A study of the effects of economic policy on inflation, currency depreciation and growth*. London/New York: MacMillan/St. Martin's Press.

Tullio, G. 1987. The long run implications of the increase in taxation and public debt for employment and economic growth in Europe. *European Economic Review* 31(3): 741–774.

Tullio, G. 1989. Smith and Ricardo on the long-run effects of the increase of government expenditure, taxation and public debt: is their theory relevant today? *History of Political Economy* 21(4): 723–736.

von Hayek, F. 1944. *The road to serfdom*. England: Routledge, Chicago: University of Chicago University Press.

Revitalising Europe's Economy: Towards Growth

Lorenzo Codogno

Abstract The Europe 2020 Strategy is under mid-term review. This paper looks at the Strategy's objectives and the means to achieve them, considering the new socio-economic reality that has emerged from the crisis along with new data on employment and social inclusion (or exclusion). It argues that any future strategy should address, at the same time, innovative ways to: (i) enhance potential growth from a lowered post-crisis level; (ii) improve finance for growth given tight budgetary constraints and high levels of public and private debt; and (iii) ensure social and environmental sustainability. The paper contains suggestions for a new approach to Europe 2020 and considers possible structural reforms to enhance growth and employment, compatible with environmental and social goals. Moreover, it discusses the need for some 'good imbalances' as by-products of economic and financial integration and includes a few remarks on the current policy mix, which appears suboptimal, and as a necessary ingredient to strengthen the reform process.

1 Introduction

Europe appears on its way to recovery from the worst economic crisis since the Second World War, and maybe even before. The recovery is still weak in some European countries, and especially in the periphery, with domestic demand lagging behind.

The article was written when the author was working for the Italian Ministry of Economy and Finance. The views expressed in this paper are those of the author and do not necessarily reflect those of the Italian Ministry of Economy and Finance. This paper was first presented at the Asia Europe Economic Forum on "Asia and Europe in Times of Global Change" held in Berlin on 15–16 May, 2014 and then at the round table on "Revitalising Anaemic Europe" at the XXVI Villa Mondragone International Economic Seminar, Rome, July 3, 2014.

L. Codogno (✉)
London School of Economics and Political Science, London, United Kingdom
e-mail: lorenzo.codogno@tesoro.it

L. Paganetto (ed.), *Achieving Dynamism in an Anaemic Europe*,
DOI 10.1007/978-3-319-14099-5_9

The crisis made it all the more urgent to launch structural reforms aimed at enhancing potential growth and making national economies more resilient and responsive to the challenges of the global economy(Varga et al. 2013). The ECB now has a firmer commitment to address adverse shocks and can use an expanded arsenal of monetary weapons if deemed necessary. The European Stability Mechanism was established as a safeguard against potential financial market instability.

Although with some initial hesitation, all Member States acknowledged that a monetary union cannot work without a banking union, that is without a single financial market. Now the Single Supervisory Mechanism (SSM) is underway, and the Supervisory Board has already drafted its operating procedures. Member States have reached a political agreement on the Bank Recovery and Resolution Directive, the Deposit Guarantee Schemes Directive, and the Single Resolution Mechanism (SRM), which will provide a Single Resolution Fund as a significant step in the direction of a full-fledged banking union. The ECB is running the Comprehensive Balance Sheet Assessment (BSA) that should strengthen confidence in the soundness of the European banking system.

European institutions and national governments are now better equipped to face systemic shocks. The crisis helped European leaders to make necessary adjustments and strengthen integration, which otherwise would likely not have occurred. Now it is time to shift gears with a renewed strategy for growth and employment.

At the European level, there is already a strategy for smart, sustainable and inclusive growth—Europe 2020—that was adopted in 2010 (European Commission 2010). The Europe 2020 Strategy sets several complementary targets, which were defined so as to promote a growth model based on a multi-dimensional perspective (European Commission 2009). As a model of growth that goes beyond GDP, it was—and still can be—considered at the forefront of policy making design.

In many EU countries, fiscal consolidation has resulted in difficult choices and often investments towards achieving the Europe 2020 targets have suffered. The Strategy itself is under mid-term review, to be completed in 2015 (European Commission 2014). This provides European policy makers with the opportunity to take a hard look—not only at the Strategy's objectives but also at the means to achieve them. This review must consider the new socio-economic reality that is emerging from the crisis, along with new data on employment and social inclusion (or exclusion), as well as future growth prospects.

Any future strategy should address, at the same time, innovative ways to: (i) enhance potential growth from a lowered post-crisis level; (ii) improve finance for growth given tight budgetary constraints and high levels of public and private debt; and (iii) ensure social and environmental sustainability.

This paper contains suggestions for a new approach to Europe 2020 and considers possible structural reforms to enhance growth and employment, compatible with environmental and social goals.

Moreover, it discusses the need for some 'good imbalances' as by-products of economic and financial integration and includes a few remarks on the current policy mix, which appears suboptimal, and as a necessary ingredient to strengthen the reform process.

2 Highlights of the Main Economic Challenges

The European answer to the unprecedented financial and economic crisis focused on the urgency of financial market stabilisation and on fiscal consolidation. Efforts made by the European Union and its Member States to overcome the short-term impact of the crisis and strengthen European governance were remarkable, although somewhat slow and not without mistakes. Significant progress has been made on the issue of financial integration, an important step in the process of strengthening institutions to achieve real economic and monetary union. Most EU Member States will be engaged in fiscal consolidation and/or efforts to reduce macroeconomic imbalances for several years.[1] In this context, policies must focus not only on current account deficits, sovereign debt and the financial sector, but also on productivity and competitiveness to allow the economy to grow out of current problems.

In order to deleverage debt in both the private and public sectors, Member States have adopted several measures which have produced non-negligible adverse near-term effects on economic activity (Varga et al. 2013). In particular, the need to encourage moderate wage developments or even a so-called 'internal devaluation', has had inevitable negative consequences on domestic demand. Sometimes Member States had no other options but to adopt policies that depressed domestic demand over the near term to achieve financial stability and fiscal sustainability. Negative economic dynamics have also contributed to an increase in unemployment and worsening of social conditions, threatening the social viability of such policies.

Emerging from a deep recession, many EU countries find themselves coping with an economic situation characterised by still relatively low growth and high debt, increased poverty, a recovering financial sector and an industrial sector needing a boost in competitiveness and modernisation. Unemployment has reached new heights, particularly among young jobseekers. The consequences of high youth unemployment are destructive, both individually and collectively, through lowered growth potential.

The financial and economic crisis shifted attention to systemic and short-run considerations, to the detriment of medium to long-term policies to support growth and employment. Policies to deal with the social costs of the crisis have lagged further behind. Current policies focused on further fiscal consolidation and additional measures to overcome imbalances, while certainly necessary, do not seem to

[1]In 2014, within the macroeconomic imbalance procedure, in-depth analyses were performed by the Commission for 17 Member States, 14 of which were deemed to be experiencing imbalances of some degree. On the fiscal front, "while the large consolidation efforts over the past years are now bearing fruit […] only two Member States have attained their Medium Term Objectives in terms of structural balance, implying that further consolidation will be necessary." Commission for 17 Member States, 14 of which were deemed to be experiencing imbalances of some degree. On the fiscal front, "while the large consolidation efforts over the past years are now bearing fruit […] only two Member States have attained their Medium Term Objectives in terms of structural balance, implying that further consolidation will be necessary."

be sufficient to the task. With the emergence from the crisis, the focus must accordingly shift to new ways to address the main economic, social and environmental structural challenges facing the EU, to increase growth, jobs, competitiveness and sustainability over the long-term.

3 Overview of the Europe 2020 Strategy

The Europe 2020 strategy is based on the Lisbon Strategy for growth and jobs which was adopted in 2000, renewed in 2005 and still in place up to 2010 (European Commission 2005). The current Strategy outlines "a vision of Europe's social market economy for the 21st century" aimed to "turn the EU into a smart, sustainable and inclusive economy delivering high levels of employment, productivity and social cohesion". Europe 2020 is an effort based on three mutually reinforcing attributes for growth: (1) smart, through investments in education, research and innovation; (2) sustainable, through a move towards a low-carbon economy; and (3) inclusive, by emphasising job creation and poverty reduction.

The Strategy sets out five interrelated and exemplary headline targets intended to be "representative", but not exhaustive, of the EU priorities in the areas of employment, R&D, climate change and energy, education and the fight against poverty and social exclusion.[2] The Strategy also sets out seven flagship initiatives at the EU level that include specific work programmes in important areas for growth (skills and jobs, youth, innovation, digital agenda, industrial policy, resource efficiency, fight against poverty and social exclusion). National targets reflect the different starting points and capacities of individual Member States.

The Europe 2020 strategy was intended to be the medium- to long-term growth strategy in the EU, but almost five years since its launch it is still far from delivering its objectives (European Commission 2014). It was also the starting point for the European semester that has become the overall framework for coordination and convergence of Member States' policies, and is the building block from which a revised strategy can be designed.

4 Assessment of Europe 2020

The Commission notes the "mixed progress" in achieving the Europe 2020 goals (European Commission 2014) (see Table 1 in the Appendix), but a review of the progress on each target shows a somewhat less optimistic assessment of performance, with only the climate change and energy indicators likely to be reached given current efforts and slower growth. Indeed, we should acknowledge that the

[2]For a discussion about targets see Codogno et al. (2009).

climate change and energy targets are binding, given that they were defined on the basis of a legal framework at both the EU and the Member State level.

The protracted economic crisis has played a major role in hampering the progress towards the achievement of other Europe 2020 targets. Even in cases in which there seems to be progress, the situation may in reality be less clear cut. For example, the seemingly satisfactory progress in reducing the drop out and educational attainment rates is attributable in large part to increased demand for education, as a result of the reduction in employment opportunities that might otherwise encourage would-be students to enter the workforce. To some extent the crisis has even helped Member States move closer to reaching climate change and energy targets, given lower production (and thus CO_2 emissions) and lower overall energy demand. Moreover, achieving targets may not necessarily make the ultimate goal of sustainable, smart and inclusive growth any closer as the relationship between targets and the ultimate policy goal is rather loose.

At any rate, the most worrisome performances are those towards the social targets, with an expected failure to reach the employment target and an increase in the population facing poverty and social exclusion. The current at-risk-of-poverty indicator may underestimate the social costs of the crisis, as this category is defined to include those earning below 60 % of median income. As median incomes fell during the crisis, the poverty line automatically shifted downward as well.

The crisis has also meant falling resources dedicated to research and innovation. While immediate fiscal consolidation warranted spending cuts, the consequences of reduced R&D investments may manifest themselves in the long term via lowered innovative capacity and slower rates of potential growth. Moreover, the fragmentation of markets has exacerbated the crisis at the time major restructuring efforts were underway in many countries to respond to the challenge of globalisation.

There is thus a need to assess how to strengthen and realign the strategy to make growth, employment, productivity and social cohesion again the top policy priority. The Commission's stocktaking Communication is a good starting point, but further analysis and debate will be needed to develop the EU's post-crisis growth strategy for the 2015–2020 period and beyond.

Implementation of the Strategy in the past years has revealed a number of weaknesses that need to be tackled. While policy priorities have changed as a result of the new economic conditions, the methods and overall approach to structural reforms have only slightly changed since the Lisbon Strategy. Additionally, the incentives for Member States to effectively reach the proposed targets have in some cases progressively weakened, while in others the budgetary means—both at the national and the EU level—are not sufficient.

To make the Europe 2020 Strategy more effective, greater ownership by Member States is needed, in particular by strengthening peer interest and pressure. At the same time, the European dimension needs to be reinforced. It is evident that, partly because of the economic crisis, governments tend to focus mostly on the implementation of their own reforms and recommendations. Attention to the EU-wide framework by individual Member States (and also by EU institutions) has been insufficient, particularly given the potentially positive spill-over effects of reforms by other EU countries. Moreover, there are reforms that are strictly competence of the Union, such as the strengthening of the Single Market for goods and services. Overall, evidence from Member States reveals that the governance structure of the Strategy has not necessarily led to an alignment between national policies and EU objectives.

While it is clear that the achievement of the Europe 2020 targets would benefit all EU countries, these potential benefits have not been emphasised, nor have the overall benefits of reaching the Europe 2020 targets been properly estimated at EU level. The Europe 2020 Strategy ignores the integration and regulation of financial markets and does not directly incorporate Single Market considerations. Moreover, the recommendations in the context of the Europe 2020 Strategy have not been adequately tailored to needs of each individual Member State.

5 Suggestions for a New Approach to Europe 2020

The overarching goal of the Europe 2020 Strategy is the creation of favourable conditions to raise the growth potential of the Member States and therefore it is of the utmost importance giving credible signals to create and strengthen expectations of future growth and prosperity. The Commission has launched an EU-wide public consultation of stakeholders on the review of the Europe 2020 Strategy. It will then propose revisions to the Strategy by early 2015 taking into account the results of the public consultation and the discussion in technical committees.

While acknowledging that the economic crisis has limited the capacity of the EU collectively and of each individual Member State to achieve Europe 2020 targets, the current situation calls for renewed efforts by Member States and the EU as a whole to implement structural reforms focusing on strengthening productivity and competitiveness to enhance growth and employment.

This would require, among other things, greater accountability of Member States through strengthened peer pressure and benchmarking of policies. The European Semester, which initially focused on the objectives and targets of the EU growth strategy (and related bottlenecks), has become the forum to enforce governance procedures related to the Stability and Growth Pact and, more recently, the Macroeconomic Imbalances Procedure due to the crisis. As a result, attention to growth, other than national fiscal concerns, has been greatly reduced. The rebalancing of EU priorities towards growth and employment may thus require a rebalancing of the European Semester as well. Indeed, the review, to begin later this year, of governance structures related to the so-called Six Pack and Two Pack should reinforce the central role of the Europe 2020 Strategy.

The review of Europe 2020 must consider the current status and validity of targets, the role of, and possible successors to, flagship initiatives, as well as ways to improve the governance of the Strategy (Codogno et al. 2009). In doing so, the consequences of the crisis must be duly taken into account. Communications should be made more effective and easily accessible to all stakeholders, including the general public that often associates the EU with fiscal constraints but not necessarily with greater growth and employment opportunities.

More attention than in the past should be dedicated to those targets that have become increasingly difficult to reach, namely employment and social inclusion targets, to put in place the means by which they can be met. Other objectives regarding research and innovation, as well as education attainment, will also be difficult to meet in a number of Member States. Accordingly, there may be room for not only prioritising, but also redesigning the applicable flagship initiatives to provide greater support at the EU level towards meeting these goals. Headline targets simply represent the direction to follow but they can, by no means, be considered comprehensive. They should be complemented by a much broader set of indicators, some of which highly complementary while others would require some trade-offs (Codogno et al. 2009).

The 2015 mid-term review of Europe 2020 provides an opportunity to institutionalise and formalise an increased emphasis on growth and employment by making it the core of the EU growth agenda. More specifically, it could elevate employment to an overarching priority, not solely through labour market policies, but rather more broadly through employment-friendly policies, defined as policies that create the necessary conditions for generating employment opportunities. For instance, improving SME access to credit would allow additional investments and generate growth and jobs.

A new Europe 2020 Strategy with employment-friendly growth policies as the top priority would provide Member States with a mandate to focus on the most beneficial reforms, while avoiding extraneous or ancillary initiatives. High unemployment and inactivity, particularly among the youth, is one of the most serious challenges now facing the EU. The competitiveness of EU economies, the future prosperity of its society and the sustainability of its welfare systems rest upon the participation and productivity of the labour force.

In order to trigger positive expectations for improved growth, more resolute structural reforms at the national level are, of course, needed. For national reforms to be effective, however, they must be implemented in a supportive macroeconomic environment of stronger aggregate demand and confidence, which also means confidence in the future of the Union (Padoan 2012a, b). Against this backdrop, the debate should also focus on what can be done to rebuild a positive relationship between the Union and its citizens and rebuild a strong sense of common purpose. This would call for further deepening of the Union.

Following such an unprecedented shock and the resulting structural policy response, the European economy and society must deepen integration with speed and conviction. The risk of multiple equilibria is still looming, and if it materialises, it would bring to an end the European project. European governments could accept the current stabilisation in financial markets and the structural reforms completed so far, abandoning more ambitious programmes to foster economic growth and integration. At the current juncture, it is vital to link the short term with the long term in order to jump on a different development path, which would lead to a better equilibrium. Achieving smart, sustainable and inclusive growth does not imply just a one-time choice, but requires a coherent and shared long-run commitment.

The alternative is instead years and years of subdued growth, with increasing imbalances and divergence among Member States and with progressive weakening of the role of Europe in the global political and economic arena. Policy makers need to revive a vision of the future of the Union, where common institutions and decision making are perceived as engines of prosperity and not as obstacles, or worse, as constraints on well-being.

6 Deepening the EU Single Market for Services, Networks and the Digital Economy

Coherent with this vision is the deepening of the Single market, particularly in services, networks and the digital economy, as these are the areas that would, by all analyses, greatly improve growth potential and increase employment opportunities (Monti 2010). The EU Single Market is not directly contemplated in the Europe 2020 targets and initiatives (with one exception being the Digital Agenda flagship). Rather, the single market is considered as a 'tool' that can promote the objectives of Europe 2020 and integrate existing initiatives.

A strengthening of the internal market would generate greater economic growth and produce more employment opportunities. Its exclusion from Europe 2020 appears therefore to be a glaring omission that could undermine the entire framework. Furthermore, the strengthening of the internal market would facilitate a greater integration of EU industries within global value chains. Indeed, a greater presence in these value chains is possible only if markets for products and services are open and interconnected, investment in research and innovation is fostered and a suitably qualified workforce is available.

Given the significant benefits to be derived from fully implementing the Services Directive, furthering the integration of services should be incorporated into Europe 2020. The Commission has analysed individual services and professions to assess the implementation of the Services Directive. On technical ground, it is already possible to launch specific initiatives in sectors that offer the highest potential.

More specifically, the Single Digital Market is also an area to be included in Europe 2020. Currently, the Digital Agenda is only included as a headline initiative under the Smart Growth priority. Given the expanded role of the digital economy since the original Europe 2020, this could potentially be elevated among Europe 2020 main priorities. Alternatively, the Digital Agenda initiative could be expanded to become part of a broader initiative to integrate markets in network industries.

The EU published the first Transport Scorecard in April 2014 to compare member-state performance. Similar to the Single Market Scorecard, these indicators capture compliance with EU directives as well as provide a snapshot of transport integration. Such integration indicators should be applied also in other areas in order to accelerate progress towards fully integrated network industries.

Moreover, although renewable energy is included as one of the environmental targets in Europe 2020, oddly the integration of energy markets is not part of

Europe 2020. Given the time required to fully integrate energy markets and the importance of energy security, this could be a good candidate for inclusion.

To sum up, many important areas instrumental in stimulating potential growth are noticeable for their absence from the current version of the Europe 2020 strategy.

7 Finance for Growth

A 'Finance for growth' initiative, launched at the EU and national level, could decisively eliminate financial market fragmentation and create a favourable conditions for longer term investment.

The ultimate objective is having single financial and capital markets where economic agents can make investment choices without unjustified credit constraints: credit should be allocated competitively, irrespective of location/nationality, based entirely on the borrowers' capacity to produce wealth and cash flows upon which credit can be safely repaid. This is the best way to ensure that productive projects, including long-term ones, can be effectively pursued while protecting savers and investors. Of course this requires an integrated and effective financial system involving both the private sector, through financial markets and intermediaries, and the public sector, through supervisors and regulators.

The progress made in the past towards integration has been impressive, not only driven by the introduction of a common currency but in reaction to the global financial crisis. The creation of a Banking Union is the most visible and recent achievement, although starting from a situation of dis-integration following the financial crisis.

Now that the major reforms for the banking sector are about to be completed, there is a need to increase efforts to further develop and integrate EU non-bank finance, including long-term institutional investment and direct capital markets. Promoting further progress must focus on the need to ensure ample availability of credit to small and medium enterprises, which are the backbone of the European economy. The global financial crisis has highlighted that the 'regime shift' to a new risk-adverse steady state in the financial system is particularly challenging for otherwise creditworthy SMEs.

There is plenty of room for European initiatives in the area of research, innovation, human capital development, green economy, energy, transport and digitalisation. Recently the need for financing long-term investment projects are also related to new areas of development such as health care services, full information-technology integration among different level of government and the EU, network systems in the energy and communication fields and a new effort on the digital agenda. They are all areas of potential growth that require private and public capital for their development. Refocusing the EU budget could be a source of financing for these initiatives as well as the set-up of a European infrastructure fund and the recapitalisation of the European Investment Bank.

8 Greening of Growth

The recent economic crisis has provided an opportunity for Member States to define policies aimed at promoting the transition to a 'green economy'. A strategic vision, in this sense, would require that policies to overcome the crisis are environmentally sustainable.

In this sense, green growth can be a tool to achieve economic growth while preventing environmental degradation, biodiversity loss and the unsustainable use of natural resources. To facilitate the transition to this idea of economic growth it is necessary to explore all opportunities. Therefore, it is crucial to have data and indicators that appropriately measure progress towards 'green growth'.

The aim would be to promote a better use of natural capital, through a mix of policies that internalise environmental externalities, and to emphasise certain strategic productive sectors, such as agriculture, food, tourism, services with high value added and employment potential, as well as the industrial system as a whole.

The full incorporation of policies oriented to green growth into the Europe 2020 strategy can create new business opportunities and increase the competitiveness of enterprises, reducing the cost of energy and the exposure of the economy to fluctuations in energy prices. Among the sectors with the most potential are the upgrading of energy efficiency of buildings, the efficient management of water sources and waste, activities related to adaptation to climate change and the development of renewable energy sources.

'Green growth' cannot be promoted in isolation from other public policies, but must be part of a broader strategy addressing both supply and demand. It must become an essential element in production dynamics and the behaviour of businesses and individuals. In this sense, it must also be tailored to national circumstances.

Green growth can be promoted through: (i) a change in the composition of taxes, in particular through a well-designed increase in environmental taxes and a corresponding decrease in income taxes; (ii) the creation of long-term price signals through economic instruments, putting a price on externalities and applying the principle of 'polluter pays', providing strong indications to the market in terms of investment opportunities; (iii) the focus on sustainability of growth to prevent an eventual reduction in the growth rate once the limits of natural resources are reached.

9 Imbalances Versus Integration

In general, policies to correct imbalances can reduce macroeconomic risks related to these imbalances, thus fostering better economic conditions. The same holds true for excessive fiscal imbalances. Fiscal adjustment becomes the precondition for future economic growth. There is nevertheless a thin line between addressing economic imbalances on the one hand and damaging potential growth or undermining social cohesion and sustainability on the other. The quality and composition of the response to imbalances becomes pivotal. Measures to correct external and internal macroeconomic imbalances, as well as excessive fiscal imbalances, should draw from the improved economic outlook to encourage growth and convergence to a greater extent than past practices.

In a context of economic integration, divergent patterns of sectoral specialisation enhance economic growth but also contribute to produce divergent productivity growth rates and current account balances, implying co-existence of different industrial and economic structures and a different pace of employment creation and output generation in different countries. In the long run, the literature suggests that sectoral composition also has a substantial impact on TFP growth. Moreover, greater specialisation could result in a de-synchronisation of business cycles across countries and non-synchronous reactions to common shocks within the economies of the market union, which would have ultimately to be offset by fiscal policy.

The benefits of specialisation would be evident for a currency union, in terms of productivity growth and competitive advantage, and would not make the whole-area economy weaker. Imbalances, to some extent, could be considered as a by-product of integration.

The crisis urged decisive action to prevent the collapse of the European Economic and Monetary Union. Country-specific imbalances (especially fiscal and trade) are often pointed out as being prominent sources of problems within the Euro Area. While imbalances are certainly at the root of the current crisis, we must also acknowledge that the economic recipes currently proposed to reduce imbalances do not fully consider the economic effects of increased market integration and specialisation. For the above reasons, different growth rates and output trends across Member States, within certain limits, should be expected as a result of greater product and services market integration (Codogno 2011a, b).

In other words, there are also 'good imbalances' that reflect increased economic integration and product market specialisation, together with greater financial and banking integration.

10 Finding the Appropriate Policy Mix

The key for EU economic success lays on structural supply-side measures, which may sometimes have negative effects on aggregate demand over the near term. Moreover, private and public sector deleveraging must continue. In this situation, tight fiscal policy and insufficiently accommodative monetary policy/fiscal fragmentation may leads to:

(i) Weakness in consumer spending.
(ii) Insufficient recovery in investment activity.
(iii) Uncomfortably high unemployment.
(iv) Continuing disinflation (and risks of deflation).
(v) Rising Euro Area C/A surpluses.

(vi) Strengthening of the euro exchange rate.
(vii) More problematic debt dynamics.

In the Euro Area there is evidence of all these phenomena, and thus there is a need to combine structural policies with an appropriate policy mix over the near-term to facilitate the transition towards higher potential growth. The above mentioned phenomena (Fig. 1, 2, 3, 4, 5, 6, 7, 8, 9 and 10 presented in the appendix) seems to suggest that the current policy mix is suboptimal and is not facilitating the reform process.

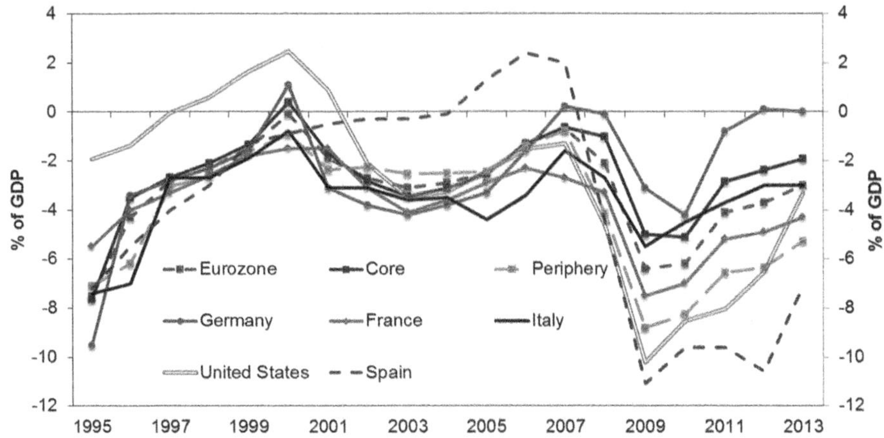

Fig. 1 Additional fiscal consolidation is unavoidable. *Note* Deficit data Greece, included in Pheriphery, are not available for the period 1995–1999. *Source* Eurostat, US Department of the Treasury, Bureau of Economic Analysis

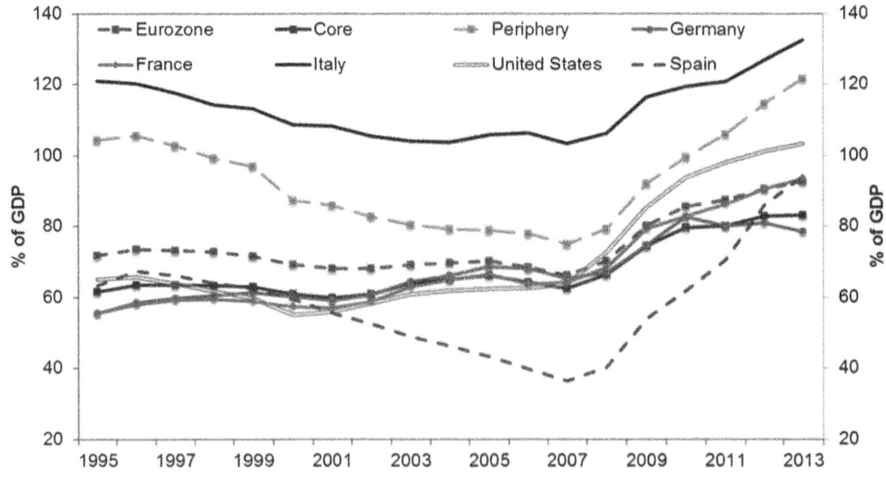

Fig. 2 Public debt deleveraging has yet to start. *Source* Eurostat, US Department of the Treasury, Bureau of Economic Analysis

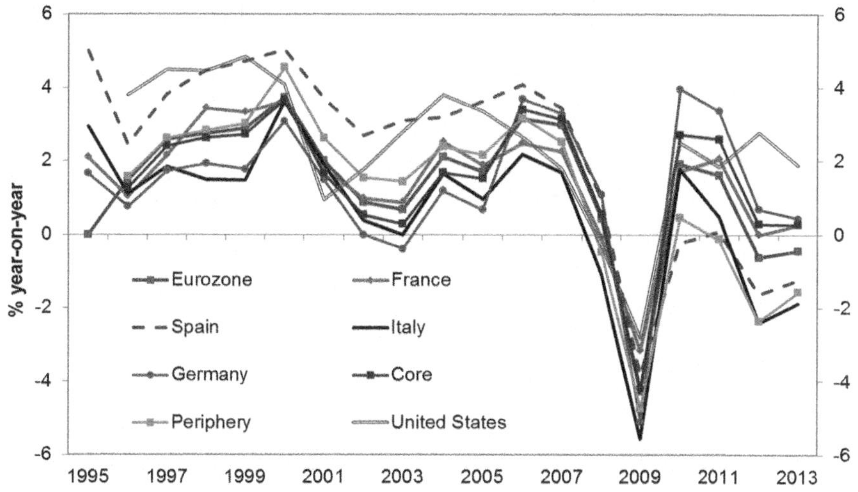

Fig. 3 Is GDP going back to its pre-crisis potential? *Source* Eurostat, BEA

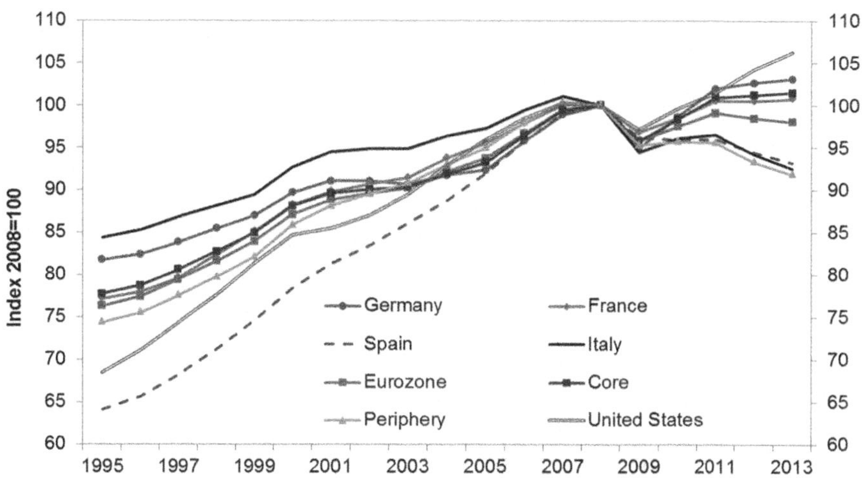

Fig. 4 Are GDP level losses going to be recovered? *Source* Eurostat, BEA

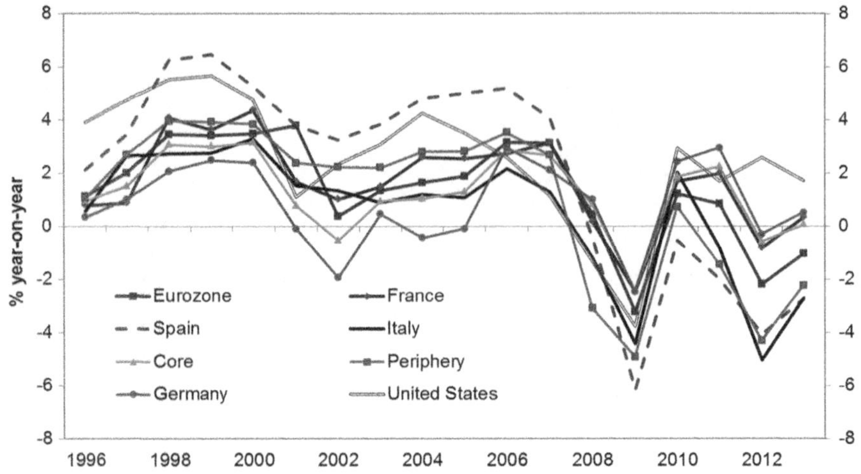

Fig. 5 Domestic demand improving slowly even in core EA countries. *Source* Eurostat, Oxford Economics

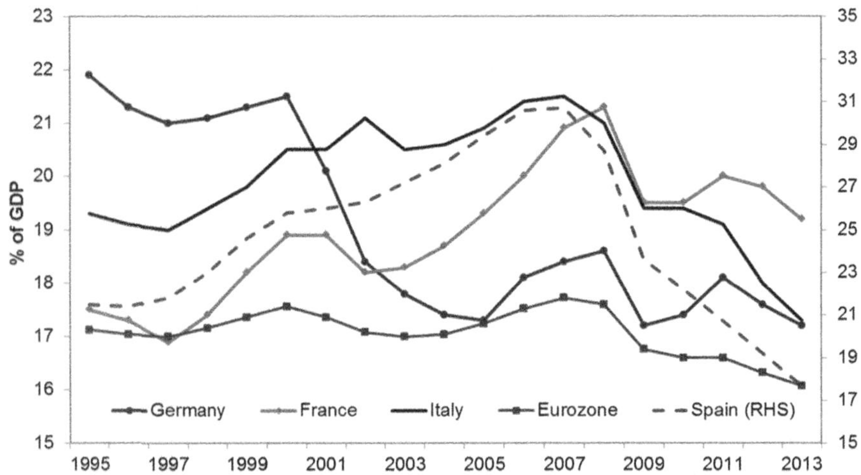

Fig. 6 Investments for growth: the challenge to reverse current trends. *Source* Eurostat

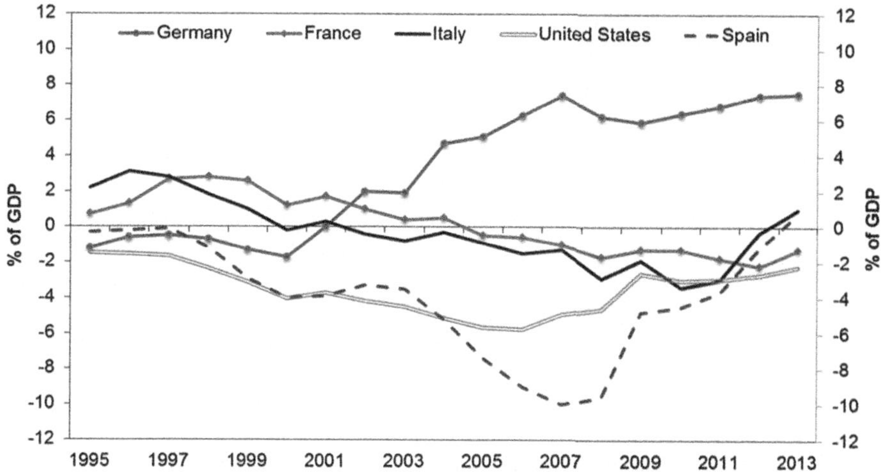

Fig. 7 Policy mix leading to current account surpluses. *Source* Eurostat, ECB, IMF

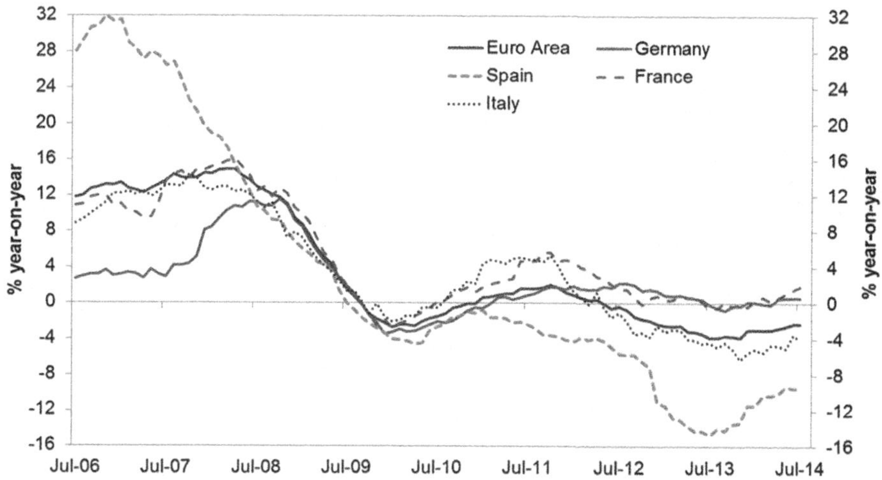

Fig. 8 Contraction in credit growth: still no turning point. *Source* ECB

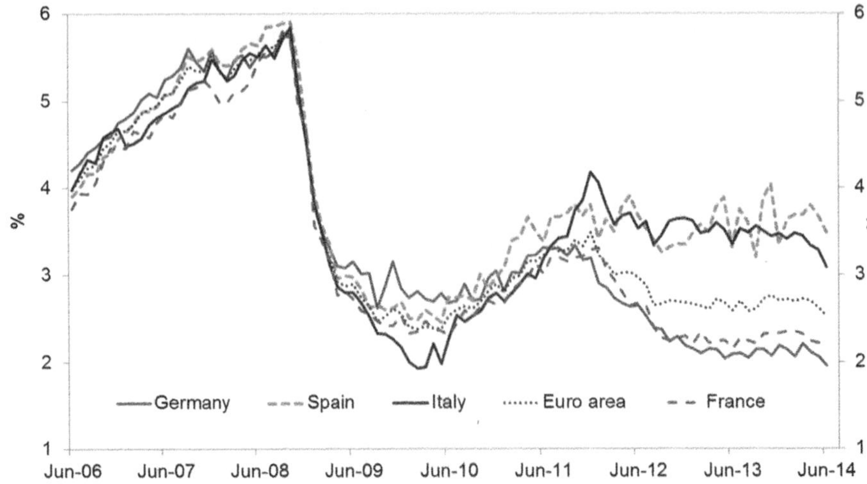

Fig. 9 Cost of credit: the gap among Euro Area countries remains wide. *Source* ECB

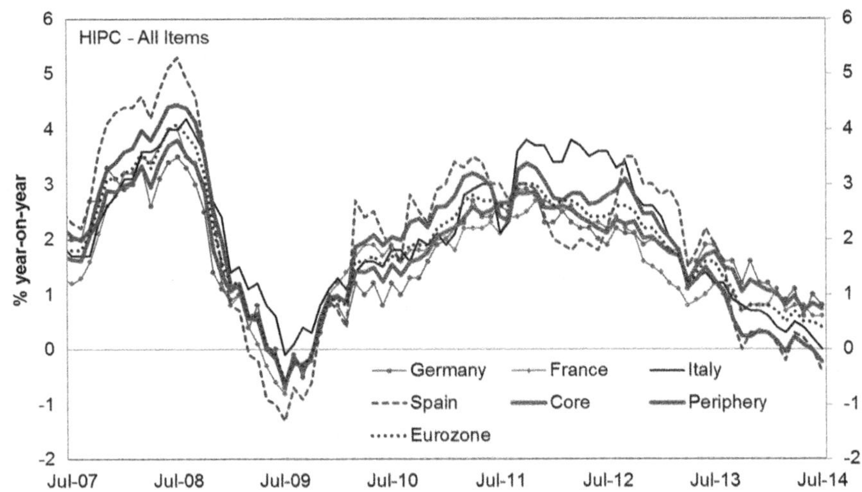

Fig. 10 Disinflation continues (with non-negligible risk of deflation). *Source* ECB

11 Conclusions

The pre-crisis paradigm was unsustainable, economically, socially and environmentally, and Europe needs a new vision of well-being that recognises new challenges, new opportunities and new sources of growth.

A renewed focus on promoting growth should take into account areas such as the efficient functioning of the labour market, addressing issues such as the skill mismatch (for example, by redefining a flagship such as "an agenda for new skills and jobs"), areas related to the strengthening of the single market, increasing the integration of financial markets (i.e. banking union) and policies to promote a transition to a 'green economy'.

Inequality has increased in many European countries in recent years. In order to make the recovery sound and sustainable, policies must boost long-run GDP growth and reduce inequality as well. Investing in education and skills, promoting the integration of immigrants and helping more women into decent employment, are just a few examples of such policies.

But it is not only revisions to its content that would provide added momentum to the Strategy. For Europe, complete recovery is not a return to normality; there is a need to foster new sources of growth and competitiveness, based on knowledge-intensive activities, high productivity and environmental sustainability. The new vision must be rooted in the medium to long run. The review of the Europe 2020 strategy is an important opportunity in this sense.

Europe has learnt some lessons from the crisis. Inter-connectedness touch on every dimension of Europe's economic and social lives, so that nationally-oriented policies proved to be not only ineffective, but made the imbalances worse. It follows that national imbalances cannot be corrected only by means of asymmetric mechanisms, particularly those that place the entire burden of adjustments on a few countries. Indeed, experience shows that such asymmetry jeopardises growth and even social cohesion in the adjusting countries and also risks spreading the slowdown to other countries. Only well-coordinated policies will be successful in achieving further integration and enhancing potential growth for the whole area.

Sufficient leeway must be allowed for imbalances that are necessary to make an efficient allocation of factors of production and financial resources within Europe.

Finally, to help this process, some rebalancing of the current policy mix may be desirable to maintain price stability, prevent further increases in the Euro Area current account surplus, discourage further appreciation of the euro exchange rate, facilitate deleveraging and, finally, provide some near-term support to demand to strengthen the economic recovery and the citizens' support to much-needed reforms.

Appendix

Europe 2020 Background (Table 1).

Table 1 Summary of Italy's key results on Europe 2020 targets

Target	Flagship	EU-wide status (2012)	Expected EU-wide status (2020)	IT status (2012)
Employment: at least 75 % of working age population (ages 20–64) *IT Target*: 67–69 %	Innovation union Digital agenda for Europe Youth on the move Agenda for new skills and jobs	**68.40 %**	**Expected 72 % (74 % if national targets met)**	61 %
Investments in R&D: 3 % of GDP *IT Target*: 1.53 %		**2.06 %**	**2.6 % at best**	1.27 %
School drop-out rates (<10 %); **Completing tertiary education** (at least 40 % of 30–34 year olds) *IT Targets*: **Drop-out rate**: 16 % **University graduates**: 26–27 %		**Drop-out rate**: 12.7 % **University graduates**: 35.7 %	**Drop-out rate**: "Target Broadly Achievable" **University graduates**: "Target Likely to be met"	Drop-out rate: 17.6 % University graduates: 21.7 %
Reducing GHG (by 20 or 30 % "if conditions are right"); **Increased Renewables Share** (to 20 %) **Energy Efficiency** (+20 %) **IT Targets**: **GHG**: −13 % **Renewables**: 17 % **Energy Efficiency**: 158.0 mTOE	Resource-efficient Europe An industrial policy for the globalisation era	**GHG reduced by 18 %** **Renewables**: 14.4 % **Energy Efficiency**: primary consumption fell; energy intensity increased	**GHG**: −24 % **Renewables**: 21 % **Energy Efficiency**: on target (not specified)	GHG: −4.7 % Renewables: 13.5 % Energy Efficiency: 155.2 mTOE
Poverty and Social Exclusion: 20 million lifted from at-risk group *IT Target*: **Poverty reduced by 2.2 m**	European platform against poverty	**Increased from 2009**: 114 million to 124 million	No evidence of a "quick-fix solution"	Poverty *increased* by 3.4 million (from 14.8 m in 2010 to 18.2 m)

In addition to the summary provided in the Stocktaking Communication, Eurostat prepares an annual report on Europe 2020 progress. http://epp.eurostat.ec.europa.eu/cache/ITY_OFFPUB/KS-02-13-238/EN/KS-02-13-238-EN.PDF

References

Alesina, Alberto, Ignazio Angeloni, and Ludger Schuknecht. 2005. What does the European Union do? *Public Choice* 123(3–4):275–319.

Alesina, Alberto and Roberto Perotti. 2005. The European Union: A politically incorrect view. *Journal of Economic Perspectives* 22.

Barrel, Ray, and Simon Kirby. 2007. Notes on the Lisbon process: An analysis of the impacts of reaching the Lisbon targets for skills, R&D and the administrative burden in the European Union. In *Industrial policy and economic reforms papers*, no. 7, DG ENTR.

Barroso, J.M. 2010. Presentation to the informal European Council of 11 Feb 2010.

Brülhart, M. 2001. Growing alike or growing apart? Industrial specialisation of EU countries. In *The impact of EMU on Europe and the developing countries*, ed. Wyplosz, C. Oxford: Oxford University Press.

Codogno, L., and G.J. Koopman. 2008. European economy occasional papers n. 41 by the European Commission forewords on "The LIME assessment framework (LAF): A methodological tool to compare, in the context of the Lisbon strategy, the performance of EU member states in terms of GDP and in terms of twenty policy areas affecting growth".

Codogno, L., G. Odinet and F. Padrini. 2009. The use of targets in the Lisbon strategy. Rivista di Politica Economica, pp. 3–21, Issue I–III, January–March 2009.

Codogno L. 2011a. Iniziative per rafforzare la governance economica in Europa: alcune considerazioni (Initiatives to strengthen economic governance in Europe: Some considerations). In "Ripresa dopo la crisi?" (*Recovery after the crisis*? ed. Luigi Paganetto, Eurilink, 73–92).

Codogno L. 2011b. Speech at the concluding policy panel "Perspectives on European growth: One currency, several growth models? In *DG ECFIN annual research conference on "new growth models in Europe*. Brussels, 21 Nov 2011. http://ec.europa.eu/economy_finance/events/2011/2011-11-21-annual-research-conference_en/pdf/arc2011_conc_panel_enl.pdf.

Codogno L. 2013. La governance economica in Europa: come supportare le riforme strutturali? (Economic governance in Europe: How to support structural reforms?) In "Patto per l'Euro e Crescita. L'austerità conviene?" ed. Luigi Paganetto, Eurilink.

Codogno L. 2013. Beyond the austerity versus growth debate: Is it possible a marriage? (Oltre il Dibattito su Austerità e Crescita: è Possibile un Connubio?), "Politiche di Austerità e Dinamismo dell'Economia" (Austerrity policies and dynamism of the economy, ed. Luigi Paganetto, Eurilink).

Darvas, Z., E. Vihriälä. 2013. Does the European semester deliver the right policy advice? Bruegel policy contribution.

Economic and Financial Affairs Council (ECOFIN). 2009. The Lisbon strategy post-2010. Ecofin view.

European Commission. 2005. Working together for growth and jobs. A new start for the Lisbon strategy. Communication for the Spring European Council.

European Commission DG ECFIN. 2009. Improving incentives to implement structural reforms: the role of targets and indicators. Note for the EPC working group on methodology to assess Lisbon related structural reforms.

European Commission. 2010. Europe 2020, A strategy for smart, sustainable and inclusive growth.

European Commission DG ECFIN. 2014. Taking stock of the Europe 2020 strategy for smart, sustainable and inclusive growth. Communication from the Commission to the European Parliament, the Council, the European Economic and Social Committee and the Committee of the Region.

European Council. 2000. Presidency conclusions of the Lisbon European Council, 23 and 24 Mar 2000.

European Council. 2005. Presidency conclusions of the Brussels European Council, 23 Mar 2005.

Frankel, J., and A. Rose. 1998. The endogeneity of the optimum currency area criterion. *Economic Journal* 108: 1009–1025.

Gelauff, George M.M., and Arjan M. Lejour. 2006. Five Lisbon highlights—The economic impact of reaching these targets, CPB Document.
International Monetary Fund. 2013. Euro area policies 2013 article IV consultation, IMF Country Report no. 13/231.
International Monetary Fund. 2014. Jobs and growth: Supporting European recovery.
Krugman, P. 1993. Lessons of Massachussetts for EMU. In the transition to economic and monetary union in Europe, ed. Giavazzi, F. and Torres, F., 241–261. New York: Cambridge University Press.
Mongelli F.P., Vega J.L. 2006. What effects is EMU having on the Euro area and its members countries?, ECB working paper series no. 599.
Monti M. 2010. A new strategy for the single market. Report to the President of the European Commission, José Manuel Barroso.
MPC task force of the ESCB. 2004. Sectoral specialisation in the EU, ECB occasional paper series no. 19.
Mundell, R.A. 1961. A theory of optimum currency areas. *American Economic Review* 51: 657–665.
OECD/The World Bank. 2012. Promoting inclusive growth: Challenges and policies, Paris.
Padoan P.C. 2010. Beyond the crisis: Shifting gears, OECD Observer No. 278.
Padoan P.C. 2012a. Speech on from crisis management to global sustained growth. The Hague, 7 Nov 2012.
Padoan P.C. 2012b. The evolving paradigm, OECD Yearbook.
Puga, D. 1999. The rise and fall of regional inequalities. *European Economic Review* 43: 621–634.
The World Bank. 2012. Golden growth—restoring the lustre of the European economic model.
Varga, J., W. Roeger and J. in't Veld. 2013. Growth effects of structural reforms in Southern Europe: The case of Greece, Italy, Spain and Portugal. European commission, Economic papers 511.

The Corporatist Antagonism to Economic Dynamism

Juan Vicente Sola

Abstract This paper intends to describe the common traits of 'corporatism' both as an economic and political movement. The essence of corporatism is confusion in its theories and institutions and that characteristic has made its definition very complex. The paper indicates the existence of nine political myths in corporatist systems: the myth of unity, the myth of populism, the myth of the charismatic forms of power, the myth of politics as epic; the myth of progress against capitalist individualism, the myth of autarky, the myth of industrialization and the myth of politics as the dialectics of friend-enemy. Many of these political myths are effective in many present day democratic societies and prevent the development of a healthy and dynamic economy. Corporatist doctrines and institutions are the cause of the economic stagnation around the world. Corporatist doctrinaires are the "long defunct economists" that influence present day statesmen even beyond their conscious knowledge, having serious consequences in the dynamism of their economies. Corporatism is the adversary of individualism and a dynamic economy.

1 The Corporatist Challenge to Open Economic Institutions

Modern democratic societies accept individualism, pluralism and constitutionalism as the legitimate political system. Pluralist political systems require the self-limitation of governments, introducing separation of powers and checks and balances

How to avoid mentioning the whole paragraph of Keynes General Theory: *Practical men, who believe themselves to be quite exempt from any intellectual influences, are usually the slaves of some defunct economist. Madmen in authority, who hear voices in the air, are distilling their frenzy from some academic scribbler of a few years back.*

J.V. Sola (✉)
University of Buenos Aires, Buenos Aires, Argentina
e-mail: Juansola@hotmail.com

L. Paganetto (ed.), *Achieving Dynamism in an Anaemic Europe*,
DOI 10.1007/978-3-319-14099-5_10

into an otherwise monopolistic concentration of power. Self-limitation has an ancient tradition, going back to the metaphor of Ulysses in the Odyssey introduced by the XVII century philosopher Benedict Spinoza as the justification of a correct moral behavior when voluntary restriction and control prevents a greater evil; he proposed the use of this principle by authorities. Following this metaphor modern constitutions are often associated to Ulysses binding himself to the mast in order to resist the fatal call of the Sirens. But what is the equivalent of Ulysses' ropes that might enable a political community to bind itself to constitutional rules? The positive puzzle of constitutionalism lies in explaining the willingness and ability of powerful political actors to make sustainable commitments to abide by and uphold constitutional rules even when these rules stand in the way of their immediate interests. That is to say, how political communities can credibly and durably commit itself to repaying its debts, respect human rights or refraining from war (Levinson 2011)

Individualism, pluralism and constitutionalism have a strong adversary. Corporatism[1] is a traditional and recurrent form of governance that pretends to solve the same problems than pluralism and constitutionalism but with entire different answers. Corporatism connotes a system in which major societal groups, for example, clan, ethnic, religious, economic, or military structures, are integrated into the governmental system for the purpose of achieving coordinated national development. It remains a distinct political system.

In the Odyssey, Ulysses faced a problem of time inconsistency in his optimal plan. His optimal plan was to listen to the sirens and then continue his journey. But this was time inconsistent because, once he had embarked on the plan by listening to the sirens; he would not have been able to implement the later part of the plan, the rest of his journey. The time inconsistency arises because the sirens affect Ulysses' preferences. His perception of the best action changes in the middle of the plan and this leads him to deviate from the original version. Ulysses implemented his optimal plan by denying himself freedom at the later stage of the plan. Having instructed his men to tie him to the mast and to ignore any orders to do anything other than sail past the rocks, he told them to plug their ears and row. Thus, Ulysses established for himself a private constitution, a set of more or less binding rules that constrain his future choices. By exploiting elements of his natural and social environment, Ulysses was able to subvert certain inclinations of his future self, inclinations that he knew would be destructive of his overall interests but which would nevertheless prove irresistible when they arose (Van den Hauwe 2005). The use of the metaphor of Ulysses and the sirens as an explanation of the need of self-limitation of power although developed by Jon Elster it was originally mentioned in Benedict Spinoza (Elster 1984).

But Ulysses and the sirens is not a universally accepted metaphor, contrary to individualism, pluralism and constitutionalism Corporatism is not a doctrine for the

[1]In this paper we shall use the terms "corporatism" and "corporativism", as synonyms although in English the word "corporatism" may have other meanings that are not referred to here.

limitation of power it is mainly a doctrine for the justification of unbounded power. It was born as a denial of individualism and constitutionalism, with serious restrictions to, among others, economic freedom.

1.1 The Response to the 'Social Question'

Since Corporatism pretends of ancient indeed medieval origins it is difficult to indicate its origins. Modern corporatism appeared as an alternative to socialism to give an answer to the social conflicts at the end of the XIX century. In 1891 Pope Leo XIII wrote the Encyclical letter *Rerum Novarum* as a solution of the 'social question', it raised the possibility to establish 'class harmony' between the capitalistic entrepreneurs which challenged the ordered system of the state and the revolutionary labor organizations. These proposals used some traditional pre capitalistic images, medieval corporations that would give a different scope to trade unions that would accept the natural order, at the same time medieval disdain against greed and illegitimate usury. This root of corporatist doctrine preserved traditional power hierarchies but permitted the inclusion of the social question. It intended a third way beside capitalism that would adopt a humane form, and against the new forms of socialism.[2] Following this medieval metaphor, although it could not be a possible transplantation of the feudal orders to the late XIX century social problems, the new corporatism defined each person by his rank in society. If in ancient times one was born and lived in a certain status and had to accept this place in life, the new corporatism was based in function or occupation. Persons were to be represented in the political decision made not by their convictions or interests but according to their occupations. It was therefore considered that political parties did not represent the whole of society, on the contrary they fractured opinion and tended to disunion and conflict, but corporatist representation tended to political unity and social harmony. The process started by giving legal status to trade unions, this 'legal personality' allowed them to participate in the political process and to be recognized by employers and business organizations. At the same time the state would order employers to give better salaries and working conditions. Strikes the main revolutionary weapon of trade unions, were forbidden. Employers were compensated both with high tariffs that would impede the competition with foreign imports and by the limitation of the access to the market by new enterprises. As in the widely used medieval metaphor society would be hierarchical, if in the past the three orders were the clergy, the nobility and the third state,[3] in the new corporatist regime the three orders would be the State, the centralized business conglomerates

[2]This late XIXth, century debate on the social question coincided with the debate of the future of socialism between the more aggressive forms proposed by Karl Kautsky and the social democracy of Eduard Bernstein in 1899 and 1900.

[3]According to Duby (1980), the three medieval orders were a product of imagination of contemporary authors but had no strict basis in reality.

and the general confederations of trade unions. Each hierarchy formed a pyramid that would peak in the centralized confederation and in the State. New business and new trade unions were excluded of the system and had to accept the existing order were incorporated to the existing structure. The tripartite hierarchical organization tended to unity, the unity of the State that represented all human activities.

1.2 Political Parties and the "Unity of the State"

Corporatist legal doctrine, in spite of its older roots, developed actively in the Weimar Republic in Germany as a reaction mainly by authors who cherished the imperial past, to the new significance and influence of the political parties within the state. The new political parties appeared to be a necessary consequence of the emancipation of all classes and social strata, the legitimacy of state rule was no longer conceivable merely as a natural rule from above; at the same time, after the crisis at the end of World War I there was no longer a unified bourgeoisie, and it thus seemed impossible for the political whole to be represented by people who felt beholden exclusively to the common good. The homogeneous "people" had become a heterogeneous "mass." The parties appeared to be a necessity for active citizens to articulate themselves in the political system bringing a risk for state unity to be torn apart by the power of a plurality of interests leaning in many different directions. In the new constitutional order parties could be conceived as a prerequisite for state organization and the idea of the "party state" was born. One important protagonist in the discussion in favor of the status of parties within the state structure was the constitutional legal scholar Gerhard Leibholz (1901–1982). For Leibholz, the only valid dimension of the term representation is one that is geared towards representing, or "mirroring" the people in parliament, in the sense that a randomly drawn sample in empirical research is said to represent the population it was drawn from. His party state doctrine hence aims at allowing the institutions representing the people to become in a certain sense identical with the people itself by way of the new political parties, so that it becomes an inescapable condition that only such decisions can be made that lie in the interest of the people (Towfigh 2012).

Against this theory stood Carl Schmitt. He developed the theory of the President as the custodian of the Constitution, and the theory of the 'fundamental decision' of the people as the base of the Constitution. These were the basis of the legal doctrine that justified the corporatist attack to political parties considering they broke the unity of the "people", what in later times was derisibly called the 'partidocracy'.[4] He established the first orderly description of the corporatist state, his doctrines subsist and have new readers.

[4]Partidocracy in Italian *Partitocrazia* means a political regime in which the real power has its centers in parties and not in any organs provided for in the Constitution. Professor Joseph Maranini, which he called *Governo parlamentare e partitocrazia* in his inaugural lecture at the University of Florence in 1949.

1.3 Varieties in Corporatism

Wiarda (1997) classifies corporatism in historical or "natural" corporatism, ideological corporatism, manifest corporatism, and modern neo-corporatism. Historical or "natural" corporatism would occur in many pre modern societies that are founded on traditions emphasizing solidarity, group identity, and community. These include the ethnic, clan, and tribal basis of African politics, many of the Confucian based societies of East Asia, the group, clan, and caste based societies of South Asia, and those societies based in the tradition involving the Koran. In Western Europe, a corporatist system existed before the onslaught of the Renaissance, the Enlightenment, and the Industrial Revolution which included military orders, guilds, the Roman Catholic Church and its orders, and the aristocracy. With the emphasis on the individual and on individual rights brought about by the Enlightenment and the French Revolution, many came to regret the coming breakup of the old order. This led ideological reactionaries to create modern corporatism.

In the papal encyclicals, Quadragesimo anno and Rerum novarum[5] a religious based system of corporatism was sketched.

Manifest Corporatism had an autocratic nature; it included various regimes like Fascist Italy, Nazi Germany, Vichy France, Franco's Spain, Salazar's Portugal, Metaxas's Greece, Dolfuss's Austria, Vargas's Brazil, and Peron's Argentina in the earlier half of the twentieth century. Many of these regimes were authoritarian and involved severe human rights abuses leading many to perceive corporatism in a highly negative light. Later regimes that came to involve corporatism would reject the corporatist label despite their adherence to this ideology because of the negative connotations that became associated with the word due to the fascist regimes that operated under its principles.

Modern neo-corporatism is distinct from these authoritarian regimes and tends to be more democratic in character and is particularly useful model for understanding various regimes in Latin America, as well as in Europe.

1.4 Corporatism, Pluralism and the Dispersion of Knowledge

In opposition to corporatism pluralism is the political system that more easily adapts to the dispersion of knowledge in society. As von Hayek (1945) indicates, information is in '*dispersed bits of incomplete and frequently contradictory knowledge which all the separate individuals possess*'[6] it requires prudence and self-limitation

[5]These doctrines were reformed in latter pontifical documents, mainly '*Mater et Magistra*' Encyclical OF Pope John XXIII On Christianity and Social Progress May 15, 1961 and in '*Octogesima Adveniens.' A Call to Action Encyclical Letter of Pope Paul VI, issued on May 14, 1971.*

[6]Quoted in Sunstein (2006).

from legislators and regulators. Planning and rigid economic structures are inefficient since they consider information to be accessible not disperse and ignore the effects of uncertainty, they therefore prevent innovation and economic growth. Corporatism disregards the dispersion of knowledge, insists on harmony not competition and the search for establishing the "natural order".[7] Corporatist policies in opposition to pluralism are not based in competition but on agreements between big industries or business organizations, centralized trade unions and the government. Since the agreement is seen as the representation of the organized society, no self-limitation of government is accepted or needed. Corporatism is a process in which a limited number of monopolistic organizations representing fundamental interests engage in bargaining with state agencies over public policy outputs. In exchange for favorable policies, the leaders of these organizations agree to undertake the implementation of policy through delivering the cooperation of their members. This rigid procedure seriously curtails the possibility of the development of new companies that offer new products to the market.

Modernized versions of corporatism intended to separate it from any fascist connection were defined as the '*institutional arrangement for linking the associational organized interests of civil society with the decisional structures of the state*'.[8] In this way persons living in society participate in policy decisions only if they are organized through associations. A more comprehensive definition of corporatism would include certain characteristics as:

1. the growth of central planning;
2. the requirement of political stability by bringing both trade unions and business organizations into the decision making process and integrating them into the state;
3. the delegation of the state power to trade unions and business organizations to regulate, license and police their own members; and
4. the use by government of the corporate groups to help implement government social and economic programs.

Taking all this in consideration corporatism can be defined as a system of interest representation in which the constituent units are organized into a limited number of singular, compulsory, noncompetitive, hierarchically ordered and functionally differentiated categories, created, recognized or licensed by the state and granted a deliberate representational monopoly within their respective categories in exchange for observing certain controls on their selections of leaders and articulation of demands and supports.[9]

[7]Natural order could be defined as the moral source from which natural law derives its authority. It incorporates the natural relations of beings to one another, in the absence of law, which natural law attempts to reinforce.

[8]Schmitter (1974).

[9]Schmitter (1974) at 93.

In a corporatist system, the state confers a representational monopoly on certain organizations and grants them a presence in policy-making arenas. In the corporatist political myth these organizations are preexistent to the state and not a government creation. They are 'recognized'. For example in the making of labor law, corporatism may be understood as a system of functional participation, involving business organizations by sector and the equivalent trade unions, alongside government representatives. The problem with this idyllic version is that it favors traditional business and labor representatives of already existent and structured activities; new innovative activities or enterprises are excluded.

Corporatist policy-making is carried out through negotiations where the state is one part, or through negotiations between structures within political institutions designed to favor the realization of certain political ends. The state may further influence the outcome by taking an active part in the formation of both groups and their interests through its ability to license their existence, subsidizes their activities and include or exclude them from the policy-making. Hence, monopolized interest organizations may then act as middlemen between the Government and the members of interested organizations.

1.5 Corporatism and Fascism

The study of corporatism is often distorted by its association with fascism, although connections exist it excludes some elements of corporatism and includes other inapplicable to its modern forms. At the same time the term 'fascism' is surrounded by a charged atmosphere due to the brutal characteristics of the Italian and German versions which ended after World War II, that sometimes prevents the understanding of the surviving corporatist institutions. In this way if we can reject as fascist many movements and political parties that incorporate some of its elements in their ideology, style and organization, we must include them in the wider and more technical concept of "corporatism". Some essentials are common like populism, nationalism, anti-liberalism, anti-capitalism; the aim of national and social integration through corporative representation; a distinctive style and rhetoric, and the neglect for the constitutional and legal structures in a way that puts individual rights second to national interest; and the distorted version of the "common good'. The appeal based on emotion, myth and action and the epic vision of political activity are characteristics present in corporatism.

Renzo De Felice sustains that "*If Mussolini hadn't intervened in the war, fascism would have lasted for a long time*",[10] as was the case of the Spanish and Portuguese dictatorships that lasted forty years and the new forms of corporatism that

[10] De Felice and Ledeen (1979, p. 75).

succeeded in South America.[11] Fascism in all its forms evolved into corporatism as an ideology applicable in democratic societies.

Renzo De Felice is the main historian of Mussolini and fascism, his biography extends to seven volumes.[12] He offers general description of the corporatist social and economic model, although De Felice thinks that fascism is exclusively a European experience limited to the period between the wars. We argue that corporatism is a universal phenomenon of which fascism was only a more spectacular case. If we consider fascism as an answer assumed by some European societies to the assessed dangers of communist revolution, as such it has definitely ended with the exhaustion and later disappearance of the communist system. Corporatism to the contrary, although not always by that name, is nowadays embraced by populist democracies as a new form of leftist nationalist discourse.

Fascism is sometimes considered a parenthesis in world history, but that is not true of the social movements that follow corporatist ideas, as for example Peronism could not be considered a parenthesis in Argentine history, although those who in its origin associated it with fascism considered so. Corporatism is here to stay as a political and social doctrine that has evolved into a political myth.

2 The Political Myths of Corporatism

The political myth has a similarity to ideologies; both are beliefs that hold societies together, more so these beliefs may be inconsistent with reality and between the verbal forms and consistent meaning. In this manner Corporatism includes several, juxtaposed political myths in the same sense that Sorel describes as a political myth. In this paper we would like to describe the strong mythical beliefs that construct corporatism.

The constituting myths of corporatism are:

1. unity;
2. populism;
3. charismatic forms of political power;
4. politics as epic;
5. progress against capitalistic individualism;
6. autarky;
7. industrialization; national bourgeoisie and the iron law of oligarchies; and
8. the dialectics of friend-enemy.

[11]The Spanish version of fascism is 'falangism' after the "Falange Española" created by Jose Antonio Primo de Rivera. See Payne (1985).

[12]Mussolini, 7 volumes, 1965–1997 (Turin 1965–97).

3 The Myth of Unity

3.1 The Hostility to Constitutional Limitations and Legal Structures

The idea of the autonomy of free will that is central to constitutional thought and to private law is denied in corporatism. In traditional authoritarian regimes it is the autonomy of the will of the leader or conductor that weakens legal structures, in more modern ways of corporatism it is the will of the centralized bureaucracy or of the governing structures that regulate economic activity that override constitutional limitations. There are two ways in which the constitutional rights; especially economic constitutional rights are limited, the idea the state represents the common good and should prevail over individual interests, and the use of emergency regulations.

Initially is the idea that the state represents the common good against the private good of individuals ruled by greed. Following this principle the more vilified conception of law in corporatism is that of legal security, as the symbol of all false values of liberalism, the premises of the individual interest over the common interest which is the dogma of the satiated bourgeoisie. For example the strict compliance of contracts is considered a formalism that hides the abuse by the powerful over the weak. Courts therefore should revise contracts in order to establish a true equilibrium of benefits between the parties in accordance to the common good. In the organized community order is not based on the 'petrified formulae' of the bill of rights but in communal values structured by the state. These communal values constitute the "moral community" stated by Mussolini and the "organized community" by Peron.

At the same time the application of the doctrine of political and economic emergency allows the restrictions of constitutional rights for long periods of time.[13] The declaration of emergency by law or even by administrative decisions is generally given without precise foundations and is not and cannot be revised by legal courts. In this sense it's convenient to remember the phrase by Carl Schmitt '*sovereign is he who can declare the state of emergency.*'

Schmitt (2004) in his book Legality and Legitimacy establishes an opposition between legitimacy characterized the power in direct contact with the realities of national life, and legality as a purely rationalistic notion that allows the government to keep the right to the exercise of power without any foundation or relation with the needs or aspirations of the national community. This conflict of the legitimacy of power against the legality of institutions is resolved in favor of power, specially the power of the President against Parliament or Judges. But this is not a pure defense of dictatorship specifically Cesarist or Bonapartist dictatorship, although

[13]Hitler consolidation in power was performed by two relatively innocuous acts, the federal intervention of the State of Prussia and the Emergency powers act after the fire in the Reichstag.

Schmitt (1994) wrote a book on dictatorship indicating there was a form of government with a long tradition.[14] Corporatism is not a pure justification of dictatorship, it shows a political and economic theory as its backing and in a way it is the main challenge to a capitalist society and to the rule of law or the *Rechtstaat*. Even if its origins were essentially authoritarian nowadays corporatism has taken new forms that are in some way compatible with democratic theory although not in a pluralist society with an open economy and a constitutional organization.

Traditional constitutional definitions of Corporatism could be found in the Austrian constitution of 1934, its preamble says that the state is: '*based on the corporatist principle*'. Article 5 of the Portuguese Constitution of 1933 proclaims the Portuguese State: '*is a Unitarian and corporatist Republic based on the intervention of all the structural elements of the nation in the administration and in the making of laws.*' The idea of hierarchy is also present in the speeches of Gen Franco and Marshall Petain. They embrace a description of the destructive capacity of individualism and the virtues of a community founded on the natural groupings such as family, profession and motherland.

The description of society by different elites that fight for political power is an enduring theme in corporatist thought both in the authoritarian versions as in new populist ones. For example, Marshall Petain in his message in October 11, 1940 described the new Form of government that was to be created: '*the new Regime will be a social hierarchy. It will not anymore be based on the false idea of natural equality between men, but the new true elites that will be reborn.*'

This association between extremely different governmental institutions, from traditional authoritarian regimes to modern populist versions is not an accidental coincidence they all include an open attack to pluralism and competition in the creation and search of wealth. They despise the innovation and creativity of the dynamic segments of society as an attack to the natural equilibrium. Innovation is not easily accepted unless it is inside the regulation of the state, although scientific research is promoted, especially by public not private funding, but the translation of the results of the research into new products by new enterprises is not easily admitted. Acknowledged companies can innovate but according the conditions established in the collective bargaining between the State, businesses through its natural representatives, that is organizations or corporations; and the workers through the trade unions.

[14]Written after the Russian Revolution and during the existence of the Weimar Constitution, Schmitt analyses the problem of the state of emergency and the power of the President of the Reich in declaring it. Dictatorship, Schmitt argues, is a necessary legal institution in constitutional law.

4 The Myth of Populism

4.1 Corporatism in the Mirror of Populism

Populism is the relation between the people and its leader without constitutional constraints. Corporatism views itself in the mirror of populism usually as an association of charismatic leaders, industrialization through imports substitution and a rebellion against the constitutional system. Populism is an anti-status quo discourse that simplifies the political space by symbolically dividing society between "the people" and the "other". The identity of both the 'people' and the 'other' is a political construction in a relation of antagonism and not a strict political term. Antagonism is a mode of identification in which the relation between a group described as "the people" is by the very process of naming establishes who the enemies of the people are. And anti-status quo dimension is essential to populism giving its identity that requires the political defeat of "the other" which is deemed "the oppressor" which impedes the full presence of the people. The "other" in opposition to "the people" can be presented in political or economic terms as a combination of the oligarchy, the politicians and dominant group, imperialism and its associates, among others. Populism has its principal the notion of the supremacy of the "will of the people," and the notion of the direct relationship between the people and the government. It requires the "constitution of popular identity" against both this existent structure of power and the dominant ideas and values of society. Politics always consists of the creation of an "*us versus them*." This antagonism is a mode of identification since the existence of an oppressor renders all the others to be the same.

Populist corporatism transforms representative democracies in delegative democracies, in such circumstances the political leader having been elected by the people considers that all political power was delegated to him or her by the people and rules without limits or respect to minorities. It also takes de form of "tutelary democracies" as a form of keeping control on increasingly pluralist societies (Wiarda 1997, p. 21).

The dimension of the chain of unfulfilled demands implies the notion of politically mobilized actors advancing their demands against a political system that is unwilling to address them. The process that transforms these demands into an antagonistic relation with the established order that comes an aggregation of discontents that condenses in a new political identity. Populist practices operate within a social milieu in which people have grievances, the desires, needs and wants that have not yet been constituted as political demands, people do not know how to name what they are lacking. The populist leader offer these benefits to them, even some they had never dreamt about, this process is also called the "awakening". In spite that populism is always considered a bottom up process which includes the organization of the people to extract its demands from the established order, in reality there is always a paternalistic top-down nature in populism. The leader in this sense delivers what the audience already wants although it may not be clear to them what it is, it is the interpreter of the vague and imprecise wishes of the multitude. The metaphor of awakening suggests a dormant identity that is mobilized to constitute a new political identity and the introduction of issues that had not been previously part of the political agenda. In this way populism is not exclusively about a crisis of representation in which the people leave their whole identity and embrace a new one; but is about the beginning of a representation of those who had been ignored and now are acknowledged as political actors. In all cases there is a constitution of a new political identity that becomes possible because of the breaking of the existing political order. These failures of representation appear in times of political and economic crisis as it is in these times that previously stable forms of representation become unsettled and there is a research for new forms of identification. In crisis limited rational responses and forms of irrationality appear in political discourse. In these cases the relations of representation become dislocated and the populist and corporatist ideal becomes our dominant mode of identification.

One is hyperinflation. The traditional case is the Republic of Weimar that brought Hitler to power. High inflation produced deep social dislocation and disrupted all individual relations that depend on monetary exchange, savings, the idea of the future, and even health and education. The economy and society loses his institutions starting by the currency, the tax system and following by the legal system. Of course hyperinflation needn't end in a corporatist regime as was the case in Argentina in 1990 1991, but in all cases destroys the institutional system and the respect of the Constitution. But in generality hyperinflation comes associated with populism and with corporatist solutions.

Another situation is the exhaustion of political traditions and the discrediting of political parties. Corruptions, malpractice, the control of public life by non-accountable and self-serving political elite makes that politicians become the "other" of the "people". This is what some Italian political doctrine calls the "partitocrazia" a system in which political parties agree between themselves on policies for their own benefit, there is no real difference between majority and minority since all form part of the same political agreement. The first element for defining partitocrazia is the presence of mass political parties, tightly controlled by their leadership. The partitocrazia is generally associated with the idea of 'sottogoverno', where parties are increasingly seen as contending not so much over the government of the polity, as over its *sottogoverno* where party leaders can influence day to day administrative and policy decisions without being a direct part of the government. This strong denunciation of political parties as not representing the interests or wishes of voters but the interests of their leaders was used in Venezuela and allowed the electoral victory of Hugo Chavez in 1998, similar political discourses were used to justify the taking of power in Italy in this was in 1922 and to lesser extent in Argentina in 2003.

4.2 Who Are the People?

Populism grows as a response to the political breakdown, but then it establishes a new political and economic system. Which mediates between the leaders and the led in a way different from the constitutional institutions. The "people" becomes a metaphysical concept that incorporates this imaginary group conformed by the oppressed and prevented by the powerful from airing their grievances till they burst into history often in a brutal and uncontrolled way. This metaphysical concept of "people" should not be confused with real social upheavals and its participants, this expression is part of the political discourse which can have a relation to social phenomena but is not a description of them. It has a sense of internal homogeneity but also an outside that constitutes its reality: "the other", this threatening group against which the "people's" identity is formed. The political battles form between "us and them", or in a more technical version to the dialectics of friend—enemy. It is the "other" of the people that prevents the popular identity from achieving complete fullness. For that reason pluralism is impossible or inapplicable in corporatist and populist systems, because it would mean the dissolution of the popular identities and only lead to an atomistic society that would not enable this form of representation. The difference between the populist corporatism and the more bureaucratic forms is the presence of a leader. If the epitome of the bureaucratic corporatism is Salazar in Portugal, populist corporatism originated by Vargas and Peron and existent in some countries in South America till this day. In Europe although less successful, populism is present in the right wing populism existent in Eastern Europe, France and Austria. Perhaps a clear example is Vladimir Putin in Russia. Populist corporatism succeeds when there is an important source of wealth generated from the exports of some commodity, it could be oil, gas, mining products, or even agricultural exports like soybeans.

5 The Charismatic Forms of Power

5.1 The State, the Common Good and Political Power

The State represents the common good so individual interests are always submitted to the interest of the state, even in legal process where the state has privileges over ordinary citizens. Law is despised, the principles of the spontaneity of the new law combined with the principle of the total autonomy of the will of the leader weakens constitutional structures, specially ideas like separation of powers and checks and balances. The great jurist of corporatism to this day is Carl Schmitt, mainly by his defense of the concentration of presidential power vis-à-vis Parliamentary or congressional limitations.[15] At the same time the President is the custodian of the

[15]For a contemporary application of Schmitt's ideas on presidential power and the Constitution see Eric (2011, p. 4 and 113 onwards).

Constitution and not the legal courts, therefore any control of the presidential will should be made ex post by political limitations and not ex-ante by strictures established in a constitutional document that could be interpreted by the courts of justice.[16] Corporatist governments or institutions apply Schmitt doctrines as the justification of the augmentation of the regulatory powers of the president. There is a necessary relation between the enhancement presidential power and corporatist economy, this relation evolved from the original authoritarianism to populism.

6 The Myth of Politics as Epic

6.1 Epics, Youth and Energy

Corporatism reveres an ideal both of traditionalism and revolution. In the mid '30s it was a medieval ideal of a structured society through the 'natural' institutions of family, guild and paternalistic government, in newer times it praises indigenism and nationalism in Latin American countries, and in all cases a dogma both anti-capitalistic, anti-individualistic and describing of greed as a cause of evil in society. In spite of its traditionalism it intends to show that something new is created, the idea of government actively running the economy through regulation and not by socialist property. Corporatist structures looks for the inclusion of the young. In all corporatist movements youth organizations are found. The Opera nazionale Ballila in Italy,[17] "Fascist education is moral, physical, social and military. It is designed to create complete harmonious man, the fascist we want," indicated Mussolini. But to form the "character" was essential to raise the emotions of youth, no critical sense. To Mussolini, "childhood and adolescence (…) cannot be fed only of concepts, theories, abstract teachings. The truths that we teach should go first to his fantasies, his heart, and then his mind". Salazar in Portugal[18] and Vargas in the Brazil of the

[16]The classical defense of the power of the President as a custodian of the Constitution against judicial Review in the American tradition is Schmitt (1931) and widely translated. The title referring to the President means de Defender of the Constitution.

[17]Opera Nazionale Balilla was the student and paramilitary organ National Fascist Party (PNF) of Italy. Mussolini's youths were called Balilla after Giovan Battista Perasso, "Balilla" young Genoese who had begun the uprising against the occupying Austrians in 1746. Balilla was a revolutionary image very seductive to the fascist dictatorship.

[18]The *Estado Novo* ("New State"), or the Second Republic, was the corporatist authoritarian regime installed in Portugal in 1933. It was established following the army-led coup d'état of 28 May 1926 against the democratic but unstable First Republic. The Estado Novo, greatly inspired by conservative and authoritarian ideologies, was developed by António de Oliveira Salazar, ruler of Portugal from 1932 to 1968. The motto of the regime was "Deus, Pátria e Familia".

"Estado Novo"[19] had youth organizations that included even schoolchildren in spite that many of policies applied were traditionalist and even reactionary. Peron spoke of the "new Argentina", his party had three branches the political, the trade unions and women, and the 'peronist' youth existed in the organizations like the "Union of Secondary Students" (U.E.S) and the "General University Confederation" (C.G.U.) which had much lesser importance.[20] The 'Juventud Peronista' had particular relevance later particularly from the late '60s to this day.[21] The epic element is shown in the use of battle metaphors by Mussolini established "The battle of wheat, the battle of the lira, L'Oro alla Patria".[22]

There is also a cult of energy, the idea that the public intervention in the market activates and regenerates a drowsed economic system. Some ideas taken by corporatists have an improbable and non-fascist origin for example the "animal spirits" and "euthanasia of the rentier" that come from Keynes' General Theory.

The regeneration of the national values is also an argument used by corporatism; defining the idea of law in the real nation, in the "fundamental decision" of the people and not in the 'caricature' of the assemblies. The need of an elite which knows the public interest and the national spirit, associated with the 'national bourgeoisie', excluding intermediate organisms or legal fictions that could interpose between the leader and the people or the nation. Although cases of bureaucratic corporatism exist they were not common in the origins of corporatism, the main example is Salazar in Portugal, the very unusual case of an economist being dictator. Once the system is established a strong bureaucracy is created and used to apply corporatist regulations in order to prevent the developing of an open economy. At the same time the official party acts as the political structure that would apply the leader's ideas in society. In some cases the official parties use directly the names of the leaders, "Peronismo" in Argentina, "Getulismo" in Brazil (Levine 1998, p. 81).

Corporatist ideology changes the elementary concepts of an open democratic society, the citizen is changed into a 'worker' or 'producer', and the word of reference to people of similar ideas is 'companion' in Spanish 'compañero'. Society is transformed into a hierarchical group following the unchanging laws of economic life; there is no freedom of work or freedom of association in trade unions. The state

---

[19]Estado Novo (New State) is the name of the political regime founded by Getulio Vargas on November 10, 1937, which lasted until October 29, 1945. The 1937 Constitution had the nickname "Polish" designation used to show that the Brazilian Constitution of 1937 was largely influenced by the authoritarian constitution of Poland.

[20]Union de Estudiantes Secundarios and the Confederacion General Universitaria.

[21]Gillespie (1982). See especially chapters 1 and 2 on the evolution of the youth from the original catholic nationalism to the left, from the '50s. onward. The name "Montoneros" came from informal militias used by provincial strongmen and governors in the XIX century.

[22]Oro alla Patria was a manifestation of national character, organized by the fascist regime, which took place in Italy December 18, 1935, during which the Italians were called to donate to donate their wedding rings in order to support the costs of war and cope with the difficulties of sanctions. Iron wedding rings were used instead.

is confused with a political party, the party takes the colors of the national flag as is the case pale blue and white with a rising sun of Peron in Argentina, Vargas in Brazil uses the green as a party color, in Mexico the PRI takes both the name of the Mexican revolution and uses the national colors as the party's.

7 The Myth of Progress Against Capitalist Individualism

7.1 The Evolution from the Reactionary Thought to Modern Neocorporatism

Corporatism is the distant heir of a long tradition of political thought which originated as an attack to the American and French revolutions, and based in the impossibility of rationalizing political power. These enemies of the revolutions, that considered impossible to submit governments to an abstract logic since the equilibrium of societies and its prosperity could only be found in the respect of traditions and in the safeguards of their historical originality, were called *Reactionaries*. The elegant pages of Joseph de Maistre[23] and in the dogmatic ones of the Viscount de Bonald[24] and Juan Donoso Cortes,[25] would influence nationalist thought through the XX Century both in Europe through Gaetano Mosca[26], Charles Maurras[27] and a number of nationalist writers particularly active from the '30s to the '60s in Latin America.[28] James Burnham,[29] an American writer very active in the in the middle of XXth. Century had also readers in Latin America.

The answer to the 'social question' made by Fascism was the theory of the corporations and its movement was corporatism, 'corporativismo'. The XXth

[23]See Particularly the Study on Sovereignty p. 93 and The Saint Petersburg Diaries p. 183. Cioran (1992, p. 22).

[24]Vicomte de Bonald 1796.

[25]Cortés (1837). In his Political Theology (1922), Carl Schmitt devotes large portions of his final chapter ("On the Counterrevolutionary Philosophy of the State") to Donoso Cortés, praising him for recognizing the importance of the decision and of the concept of sovereignty. He also influenced Georges Sorel.

[26]His book Elementi di scienza politica published in 1896, was translated as The Ruling Class, he is credited as the developper of the theory of elites. He influenced american authors as Seymour Martin Lipset, C. Wright Mills.

[27]See Maurras (1973).

[28]For the traditional nationalist thought see Marysa (1964). In the Spanish version Los Nacionalistas. Buenos Aires 1968, indicates the year 1964 as the date of the association between nationalists and Marxist militants. See also Rock (1993).

[29]James Burnham started being a Trotskyite and ended as probably the first neo conservative. His books widely translated and read in Latin America are: The Managerial Revolution: What is Happening in the World. New York: John Day Co., 1941. The Machiavellians: Defenders of Freedom New York: John Day Co., 1943, where he analyses the work of Gaetano Mosca, Sorel, Michels and Pareto.

century was hailed as the century of corporatism and was offered as a third path between capitalism and socialism and in such a way it was very attractive to trade unionists and labor leaders on the one side but also to both businessmen and the Catholic Church which were opposed to socialism. The corporations indicated a rejection of class warfare and the reunion of all 'productive activities' in a sole organization. Both the fear by trade unionists of Communist assailment of their organizations and also the evolution of Christian thinkers worried by social questions and willing to build a new Christian social order, accepted the new corporations. This was particularly fertile in Latin American nations and in Spain with the development theory of national syndicalism 'nacionalsindicalismo'. Corporatism social order required one trade union by activity and all these trade unions into one hierarchical central organization. As a mirror one centralized business association by activity was established and one 'economic confederation' which centralizes all business activities in the country. This structure is associated with of the intervention of the state in the economy following the economic regulation during World War I but popular also in nations that did not participate in the struggle. This paternal view of the state started probably by Bismarck, which established the National system of economy proposed originally by List.

Although it had a romantic mediaeval presentation with reference to mediaeval corporations in reality it was a completely modern institution structured to organize a trade union movement against socialism, industrialize the nation through a closed economy, and justify authoritarianism. The great moment of the social policy of corporatism is the *Carta del Lavoro* of 1927, which was a model of the legislation on the workers' labor contracts to governments as different as Franco in Spain, Petain in France, Getulio Vargas in Brazil and Peron in Argentina. The model is still applicable in South America. Mussolini defined his 'Carta' as an 'original provision to the evolution of humanity'. Strikes and lock out are symmetrically prohibited as is the case in the Argentine Constitution of 1949, where the right to strike was not included in the long description of workers' rights.

Surprisingly enough these nationalistic tones would have a leftist interpretation from the late '60s onward in South America, through an hybrid discourse that would unite nationalism and populism, using Marxist categories and indigenistic movements. Although applied to different circumstances the corporatist myths survive. It exalts nationalism, the nobility of family, the dignity of work or the circumstances that contained individual but eliminate individualism, inspiring a sentimental solidarity that unite all the members of the community. This 'moralizing effect' of corporatism has sometimes brought the sympathy and influence of the Catholic Church especially in the Catholic nations of Latin America. Some sectors of Catholic nationalists evolved into a leftist version from the 1950s onwards. Extreme examples of this could be found in the works of Ernesto Cardenal about Cuba,[30] and in the theology of liberation in the case of Leonardo

[30]Cardenal (1974), also Castro (1974). Cardenal a priest from Nicaragua he wrote this book in defense of the Cuban revolution. Pope John Paul II publicly chastised him in 1983.

Boff.[31] Apart from these extreme cases, more moderate versions that include the attack on individualism, the need of social equality, and the virtues of poverty could be widely found in political and religious thought in South America.[32]

In the corporatist organization to be a citizen is not the main form of representation of an individual, but it his or her activity in the social cells such as family and professional activity. It is at the interior of these cells then the individual takes its true significance, it is there he finds his role in society and consequently his rights. Therefore the organization of state should be based in those structures and establish a hierarchical organization. So a small company should enter the chamber of its trade, and then be part of a federation of similar business organizations and finally a confederation of all business activities. Professions should be organized in colleges or orders, and then federations of each profession. Each worker should be a member of a single trade union that includes all of those who work in the same activity, then Federation that groups the trade unions by branch of industry and finally a general confederation of Labor. In what was to be Peron's main discourse in political theory, his speech on the 'organized community' in the International Congress of philosophy in 1949 rejected individualism and proposed the creation of a new hierarchy.[33] He attacked individualism: "*The ultimate meaning of ethics is correction of egoism. The platonic idea that man and the community to which he belongs are in irresistibly mutual integration seems to us fundamental.*" And he proposed a third way between individualistic capitalism and Marxist collectivism.[34] On top of this hierarchy is the conductor, the leader.[35] In corporatism the individual wants revenge over that mediocrity of his condition and it is a medium to punish those who succeed in open competition. Conflict between workers and business continue but the national businessman is accepted as a national alternative to foreign companies and products. The corporatist theory of an 'organized community' is in obvious opposition to the spontaneous order. It is the case in Latin America where the cases of Vargas in Brazil and Peron in Argentina established the corporatist economic structure with consequences that survive to the present.

Individualism is condemned as a form of moral degradation and as an agent of political instability, personal freedoms only accepted as part of collective rights. Every person must acknowledge his place in society and not envisage personal progress over the rest of his or her equals. In Peron's words: *7. No Peronist should*

[31]Boff is a Brazilian Franciscan Priest and professor of Theology. See Boff (1987).

[32]For example the cover of the respected Catholic review Criterio stated in the Christmas number of 1976 'to learn to be poor' meant as a virtue. Criterio, Diciembre 1976, "Aprender a ser pobres". Buenos Aires.

[33]La comunidad organizada. Conferencia magistral del Excmo. Señor Presidente de la Nación, general Juan D. Perón, al cierre del Primer Congreso Nacional de Filosofía. Mendoza, 9 de abril de 1949.

[34]*El sentido ultimo de la ética consiste en la corrección del egoísmo.*

[35]Although corporatism can flourish without a formal leader, it could be a bureaucratic system that can survive the original creator. The possibility is rare but the case of Portugal with Oliveira Salazar is an example.

feel more than what he is, nor less than what he should be. When a Peronist begins to feel more than what he is, starts becoming an oligarch.[36] Dedication till death to the leader, the loyalty, is a virtue since he or she has the sagacity, the selflessness and the patriotism that legitimated the exercise of power. For example, the main political festivity in argentine Peronism is the 'day of the loyalty'.[37]

Corporatism inspires patriotism, national pride, the respect of national traditions and the reject to foreign ideology. It created a dialectic theory of national historic, for respect of leaders that fought against foreign intervention, as opposed to politicians who accepted and negotiated with foreign powers. The need of economic independence, throws against the domination of capital and foreign enterprises but also against the spiritual colonization of the intellectual elite. Imposes a dialectic struggle of "imperialism versus nation", where certain social classes represent the 'nation' opposing imperialism and their local allies.[38]

8 The Myth of Autarky, from List to Keynes

8.1 A Distant Mirror: Dictator Francia a Hero in Carlyle

The oldest reference of South American corporatism is a Paraguayan dictator José Gaspar Rodriguez de Francia, whose life was written by Carlyle, and published in the 4th volume of his Critical and Miscellaneous Essays published in 1840.[39] Apart from being brutal tyrant who ruled his country with an iron fist for 30 years he closed its frontiers to all external influence including all type of imports. He was a strict applicant of autarchy and is influenced lasted till the War of Paraguay or War of the Triple Alliance which lasted from 1865 to 1872 long after his death in 1840. Carlyle considered him one of his models of hero in the same standing as Cromwell. Luis María Drago a Foreign Minister and creator of the Drago doctrine translated Carlyle's essay into Spanish, it was published in Buenos Aires in 1905.[40] In Argentine nationalist authors Paraguay was considered as a distant originator of the theory of substitution of imports and successfully created some military industrial organization.[41]

---

[36]The seventh of the Twenty Peronist Truths says: *7. Ningún Peronista debe sentirse mas de lo que es, ni menos de lo que debe ser. Cuando un Peronista comienza a sentirse mas de lo que es, empieza a convertirse en oligarca.*

[37]Día de la Lealtad, October 17th, after the popular movement in 1945.

[38]Cooke (1972, p. 27). Also Gillespie (1989, p. 32).

[39]Carlyle (1857). Dr. Francia, p. 249.

[40]Carlyle (1905).

[41]For example Jose Maria Rosa who wrote eight volumes of Argentine History finalized in 1980 and is an intellectual transition from the traditional Catholic nationalism to populist corporatism. Francia is best described in the novel by Bastos (1985). English version: 1986.

8.2 List: The National System of Economy

In "The National System of Political Economy", Friedrich List addresses the differences between the political economy of a nation and a "cosmopolitical economy" of the earth. List rejects the earth-wide approach as impractical. While agreeing that in a confederation of all nations, the principle of international free trade would be justified, List points out that such a confederation does not yet exist. Given contemporary conditions in the world, he fears that free trade in manufactured products would lead to "*a universal subjection of the less advanced nations to the supremacy of the predominant manufacturing, commercial, and naval power*" (i.e., Great Britain). Thus, List condones the use of protection to develop the national economy until all nations reach the same stage of industrial development. Then, a union of nations would be positioned to promote "true freedom of trade," he theorizes.

List's denunciation of the British politicians and economists of his day (the latter being intellectual forebears of the neoclassical school) is worth quoting at greater length:

> It is a very common clever device that when anyone has attained the summit of greatness, he kicks away the ladder by which he has climbed up, in order to deprive others of the means of climbing up after him. In this lies the secret of the cosmopolitical doctrine of Adam Smith, and of the cosmopolitical tendencies of his great contemporary William Pitt, and of all his successors in the British Government administrations. Any nation, which by means of protective duties and restrictions on navigation has raised her manufacturing power and her navigation to such a degree of development that no other nation can sustain free competition with her, can do nothing wiser than to throw away these ladders of her greatness, to preach to other nations the benefits of free trade, and to declare in penitent tones that she has hitherto wandered in the paths of error, and has now for the first time succeeded in discovering the truth.[42] (List 1841, 295–296)

As Friedrich List argued, "the principle sell manufactured goods, buy raw materials has been the substitute for a theory [of growth] in England for centuries" (1841, Preface). List was a direct influence on the "Dependency Theory" sustained originally by Raul Prebisch and developed by Cardoso and Enzo Faletto 1969.[43] "Dependency theorists" argue that different "situations of dependency" exist and that the exact nature of dependency depends on the nature of alliances between governmental elites and foreign capitalists and other prominent economic and political groups in the society. Although it has wider scope it emanates from the economic theories by Friedrich List. At its core, this theory submits that the world capitalist economy is a resultant of the domination by a few countries ("The Center") over most of Africa, Asia and Latin America ("The Periphery"). They contend that the "Center" has dominated the "Periphery" by employing various tactics and strategies including the formulation of an international division of labor

---

[42]See also Chang 2002, pp. 19–51, 59–66), also see Henderson (1983).

[43]It must be said that when President of Brazil Fernando Henrique Cardoso, acted in a much different manner that what his book promoted.

(starting from the 16th century) in which countries of the "Periphery" were "condemned to agriculture." Thus, the "Periphery" was prevented from attaining industrialization and remained in the capacity of supplier of primary products. '*The result of general free trade would not be a universal republic, but, on the contrary, a universal subjection of the less advanced nations to the supremacy of the predominant manufacturing, commercial, and naval power...*' "*Globalism is thus the product of unilateral parochialism.*" Suzuki (2001).

8.3 Keynes Through Prebisch: The Closed Economy

The great theorist of economic autarky en Latin America is Raul Prebisch, although his own intellectual work had a paramount influence in the continent for many years, he also played an important role as the introductory of Keynes. The influence of Keynes in Latin America was due to his book Introduction to Keynes. Prebisch did appreciate the importance of Keynes' theoretical framework but he was not convinced that it was adequate for what he called 'the periphery'. In 1947 he published his "*Introducción a Keynes*",[44] the small book was an instant and lasting success because it was the first introduction of Keynes in Spanish. This introductory work led local economists and politicians to read the General Theory and many were particularly attracted to the last chapter of Keynes' General Theory, *Final notes about the Social Philosophy...* which is easier to read than the previous parts of the book and has a clear normative instruction on economic policy. This chapter 24 had a vast influence in Prebisch and was at the origin of his theory of 'peripheral capitalism', especially in both the substitution of imports[45] and in the 'euthanasia of the rentier'.[46] It would be unfair to call Prebisch authoritarian since he was a victim of political persecution and expelled from his country by Peron in 1948, (Dosman 2008, p. 228). Nevertheless his doctrine on the substitution of imports and the declining terms of trade in the international system were central in the justification of autarky in Latin America.

---

[44]Prebisch (1948). See also Dosman (2008).

[45]Probably the most quoted phrase written by Keynes is '*But let goods be homespun whenever it is reasonably and conveniently possible, and, above all, let finance be primarily national.*' in Keynes (1933, pp. 755–769).

[46]Krugman (2006) says: *Book VI, at the opposite end of The General Theory, really is a kind of dessert course. Keynes, the hard work of creating macroeconomics as we know it behind him, kicks up his heels and has a little fun. In particular, the final two chapters of The General Theory, though full of interesting ideas, have an impish quality. Keynes tells us that the famous victory of free trade over protectionism may have been won on false pretenses—that the mercantilists had a point. He tells us that the "euthanasia of the rentier" [376] may be imminent, because thrift no longer serves a social function.* One cannot really blame third world politicians of being of being mercantilists if protectionism is sustained by both a historic economist like Keynes and a Nobel laureate like Krugman.

9 The Myth of Industrialization, the Creation of a National Bourgeoisie and the Iron Law of Oligarchies

In the new versions of corporatism and particularly in developing nations the idea of elites is established especially in the building of a national bourgeoisie that will allow the growth of an industrialized and independent economy. The rents obtained by industrial business and the subsequent inequalities are accepted as a condition to create the national bourgeoisie that will develop enterprises opposed to foreign rivals. The national bourgeoisie was defined within dependent countries is the sector or the bourgeoisie that owns the industrial means of production whose interests are antagonistic to foreign capital. In a nutshell, corporatist economic theory requires the existence of a true National Industry with a strong domestic market and a government in control of the economy (Sergio de la Peña 1976, pp. 167–170).

9.1 Pareto's Theory of the Circulation of Elites

In his book "The Machiavellians" American writer James Burnham associates the thought of Gaetano Mosca, Georges Sorel, Robert Michels and Vilfredo Pareto, as all being disciples of Machiavelli. Pareto describes the theory of elites and that political changed is basically our circulation of elites; Michels described the iron law of oligarchies, finally Sorel explained the role of myths in providing a unifying force for political action, particularly referring to a general strike. The political struggle invariably results in a minority coming to power monopolizing as much as possible political, economic and military power excluding and oppressing the rest. The rule of elites in human societies is inevitable and therefore an oligarchy is the only possible distribution of power through the iron law. Although one elite may loose its supremacy sooner or later another minority takes its place through what Pareto calls the circulation of elites, thus establishing an unending rise and fall of ruling minorities.

In his '*Traite de Sociologie Generale*' Pareto describes the circulation of elites, whereby new elites "*rise up from the lower strata of society, mount up to the higher strata, flourish there, and then fall into decadence,*" *as* "*one of the motive forces of history*" to which due weight must be given "if we are to understand great social movements." From a leftist indeed Marxist perspective, T. B. Bottomore emphasizes Pareto's and Mosca's concept of the elite:

> In every society there is, and must be, a minority which rules over the rest of society; this minority–the "political class" or "governing elite", [is] composed of those who, occupy the posts of political command and, more vaguely, those who can directly influence political decisions…

These conceptions strongly influenced the traditional corporatist thought because they described and justified the failure of parliamentarism and democracy.

Nevertheless the 'iron law' is also associated to the new forms of populist corporatism. Because it describes modern democracy as a form of disguised oligarchy not fundamentally different from earlier kinds of elitism and therefore a justification of a political system created to oppress the 'people' and therefore could be replaced by a different and populist elite.

In this view elites are an inherent part of social and political organization, elites do not hold power simply through force and intimidation but through doctrines that rationalize or justify their control into logical, moral or even theological terms. Their purpose is not to express or explain reality in a way that can be proved or disproved but to offer rationality for the existence and power of the dominant elite. Elites must always invent their own validating myth. Institutions inconsistent with the perceived interest of an elite are abolished or changed while those that are consistent with its perceived interest are created or promoted. Politics is seen in terms of struggle for power, and the struggle for power is central to the nature of new elites or to the consolidating of existing ones when they are challenged. This struggle creates a form of political determinism, it is the will of the people or the wheels of history that impose the rule of the existing elite.[47]

Pareto developed a psychology of elites that is at the root of the theory of the circulation of elites. But he distinguished between derivations or ideologies that we can call myths and residues that are constant as universal psychological instincts or impulses. Among the six classes of residues of the most important were the class I, the instinct for combinations and class II association with other systems.

Class I residues include behavioral patterns such as philosophical development and financial manipulation. This type of class are elites that exhibit intellectuals and administrators and would try to preserve their own power through discourse and administrative behavior. Class II residues tend to sustain and perpetrate existent combinations and are sociologically conservative. They would use groups like the family, church or nation to consolidate their power. These differences indicate also a variation between the conservative elites of class II represent the more traditional forms of corporatism against the more intellectual and discourse driven versions nearer populist corporatism. In the second group could include leadership oriented corporatism and the name of Mussolini comes easily to the mind, but also the bureaucratic way of corporatism which could also mean a very strong leadership and brutal repression, and the name of Salazar could be considered a good example. In the first group where the leads are more driven to discourse the corporatist populist regimes could be included. First is the case of Vargas in Brazil and Peron in Argentina, but even more connected to a more sophisticated political discourse are the new forms of populist corporatism both in South America and Europe in more recent times.

The main criticism to the theory of elites in Pareto is that elites prevent innovation and dynamism in the economy. Since we cannot imagine what new

---

[47]The term "wheels of history" (*ruedas de la historia*) was used by Fidel Castro to define the triumph of the revolution.

commercial products would appear and therefore cannot plan their appearance, the existence of elites is necessarily conservative and a source of economic stagnation. The maintenance of present day elites is contrary to the spontaneous order, since the mere existence of elites supposes that innovations can only occur in their midst and that is of course a strong limitation to economic dynamism. The existence of the new elites that would appear out of the spontaneous order would be limited and fought by the existing elites. And this is a problem both to the conservative theory of elites in Mosca and Pareto, as to the more recent theory of populist elites.

James Burnham proposed the managerial class as the rising elite. This new leading group would include the production executives and organizers of the new industrial processes, the officials trained in the manipulation of the great labor organizations, and administrators, bureau chiefs and commissars developed in the executive branch of the unlimited modern state machineries (Burnham 1943, p. 232). This managerial elite composed by the leaders of great organizations leaves little place for innovation and dynamism.

9.2 The Iron Law of Oligarchy

Giving a further twist to Pareto's idea of the circulation of elites Robert Michels in his 1911 book, *Political Parties* indicates that rule by an elite, or oligarchy is inevitable within any organization as part of the "tactical and technical necessities" of organization, this inevitability expresses an "iron law". Michels particularly addressed the application of this law to representative democracy, and stated: "*It is organization which gives birth to the dominion of the elected over the electors, of the mandataries over the mandators, of the delegates over the delegators. Who says organization, says oligarchy.*" Michels indicated that the avowed objective of representative democracy of eliminating rule by elites was impossible, that in reality representative democracy is a disguise of legitimacy to the rule of a particular elite, but the rule by oligarchic elites is unavoidable.

Therefore there is an inherent tendency of all complex organizations, including radical or socialist political parties and labor unions, to develop a ruling group of leaders with their own personal interests rather than what is publicly announced. These leaders desire leadership and its status and rewards more than any commitment to goals. Inevitably, their influence was conservative, seeking to preserve and enhance the organization and not to endanger it by any radical action. Michels based his argument on the observation of the behavior of the leaders of the German Social Democratic Party in the times of Imperial Germany. The professional full-time leadership required in the management of the most important opposition party with vast representation throughout the German Empire, with many working class members, required a ruling oligarchy even in a popular party. In theory the leaders of the organization were subject to control by the mass membership, through delegate conferences and membership voting, but, in reality, the leaders were in the dominant position. They possessed the experience and expertise in running the organization, they came to control the means of communication within the organization and they monopolized the public status of representing the organization. It became difficult for the mass membership to provide any effective counterweight to this professional, entrenched, leadership. Michels also argued that these inherent organizational tendencies were strengthened by a mass psychology of leadership dependency, he felt that people had a basic psychological need to be led.

> society cannot exist without a ...dominant... or... political class, and that the ruling class, while its elements are subject to frequent partial renewal, nevertheless constitutes the only factor of sufficiently durable efficacy in the history of human development. [T]he government, or, ... the state, cannot be anything other than the organization of a minority. It is the aim of this minority to impose upon the rest of society a "legal order" which is the outcome of the exigencies of dominion and of the exploitation of the mass ... Even when the discontent of the masses culminates in a successful attempt to deprive the bourgeoisie of power, this is ... effected only in appearance; always and necessarily there springs from the masses a new organized minority which raises itself to the rank of a governing class... (Michels 1915, pp. 353–354)

10 The Myth of Politics as the Dialectics of Friend-Enemy

There is a paradox in the corporatist theory of the state, first it proposes the idea that the state is magnified to the point that it represents the common good and therefore should not subject to constitutional limitations. At the same time the state itself is limited by the political process, without any institutions outside the mere exercise of power by the government, only the struggle between friends and enemies. The power of the state is not limited but it is also without the justification of the constitutional institutions. This reduction of the state to distinction between those who govern and to those who obey is outside the limits of constitutional government. Carl Schmitt established that the theory of government is the difference between command and obedience, a few who command and many who obey. Politics is understood as the 'science of command', and '*command and obeisance are the essence of politics, we can't protest against the inevitable*' (Freund 1981, p. 104). "*Only one person or one will is given the power to command.*" It is impossible for a law or a principle to command, and also for a number or persons, especially for a great number of persons. "*Without obedience the order is pure desire, to obey is to receive an order and execute it*" (Julien Freund. Id, p. 155).

In this corporatist political theory political debate is the opposition between friend and enemy. This dialectical relation between friend and enemy is the 'essence of politics' in corporatist political theory.[48]

[48]The titles of the chapters in Julien Freund. L'Essence du politique. 1981, are very eloquent. Chap. III, Le Commandement et l'obeissance, p. 101. Chap. VIII, La dialectique de l'ami et de l'ennemi: la lutte, p. 538.

For Carl Schmitt the act of distinguishing between friends and enemies was the essence of the political (Schmitt 1996). He recognized that collectivities have external friends ('allies') and enemies. The ally is important because he can provide not merely material support but also recognition and legitimacy. The enemy is the 'other', which a collectivity 'potentially' fights. The word 'potentially' indicates that for Schmitt the political does not reside in armed struggle itself—let alone in glorifying war—but 'in the mode of behavior which is determined by this possibility', by the ever-looming possibility of armed conflict.

While we delimit the political in a way indebted to Schmitt, we also deviate from his understanding of politics in an important respect. For Schmitt, the friend-enemy distinction constitutes the essence of the political—it signifies what politics is. Our reading of the political is less essentialist: there is more to politics than friend-enemy distinctions, for example the organization of the polity or the art of bringing a political community together. Jürgen Habermas considers that the friend/enemy distinction is an instrumental tool for politics rather than a theory, a strategic position that resonates all too well with Schmitt's Nazi sympathies and opportunistic political adventures.

Carl Schmitt argued that the fundamental distinction on which political life rests is that of friend and enemy. The enemy is "the other, the stranger; and it is sufficient for his nature that he is, in a specially intense way, existentially something different and alien, so that in the extreme case, conflicts with him are possible." As for the friend side of the equation, the "us" in a democratic polity, Schmitt argued that homogeneity was crucial and necessitated—"if the need arises—elimination or eradication of heterogeneity."

10.1 The "Anti" Character of Corporatism

The ideology of corporatism is an anti movement. It defines itself that the things against which it stands. Anti-individualistic, anti greed, anti-bourgeois, antidemocratic authoritarianism in combined with strong populist appeal. If traditionally fascism was viewed as strictly anti communist, the latter versions are not generally anti- Marxist, on the contrary it uses Marxist discourse to justify some policies, is not anti-proletarian and has a certain ambivalence vis-à-vis religion. The new forms of corporatism are not the consequence of a war, be it a defeat in the international one or a civil conflict. The epic of corporatism includes the struggle for industrialization, national development, and the need to defeat individual greed in order to build a more equal society. The anti-positions of corporatism on their own are not sufficient to define the phenomenon, they are certainly decisive in its capacity to attract a following but they probably would not be sufficient to its evolution if they had not been combined with other characteristics.

If fascism was anti-rationalist and anti-intellectual, the new forms of corporatism can have an intellectual justification through the new forms of the justification of emotion, epics, and struggle against the common enemy. It continues the idea of the foundation of a new a right age but with some differences, if in traditional forms of corporatism the state was to go back to some form of medieval times with honor, chivalry, respect of religion in military courage; this new age is more associated with the struggle of the productive classes including workers and "national businessmen" against and to eliminate the parasites of society. It is a fight between the real economy against the speculative economy.

10.2 The Opposition to Parliaments and Political Parties

Corporatism was traditionally established in opposition to parliamentarism and political parties against the oligarchy and professional politicians who controlled those institutions. The idea that political parties did not represent the "people" but were controlled by corrupt local chieftains who manipulated elections which produced it that is heavily dependent on the government that had made possible their election. The first corporatist writers like Pareto or Gaetano Mosca came from societies that had very underdeveloped political systems. It came to Latin America were the influence of political leaders, including local political leaders on Parliament or Congress remains to this day even after great social changes. For that reason the criticism of Carl Schmitt to parliamentary and is still read and followed in South America. Corporatism is an ideology of concertation and agreement between powerful political, business and social sectors and stands against competition, both economic competition and political competition in a constitutional system. The terms used in corporatism are "struggle" between the "people" and the "rest". Inside the field of the "people" there is this agreement, organization, following of a leader, outside this field is the "enemy', imperialism and its "neoliberal" followers. There are of course psychological characteristics before the appeal of corporatism special in particular social groups like students, workers, intellectuals, which tend to rationalize the lack of appeal of capitalism in these societies. In many cases it is more a matter of style, of rhetoric, of action, than of ideas. An example is the defense of autarky, a defense by sectors that are damaged by it. A type of defense which is in a way metaphysic, associated with independence, industrialization, growth, social equality; in spite that he will benefit a fairly small group of industrial rent seekers.

Corporatism offers a new style in politics, new symbols, new rhetoric, new forms of action, new patterns of social relations, many of them taking from Marxist intellectuals that are left with our political leadership after the demise of the Soviet Union and other socialist countries. This new mixture of nationalism, populism, epic and youth is a fertile amalgam that tends to the new forms of corporatism. It has a strong romantic complement, an appeal to emotions and sentiments, to the love of adventure and heroism, the belief in action rather than words, elements not alien to the romantic nationalist movement of the 19th century in Europe and of the middle 20th century in Latin America, together with anarchism, that has attracted students and the Bohemian intelligentsia. It excludes personal development, considered individualistic and the creation of wealth, considered greed.

There is a misunderstanding surrounding the perception of corporatism whether it is right wing or left wing movement that sometimes creates sympathetic views in academic and political circles in developed societies that ignore its deleterious consequences. Corporatism is an economic policy more active in less developing societies, although its influence is felt throughout. It proposes an economy of economic controls which is associated with left-wing governments. At the same time the denial of parliamentarism, freedom of expression, political pluralism and the promotion of rent seeking is a characteristic of right wing thought. Although it would seem irrelevant and in some point of pure intellectual fantasy, a leftist image is very useful to attract popular public opinion. That attraction would be impossible if corporatism was correctly perceived as a conservative movement that favors and gives privileges to businessmen. Corporatism economic policy is associated with national aspirations thwarted by the failures in industrialization and periodic economic and financial crises. The modernization of the economy, which is the avowed objective of corporatism, is an intensely nationalistic one in which goals as self-sufficiency and industrialization receive the highest economic priority. For corporatism the model worker is an industrial worker and the favorite businessmen is that who creates factory intensive in the use of manpower. And it favors the existence of protected oligopolies that would create employment within the formalities of the legal labor contract. One of the characteristics of corporatism is this idea of the stability of employment and that the separation of a worker from an enterprise should be compensated by the owner. This was the principal of the Italian *Carta de Lavoro* and continues as the ideal form of labor contract to this day.

11 The Exhaustion and Revival of the Corporatist Organization of Labor

11.1 Obligatory Collective Agreements Between Trade Unions and Business Organizations

Collective negotiation extends beyond the single factory. If a group of employers of a certain area bargain a level of salaries with their employees, how could workers of another factory, even of the same area and the same productive branch, secure the same wage? And also within the same factory: is a collective agreement signed today binding for individual contracts concluded tomorrow? The Italian literature is accustomed to call "subjective" the effect in the scope of the agreement, and to call "objective" the effect to the relationship between the collective agreement and the individual employment contract.

The dual issues of the *erga omnes* effect[49] and the problem of the so-called "inderogability" had been settled by the corporatist system through the denial of

[49] A Latin term literally meaning "against all", it indicates that the contracts are obligatory even to those that did not agree to them or signed them.

trade union freedom. Thus, the Constitution had to reconcile freedom of association with the described effects of collective agreements. It guaranteed the *erga omnes* effect while leaving the resolution of the ensuing questions to the legislature.

These last rules can also be considered a buttress for freedom of association. It might have been the case that a plurality of registered unions would have resulted. But, because only one collective agreement can bind all those it purports to govern or affect, which of the many registered unions would have been authorized to bargain and sign it?

Like many others questions, corporatist labor relations leaves this problem in a great way unresolved. These are institutions developed for authoritarian regimes and cannot easily be translated into the competitive and democratic.

11.2 Corporatism in the International Labor Organizations

The International Labor Organization has established in the international scene a corporatist structure, ensuring that employer and worker representatives share in standard-setting alongside government representatives. This corporatist arrangement, probably understandable when the ILO was created in 1919, continued in the formulation of European Community social policy that has a predominantly bipartite process of social dialogue between management and labor. Despite significant differences in approach, both organizations give priority to the participation by trade unions and employer representatives within designated bargaining structures ostensibly designed to achieve some balance in their relative influence.[50]

In national and transnational systems representatives of business and trade unions have privileged participation in the creation of labor law. Labor law more than any other policy areas is where corporatist practices are more visible and still active[51].

Corporatism has developed in democratic societies following a contemporary legitimating discourse around the concepts of 'civil society' and 'civil dialogue'. This rhetoric is prevalent now not only in the ILO but also within European Union institutions. The participation of groups, the new 'corporations', may arise through forms of partnership and delegated power, such that those who claim a legitimate interest in the outcomes of a particular policy can shape its content. In this way the better-organized groups can impose their will against the least organized ones.

Corporatism also refers to policy creation through concertation. Within a corporatist structure, interest groups cooperate with each other and with public authorities in the articulation of interests, allocation of values and implementation of policy. The structural framework determines the magnitude to which benefits can be expected to derive from the process. It is often argued that unless the number of

[50]Falkner (1998), Lavdas (2005), Ottaway (2001), Smismans (2004), Yee (2004).

[51]Smismans (2003) and Compston (2003).

participants remains limited, bargaining becomes unmanageable, and that unless there is a hierarchical structure, binding commitments cannot be made. As part of the corporatist deal, business organizations and trade unions persuade, or more probably coerce, their members to conform to the agreed policies and permit to the agreed policies operate effectively. Hierarchical structures especially within trade union movements are critically important. Strong vertical integration ensures that union leaders are able to use wage restraint and industrial peace as bargaining tools, almost regardless of the individual views of their members. Corporatist pacts might provide a benefit for the state by serving to 'reduce uncertainty among competing elites' and by broadcasting 'an image of orderly cooperation to the citizenry at large'. There may also be potential for corporatist structures to lend credibility to the norms adopted. In other words, the ways in which particular interest groups are included in decision-making might afford not only performance, but also regime and polity legitimacy to the state.

Pluralism, unlike corporatism, envisages participation by a multitude of voluntary, competitive, non-hierarchically ordered and self-determined interest groups that do not exercise any monopoly of representation or special state endorsement.

It is possible to distinguish corporatism from deliberative democratic theory in at least three respects. Primarily, deliberative democracy indicates that policy-making should be responsive to groupings of all interests that spontaneously emerge within civil society, and like pluralism, calls into question the privileged representation of management and labor under corporatist structures. Moreover freedom of speech that guarantees the fundamental basic rights and the free exchange of views. Rather than reach a bargain, as they would within a standard corporatist framework, participants in the deliberative process are expected to debate beyond their own vested interests and prejudices. Finally, a deliberative framework of analysis would seem to cast doubt on the notion prevalent in corporatist theory that one should aim to provide a balance in bargaining power between management and labor. Within such a framework, it is arguable that bargaining power is irrelevant Habermas (1997, p. 36).

Although International and regional organizations, cannot exercise the same bureaucratic influence within transnational corporatism, as states do in relation to corporatism at the domestic level, some features of corporatism prevail.

Three key characters of corporatism are applicable to transnational governance:

(a) bureaucratic and hierarchical control;
(b) privileged access of management and labor to decision-making; and
(c) the importance of bargaining power to policy outcomes.

Corporatist structures depend on some degree of bureaucratic control. Within any corporatist structure, someone must select the participants and establish mechanisms within which they are provided with voice. The view taken of what amounts to balanced participation and the steps taken to achieve such balance will also be significant, as will the demarcation of subjects deemed appropriate for discussion. Any corporatist process also requires some degree of hierarchical control coordination within participant organizations, as regards the consultation of members, representation of members' views and communication to members of decisions reached. Without this organizational capacity, the process could not deliver policy outcomes. In these ways, bureaucratic and hierarchical controls play a role in transnational corporatism, even though it is limited.

The privileged participation of business organizations and trade unions in the making of labor law is most commonly justified in terms of performance. It is traditionally argued that Employer and worker representatives possess knowledge, expertise and experience that government officials lack. However, at a transnational level, the consultation that leads to any position being taken by employer or worker sides is on such a large scale that specific concerns are unlikely to be directly represented. The process offers no more than a general overview of commonly held views and accepted practices, practices that are going to be written into international law therefore with little possibility to be changed if new conditions, produced as a result of innovation, appear. The privileged access of business organizations and trade unions is also defended as an answer to the fear that without specific representation of workers' interests in the making of labor law, business might predominate. As an example of what happens when this sort of representation does not exist the activities of international financial institutions are generally mentioned (Morgan-Foster 2003, 643–646). The idea of a consensus in society to assemble all social forces behind a decisive purpose is widely mentioned in defense of both European and Latin American corporatism. A non-corporatist or pluralist vision raises two objections to this justification of a corporatist international structure: First, the illegitimacy for a state or international organization to identify those who should be allowed access to policy-making to the exclusion of others. Second, whether it is appropriate that business organizations and centralized trade unions should be afforded priority at the expense of other interested but much less organized groups, among them notably consumers and new innovative enterprises. The international tripartite structure in the creation of labor law is an obstacle to economic dynamism and innovation since a traditional business structure is crystalized in international regulations and limitations are imposed to new business forms and the creation of new products.

In the European Union the legislative process under the social dialogue has three distinct stages; a consultation stage, a negotiation stage and an implementation stage. Where business organizations and trade unions are privileged above other groups, at the same time the organizations requires a formal balance and equality of bargaining power (Novitz 2006).

12 The Economics of Regulation in Corporatism

Economic theory of regulation is primary an issue of pluralism. By pluralism, when interest group have certain common traits:

(i) The political arena is open for a multiplicity of conflicting interests that compete to deliver favorable policies;

(ii) Interest groups have no political status and the membership is voluntary;
(iii) The political process is characterized by external lobbying making the division between the public and the private realm distinct.

The neo-corporatist schools criticize pluralist explanations because the role for the state is too passive and neglect the influence that government exerts on the development of interest groups in society. This opposes the adversary political system of the United States and the more structured consensual political context of some European countries and even more so in Latin America. The strong elements of corporatism in these societies prevent the existence of pluralism and the development of economic dynamism. In corporatism selected private interest groups are given political status and take part in public policy-making, in law making and in the implementation of the law. Corporatist Governments chooses the economic winners in society.

In a corporatist state politicians and government officials offer regulatory benefits if interest organizations comply with the policies pursued. In this respect, ideologies play a significant function in determining political objectives, as is the establishment of the Welfare State or the industrialization of the national economy through the substitution of imports. Government officials pay for the interest groups' willingness to co-operate in fulfilling such political ends. The logic of collective action is then made dependent on interest organizations' ability to oppose and obstruct the implementation of these policies. Therefore the means usually important in the United States, such as campaign contributions, employment of party workers, have a lesser role. Additional provocative characteristic is that the power of collective action is generally invalidated by state actions in a corporatist system. Only interest groups invited, subsidized or created to take part in corporatist negotiations may have direct access to political influence. Corporatism techniques can then be used to alter organizations' bargaining power and strengthen particular interests such as disperse consumer interests. Moreover, corporatist institutions may result in cooption of organization representatives into the sphere of interests of government officials, entailing that the top of the hierarchy is detached from the groups they are supposed to represent. Corporatist structures of political bargaining reverse the capture process, making business or labor representatives into servants of state interests, in divergence with the interests they are supposed to legitimately represent.

References

Boff, Leonardo. 1987. *Introducing liberation theology*. Maryknoll: Orbis Books.

Burnham, James. 1941. *The managerial revolution: what is happening in the world*. New York: John Day Co.

Burnham, James. 1943. *The machiavellians: defenders of freedom*. New York: John Day Co.

Cardenal, Ernesto. 1974. *In Cuba*. New York: New Directions Publishing.

Cardoso, Fernando Henrique, and Faletto, Enzo. 1969. *Dependencia y desarrollo en América Latina: ensayo de interpretación sociológica*. Buenos Aires: Siglo XXI Ed. English translation.

1979. *Dependency and Development in Latin América*. California: University of California Press.

Carlyle, Thomas. 1857. Critical and miscellaneous essays, Vol. IV. In *Dr. Francia*, Collected and republished by Thomas Carlyle, 249.

Carlyle, Tomás. 1905. El doctor Francia. Traducción del inglés por Luis María Drago, Buenos Aires.

Castro, Fidel. 1974. En cristianismo y revolución.

Chang, Ha-Joon. 2002. *Kicking away the ladder: development strategy in historical perspective*. New York: Anthem press, 19–51, 59–66.

Cioran, E.M. 1992. Joseph de Maistre. An essay on reactionary thought. In *Anathemas and admirations*, 22. Palestine: Quartet Books.

Compston, H. 2003. Beyond corporatism: a configurational theory of policy concertation. *European Journal of Political Research*:787.

Gillespie, Richard, J.W. Cooke. 1989. El peronismo alternativo, 32. Buenos Aires: Cántaro.

Cooke, John William. 1972. *Apuntes para la militancia*, 27. Buenos Aires: Schapire Editor, Cambridge.

Cortés, Juan Donoso. 1837. *Marqués de Valdegamas*. Lecciones de derecho politico.

De Felice, Renzo. Mussolini, 7 volumes, 1965–1997 (Turin, 1965–97). Vol. 1, Mussolini il rivoluzionario, 1883–1920; Vol. 2, Mussolini il fascista, pt. 1, La conquista del potere, 1921–1925, pt. 2, L'organizzazione dello Stato fascista, 1925–1929; Vol. 3, Mussolini il duce, pt. 1, Gli anni del consenso, 1929–1936, pt. 2, Lo stato totalitario, 1936–1940; Vol. 4, Mussolini l'alleato, 1940–1945, pt. 1, L'Italia in guerra, 1940–1943, bk. 1, Dalla guerra "breve" alla guerra lunga, bk. 2, Crisi e agonia del regime, pt. 2, La guerra civile, 1943–1945.

De Felice, Renzo, Michael Ledeen, . 1979. Entrevista sobre el Fascismo. In Original version Intervista sul fascismo, ed. Michael Ledeen. Buenos Aires: Editorial Sudamericana.

Dosman, Edgar J. 2008. *The life and times of Raul Prebisch*. Montreal: McGill-Queen's University Press.

Duby, Georges. 1980. *The three orders: feudal society imagined*. Chicago: University of Chicago Press.

Elster, Jon. 1984. *Ulysses and the sirens: studies in rationality and irrationality*. Cambridge: Cambridge University Press.

Falkner, G. 1998. *EU social policy in the 1990s: towards a corporatist policy community*. London: Routledge.

Freund, Julien. 1981. *L'Essence du politique*, 104. Paris: Sirey.

Gillespie, Richard. 1982. *Soldiers of peron, Argentina's montoneros*. Oxford: Oxford University Press.

Habermas, Jurgen. 1997. *Between facts and norms*, 36. Cambridge: Mit Press.

Henderson, W.O. 1983. *Friedrich list, economist and visionary*, 1789–1846. Amsterdam: Psychology Press.

Keynes, John Maynard. 1933. National self-sufficiency. *The Yale Review* 22(4): 755–769.

Krugman, Paul. 2006. In his Introduction to the General theory of employment, interest, and money by John Maynard Keynes.

Lavdas, C. 2005. Interest groups in disjointed corporatism: social dialogue in Greece and European competitive corporatism. *West European Politics* 28(2):297.

Levine, Robert M. 1998. *Father of the poor? Vargas and his era*. Cambridge: Cambridge University Press, 81.

Levinson, Daryl J. 2011. Parchment and politics: the positive puzzle of constitutional commitment. *Harvard Law Review* 124:657.

List, Friedrich. 1841. The national system of political economy, (Trans. Sampson Lloyd), 295–296. London: Longmans, Green, and Company.

Marysa, Navarro Gerassi. 1964. *Argentine nationalism of the right: the history of an ideological development*. New York: Columbia University Press.

Maurras, Charles. 1973. Romantisme et Revolution. Realités. In *Oeuvres Capitales. Essais Politiques*. Paris: Flammarion.

Michels, Robert. 1915. *Political parties: a sociological study of the oligarchical tendencies of modern democracy*, 353–354. New York: Hearst's International Library Company.
Morgan-Foster, J. 2003. The relationship of IMF structural adjustment programs to economic, social and cultural rights: the argentine case revisited 24. *Michigan Journal of International Law* 577:643–646.
Novitz, Tonia. 2006. Assessing legitimate structures for the making of transnational labour law: the durability of corporatism. *Industrial Law of Journal* 35(4):367–394, 387.
Ottaway, M. 2001. Corporatism goes global: international organisations, nongovernmental organisation networks and transnational business. *Global Governance* 7:265.
Payne, Stanley. 1985. Falange, a history of Spanish Fascism. There is an Spanish version published in 1985, before it was prohibited in Spain.
Van den Hauwe, L. 2005. Constitutional economics. In *The Elgar companion to law and economics*, 224.
Vicomte de Bonald, Louis Gabriel Ambroise. 1796. *Theorie du pouvoir politique et religieux*, Vol. 3.
von Hayek, Friedrich. 1945. The use of knowledge in society. *American Economic Review* 35: 519.
Sergio de la Peña. 1976. Burguesía nacional y reproducción capitalista. Revista Mexicana de Sociología. Vol. 38, No. 1, 167–170, Jan–Mar 1976.
Bastos, Augusto Roa. 1985. Yo el Supremo. Editorial Sudamericana Buenos Aires. English version: I the Supreme. New York: Knopf 1986.
Perón, Juan Domingo. 2006. La comunidad organizada. Conferencia magistral del Excmo. Señor Presidente de la Nación, general Juan D. Perón, al cierre del Primer Congreso Nacional de Filosofía. Mendoza, 9 de abril de 1949. Instituto nacional "Juan Domingo Perón" De estudios e Investigaciones Históricas, sociales y Políticas Buenos Aires.
Posner, Eric A. 2011. *The executive unbound: after the Madisonian Republic*. Oxford: Oxford University Press.
Prebisch, Raul. 1948. *Introduccion a Keynes*. Mexico: Fondo de Cultura Economica.
Rock, David. 1993. *Authoritarian Argentina: the nationalist movement. Its history and its impact*. California: University of California Press.
Schmitt, C. 1996. *The concept of the political* (trans: Schwab, G.).
Schmitt, Carl. 1931. *Der Hutter der Verfassung*, published in Germany in 1931.
Schmitt, Carl. 1994. *Die Diktatur: von den Anfängen des modernen Souveränitätsgedankens bis zum proletarischen Klassenkampf*. Duncker and Humblot.
Schmitt, Carl. 2004. *Legality and legitimacy*. Duke University Press. Original edition Duncker und Humblot 1932.
Schmitter, Phillipe. 1974. Still the century of corporatism? *Review of Politics* 36:85 at 86.
Smismans, S. 2003. What is alive and what is dead in the theory of corporatism. *British Journal of Industrial Relations* 41:683.
Smismans, S. 2004. *Law, legitimacy, and European governance: functional participation in social regulation*. Oxford: OUP.
Sunstein, Cass. 2006. *Infotopia. How many minds produce knowledge*, 119. Oxford University Press, Oxford.
Suzuki, Eisuke. 2001. The Fallacy of Globalism and the Protection of National Economies. *Yale J. Int'l L.* 26:319, 321–22.
Towfigh, Emanuel. 2012. Old Weimar meets new political economy: democratic representation in the party state. *German L.J.* 13:237.
Wiarda, Howard J. 1997. *Corporatism and comparative politics: the other great "Ism"*. New York: M. E. Sharpe.
Yee, A.S. 2004. Cross-national concepts in supranational governance: state-society relations and EU policy making. *Governance* 17:487.

Growing-by-Unleashing Grassroots Entrepreneurship and Alibaba Innovations

Ying Lowrey

Abstract Inspired by Phelps' book (Mass flourishing: how grassroots innovation created jobs, challenge, and change. Princeton University Press, Princeton, 2013) and drawing upon Alibaba's experience, this paper discusses a small-business-based and digital-technology-driven new growth model—growing by unleashing grassroots entrepreneurship. Small business is an important expression of individuals' will, capacity, and aspiration to innovate. In the digital age, technology-driven platform can assist small business to thrive. From Alibaba's experience, building credibility and trust, providing open, transparent, efficient, and accountable finance services and establishing rules of games are crucial in the digital age for unleashing grassroots entrepreneurship and innovation that can bring sustainable mass flourishing.

1 Introduction

This paper was inspired by Professor Phelps' 2013 new book, *Mass Flourishing: How Grassroots Innovation Created Jobs, Challenge, and Change*. Phelps focuses on dynamism, innovation, and personal growth as well as economic growth. Innovation is "a new method or new product that becomes a new practice somewhere in the world." Dynamism is about people's participation in economic activities and "the will and the capacity and aspiration to innovate" (Phelps 2013, p. 19). According to Phelps, one way to measure dynamism is the inputs producing dynamism. Businesses that entrepreneurs start and operate embody such inputs. The pervasiveness of business is the base for generating dynamism and producing mass flourishing. A nation to have a high degree of dynamism must be full of small

Y. Lowrey (✉)
School of Social Sciences, Tsinghua University, Haidian, Beijing 100084, China
e-mail: Ying-Lowrey@tsinghua.edu.cn

L. Paganetto (ed.), *Achieving Dynamism in an Anaemic Europe*,
DOI 10.1007/978-3-319-14099-5_11

businesses providing the backbone of the economy. These owners of young therefore small business, with hope and expectation of growing larger, are major contributors to the dynamism of innovation.

The paper presents a new economic growth model—"Growing-by-Unleashing Grassroots Entrepreneurship" using Alibaba as a case study. Information technology has reshaped the world and people have had to change their ways of thinking and doing business. Confusingly, when the world was suffering from "too big to fail," beautiful "small" is "the new big." Free enterprise and free competition have become evermore important; and the prevalence of small business ownership and mass innovation have become ever more crucial to economic growth and people's economic wellbeing.

Alibaba started by 18 founders with an investment of 50,000 RMB in 1999 and grew into a 25,000-workforce giant valued at 936 billion RMB ($150 billion) in 2014. The reason for Alibaba's unusual growth was not mainly injections of large amount of capital or an exploitation of natural resources such as oil or coal. Alibaba has built a platform for innovation and created a market ecosystem that brings together over 10 million e-commerce vendor businesses, and that in 2013 alone created over 11 million jobs. This paper characterizes Alibaba's growth experience as "growing by unleashing grassroots entrepreneurship." Those unleashed entrepreneurs on Alibaba's platform have been putting goods and services on the market, servicing hundreds of millions consumers and improving people's lives.

The paper proceeds as follows. Section 2 reviews the importance of prevalence of small businesses. Section 3 provides a theoretical background for understanding the role of small businesses and technology in unleashing grassroots entrepreneurship. Section 4 examines how Alibaba created a mass of businesses and jobs. Sections 5 and 6 draw on Alibaba's experience and analyze the importance of credibility, trust and finance as well as market rules in unleashing grassroots entrepreneurship. Section 7 discusses issues appeared from Alibaba journey of growing by unleashing entrepreneurship. Finally, Sect. 8 concludes the paper.

2 From "Small Is Beautiful" to "Small Is the New Big"

Since later 1950s, when large-scale industrialization achieved unprecedented success, western economists—led by John Kenneth Galbraith—concluded that the United States had entered the era of big industry and that the traditional small business community no longer on Main Street. Further, by merely relying on government and the cheap products supplied by big industries, the American people would be able to enjoy their lives in an "Affluent Society."[1] Many scholars had opposed Galbraith's ideas and policy proposals, as well as his endorsement for the

[1]Galbraith (1958, 1967, 1973).

behaviors and stands of big business. In addition to the criticism from Nobel laureates such as Paul Krugman,[2] many scholars who believe in market and grassroots innovation and entrepreneurship proved Galbraith's ideas were factually incorrect.

Phillips (1958) in *Little Business in the American Economy* emphasized two important value of small businesses: (1) small business is "the backbone of the American system of free enterprise"; it "serves as a providing ground for new technologies and new, vigorous entrepreneurial talent." (2) The preservation of small business "is essential to the maintenance of the middle class" (p. 113–114).

Bunzel (1962) in *The American Small Businessman* pointed out that small business is as American heritage; the small businessman "appears to have few enemies and is, in fact, something of a national hero" (p. 13). He further noticed that "living in a country that places heavy emphasis on material success and pecuniary rewards, the small businessman had managed to be a symbol of success even in times when he has not … been financially successful" (p. 85–86).

In his world-awakening book in the midst of the Oil Crisis, *Small is Beautiful: Economics as if People Mattered*, Schumacher (1973) firmly believed in the "small" as basis to freedom, efficiency, creativity, joy, and enduring. He called for a "restructure [of] large-scale industrial ownership without revolution, expropriation, centralisation, or the substitution of bureaucratic ponderousness for private flexibility." In his view, "All the indications are that the present structure of large-scale industrial enterprise, in spite of heavy taxation and an endless proliferation of legislation, is not conducive to the public welfare" (p. 275).

Solomon (1986) in *Small Business USA: The Role of Small Companies in Sparking America's Economic Transformation*, claimed that "by injecting aggressive, free-market forces into a modern economy, small businesses permits the 'invisible hand' to play an important part in selecting those innovations upon which America will compete in the new global marketplace" (p. 140).

Blackford (1991) in *A History of Small Business in America* claimed that "From the time of Thomas Jefferson to the present, many Americans have seen the owners of small businesses as epitomizing all that is best about the American way of life." He noticed, "Small businesses have often received special treatment in state and national legislation" (p. 4).

Case (1992) in *From the Ground Up: The Resurgence of American Entrepreneurship* clearly saw "The economic stability that Americans once took for granted was gone. We could no longer count on big companies for what they used to provide." He envisioned that we "will need a highly dynamic business world, once characterized by high levels of innovation, technical progress, and entrepreneurship" (p. 224).

In the wake of the financial crises, the United States and European countries regained a sense of urgency to recognize the importance of small business. China shares this same sense of urgency. Under the unique circumstances after 1949,

[2]For example, Krugman (1994).

through the power of the state, China rapidly integrated its very limited resources, utilized large-scale industries, and rebuilt homes on its brutally trampled land. The heavy industry, large industrial and state-owned enterprises all have made undeniable contributions to the development of new China. However, due to the state economy's biggest setback—the lack of efficiency, let alone dynamism—China's economy was on the verge of collapse in the late 1970s. Thanks to the market mechanism, which unleashed long absent entrepreneurship, tens of millions of businesses created a very dynamic Chinese economy via market competition. Business number increased drastically from 348,000 in 1978, 7957,800 in 1990, to 60,623,800 in 2013.[3]

"Small is the new big" (Godin 2006). Big boxes, such as Wal-Mart and Home Depot once drove mom-and-pop stores out of main streets, are facing severe competitions from special niche markets and efficient e-commerce businesses. In nowadays, the successful big businesses are no longer the ones that are strongly associated with the Wall Street and the well-established supply chains internationally. Instead, those establishing platform and running two-sided markets, such as Google, Amazon, eBay and Alibaba, are the successful ones. The secrets of success in the platform economy are two folds: bringing together the most innovative grassroots entrepreneurs and creating a business territory by providing the best quality services. The small and micro enterprises that have the flexibility and vitality to face a constantly changing environment can either prosper or disappear in a drastic manner. Business as an expression of the willingness and capacity to innovate might either succeed or fail. However, the dynamism and innovation generated by a mass of entrepreneurs would agglomerate, proliferate, and spillover—thus creating the positive energy field for building a prosperous and strong society.

Small is beautiful because people matter. The U.S. Small Business Act states simply why "small is beautiful": "Only through full and free competition can free markets, free entry into business, and opportunities for the expression and growth of personal initiative and individual judgment be assured. The preservation and expansion of such competition is basic not only to the economic well-being but to the security of this Nation. Such security and well-being cannot be realized unless the actual and potential capacity of small business is encouraged and developed."[4]

"Small is the new big because small gives you the flexibility to change your business model when your competition changes theirs. … Small means you can tell the truth on your blog. … Small means that you will outsource the boring, low-impact stuff like manufacturing and shipping and billing and packing to others while you keep all the power because you invent something that's remarkable and tell your story to people who want to hear it. … A small law firm or accounting firm or ad agency is succeeding because they're good, not because they're big. So smart, small companies are happy to hire them. … A small restaurant has an owner who

---

[3]The 2013 business number is from http://www.chinanews.com/gn/2014/01-14/5734631.shtml.

[4]From *Small Business Act* as amended (1/13/13), http://www.sba.gov/sites/default/files/Small%20Business%20Act_0.pdf.

greets you by name. … A small venture fund doesn't have to fund big, bad ideas in order to put their capital to work. They can make small investments in tiny companies with good ideas. … Small is the new big *only* when the person running the small thinks big" (Godin 2006, p. 217–218).

3 A New Growth Model: Growing-by-Unleashing Grassroots Entrepreneurship

Economic theory defines economic growth and provides several economic growth models. Economic growth is the increase in the market value of goods and services produced by an economy over time. The conventional measurement is the percent rate of increase in real gross domestic product, or real GDP.

The classical (Ricardian) growth model describes production and growth in the agricultural era. Holding other variables constant and with no technological change, the theories of production and growth claim that increasing either of the factors of production (labor, capital, or land), will increase output, but at a diminishing rate that eventually will approach zero.

The neoclassical growth model is a product of the industrial revolution. In this model, labor-time, capital goods, output, and investment are all important; the law of diminishing returns to scale applies, but the role of technological change became crucial, even more important than the accumulation of capital. In this models, the long-run rate of growth is exogenously determined by either the savings rate (the Harrod–Domar model) or the rate of technical progress (Solow model). However, the savings rate and rate of technological progress remain unexplained.

Endogenous growth models strive to overthrow the "diminishing return to scale" and "steady state" dogma and incorporates "human capital"—the skills and knowledge that make workers productive. This model can explain the long lasting economic growth in many western nations. The model assumes human capital to have increasing rates of return. Overall, there are constant returns to capital, and economies can never reach a steady state. Growth does not slow down as capital accumulates. The research focus is on the determinacies that increase human capital (e.g. education and training) or technological change (e.g. innovation).

Phelps (2013) firmly believes that only sustained grassroots innovation can bring prosperity to the country.[5] Phelps does not believe in the explanatory power of either classical models that focus on the resources, or neoclassical models that emphasize on human capital or technological changes to the long lasting economic growth. He believes instead in the importance of economic dynamism, e.g. people's will, capacity and aspiration to innovate. Phelps quoted McKinsey's finding: from 10,000 business ideas, 1000 firms are founded, 100 receive venture capital, 20 go

---

[5]Professor Phelps defines "Dynamism" as "the will and the capacity and aspiration to innovate," Phelps (2013, p. 19).

on to raise capital in an IPO, and two become market leaders.[6] Massive participation in innovation is the key to nurture such market leaders for economic growth.

Lowrey (2003, 2005, 2006, and 2011) verified Phelps' idea about the role of dynamism to foster economic growth. Lowrey (2003) attempts to introduce the entrepreneur as the "economic man" into a neoclassical framework. The paper assumes the entrepreneur to behave as if he maximizes utility including his valuation of success and his desire to succeed, subject to an income constraint determined by his physical effort in subsistent production and entrepreneurial production. The paper also defines entrepreneurship as an "economic system" that consists of three components: (1) entrepreneurs who desire to achieve their goals of economic survival and advancement; (2) a societal framework that grants the entrepreneur's right of free enterprise; and (3) a government that has the ability to adjust the institutional framework that can protect each individual entrepreneur.

Lowrey (2006) further develops the 2003 idea about the entrepreneur. Focusing on entrepreneurial work, the paper challenges the neoclassical doctrine of the representative agent's utility maximization and borrows from the classical theory of the entrepreneur in the tradition of Max Weber and Joseph Schumpeter. From this classical tradition and evidences from data, the paper finds entrepreneurial work to be the intrinsic character of the entrepreneur. This paper divides the human work into "subsistence" production for standard products such as bread and butter, and entrepreneurial products and services such as iPhone, Google Map and Amazon.com. When assuming the representative entrepreneur to take pleasure in entrepreneurial work, the utility maximization requires a higher productivity of subsistence production than that of entrepreneurial production. The paper also develops a two-period and two-goods dynamic model that allows the inclusion of an initial capital to this representative entrepreneur's utility maximization problem. The model predicts that an additional unit of initial capital generates a substitution effect in the first period, but a complement effect that is positively associated with initial capital.

Lowrey (2005) asserts that people's economic well-being relies upon the strength of the economy and that behind a robust and balanced economy must be a vibrant market system, in which private business ownership is pervasive, small, and local. Using business/firm data and macroeconomic data from all 50 US states, this paper introduces a new concept—business density defined by the business number per unit of population. A spatial economic model and statistical testing demonstrate a significant correlation between business density and economic well-being at the state level. The paper estimates that increasing business density by one percent would respectively increase household income by 1.0957 %, personal income by 1.0178 %, and gross state product 1.2444 %. The estimated results also indicate that a higher business density is associated with lower poverty and disparity between the rich and the poor.

Lowrey (2011) distinguishes two kinds of jobs in the process of business creation. One is the "employment job" offered by an employer to an employee through

[6]p. 24 in Phelps (2013). U.S. Small Business Administration, Office of Advocacy released a report (2010) is a good example of such dynamism in the US.

a contractual (paid) relationship. The other is the "entrepreneurial job" created by active business owners for themselves. Only a small proportion of salaried entrepreneurial jobs are included in official employment statistics. To estimate the scale of entrepreneurial jobs, this paper examines mainly three databases: the Panel Study of Entrepreneurial Dynamics (PSED), the Kauffman Firm Survey (KFS), and the 2002 Survey of Business Owners (SBO). All three provide information in detail of both employment and business owners. In 2002, an average of 5.8 jobs (4.4 employment jobs and 1.4 entrepreneurial jobs) created by a startup employer firm and an average of 1.2 entrepreneurial jobs by a startup nonemployer firm. Each entrepreneurial job taker contributed an average of 33.1 labor hours per week to their startup firms. It estimates that at least 2.5 million people created their own entrepreneurial jobs every year between 1997 and 2008, in addition to creating more than one million paid employment jobs. The paper concludes that, to encourage job creation, policymakers need to recognize that startup business owners are creators of jobs for others, but most importantly, for themselves.[7]

Determined to become "China's greatest, most unique, 102-year-old company that exists across three centuries,"[8] Alibaba realized the need for ceaseless "routinized innovation" "in order to survive."[9] The "customer first" value does not need to be based on "altruism." Rather, it can be ecological characteristics of the e-commerce "platform economy" in the digital age.[10] From a subjective point of view, the philosophy of "customer first" guided the design a platform to bring together millions entrepreneurs for online business. Modern hardware and software enable Alibaba to use technological innovations and the economy of scale for developing a huge special customer-vendor base. This base consists of millions self-reliance, active, innovative, and dynamic businesses. Alibaba empowers a large number of grassroots entrepreneurs. The 7 million active vendors on Alibaba's platform not only created and developed their own businesses, but also fueled Alibaba's growth. In this process of empowerment and innovation spillover, Alibaba and millions of small and micro enterprises entered an interdependent and complementary relationship. Alibaba is a good example of growing by unleashing grassroots entrepreneurship.

4 Alibaba's Creation of Businesses and Jobs

Alibaba's creation of 25,000 jobs is not the whole story. Its retail e-commerce platform (Taobao.com and Tmall.com) alone brought together about 50,000 third-party e-commerce service-providing businesses for over 10 million registered

[7]An employer firm is a business with employees while nonemployer firm without.

[8]p. 14 Jin (2012).

[9]Please see Chap. "Trade Margins and Exchange Rate Regimes: New Evidence from a Panel Varx Model" in Baumol (2002) for the idea of "routinized innovation."

[10]Parker and Van Alstyne (2013). This is a good paper on the platform ecology system.

on-line retail sellers, of which, only 10 % paid a usage charge, the rest were free users on the platform.[11] These e-commerce and its service-providing businesses on Alibaba platform had created 11.76 million jobs.[12] In addition, Alibaba Group includes many other components such as the company's English language international marketplace for importers and exporters from more than 240 countries and regions.

Besides Taobao.com and Tmall.com that serve on-line retail businesses, Alibaba Group also consists of many internet and mobile related subsidiary business groups. For example, 1688.com is for B2B services; Alipay.com is for transactional payment and clearance; Aliloan.com is for micro lending services; Aliyun.com is for cloud computing service and data management; Alibaba.com is as leading global wholesale platform for small businesses; and Alixpress.com is as popular E-marketplace for international consumers.

There are key similarities and differences between Alibaba and its three American counterparties, i.e., Google.com, Amazon.com and eBay.com. Like them Alibaba uses the latest technologies, such as internet, big data, cloud computing and mobile communications, to serve its customers. However, Alibaba is not a reseller but rather provides a virtual marketplace for real economic activities. One might say that Alibaba provides a fishing platform and fishing poles to all who want to start fishing.

Alibaba became a household name in China not only because of the growing reliance on online retail and services, but more importantly because of Alibaba's unique small business vision—"to use the open nature of the Internet to level the playing field so small businesses could compete more effectively in national and global markets."[13] Following this vision, while enjoying remarkable growth, Alibaba enables people to develop online business as an expression of their creativity and unleashes grassroots entrepreneurship. In this digital age, a country can also enjoy long-term economic development via generating such dynamism nationwide.

Noting stagnant economies since the mid-1970s in the Western world, Professor Phelps inquires how to restart the economic system of "desire and dreams" that arose "the world's first modern economies." He boldly concludes that neither mercantilism nor the discoveries in science and the inventions that followed were reasons for "the take-off economies of Western Europe and North America" in the 19th century. Rather, these nations' "economic dynamism" and the resulting "indigenous innovation" made them "the marvel of the modern era" (Phelps 2013, p. 14).

---

[11] http://www.aliresearch.com/?m-cms-q-view-id-74973.html.

[12] Alibaba Research Institute 2013.

[13] http://news.alibaba.com/specials/aboutalibaba/aligroup/index.html.

Table 1 Alibaba e-commerce retail job creation by category, 2013

Category	Explanation	Number of employment (million)	Total (million)
Direct employment	Taobao.com platform vendors	9.27	9.72
	Tmall.com platform vendors	0.45	
Indirect employment	Alibaba online exchange service	0.01	2.04
	Supporting services (logistics, express delivery, payment and finance)	0.94	
	Other e-commerce services	1.09	
Total job creation			11.76

Source Alibaba E-commerce Retail Employment Research Report, November 2013, see Alibaba Research Institute, 2013.

While the world is still impacted by the aftershock of the 2007 financial crisis, Alibaba experience shows that, "economic dynamism" has been the reason for the marvel of China's economic growth since the end of 1970s.

Why Alibaba? Alibaba was created at the right time and in the right place. Alibaba was created at a time when entrepreneurship was a new concept in China; when it could apply rapidly evolving technologies to reach out to grassroots people at unprecedentedly low cost; when China was still backward enough that an industrial corporatism with special interests had not yet strongly and widely formed; and when China was open and flexible enough to combine eastern and western cultures. However, the reason why Alibaba had achieved so much is its deep belief in entrepreneurship with its core mission on "championing small businesses to help them achieve their dreams." Alibaba strives to "operate an ecosystem where all participants —consumers, merchants, third-party service providers—have an opportunity to prosper. Our success and rapid growth is built on the spirit of entrepreneurship, innovation, and an unwavering focus on meeting the needs of our customers."[14]

According to Alibaba most recent study using big data from the Taobao.com platform, Alibaba created 9.72 million direct employment in 2013, including 4.96 million employment jobs and 4.76 million self-employed jobs (Table 1). In fact, millions vendors on Alibaba platform business chose to "start and run their own businesses" already became a necessity, as well as a fashion. Alibaba platform provides the major or sole income for 42 % of Alibaba e-commerce vendors. Among all vendors, about 60 % of them had an associate or higher academic degree, near 90 % of them were below 35-year old, and more than 60 % of them were moonlighters who took e-commerce business as a second job (Table 2).

In 2011 Alibaba Research Center published the book *Light House for a New Path —The Alibaba's 100 Global E-commerce Business Vendors of 2011*, recording 100 entrepreneurial success stories (Alibaba Research Institute 2012). These cases show that Alibaba not only provided personal and household employment and livelihood, but also was associated with tremendous innovation and positive energy for society.

[14]http://news.alibaba.com/specials/aboutalibaba/aligroup/culture_values.html.

Table 2 Demographic information of Taobao.com e-commerce platform vendors, 2013

Education background		E-commerce business income nature	
College associate and above	59.7%	Sole income source	26%
High school (include associate)	30.9%	Major income source	16%
Middle school or below	9.4%	Not major income	58%
Multiple job?		Vendor's age group	
E-commerce business only	37.3 %	22-year old or below	7.2 %
Government employment	5.8 %	23–25	24.7 %
At school as student	3.4 %	26–30	35.7 %
Self-owned other business	22.4 %	31–35	20.8 %
Other's business employment	27.7 %	36–40	6.6 %
Farming	1.5 %	40–60	4.96 %
N.A.	1.9 %	Above 60	0.1 %

Source Alibaba E-commerce Retail Employment Research Dataset, 2013

Many college graduates or migrant workers returned to their villages and brought their knowledge, ingenuity, and curiosity to try new things, and experience in modern manufacturing and urban lifestyles. They led their fellow villagers to start e-commerce businesses, create a local economy, and establish a "Taobao village." Alibaba defines a Taobao village as a village where more than 10 % of local economic activity derives from e-commerce. So far, more than 20 Taobao Villages have been found nationwide.[15] These villages have become clusters using e-commerce as a driver for boosting the regional economy. A list of Taobao County are emerging; focusing on regional characteristics of Chinese organic food and other local products, China.taobao.com becomes especially popular.

5 Credibility, Trust and the Missing Microfinance Market

Credibility and trust are crucial to maintaining a functional economy with money, banking, virtual transactions, and extremely segmented productions and services providing. An efficient finance market can play an important role in assisting startup and operation activities of numerous small and micro businesses. However, in the era of financial capitalism, microfinance market was missing or imperfect, so were credibility and trust.

Using the concept of "invisible hand," Adam Smith's1776 book *The Wealth of Nations* laid out a solid theoretical ground for today's mainstream economics. Focusing on moral code or credibility, Smith's 1759 book *The Theory of Moral*

[15]Calum MacLeod, "Alibaba works magic for China's Taobao 'treasure hunters'," April 25, 2014 USA Today http://www.usatoday.com/story/news/world/2014/04/24/alibaba-china/8102033/.

Sentiments set norms for human behavior and the wellbeing of human life. The book should have been the ethical, philosophical, psychological, and methodological underpinnings of mainstream economics. Nevertheless, mainstream economics had ironically overlooked these important underpinnings.

"Greed is good" became a dangerous idea for 300-year, *The Fable of the Bees* by Bernard Mandeville in 1705 was some classroom relish; such a largely reviled story, later passed around in academia and Wall Street.[16] Smith expressed his strongly distained opinion in his 1759 book and in its later revisions of such a fable.[17] Unfortunately, this fable is still in lectures and winning applause in MBA and EMBA classes in China.[18]

There has been much written about human greed particularly in the financial sector. A financial "insider," former U.S. Treasury Secretary Timothy Geithner acknowledged this fact: "Most financial crises are caused by a mix of stupidity and greed and recklessness and risk-taking and hope", reported by Reuters on April 25, 2012.

Through reviewing annual reports and financial ratios longitudinally between 2004 and 2009, Alison Lui (2014) describes and compares the effects of the financial crisis 2007 on five UK banks.[19] The author examines two hypotheses: (1) banks moved from a customer-driven culture to a sales-driven one; (2) the banking culture during the 2004–2009 period was one of greed, recklessness, and dishonesty. The case study shows that there is evidence that both hypotheses are correct to a certain extent.[20]

The financial sector is important to economic development and growth, as pointed out by Shiller in his 2013 book, *Finance and the Good Society*. However,

[16]"'I think greed is healthy,' an apparent acolyte told the graduating class at Berkeley's business school in 1986. 'You can be greedy and still feel good about yourself.' The speaker was Ivan Boesky, who shortly thereafter would be fined $100 million, and later go to prison, for insider trading. His address was adapted by Oliver Stone as the basis for Gordon Gekko's 'greed is good' speech in Wall Street. An exhortation to shareholders of a sagging company, it reads like a corporate raider's war cry, with Gekko the grinning avatar of Agency Theory." See John Paul Rollert, "Greed is Good: A 300-Year History of a Dangerous Idea," *Atlantic*, April 7, 2014, http://www.theatlantic.com/business/archive/2014/04/greed-is-good-a-300-year-history-of-a-dangerous-idea/360265/.

[17]"Such is the system of Dr. Mandeville, which once made so much noise in the world, and which, though, perhaps, it never gave occasion to more vice than what would have been without it, at least taught that vice, which arose from other causes, to appear with more effrontery, and to avow the corruption of its motives with a profligate audaciousness which had never been heard of before." Paragraph 13, Chap. "Rebalancing and the Euro" in Adam Smith, *The Moral of Sentiments*, Sixth Edition (1790).

[18]p. 9 in Chinese version of *The Theory of Moral Sentiments*, SONG Deli translate, Yilin Publishing House, 2011.

[19]The five banks are Northern Rock, the Royal Bank of Scotland, Barclays, Lloyds Banking Group and HSBC.

[20]Lui (2014), http://www.palgrave-journals.com/jbr/journal/vaop/ncurrent/full/jbr20141a.html.

the "financial capitalism" that made the financial sector "too big to fail,"[21] also brought "the anger and resentment over executive compensation account for much of the public hostility toward financial capitalism in general."[22] These anger and resentment accumulated very negative sentiment in the society. For example, Americans are losing trust in all institutions, especially banks in the U.S. where the 2007 financial crisis started.[23] A Gallup poll in 2011 shows that more than 3 quarter of people in the poll did not believe in banks; but in the midst of financial crisis, about two third of them believed in small business. This poll reflected the international mood about the financial sector and small business.

Despite the popularity of small business ownership, microfinance has long been a missing market due to lack of collateral, credit record, and financial insurance of small business owners. These are two key ideas from Shiller (2012): (1) the finance sector ought to be about financing economic activities; (2) the financial sector is too concentrated so it must be democratized. Alibaba's Microfinance Service Group is a result of financial democratization.

Alibaba's financial innovations give hope to regaining people's confidence in modern finance. Aiming at unleashing grassroots entrepreneurship and financing economic activities, Alibaba microfinance services include: (1) establishing a payment system to build people's trust in e-commerce; (2) creating easy access to capital using a credibility based micro lending system; and (3) facilitating the public's wealth management based on individual preference and convenience.

Launched in 2003, Alipay strives to serve grassroots business and hundreds of millions online or offline consumers. Without charging transaction fees, Alipay provides online and mobile third party payment escrow service for more than 550 million registered users, about 8.5 million transactions daily. Alipay collaborates with more than 65 financial institutions including Visa, MasterCard and all national banks in China. Alipay also facilitates offline value-added services through strategic partnerships with China Post, which has coverage of rural areas and university campuses, and 24-hour convenience stores.[24] Alipay does not run credit card service, and operates in a manner similar to PayPal. The difference is that Alipay does not release payment until after the buyer actually receives the item.[25] In this way, consumer trust in the online purchase is created. China has not yet established a credit card system like that in the U.S. Alipay has successfully filled the gap between the backward credit system and advanced online retail system.

---

[21]Financial capitalism is "an economic system that is increasingly guided by financial institutions and that, in the wake of the severe financial crisis that began in 2007, appears to many to be broken." p. 67 in Shiller (2012).

[22]p. 21 in Shiller (2012), in which, Shiller mentioned the term "resentment(s)" 20 times.

[23]Ron Fournier and Sophie Quinton, "In Nothing We Trust: Americans are losing faith in the institutions that made this country great." http://www.nationaljournal.com/features/restoration-calls/in-nothing-we-trust-20120419.

[24]http://market.alipay.com/ospay/home.html.

[25]http://www.forbes.com/2010/01/18/china-internet-commerce-markets-equities-alibaba.html.

Traditional lending required borrowers to provide at least one of the following three: (1) solid collateral, (2) good credit record, or (3) sound insurance. Using the transaction records from Alibaba platforms such as 1688.com, taobao.com, and alipay.com, Alibaba's credit management team uses the big data processing and credit assessment techniques to classify credit lines for 300 million online business owners and other real-name registered online users; and creates an efficient credibility based financial system. The operational cost for processing an outstanding loan by traditional bank is about 2000 RMB; only 2.3 RMB by Aliloan.com. At the end of 2013, Aliloan.com provided micro loans to 642,000 borrowers, the accumulated outstanding loan had reached at 172.2 billion RMB (US$27.5 billion).The key characteristics of Aliloan.com service are three: small-amount, short-term, and flexible-maturity-date (http://www.aliloan.com/). Aliloan.com provides needed lending service to startups and online e-commerce small business entrepreneurs. Loans average about 13,000 RMB (US$2077) and 36,000 RMB(US$5751) per borrower.[26]

As a wealth management platform, Yu'ebao (in Chinese that means "leftover treasure") is another core innovation of Alibaba Microfinance Service Group. Established in June of 2013, Yu'ebao has become an attractive alternative to banks because it offers around 6 % in annualized return. In contrast, banks' demand deposits offer a paltry 0.36 %.[27] Up to January 31, 2014, Yu'ebao has accumulated around 350 billion RMB (US$56 billion) from over 58.95 million users.[28] Money market and fund management are not new to Chinese; the Alibaba innovation is nevertheless significant. Yu'ebao serves grassroots investors that the traditional financial sector has ignored. The characteristics of Yu'ebao are three folds: (1) simple procedure, (2) easy access, and (3) high liquidity. The cost of money market fund management is low due to highly adapted information and digital technology; ordinary, especially poor people can enjoy making their own choice between consumption and investment and gaining "return" from their savings. Many young people take their saving decision and the return to saving seriously. They would manage their fund and move any leftover cash into Yu'ebao as a last chore before getting to bed; they would check on their over-night return from computer or cell phone as first daily routine in the morning after getting up. Some even happily enjoy a nice breakfast because of the gain from Yu'ebao and view that as a free breakfast. Economic professors would never have imagined how the time preference theory and utility maximization theory could be so prevalent among ordinary people in China.

Alibaba's financial innovation apparently filled a market need in the prevailing financial capitalism world. Many great leaders, such as Mohammad Yunus, had made lifetime endeavor for establishing this market. However, this market can be

[26]Alibaba Microfinance Service Group Social Value Report (2014), p. 28–29.

[27]http://www.reuters.com/article/2014/03/20/china-banks-idUSL2N0MG0BV20140320.

[28]P. 6, Alibaba Microfinance Service Group Social Value Report (2014), "Internet Based Inclusive Finance Practice.".

facilitated only when new technologies available for eliminating the prevailing asymmetric information problem, and when transforming the monopolized financial sector. Alibaba's microfinance service innovation has had a profound impact on China's financial market, which is strongly controlled by the government. The negative spillover effect of financial crisis brought by Americans and the western nations on China is emerging. Slow growth, high unemployment, and declining export forced the government to implement limited financial democratization.

In addition to the third party guarantee system of Alipay and grassroots investment and wealth management, the most important contribution of Alibaba's financial innovation is the creation of a new format of human capital in the digital age—credibility. Relying upon a good record of credibility, one can obtain financial capital on Alibaba Microfinance Service platform for business startups and operations. Thus, modern technology can facilitate the microfinance market; and credibility can become an invisible moral standard guiding people's market conduct. Relying on the principles of openness, transparency, efficiency and accountability, finance sector will regain people's trust and become effective tool for unleashing grassroots entrepreneurship, supporting business operations, and encouraging mass innovation.

6 The Importance of Rules of Games

Baumol (1990) points out that entrepreneurship in a society could be productive, non-productive, or even destructive. The attribute of innovation in a nation depends on the political system and the incentive structure shaped by the society. Shiller (2012) addressed "Financial Capitalism" can be classified at least as "unproductive entrepreneurship." After the dot com bubble burst in the U.S., rather than studying high techs, or learning mathematics or sciences, a great number of world "best of the best" youth flooded into business schools and majored in finance. This is still the case in today's China. It reflects that there is an unusually high payoff structure for the financial sector.[29] There are two premises for unleashing grassroots entrepreneurship and promoting mass innovation: (1) it must change the unfair payoff structure; and (2) it must establish a set of rules that effectively build trust and credibility in the society.

Trust and credibility in a market economy were subject terms but now can be facilitated by digital technology recording people's conducts including transactions. Investing in most updated technologies, Alibaba has endeavored in setting up rules for promoting the efficiency of its platform, and the incentive structure for fostering a culture of productive innovations.

Alipay.com's third party guarantee in linking buyers and sellers has generated trust for the platform. The buyers can easily get on this two-sided platform and

[29]http://businessforecastblog.com/is-the-us-financial-sector-too-big/#.UkxKPcmS19A。.

make their evaluation on the services from sellers.The powerful computing system fully records the transactions of both sides, and can easily pinpoint to individuals who have broken rules, or cheated. This in turn places people to an invisible norm where being a player on the platform must follow rules and be credible. This invisible norm can greatly help to unleash productive entrepreneurship.

Aliloan.com employs the best workforce that can apply sophisticated mathematical models and computing algorithms, relying on its platform big data for screening-in those who are honest and credible, and screening-out those who cannot be trusted. Rather than maximizing profit, Aliloan.com makes tough decisions on using finance as effective tools to serve the grassroots entrepreneurs.[30] Lately, all Alibaba affiliated financial functions have merged in Alibaba Microfinance Service Group that clearly defines its serving customs and strives to assist small businesses.

In the present age based on modern technology, destructive internet and mobile businesses emerge constantly. In recent years, China's e-commerce big players such as Jingdong, Taobao, Dangdang, and Suning have been fighting in malicious blackmail incidents. These incidents included ill-intentioned orders, professional blackmailers, invoice complaints, and many other illicit online shopping activities. The evaluation system for online credit was designed to protecting the rights of the buyer, the seller, and the platform. When designing this evaluation system, the focus was only on the "expected" effects but not on the "unanticipated consequences." As a result, "the destructive innovation" seriously harm the reputation of sellers and badly hurt innocent parties. Although the e-commerce platform can adopt appropriate measures to prevent and combat illegal activities, it is still very important for the government to influence the direction of innovation by setting legal boundaries. Although e-commerce platforms are not law enforcement agencies, they can use the modern technology and big data to develop sounder incentive mechanisms for promoting good and eliminating or punishing bad behaviors.

To build a platform that can effectively govern the two-sided market as a third party, Alibaba has established its internal management and incentive systems to unleash the productive entrepreneurship and promote innovation amongst its employees. From recruitment principles, the Paten Wall (for posting names of people who applies patens), to the free-messaging board on restroom doors facing toilets, Alibaba's human resource department actively and carefully conducts initiatives to accumulate positive energy. At the same time, Alibaba resolutely cracks down on activities that are harmful to its ecosystem, corporate culture, and business principles. After verifying the fraudulent activities of a few thousand "China suppliers," Alibaba concluded that some of its B2B direct sales team employees had intentionally or negligently allowed the fraudulent companies to participate in Alibaba's platform. As a result, nearly a hundred sales personnel were held legally

[30]At a meeting with Jack Ma, the Chairman of Alibaba Group Holding Ltd., former general manager of Aliloan.com was very excited about the success of online lending. He suggested raising the ceiling of loan amount from one million to 5 million. Jack Ma responded, "If you dare to increase the ceiling, I will fire you right away!" The former general manager told this story in many occasions.

responsible. In accordance with company rules, penalties such as dismissal were imposed on these employees. Alibaba also decisively held its senior executives responsible. Both its internet network's CEO David Wei and COO Xuhui Li resigned.[31] In addition, to prevent rent-seeking activities which can be textbook case of unproductive entrepreneurship, Alibaba set up rules similar to that of the U. S. government, which regulates and prohibits government employees from receiving payments of illegal gifts or bribes.

7 Alibaba's Next 10 Years

Chris Anderson, the author of *Makers: The New Industrial Revolution*, predicted: "Here's the history of two decades of innovation in two sentences: The past ten years have been about discovering new ways to create, invent, and work together on the Web. The next ten years will be about applying those lessons to the real world" (Anderson 2012, p. 17). In the new age, "a maker movement" creates new challenges and opportunities to entrepreneurs: they can bring artisan's professional work ethic and innovation together, offer products with high-tech but low cost, with abilities to maintain a small scale but global production. "Killer app" and "3D Printing" are good examples of starting small and growing big (Anderson 2012, p. 16). Because of the nature of platform service, Alibaba can be such a "killer app." Tens of millions of "makers" connect to the platform. Taobao.com, Alipay.com, Aliloan.com and Yu'ebao all started small but got big. Despite all these successes, Alibaba has not been and should not be satisfied with what it has achieved so far.

Overall, U.S. e-commerce is the international front-runner. In 2011, U.S. e-commerce amounted to 49.3 % of sales in the manufacturing industry; 24.3 % in wholesale trade; but only 4.7 % in retail and 3.0 % in the service sector.[32] In contrast, China's e-commerce is extremely competitive in retail and service sectors. The former CEO of Alibaba's B2B platform David Wei recently said to CNN, "Unlike in the U.S., many small Chinese cities have not yet been penetrated by large retailers or brand products, which provides an opportunity for e-commerce in these cities to eventually become the mainstream retail mode."[33] While China is realizing goals of "new-four initiatives," one can foresee the irresistible force of e-commerce in other sectors.[34]

[31]See Chinese report: 《阿里巴巴CEO卫哲引咎辞职事件》,http://baike.baidu.com/link?url=hcgKNOiJpX31VjtfYhHmcOIGvEBVDK_HoNgHWTRahVR7GRld2R97SUX8DKICthGEae_z2bcgFgYytiI2HdgQo_.

[32]*Source* U.S. Census Bureau, 2011 Annual Survey of E-commerce.

[33]David Wei, "E-commerce bigger in China than United States," September 19, 2013, CNN, http://edition.cnn.com/2013/09/19/business/on-china-alibaba-e-commerce/index.html?iid=article_sidebar.

[34]The new-four initiativesare the nation's industrialization, informatization, urbanization, and modernization.

Alibaba benefited from China's "late development advantage" in certain industrial sectors. China's undeveloped retail industry has not yet been occupied by countless middle-men. This provides a great opportunity for online retail businesses. Aliresearch.com reports that the e-commerce density (online-retail seller business number per thousand population) of the Top 100 E-commerce Counties was 7.1 times that of the national level. These top counties are all in locations where the real economy are strong.[35] At the same time, e-commerce has become the new engine for real economic growth. Many villages and counties became clusters because of e-commerce development.[36] Therefore, the success of any e-commerce platform depends on how to attract to grassroots e-commerce sellers who can naturally link to real production. David Wei pointed out that "Behind these millions of merchants are hundreds of thousands of factories in China. This is why such phenomenon does not exist in the United States where you can hardly find any manufacturers."

China's retail business was less developed and marginalized. Alibaba can easily adapt the "growing by unleashing model" in this sector and become the e-commerce giant. How Alibaba is going to run its microfinance service platform remains to be seen. Two strong forces are affecting Alibaba's financial business strategies. The first is central government's strong control of China's financial sector; the second is the "financial capitalism" from the west. As a de facto traditional financial system beneficiary, the government does not want to have a strong private-owned business in financial sector. The second influence coming from the West could entice Alibaba to take the advantage of its powerful platform and grow into another Goldman Sachs. This will be trillion dollar bet: can Alibaba resist the pressure from current stakeholders of Chinese financial sector and continue its endeavor for establishing a strong microfinance market? Can Alibaba resist the temptation from financial capitalism and continue to explore a new model and provide services for a two-sided microfinance market? What would Google do (Jarvis 2009)?

How to facilitate many upcoming new "killer apps" in all different sectors? How to bring vibrant idea-producers, ingenious manufacturers, and market-know-how entrepreneurs all together and effectively assist China's industrial upgrading and product improvement? How to encourage various professional service providers, such as physicians, lawyers, teachers, accountant, and architectures, to create their businesses online so that people can enjoy a wider range of two-sided markets for modern products and services? Finally yet most importantly, how should Alibaba act as the world new business leader and establish benchmarks for running financial services where openness, transparency, efficiency, and accountability replace the "asymmetric information" of "financial capitalism"? Without doubt, the grassroots entrepreneurs on Alibaba's platform can create an unprecedented

[35]See 《县长必读: "电商百佳县哪些方面'牛'"?》 http://www.aliresearch.com/?m-cms-q-view-id-75924.html.

[36]"Alibaba works magic for China's Taobao 'treasure hunters'," this tells one of great stories in China.http://www.usatoday.com/story/news/world/2014/04/24/alibaba-china/8102033/.

demand through their novel products and services. With Alicloud in broad application and development, Internet of Things and Internet of Services would further unleash China's entrepreneurship, and become powerful engines for economic growth.

Yet, Alibaba still has a long way to go. Microsoft has entered its "middle age." Because of "big company syndrome," this once vibrant and super innovative "youth" started losing the vitality to innovate.[37] Alibaba is only 15 years old. As Alibaba has grown into a world giant, will it still be keen on entrepreneurial Lilliputians? An increasing number of platform companies have started to imitate Alibaba's business model and tried to attract online sellers. What would Alibaba's profit model be when facing with competitors? During the end of last year, 11,000 online small sellers waged a siege event toward large sellers such as Uniqlo.[38] Alibaba is constantly struggling in balancing the needs of large vs. small sellers: serving small is in Alibaba's mission statement; but serving large can be more profitable.

Alibaba recently updated its report on "Corporate Social Responsibility (CSR)." Its CSR embodies the company's free-enterprise conviction, small business passion, and the routinized innovations. Improving its ecosystem and promoting mass flourishing are important parts of Alibaba's social responsibility. Because of the internet revolution, the founders' wisdom, and employees' innovations, Alibaba has made invaluable contributions to China by "creating jobs, challenge, and change" and has become China's "David and Goliath" story. Countless new "Davids" surround Alibaba as a modern "Goliath". It is Alibaba's social responsibility and wisdom to continuously attract and serve mass entrepreneurs to innovate.

8 Concluding Remarks

Inspired by Phelps' 2013 book and drawing on Alibaba's experience, this paper discussed a small business based, digital technology driven new growth model—growing by unleashing grassroots entrepreneurship. Small business is an important expression of individuals' "will, capacity, and aspiration to innovate." Modern technologies can help create an open, transparent, efficient, and accountable microfinance market that can assist small business to thrive. Establishing and reinforcing a set of rules and regulations for an ecosystem can help the entrepreneurship of a society to be productive. Alibaba's experiences show that a nation can enjoy sustainable economic development and improved economic wellbeing by creating dynamism through unleashing grassroots entrepreneurship.

[37]Joe Wilcox, "Why former employees say Microsoft can't innovate?" http://betanews.com/2010/02/09/why-former-employees-say-microsoft-can-t-innovate/.

[38]http://www.chinaz.com/news/2013/1206/330151.shtml.

Ackowledgments I want to thank Professor Luigi Paganetto who invited me to present this paper and who created the discussion on "Anaemic Europe: how to achieve dynamism and mass flourishing." I owe a debt of deep gratitude to Professor Edmund Phelps, whose 2013 book inspired me to write this paper. Professor Phelps kindly read, edited, and provided detailed comments on an earlier version of the paper. I thank my students at Tsinghua University who participated in my research project on Alibaba, which resulted in a book, *Alibaba's Innovation: Growing by Unleashing Grassroots Entrepreneurship*. Finally, my appreciation goes to Dr. Ernst Nilsson who has been a constant source of inspiration and encouragement, and who has been generous and patient in his willingness to read, to comment on, and to help improve the paper. All errors remain my own.

References

Alibaba Microfinance Service Group Social Value Report. 2014. Internet based inclusive finance practice.

Alibaba Research Institute. 2012. *Light house for a new path—the Alibaba's 100 global e-commerce business vendors of 2011* (in Chinese: 《灯塔点亮网商路—2011年全球百佳网商案例集》). Beijing: Publishing House of Electronic Industry.

Alibaba Research Institute. 2013. E-commerce retail business on Alibaba platform employment report.

Anderson, Chris. 2012. *Makers: the new industrial revolution*. New York: Crown Business.

Baumol, William. 1990. Entrepreneurship, productive, unproductive, and destructive. *Journal of Political Economy* 98(5): 893–921.

Baumol, William. 2002. *The free-market innovation. machine: analyzing the growth miracle of capitalism*. Princeton: Princeton University Press.

Blackford, Mansel G. 1991. *A history of small business in America*. Carolina: UNC Press.

Bunzel, John H. 1962. *The American small businessman*. New York: Knopf.

Case, John. 1992. *From the ground up: the resurgence of American entrepreneurship*. Rockefeller Center, New York City: Simon & Schuster.

Galbraith, John Kenneth. 1958. *The affluent society*. New York City: New American Library.

Galbraith, John Kenneth. 1967. *The new industrial state*. Princeton: Princeton University Press.

Galbraith, John Kenneth. 1973. *Economics and the public purpose*. Boston: Houghton Mifflin Company.

Godin, Seth. 2006. *Small is the new big: and 183 other riffs, rants, and remarkable business ideas*. London: Penguin Group.

Jarvis, Jeff. 2009. *What would google do*? New York City: HarperColline e-books.

Jin, Cuodao. 2012. *Jack Ma's business idea* (金错刀《马云的创业逻辑》，中信出版社).

Krugman, Paul. 1994. *Peddling prosperity: economic sense and nonsense in an age of diminished expectations*, 10–15. Scranton, Pennsylvania: W. W. Norton.

Lowrey, Ying. 2003. The entrepreneur and entrepreneurship: a neoclassical approach. Presented at the Allied Social Science Associations (ASSA) Annual Meeting, January 2003, Washington, DC. Office of Advocacy, U.S. Small Business Administration Working Paper, http://archive.sba.gov/advo/stats/wkp03yl.pdf.

Lowrey, Ying. 2005. *Business density, entrepreneurship and economic well-being*. In: The 2005 American Economic Association Meeting in Philadelphia.

Lowrey, Ying. 2006. *An examination of entrepreneurial effort*. In: The 2006 American Economic Association Annual Meetings in Boston.

Lowrey, Ying. 2011. *Estimating entrepreneurial jobs—business creation is job creation*. In: The 2011 American Economic Association Annual Meetings in Denver.

Lui, Alison. 2014. Greed, recklessness and/or dishonesty? An investigation into the culture of five UK banks between 2004 and 2009. *Journal of Banking Regulation*.

Parker, Georey and Marshall Van Alstyne. 2013. *Innovation, openness and platform control*. http://papers.ssrn.com/sol3/papers.cfm?abstract_id=1079712.

Phelps, Edmund. 2013. *Mass flourishing: how grassroots innovation created jobs, challenge, and change*. Princeton: Princeton University Press.

Phillips, Joseph. 1958. *Little business in the American economy*. Urbana: University of Illinois press.

Schumacher, Ernst Friedrich " Fritz". 1973. *Small is beautiful: economics as if people mattered*. New York: Perennial Library, Harper & Row.

Shiller, Robert. 2012. Finance and Good Society. Princeton: Princeton University Press.

Solomon, Steven. 1986. *Small business USA: the role of small companies in sparking America's economic transformation*. New York: Crown Publishers.

U.S. Small Business Administration, Office of Advocacy report. 2010. *Race/Ethnicity and establishment dynamics, 2002–2006*.

The Evolution of European Energy and Climate Policies: The View of a Market Player

Simone Mori and Giuseppe Montesano

Abstract In the late 1990s the EU re-designed its energy system (electricity and gas) to take advantage of the internal market by enhancing competition, transparency and efficiency. As climate change broke into the international agenda, the objective of decarbonization of the energy supply was added to this design resulting in a long-term comprehensive articulation of climate and energy policies, addressing competitiveness, sustainability and security of supply. The 2014 deadline for the completion of the internal energy market is approaching and the debate on the climate and energy policy framework to 2030 is getting into its crucial phase. It is therefore timely to assess what has been achieved so far, also to learn from the past. The European market is still fragmented, the EU ETS is in trouble and industry and consumers complain about high energy prices. Are the objectives of decarbonization and fully integrated European energy markets compatible? Has a good design been undermined by failures of implementing instruments? This paper examines the evolution of energy and climate policies in the Union in the last decades with the eyes of one of the largest electricity players in the Continent. We believe decarbonization and a functional pan-European electricity market are both achievable with a serious rethinking of the current market model toward an 'Energy Plus Capacity' market with a strengthened ETS. This approach can also help in reducing the wedge between the costs of producing electricity (wholesale prices) and end-users prices resulting in electricity bills reflecting more closely the costs of generation and supply.

S. Mori (✉) · G. Montesano
European Affairs, Enel SpA, Brussels/Rome, Belgium/Italy
e-mail: simone.mori@enel.com

G. Montesano
e-mail: giuseppe.montesano@enel.com

L. Paganetto (ed.), *Achieving Dynamism in an Anaemic Europe*,
DOI 10.1007/978-3-319-14099-5_12

1 Introduction

In the EU legislation about energy and climate was initially developed separately.

The internal energy market (IEM) was designed in the late 1990s when climate change mitigation was just appearing in the policy arena. The Kyoto Protocol was agreed in 1997 but it took eight years to come into force in 2005.[1]

1.1 Unity Makes Strength

The idea underlying the achievement of the IEM is simple and unquestionable: a European market would be much more efficient than a patchwork of national jurisdictions. There would be at least three core advantages: competition would drive efficiency; there would be greater diversity and hence greater security of supply; and a fully integrated electricity network would reduce the need for capacity margins, and hence a given level of security of supply would require a significantly reduced installed electricity generation capacity (Helm 2014).

To this end, the EU released three energy packages. The first package was adopted in the late 1990s and mainly consisted of a gas directive (European Parliament 1998) and an electricity directive (European Parliament 1998) in order to privatize and liberalize markets that had been originally designed as national monopolies. Two additional energy packages were adopted in 2003 (European Parliament 2003b, c) and 2009 (European Parliament 2009c, d), while in February 2011 the European Council set the target to integrate European energy markets by 2014.

Consequently, the EU Council gave mandate to the European Commission, the European Agency for the Cooperation of energy regulators (ACER) and the European associations of Transmission System Operators for electricity and gas (ENTSO-E and ENTSO-G) to establish common and harmonized rules (i.e. EU network codes) in order to tackle cross-border issues in a systematic manner thus enabling and facilitating the integration of national energy markets into a single EU-wide energy market.

EU policy makers, through a participative process involving stakeholders, established a target model for both sectors, gas and electricity, which depicts how EU energy market structure and rules should look like in the coming future and defines an end-point of the liberalization process. In December 2009, the **Electricity Target Model** (ETM) was presented at the Florence Forum. The model is mainly based on two broad principles: the energy-only model which implies that the remuneration for the overall system costs should be covered by the short-term price resulting from competitive markets; and the market coupling process that would link zonal spot markets into a virtual market determining volumes and prices in all

[1]The Kyoto Protocol entered into force when Russia, the fifty-fifth Country representing with other fifty-four industrialized Countries 55% of 1990 carbon dioxide emissions, ratified the treaty.

relevant zones and allowing electricity to flow from high- to low-price areas provided that grids are not constrained.

Regarding the gas sector, in December 2011 the Council of European Energy Regulators (CEER) presented the **Gas Target Model** (GTM) which was endorsed by the Madrid Forum in March 2012. The objective of CEER GTM is to foster the emergence of competitive gas markets, reduce the predominant role of long-term contractual arrangements, establish functioning wholesale markets and connect them with one another while ensuring secure supplies and investments. According to the GTM, the creation of wholesale markets and their connection would be ensured mainly through the implementation of the third energy package and the application of the EU network codes on Capacity Allocation Mechanisms (CAM) and Congestion Management Procedures (CMP). Additionally, efficient investments in network interconnection capacity would be favored by a market-based mechanism (e.g. regular "bidding" process) in order to test network users willingness to pay for the additional capacity.

1.2 Climate on the Rise

While the IEM has progressed, the EU has been actively engaged in the UN multilateral negotiations on climate change, participating as a single block on the basis of common positions. Also due to the non-ratification of the Kyoto Protocol by the US, the EU became soon one of the main actors in the negotiations calling for a legally-binding climate agreement with global coverage aimed at limiting the increase of global temperature to 2 °C by the end of the century.

During the course of the negotiations, the EU strongly supported the Kyoto Protocol and after the substantial failure of the Copenhagen Conference[2] was one of the few Parties in favor of its continuation after 2012 in Cancun (COP17) and Doha (COP18).

1.3 A Long-Lasting Marriage?

At the time when the UN Framework on Climate Change Convention (UNFCCC) was signed (1992), the EU had not yet adopted any internal legislation to deal with climate change. Its common position was based on political consensus between the Member States and an aggregation of their emerging national policies.

In the same year of the adoption of the third energy package, the EU made its first attempt to integrate energy and climate policies in its legislation with the

[2]The Copenhagen Conference was aimed at agreeing a successor of the Kyoto Protocol after the expiration of its first commitment period in 2012. However, the Conference did not succeed in reaching consensus among Parties and just "took note" of the "Copenhagen Accord", a non-binding declaration of emission reduction pledges by Developed Countries.

"Climate and Energy Package". The package proposed legislation to implement by 2020 the 20-20-20 targets: 20 % greenhouse gases (GHG) emission reduction on 1990; 20 % EU energy consumption from renewable and 20 % reduction in primary energy use compared to the projected level through energy efficiency improvement. It should be noted that this last target was not set as binding.

The centerpiece of the 20-20-20 package is the EU ETS (European Parliament 2003a), the world's first large scale emission trading system.

Targets were also set for Member States at national level for renewables, to enable the EU as a whole to reach its 20 % renewable target and for emission reduction in non-ETS sectors, such as agriculture, waste and transport (European Parliament 2009a).

The package was also intended to send the message to the outside world that, in the eve of the Copenhagen Conference, the EU was willing to lead the climate change struggle with the example of its domestic policy. Directly linked to this was the EU's offer to step up its emission reduction goal to 30 % provided other developed and developing Countries implemented ambitious emission reduction policies as well.

1.4 Decarbonization, the Mantra of European Energy Policy

After the package adoption, a number of Commission papers and European Council Conclusions reiterated the importance of climate change. Reflecting the fact that on average the burning of fossil fuels accounts for two-thirds of all man-made GHG emissions globally (IPCC 2007), policies were specifically targeted to the energy sector and particularly to de-carbonizing energy supply (e.g. roadmaps for 2050 European Commission 2011a, b).

Gradually, decarbonization became the *mantra* of European policies grounded on the conviction that a low-carbon energy system can foster de-carbonization of the overall economy and that innovation and technologies would spread more quickly through the market, creating jobs and welfare for all the EU citizens.

This paper examines the evolution of energy and climate policies in the Union in the last decades with the eyes of one of the largest electricity players in the EU. Our analysis focuses on the impact of policies on the electricity wholesale market and does not address specifically downstream aspects, without intending that these are less relevant.

2 Where We Are

Looking at the results obtained so far, both the IEM and the climate and energy package have had limited success.

2.1 Progress on the Internal Energy Market

With few months left before the deadline of 2014, the IEM is far to be a fully integrated market.

By using the convergence of wholesale electricity prices as an indicator of market integration, it can be noted that a "reverse trend" is under way: in the Central West region (CWE), for instance, prices convergence declines from 68 % in 2011 to 50 % in 2012, following the important increase in 2011 compared to 2010 (Fig. 1). In addition, the number of hours with high price differentials (more than 10 €/MWh) was considerably higher in 2012 (27 %) compared to 2011 (16 %, ACER 2013).

2.2 The Triple-20 Objective

Current distance from 2020 targets in the areas of emission reduction, renewable energies and energy efficiency are shown in Fig. 2. In 2012 GHG emissions were already 19.2 % lower than in 1990 suggesting the EU will meet its objective of 20 % reduction earlier than expected. It should be noted that these results have

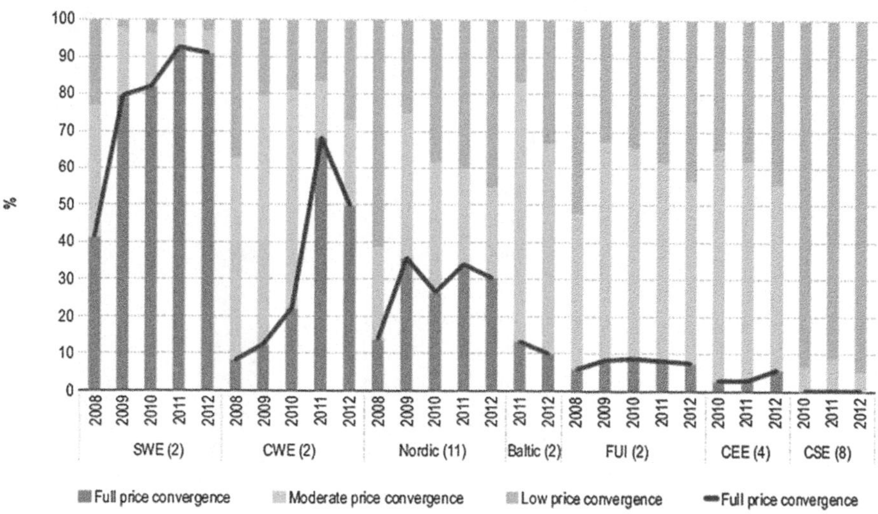

Fig. 1 Price convergence in Europe by region (ranked)—2008 to 2012 (%) Legend: Baltic region (Estonia and Lithuania), CEE region (the Czech Republic, Hungary, Poland and Slovakia), CSE region (Greece, Italy, Slovenia and Switzerland), CWE region (Austria, Belgium, France, Germany, and the Netherlands), FUI region (United Kingdom and the Republic of Ireland), Nordic (Denmark, Finland, Norway and Sweden), SWE region (Portugal and Spain). *Note* The numbers in brackets, e.g. SWE(2), refer to the number of bidding zones per region included in the calculations (from ACER 2013). *Source* Annual Report on the Results of Monitoring the Internal Electricity and Natural Gas Markets in 2012, November 2013, Agency for the Cooperation of Energy Regulators and the Council of European Energy Regulators, 2013

Fig. 2 Current distance from the 20-20-20 targets **a** reduction of greenhouse gas emissions, **b** share of renewable energy in energy consumption; **c** energy efficiency improvement (targets in *red*). *Source* Enel elaboration on Eurostat data

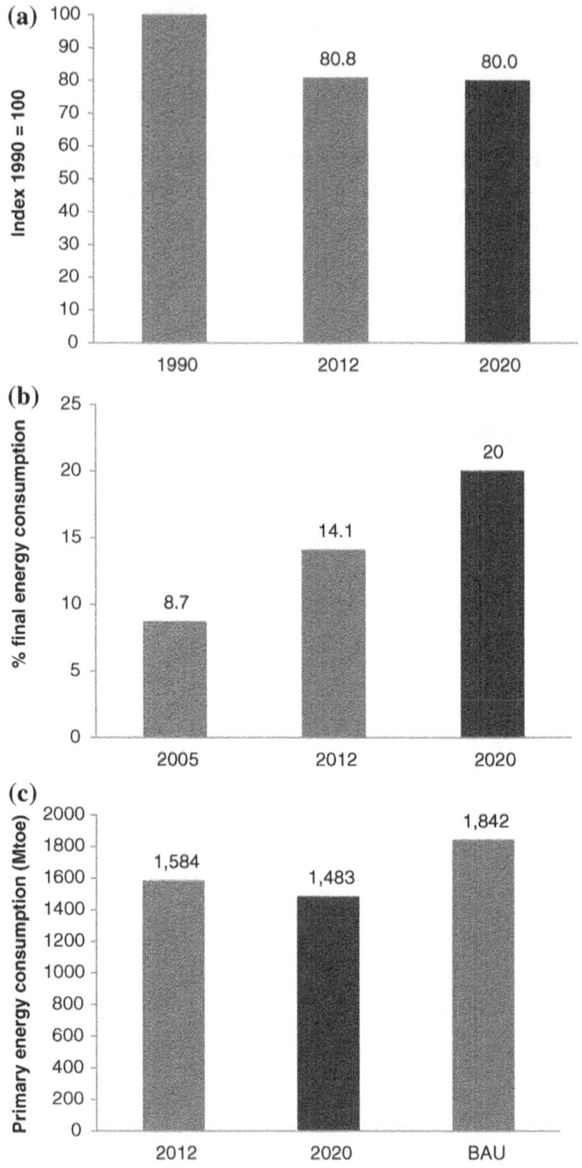

certainly been helped by the economic crisis and the decrease in industrial production in almost all EU Member States. This also resulted in industry using less allowances that those issued in the Emission Trading Scheme (ETS), generating a surplus estimated, without targeted interventions, at more than 2.5 billion allowances by 2020 (Fig. 3). Consequently carbon prices have collapsed (Fig. 4) and have not provided a signal robust enough to promote low carbon technologies.

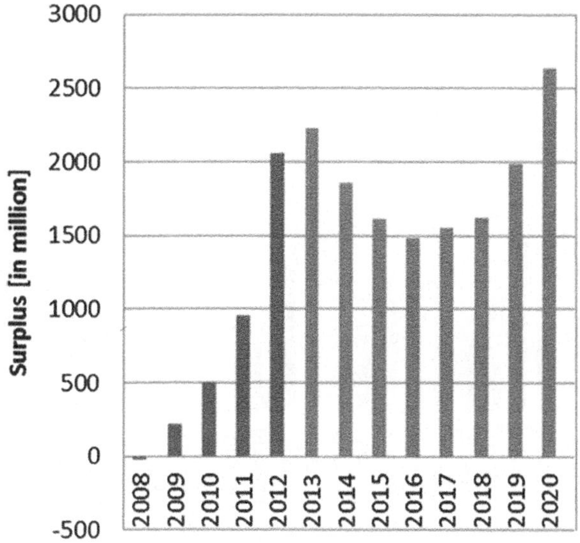

Fig. 3 Current and projected surplus of EU allowances. Actual figures 2008–2012, estimated ones 2013–2020. *Source* http://europa.eu/rapid/press-release_MEMO-14-39_en.htm

Fig. 4 EUAs prices, 2008–2014 (Spot OTC + ICE). *Source* Enel elaboration on Reuteurs data

With respect to the renewables target, the EU reached the share of 14.1 % of renewable energy in final energy consumption in 2012. Many analysts think the 20 % target will thus be met while others argue that the spread of RES in the Union will be constrained in years to come due to difficult access to finance. In fact, in the course of the economic crisis, many Member States have curtailed their support schemes and in some cases even retroactively, thus not only reducing funds for future projects but

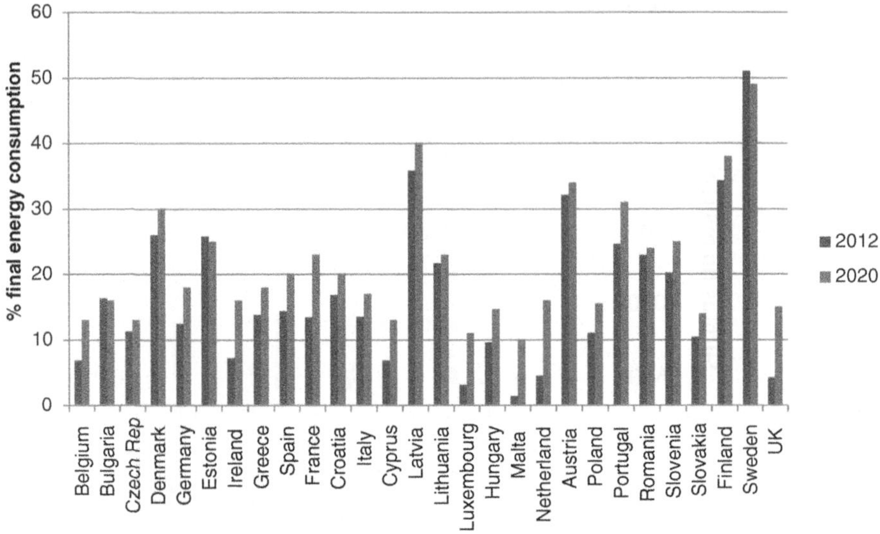

Fig. 5 Distance from the RES target in Member States. *Source* Enel elaboration on Eurostat data

also cutting promised support for facilities that had been already installed (e.g. Bulgaria, Greece, the Czech Republic. These measures severely affected investor's confidence and led to a more cautious outlook for the development of renewables. Due to the change in circumstances, even some of the former pioneering States in the area of renewable energy, such as Spain, are now unlikely to achieve their national renewable targets (Fischer and Geder 2013; Fig. 5).

As for the 20 % improvement in energy efficiency, it is very likely that this non-binding target will not be met. Projections before the adoption of the Energy Efficiency (EE) Directive in 2012 (European Parliament 2012), indicated only a 10 % energy saving achievable while, according to the European Commission, the implementation of the EE Directive would probably reach a 17 % saving in 2020. While there is still a significant untapped potential to be harnessed, energy efficiency policies in the EU remain a fragmented set of individual and incoherent measures. It is also uncertain if the transposition of the EE Directive in national legislation due by early June 2014, will lead to effective energy efficiency regulation in Member States.

3 Impact on the Power Sector

The EU 2020 energy and climate legislation along with other market factors interacted with the current crisis of the EU electricity sector, which can be clearly seen on the stock markets. Since their peak in 2008, the stock values of the top twenty utilities in the EU has declined by 50 % (Spencer et al. 2013).

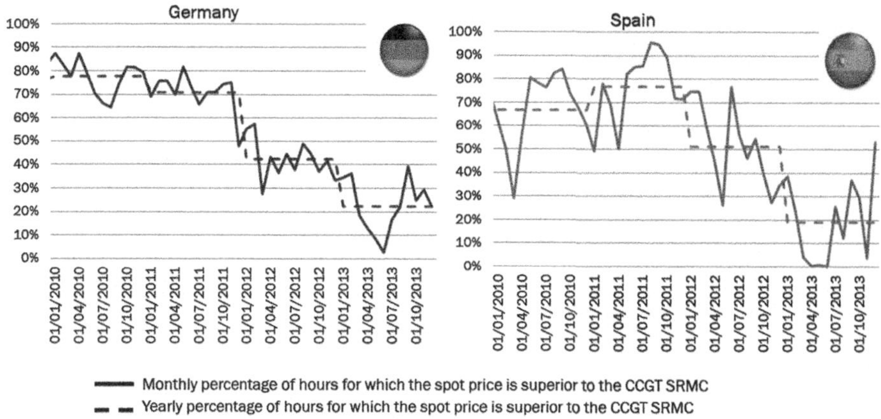

Fig. 6 Comparison between spot prices and CCGTs short run marginal costs. *Note* Theoretical utilization rate of a 56 % efficiency CCGT; For Germany NCG gas price, for Spain, PEG Sud + transit costs estimated from CNE, starting Jan 2013, gas tax included. *Source* Roques F (2014)

In particular, conventional generation, especially gas-fired, is becoming unprofitable to operate. Over the course of 2012–13 ten major EU utilities implemented or announced mothballing and closure of over 20 GW of CCGT capacity in response to persistently low or negative clean spark spreads.

This has been caused by several factors. The economic crisis resulted in significant reductions in electricity demand compared to the levels projected in 2008–09 depressing wholesale electricity prices in many countries. The impact on CCGTs has been amplified by the shift in the merit order due to increasing renewable energy capacity, which has further curtailed operating hours and depressed wholesale prices (Fig. 6). In other words, the 2020 package prompted new renewables capacity in the electricity sector at an unexpectedly high rate in several Countries. This has de facto resulted in "stranded" generation assets.

This situation has been even further exacerbated by increased coal-gas spreads (Fig. 7). Prices of imported coal in the EU dropped also as a consequence of reduced domestic demand for US thermal coal driven by the boom in US shale gas extraction (Figs. 8 and 9).

All these developments have increased the share of generation from coal plants at the expense of CCGTs. As an example: between 2009 and 2011 electricity generation from coal grew by 3 % while it fell by 3 % for gas in the same period (Spencer et al. 2013). Consequently, power generation in the EU has evolved towards an odd mix of coal and renewables.

Governments across the EU are undertaking different measures to remunerate thermal generation in order to ensure capacity for adequacy and security of the

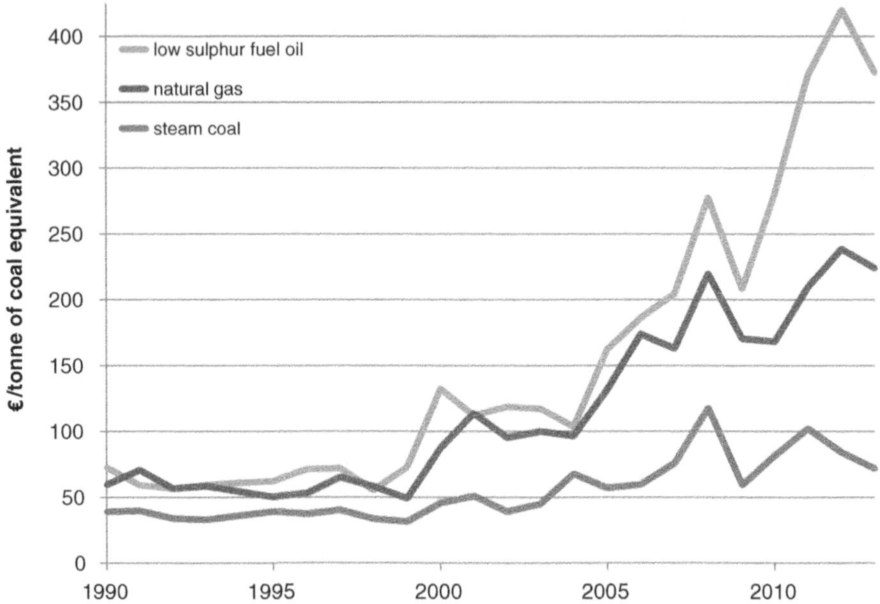

Fig. 7 Import prices for oil, gas and coal in the EU, 1990–2013. *Source* (EURACOAL 2013) from IEA oil product spot prices database for Northwest Europe—Rotterdam; average price of gas imports at German border as reported by BAFA—German Federal Office of Economics and Export Control; and IHS McCloskey Northwest Europe coal import prices)

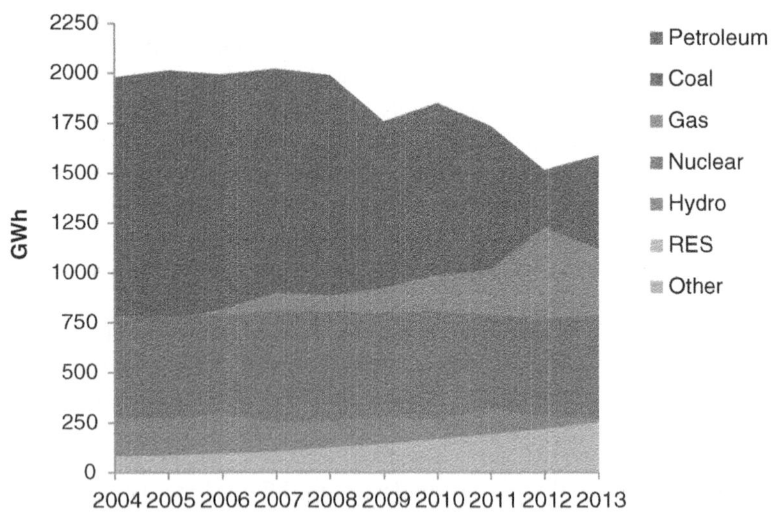

Fig. 8 US net generation by energy source. *Source* Enel elaboration on U.S. Energy Information Administration, EIA data

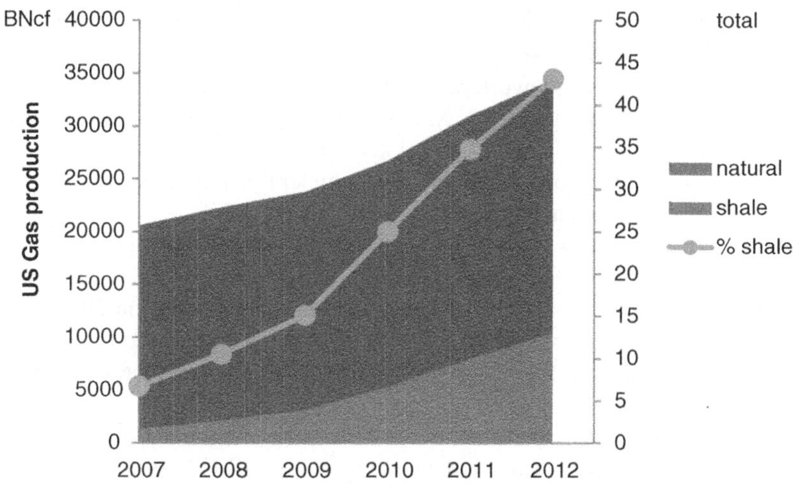

Fig. 9 US shale vs total gas production. *Source* Enel elaboration on U.S. Energy Information Administration, EIA data

electricity system including France, the UK and Germany. Italy is planning to implement similar measures.[3]

However, these initiatives, if not properly coordinated, may lead to a fragmentation of the IEM. In any case, they highlight the need for a well-thought reconsideration of the EU's vision of a single electricity market based on an energy-only model.

4 Lessons Learnt

In January 2014, the Commission, in line with the need to have long-term perspectives to plan investments in sectors such as the energy one, presented its proposal for the framework for energy and climate policies to 2030 (European Commission 2014c). It consists of two targets to be achieved by 2030: (i) reduction of GHG emissions by 40 % below the 1990 level and (ii) increase of the share of renewable energy to at least 27 % of EU's energy consumption. There are no provisions for energy efficiency in the proposal as the role of energy efficiency in the 2030 framework will be further considered in a review of the EE Directive due to be concluded in September 2014, also taking into account the ongoing debate on

[3]Decree n. 379/03 established the main criteria for a capacity payment model, whose rules have been defined by Italian TSO Terna, discussed among stakeholders in public consultations and then endorsed by the Italian Regulatory Authority in 2013 (Deliberation 375/2013/R/eel). Afterward the model has been submitted to the Italian Ministry of Economic Development for the final approval (not yet issued).

energy security, which is further highlighting the benefits of both renewables and energy efficiency in this respect.

A new governance framework has been envisaged by the Commission, based on national plans to be prepared by Member States under a common approach to ensure coherence at the EU level. An iterative process between the Commission and Member States will ensure the plans are sufficiently ambitious, as well as their consistency and compliance over time.

The Commission also proposed to establish a "market stability reserve" at the beginning of next ETS trading period in 2021 to make the EU ETS more robust and effective. The reserve would both address the surplus of emission allowances that has built up in recent years and improve the system's resilience to major shocks by automatically adjusting the supply of allowances to be auctioned (European Commission 2014a).

While objectives and instruments are still being negotiated among European Institutions, it is timely to draw on the lessons from the 2020 experience and frankly recognize that a fully integrated climate and energy policy, relying on the internal market requires a serious re-thinking of the current approach in terms of both IEM target models and instruments for climate policies.

4.1 Unexpected Circumstances or Policy Failures?

Both the IEM and the 2020 Climate and Energy package have not delivered as expected for a number of reasons. One can argue that the recession that hit Europe in 2008, the most severe during the past fifty years, was a significant factor in undermining the assumptions on which the European Commission had based the impact assessment of current energy policies made by before their adoption. In other words much of what materialized was not at all envisaged by EU policy-makers.

The economic and financial crisis produced two remarkable effects on the implementation of energy and climate policies. On one side it made investments in new conventional power generation capacity much less profitable; on the other side it made climate change slip down the political agenda. Moreover it made industry and consumers more sensitive about the level of energy prices which are unanimously blamed to be too high and ultimately to be one of the counter-forces hampering EU competitiveness and recovery from the crisis.

This is especially evident when the EU compares with the US, where the so-called "shale revolution" drove gas prices to widen even further a structural gap, bringing them to levels four times lower than in the Union (Fig. 10).

Without omitting to note that the crisis quite substantially contributed to reduce GHG emissions, its effects should however not be used to hide root causes of policy inefficiencies.

The first and the foremost was the underestimation of the conflicts between the multiple 2020 package objectives and both the European wholesale electricity market and the IEM.

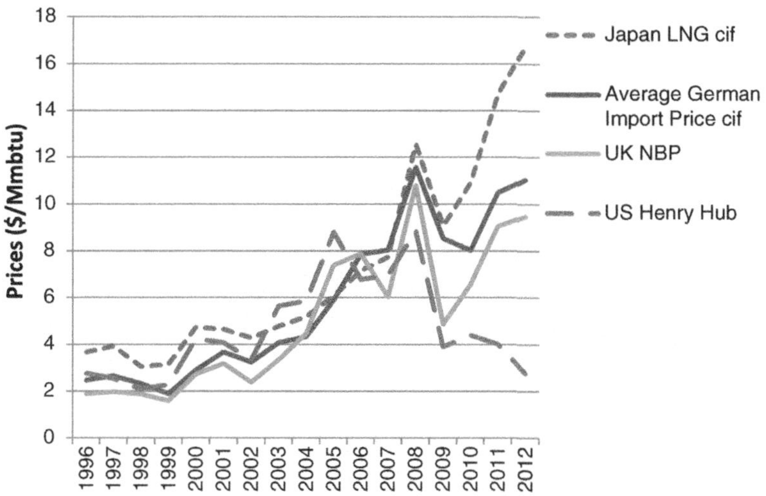

Fig. 10 Annual gas prices are given for benchmark natural gas hubs together with contracted pipeline and LNG imports. The benchmark hub prices incorporate US (Henry Hub) and the UK (NBP). Contract prices are represented by LNG imports into Japan and Average German Import Prices. The prices for LNG at European border are calculated as cif prices, where cif = cost + insurance + freight (average freight prices) in US dollars per million British thermal units (*Btu*). *Source* Enel elaboration on BP energy statistics (2013)

4.2 The RES Revolution

According to the RES Directive, RES targets in the Union were declined at national level so that individual Member States had their own target determined on the basis of the respective stage of development of their renewable energy sector in 2005 and their economic performances at the time (Dir. 2009/28/EC). Consequently Member States established support scheme for RES, especially in the electricity sector (RES-E, Table 1). At the same time, the cost of RES technologies, especially solar, dropped significantly and with an unexpected rate (Fig. 11).

Both factors pushed a significant penetration of RES-E in the generation mix (Fig. 12), mainly in Countries such as Germany, Spain and Italy where incentive schemes were particularly generous especially for solar technologies. Latest available data on net renewable support payments (2013) show figures in the order of 15 €bn/year for Germany (50 % solar PV), 9 €bn/year for Italy (53 % solar PV) and 7 €bn/year for Spain (50 % solar PV), as opposed to just over 2 €bn for France and UK.

The development of RES has contributed to reduce GHG emissions. However, abatements were often obtained at very high cost especially if compared to those that would have been achieved by the EU ETS (Fig. 13).

This has resulted in increasing the electricity bill for European industry and consumers, who are assisting at an “electricity price paradox”: prices on wholesale

Table 1 Renewable electricity support instruments in Member States

		AT	BE	BG	CY	CZ	DE	DK	EE	ES	FI	FR	GR	HU	IE	IT	LT	LU	LV	MT	NL	PL	PT	RO	SE	SI	SK	UK
Electricity	FIT	x	x	x	x	x	x		x	x		x	x	x	x	x	x	x	x	x			x			x	x	x
	Premium					x		x	x	x											x					x		
	Quota obligation		x													x						x		x	x			x
	Investment grants		x		x	x					x		x	x			x	x	x	x								
	Tax exemption		x							x	x		x						x		x	x			x		x	x
	Fiscal incentives			x			x		x											x	x	x				x		

Source European Commission (2012)

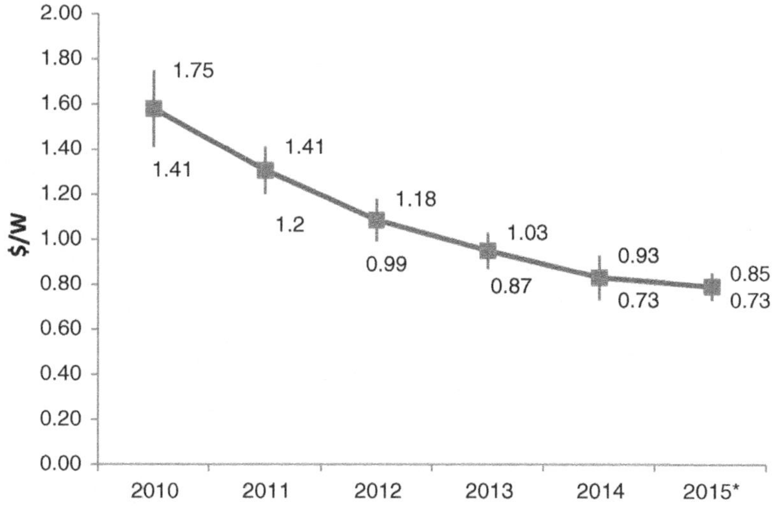

Fig. 11 Price of crystalline silicon PV modules. Higher costs refer to European, North American and Japanese manufactures, lower costs to low-cost manufactures (e.g. China). *price projection. *Source* Enel elaboration on IRENA data

markets are decreasing for power producers while those to end users are increasing as subsidies for renewables, as well as other levies, are charged on the retail electricity price (Figs. 14 and 15).

4.3 RES Impact on Wholesale Markets

Notwithstanding benefits in terms of emission reduction and energy independence, RES pose challenges to the electricity system from different perspectives. First of all, high penetration of intermittent RES, especially in certain hours (Fig. 16) modifies quite substantially the patterns to keep the balance between supply and demand on the networks and guarantee reliability of supply. From the perspective of the market, high penetration of RES modifies the way it works and provides price signals.

Since RES typically have zero or low marginal generation costs, they generally displace conventional generation, since the latter typically takes place by burning fossil fuels at marginal costs well above zero. In marginal pricing systems this generally contributes to reduce prices and margins. This trend is enhanced if RES enjoy grid priority access and are subsidized, in particular if subsidies are addressed to technologies having marginal costs above zero, such as biomass. In this case, in fact, RES generators may be willing to accept even negative prices up to concurrence with the level of the granted incentive, leading to market distortions.

Prices below zero have in fact started to appear in wholesale markets (Fig. 17).

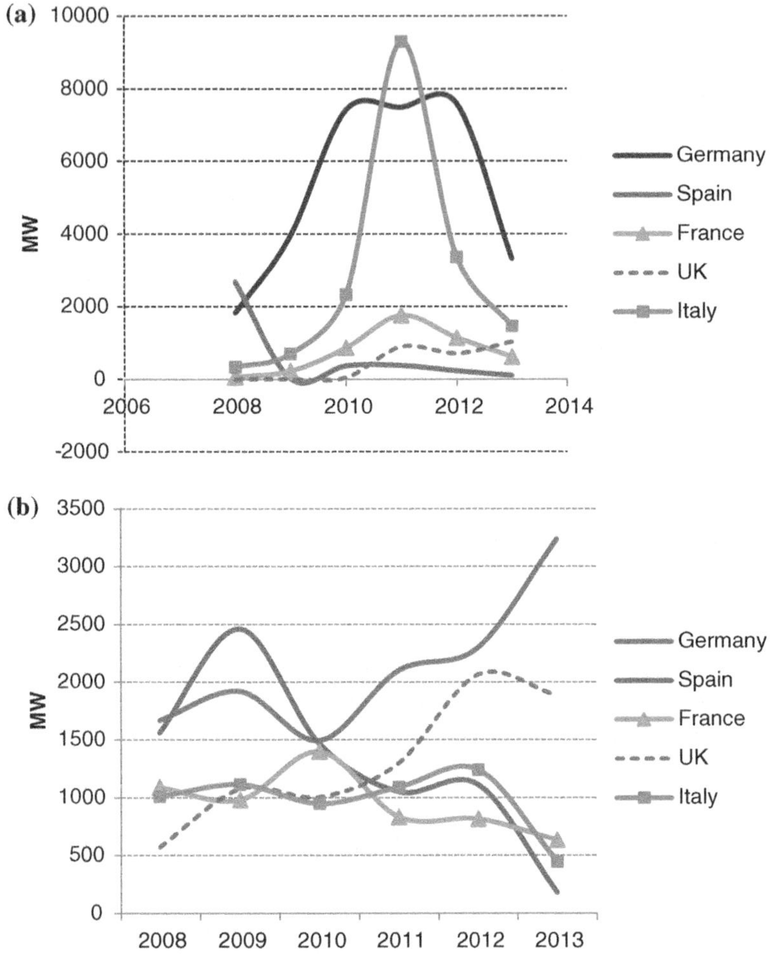

Fig. 12 Penetration of solar and wind renewable energy in the electricity mix of selected Member States: **a** capacity additions of installed photovoltaic power (*Source* Enel elaboration on EurObserv'er data); **b** capacity addition of installed wind power (*Source* Enel elaboration on European Wind Energy Association, EWEA data)

In such context an energy-only market allows conventional generators to remunerate their investments, which are necessary to guarantee the security of the system, only if prices are free to reflect scarcity situations when these occur, i.e. to reach high levels in a limited number of hours.

However high price levels are rarely politically accepted. The experience teaches that regulators are very often tempted to impose caps. Caps exist in day-ahead markets in Europe (including Belgium, Germany, Denmark, Spain, Portugal, France, The Netherlands, Switzerland, and Italy), Australia (AER 2012) and in the

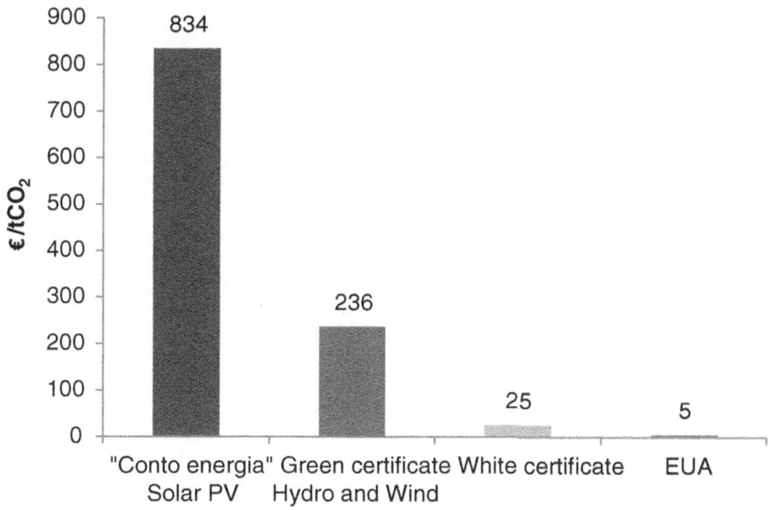

Fig. 13 Examples of abatement costs for different options in Italy. *Note* Conversion of carbon intensity based on CCGT equal to 0.36 tCO_2/MWh,"Conto energia" average value of the scheme; Green certificates (average value of 2013); EUA (average value 2013). *Source* Enel elaborations on Terna, Gestore Mercati Elettrici GME data

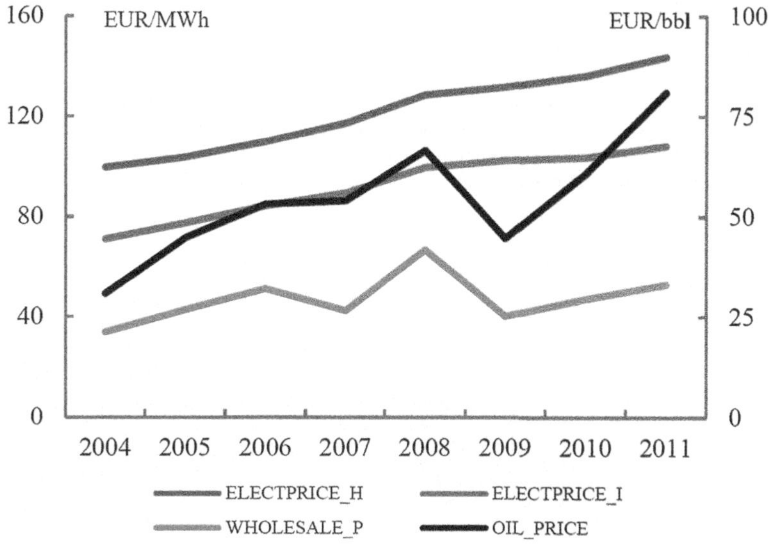

Fig. 14 The "price paradox". *Note* The consumption bands used were DC for Households (2500 kWh < Consumption < 5000 kWh) and IC for Industry (500 MWh < Consumption < 2000 MWh), wholesale prices are average spot prices from different European power exchanges and pools. *Source* European Commission (2014b)

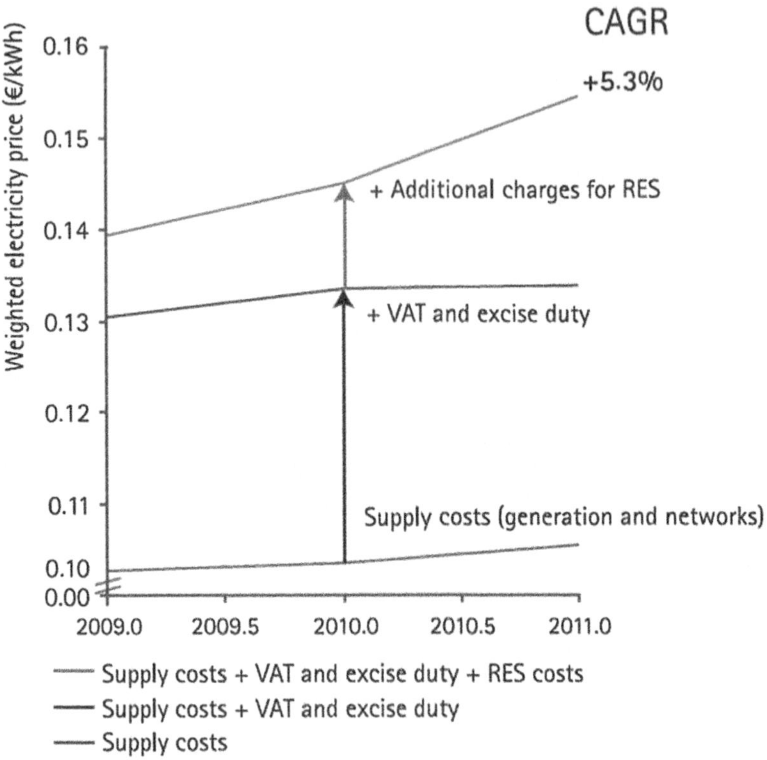

Fig. 15 Weighted average electricity prices by component (2009–2011)*. *The weighted price represents the average costs over different user categories, weighted by their relative consumption. The renewable energy costs represent the total costs for supporting renewables in the country distributed evenly over total consumption. *Source* EURELECTRIC (2014)

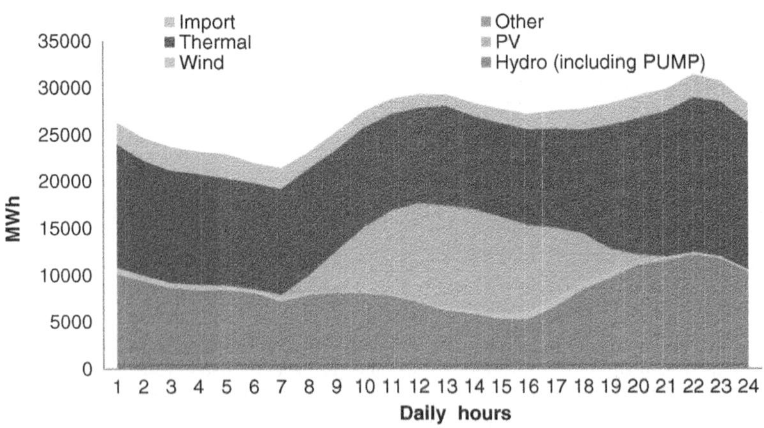

Fig. 16 Load coverage, Italy—16 June 2013. *Source* Enel elaboration on European Energy Exchange EEX, Terna

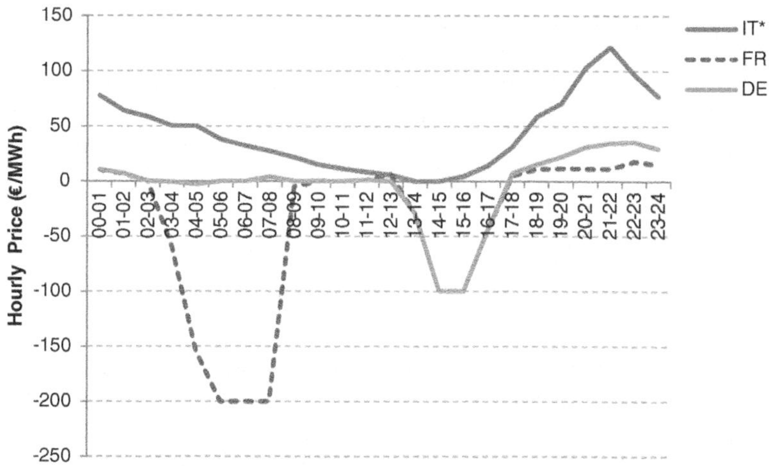

Fig. 17 Hourly pricing on day-ahead wholesale markets (16 June 2013). *PUN = *Prezzo unico nazionale*. *Source* Enel elaboration on European Energy Exchange EEX, Terna

US, where it is worth to mention the case of Texas. The Electricity Reliability Council of Texas (ERCOT), indeed, recognizing the need for generators to be compensated, is in the process of raising the existing cap of 1,000 $/MWh to 9,000 $/MWh (Keith and Michaels 2013).

If price ceilings are in place, the only way to ensure that necessary back up capacity is not mothballed or withdrawn because of unprofitability is to guarantee additional revenue streams, e.g. through capacity remuneration mechanisms.

Last but not least, renewables and their subsidies significantly interact with the IEM achievement. 28 RES national policies and related attempts of Member States to respond to the above-mentioned missing-money problem for thermal generation are undermining the fundamentals of the EU project of a single energy market.

Finally, coming back to the question whether circumstances prevail on policy failures as causes of the current situation, our conclusion is that the change of circumstances made inherent policy failures more evident.

5 Thinking Ahead

EU electricity markets are experiencing fundamental changes whose impacts are arising faster and in larger proportions than expected. With a growing share of RES, conventional generation is facing varying degrees of overcapacity, low load factors and margins insufficient to recover costs, including investments needed to cope with RES intermittency.

Is the current difficulty in electricity markets an inevitable consequence of pursuing the EU decarbonization objective?

We think it's not. Decarbonization and a functional electricity market are compatible goals but they require policies that do not create tensions among each other, especially when they are turned from principles into implementation measures.

5.1 Competitiveness Is Back on the EU's Agenda

While the 2020 package has only been a first attempt to integrate climate and energy policies, the 2030 framework includes some openings to ensure that competitiveness, security of supply and climate objectives are better balanced than in the past. It is worth to mention that the package was accompanied by a report on energy prices and costs which assessed the key drivers and compared the EU prices with those of its main trading partners, indicating a renovated intention by the EU policy makers to ensure that the energy system contributes to the competiveness of the EU economy.

The new 2014–2020 Guidelines on State aid for environmental protection and energy are also a positive step since they address specifically the issue of making RES support schemes sustainable, well-targeted to less mature technologies and harmonized among Member States, while promoting better integration of RES in electricity markets through participation in balancing.

5.2 Toward a Low-Carbon Future

The GHG emission reduction target of 40 % proposed by the 2030 framework goes in the right direction and should consistently be followed by further objectives for years to come in line with the 2050 Low Carbon Roadmap. They are essential to give a clear, long-term signal to investors on the direction of the EU energy and climate policy.

Concerning RES, they are an essential option for decarbonization. Benefits in terms of diversification of the electricity mix, emissions reduction of GHG and traditional air pollutants, promotion of innovation are all out of discussion. However, badly designed support or incentive levels have proven to have undermined market dynamics and reduced the benefits of market liberalization and integration. Moreover in a general climate of austerity and budget constraints, several Member States have decided to intervene abruptly in RES markets reducing or removing retroactively support to RES. Such move obviously undermined existing investments and investors confidence.

6 Remedies

Remedies should focus primarily on two objectives.

Firstly, for future investments, RES subsidies should be differentiated on the basis of the technological development stage along the path to full competitiveness and integration into the market, and phased-out for mature technologies.

The provisions of the 2014–2020. Guidelines on State aid for environmental protection and energy (European Commission 2014d) are in line with this aim, as they foresee the gradual introduction of competitive bidding processes for allocating public support and the gradual replacement of feed-in tariffs by feed-in premiums.

6.1 A Dynamic Approach to RES

More concretely, we believe that up to 2020 deployed technologies should receive investment aid through bidding processes in order to limit distortions and to promote more competitiveness in the market. Beyond 2020, we believe that RES incentives should be progressively phased out when renewable technologies become competitive. Their development should be substantially supported by a strong CO_2 price in a framework of markets evolving towards conditions which enable a level playing field among all participants.

Technologies in the demonstration phase should be able to benefit from low-risk incentives, such as feed-in tariffs, as long as cost or volume control mechanisms are in place to avoid excessive burdens or market distortions. Technologies in the deployment phase instead can be gradually exposed to market risks (e.g. using a feed-in premium or tradable green certificates systems). Mature renewables should be developed only through tendering on capacity in order not to distort short-term market signals and to capture the learning curve of technologies.

6.2 An 'Energy Plus Capacity' Market

Secondly, the European electricity target model should be reviewed and consider market-based capacity remuneration mechanisms (CRMs) as a pillar of future market design.

The way forward is to re-think the European market design by allowing the implementation of sound and coordinated market-based CRMs across the EU and its borders.

Properly designed CRMs are a market design option that can complement energy markets in a stable and long term manner as well as an important tool to bridge a secure transition to decarbonisation. The key arguments rely upon the potential role of imperfections, failures and real conditions of European electricity markets which are far from ideal. Market based mechanisms appear frequently to be the most desirable solution and better able to address the most significant challenges posed by the context. Moreover, CRMs should be technology neutral, ensure equal treatment of different market players, take into account interconnectors and be established as a stable framework.

6.3 Strengthening the EU ETS

Decarbonization needs also devoted policies for reduction of carbon emissions at source level.

We maintain that the EU should set a post-2020 CO_2 target of reasonable ambition and negotiate it for the purposes of the Paris Climate Conference (COP-21) in December 2015, where the Parties of the UNFCCC will meet to agree a global agreement against climate change to be adopted in 2020.

The ETS should remain the cornerstone of EU climate policies and its price signal should be used to drive policy and measures in non-ETS sectors. A reform is being undertaken by the European Commission to restore the effectiveness of the system after the creation of huge oversupply since 2009. It consists in (i) the so-called "back-loading", i.e. the postponement of the sale of 900 mln allowances from 2013–2015 to 2019–2020 aimed at redressing the oversupply of allowances in the short term, and (ii) the establishment of a "market stability reserve (MSR)", i.e. an automatic adjustment of auction volumes triggered by level of surplus outside a predefined range (Fig. 18).

While the back-loading is entered into force in March 2014, the MSR is under discussion like all other measures encompassed in the 2030 framework.

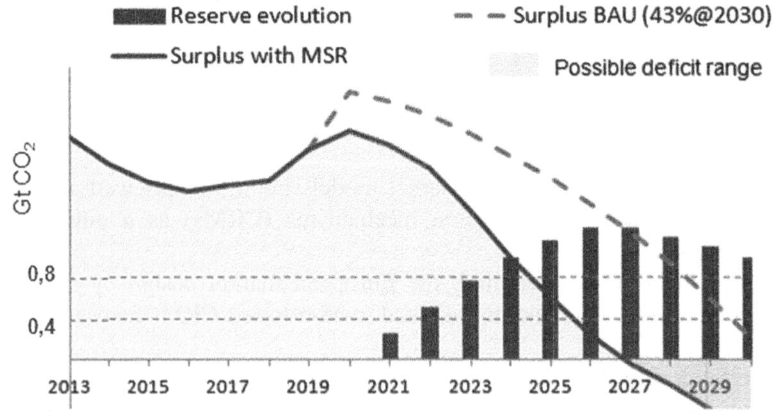

Fig. 18 The market stability reserve. *Source* Enel elaboration based on the EC proposal

We have analyzed these measures and concluded that they are valuable interventions, although they do not tackle the surplus issue quickly enough and they should be accompanied by a longer term view to align the ETS cap reduction path with the ambition of climate policy embedded in the 2050 EU Roadmap.

All these measures will help to address the energy and climate policies in one coherent structure ensuring benefits for conventional and renewables producers but also for industry and consumers. Improved policies will also contribute to reduce the wedge between the costs of producing electricity (wholesale prices) and the end-user price so that energy bills will better reflect the cost of electricity. All other costs should be left out, including those generated by ineffective policies.

Acknowledgements We wish to thank Vanessa Tedeschi and Michel D'Ausilio for their invaluable contribution and assistance in drawing up the paper. We also thank Sandro Libratti, Andrea Villa, Giovanni Bertolino, Giorgio Vitali and Giulia Barone for their help in collecting data and evidences.

References

ACER. 2013. Annual Report on the Results of Monitoring the Internal Electricity and Natural Gas Markets in 2012.

BP Energy Statistics. 2013. http://www.bp.com/en/global/corporate/about-bp/energy-economics/statistical-review-of-world-energy-2013.html.

Helm, Dieter, 2014. The European framework for energy and climate policies. *Energy Policy* 64: 29–35.

EURACOAL. 2013. Coal Industry across Europe.

EURELECTRIC. 2014. "Forging A Joint Commitment To Sustainable And Cost-Efficient Energy Transition In Europe" report prepared in collaboration with Accenture.

EurObserv'er 2009–2013 "Photovoltaic barometers".

European Commission. 2011a. Communication to the European Parliament, the Council, the European Economic and Social Committee and the Committee of the Regions: "A roadmap for moving to a competitive low carbon economy in 2050" (COM(2011) 112 final/2).

European Commission. 2011b. Communication from the Commission to the European Parliament, The Council, The European Economic and Social Committee and the Committee of the Regions "Energy Roadmap 2050" (COM(2011) 885 final).

European Commission. 2012. Communication from the Commission to the European Parliament and the Council: Renewable Energy: progressing toward the 2020 target (COM(2011) 31 final.

European Commission. 2014a. Proposal for a decision of the European Parliament and of the Council concerning the establishment and operation of a market stability reserve for the Union greenhouse gas emission trading scheme and amending Directive 2003/87/EC COM(2014) 20/2.

European Commission. 2014b. (DG for Economic and Financial Affairs), 2014 "Energy Economic Developments in Europe".

European Commissions. 2014c. Communication from the Commission to the European Parliament, the Council, the European Economic and Social Committee and the Committee of the Regions: a policy framework for climate and energy in the period from 2020 to 2030 (COM/2014/15 final).

European Commissions. 2014d. Guidelines on State aid for environmental protection and energy 2014–2020 (C(2014)2322)European Commission, 2014 Communication on energy prices and costs in Europe COM(2014) 21.

European Parliament. 1996. Directive 96/92/EC of the European Parliament and of the Council of 19 December 1996 Concerning Common Rules for The Internal Market in Electricity Official Journal of the European Union L027, 20–29.
European Parliament. 1998. Directive 98/30/EC of the European Parliament and of the Council of 22 June 1998 Concerning Common Rules for the Internal Market in Natural Gas. Official Journal of the European Union, L204, 1–12.
European Parliament. 2003a. Directive 2003/87/EC as amended by 2009/29/EC reviewing the EU emission trading scheme by defining an emissions cap and harmonising allocation of allowances to companies. Official Journal of the European Union, L140,63–87.
European Parliament. 2003b. Directive 2003/55/EC of the European Parliament and of the Council of 26 June 2003 concerning common rules for the internal market in natural gas and repealing directive 98/30/EC. Official Journal of the European Union L176,57–78.
European Parliament. 2003c. Directive 2003/54/EC of the European Parliament and of the Council of 26 June 2003 Concerning Common Rules for the Internal Market in Electricity and Repealing Directive 96/92/EC. Official Journal of the European Union,L176,37–56.
European Parliament. 2009a. On the Effort of Member States to reduce their greenhouse gas emissions to meet the Community's greenhouse gas emission reduction commitments up to 2020 (Dec. n. 406/2009/EC)
European Parliament. 2009b. Directive 2009/28/EC of the European Parliament and of the Council of 23 April 2009 on the promotion of the use of energy from renewable sources and amending and subsequently repealing directives 2001/77/EC and 2003/30/EC. Official Journal of the European UnionL 140, 16–62.
European Parliament. 2009c. Directive 2009/73/EC of the European Parliament and of the Council of 13 July 2009 Concerning Common Rules For The Internal Market In Natural Gas And Repealing Directive 2003/55/EC. Official Journal of the European Union L211,94–136.
European Parliament. 2009d. Directive 2009/72/EC of the European Parliament and of the Council of 13 July 2009 Concerning Common Rules for The Internal Market in Electricity and Repealing Directive 2003/54/EC. Official Journal of the European Union L211,55–93.
European Parliament. 2012. Directive 2012/27/EU of the European Parliament and of the Council of 25 October 2012 on energy efficiency, amending Directives 2009/125/EC and 2010/30/EU and repealing Directives 2004/8/EC and 2006/32/EC Official Journal of the European Union L315, 1–56.
European Wind Energy Association (EWEA). 2009–2013. Wind in power: European statistics .
Eurostat. 2020. Europe 2020 indicators: http://epp.eurostat.ec.europa.eu/portal/page/portal/europe_2020_indicators/headline_indicators.
Fischer S. and Geder O. 2013. Updating the EU's Energy and Climate Policy. International Policy Analysis, Friedrich Ebert Foundation.
IPCC. 2007. Fourth assessment report.
IRENA. 2012. Renewable energy technologies: cost analysis series—Solar photovoltaics, vol. 1: power sector issue 4/5.
Keith AN. and Michaels R. 2013. Does Competitive Electricity Require Capacity Markets? The Texas Experience.Texas Public Policy Foundation.
European Energy Exchange EEX, power data https://www.eex.com/en#/en.
Gestore Mercati Elettrici—GME data https://www.mercatoelettrico.org/en/Default.aspx.
Roques F. 2014. European Electricity Markets in Crisis—Which Direction for Reform? Presentation at the Conference "Energy Public Policies in Portugal—Electricity Sector" Lisbon, 25 Mar 2014.
Spencer T., Colombier M., Ribera T. 2013. The 2030 EU Climate and Energy Package: why and how? Policy Brief n.16 Istitut du developpement durable et des relations internationals (IDDRI).
Terna spa, Statistical data http://www.terna.it/default/home_en/electric_system/statistical_data.aspx.
U.S. Energy Information Administration, EIA Energy Statistics, http://www.eia.gov/.

Towards a Fair and Rigorous International Emissions Trading System: A Blueprint for Success

Odin K. Knudsen

Abstract The international negotiations to mitigate the emissions of GHGs are reaching a critical phase. But to be successful the outcome must be fair and rigorous, taking into account not only a country's historic emissions but also its capacity to pay. Furthermore, any agreement must be enforceable with failure to comply involving economic consequences. In this paper, the necessary elements of such an agreement are presented demonstrating that Europe and the United States must reduce emissions much more vigorously and an international emissions trading scheme is an absolute necessity to meet a 2 °C pathway.

1 Introduction

In late 2015, one of the most critical meetings for the future of the planet will be held in Paris. This United Nations Conference of the Parties (COP) is charged with negotiating a new climate agreement to keep global temperatures from exceeding 2 °C. As part of the negotiations, the developed nations are to create financial assistance to developing countries so they can invest in carbon reducing technologies. Sadly the chances of real success at Paris are low despite the critical and urgent need to check the growth of greenhouse gas (GHG) emissions.

Already the UN process leading to the Paris COP is in trouble. Countries have made weak, uneven and unenforceable pledges under Kyoto and few have pledge anything for the second commitment period despite numerous meetings of the Parties.[1]

While there are modest expectations for this COP, any realistic assessment says that international negotiations have failed and will continue to fail under the current

[1]As of May 1, 2014 only 9 countries with minor amounts of emissions have ratified CP2. 144 are need for CP2.

O.K. Knudsen (✉)
Real Options International, 6820 Wisconsin Avenue, Suite 8006, Bethesda, MD 20815, USA
e-mail: oknudsen@realoptionsinternational.com

L. Paganetto (ed.), *Achieving Dynamism in an Anaemic Europe*,
DOI 10.1007/978-3-319-14099-5_13

format of multiple agendas, long and diplomatically laden documents, and parties intent on scuttling any agreement. And even if they did succeed, they are unenforceable under the current format as Canada demonstrated clearly under the Kyoto Protocol by exiting at their convenience, preferring oil sand revenue to meeting an international "legally" binding commitment.

For the world to collectively check the growth of global emissions consistent with a 2° pathway, the ambition of countries in reducing emissions must increase and their efforts be linked internationally. Also there must be an enforcement mechanism that has teeth.

The negotiations must:

1. **Be simplified and viewed as fair**, resulting in an agreement consistent with responsibility for existing levels of GHGs in the atmosphere and with the ability to pay;
2. **Result in the substantial transfer of finance** from developed to developing countries with active participation of the private sector; and
3. **Be enforceable with economic consequences** for nations not achieving their targets in emission reductions.

2 Simplification

To simplify the negotiations, common standards must be established that are applicable to all countries. These standards can be broken down to three parameters for negotiation:

1. **Responsibility**: ***The base year from which emissions*** will be counted, meaning countries should have responsibility for emissions from that year onward. A reasonable base year could be 1990 when all countries should have known that their GHG emissions were responsible for climate change (as was confirmed in the Rio UN Convention of 1992). This is one logical suggestion and I am sure that there could be others equally forcibly argued. Once the base year is negotiated then it is well known what each country's contributions to global emissions are up to the COP meeting in Paris.
2. **Capacity to Pay**: ***The minimum income*** level above which people should have the capacity to pay for the efforts to reduce emissions. All countries have rich and poor. Those whose income is above a certain level, say $7,500, should have the capacity to pay. By taking a measure of income distribution (the Gini Coefficient) and total income, this capacity to pay can be estimated. Once the negotiators agree upon the cutoff income level, the capacity to pay falls out of the calculation.
3. **Weighting**: ***The relative weights assigned to responsibility and capacity to pay.*** A simple proposal would be to give equal weights to both.

By isolating to three parameters, the base year for emissions, the minimum income level and the weight to be given to each, the negotiations would be immensely simplified. Once these parameters are agreed, emission caps for every country, rich and poor, would be set. Some of these emission targets would be very low for low-income countries and could be disregarded if the negotiators so chose.

3 Finance

As will be shown shortly, choosing reasonable parameters for responsibility and capacity to pay would mean that the annual emissions of the United States and Europe would need to be negative, that is, these countries would need to be withdrawing GHGs from the atmosphere. Under current technologies, this is not possible.[2] The only way to achieve negative emissions is to buy allowances from other countries as under the Kyoto Protocol, meaning that there would need to be an international carbon market which would allow Europe, the United States and other developed countries to purchase allowances from developing countries or from other developed countries that overachieve their target.

Thus, the adoption of the three parameter negotiations sets up the necessity for an international carbon market where large amounts of funds can flow to technologies and investments to reduce carbon emissions so as to free-up allowances for trading. The specific parameters negotiated on responsibility and capacity to pay along with the weight to give to each would determine the amount of these financial flows.

Let's illustrate how this approach would play out for four important parties in the negotiations: the European Union, the United States, China and India. Assume that the negotiators reach an agreement for the base year being 1990, the cutoff per capita income level of $7,500, and a neutral weighting scheme of 50/50, equal weights for responsibility and capacity to pay. Fortunately converting these parameters to obligations on emission reductions has been facilitated by the Stockholm Institute of Environment. The Institute has developed an online tool to calculate any country's burden in reducing greenhouse gases by 2030 under the fair standard of responsibility and capacity to pay as specified above.

4 The European Unions' Responsibility and Capacity to Pay

EU 27 emissions will be at about 5.4 billion tons by 2030. For a 2° weak pathway to global reductions (meaning that emissions are gradually reduced), *global* emissions by 2030 will need to be reduced below baseline by 45 billion tons of which Europe (based on its historic contribution to global emissions) would need

---

[2]Forestry and land management could sequester carbon but not at the magnitudes needed.

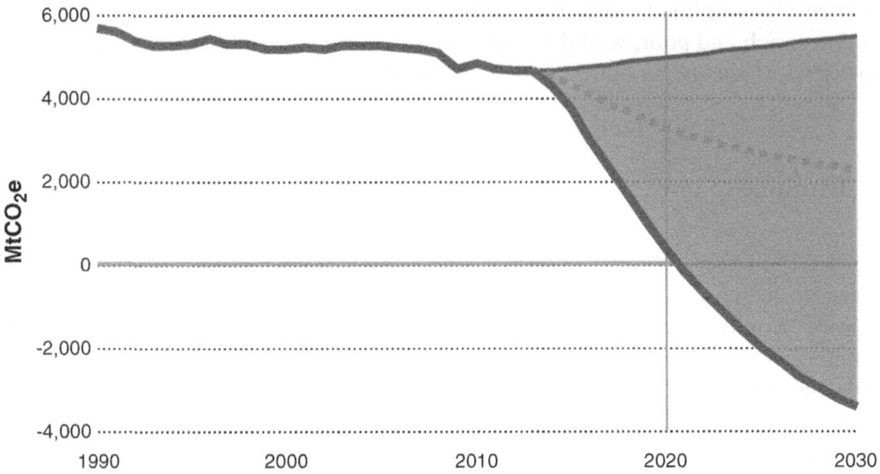

Source for data: Stockholm Environmental Institute Calculator
____ Fair Share Obligation
…….. Domestic Feasible Obligation
IIIIIII International Purchase

Fig. 1 Europe's fair obligation to 2030 for a weak 2 °C pathway

to reduce its emissions by about 8 billion tons, that is achieve negative emissions of 3.4 billion tons. This is clearly impossible without purchasing offsets or allowances from other countries that have overachieved their reductions or legitimately escape a hard cap on emissions. A 'realistic' scenario is that Europe reduces emissions to about 2 billion tons (a 60 % reduction from 1990 emissions) and purchases about 6.4 billion tons of emission reduction offsets or allowances from other countries. At a 25 Euro price (currently the price is less than a half of a Euro) for international credits, this would result in just over €160 billion of purchases in 2030. While less than 1 % of European GDP, €160 billion Euro would represent a substantial incentive for climate friendly investment in developing countries (Fig. 1).

5 The United States' Responsibility and Capacity to Pay

The same criteria can be applied, as with Europe, that is fair historic responsibility and capacity to pay. The United States' project emissions are about 8 billion tons by 2030. To fulfill its historic responsibility and utilizing its capacity to pay, the United States should reduce annual emissions by 10 billion tons. Realistically the United States could reduce by 4 billion tons domestically (about a 25 % reduction from

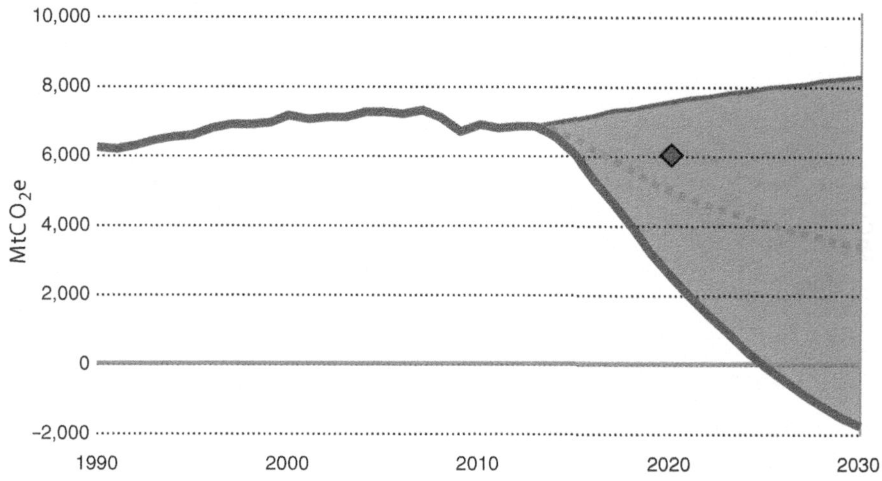

Source for data: Stockholm Environmental Institute Calculator
____ Fair Share Obligation
…….. Domestic Feasible Obligation
IIIIIII International Purchases

Fig. 2 US's fair obligation to 2030 for a weak 2 °C pathway

1990 or 50 % reduction from projected 2030 emissions) and then purchase internationally about 6 billion tons.

Again at a price of €25 per ton for an allowance, this would obligate the United States to transfer through the international carbon markets about €150 billion to developing and over-achieving developed countries (Fig. 2).

6 The China's Responsibility and Capacity to Pay

For China, emissions are projected to reach 26 billion tons by 2030 with a historical responsibility and capacity of a reduction by 8–18 billion tons. By implementing a national international trading scheme and at the same time, moving increasingly to natural gas, China could reduce its emissions significantly. If China makes a concerted effort to reduce emissions beyond the 18 billion tons then it has excess carbon tons available to sell to the US and Europe. With these sales giving additional financial incentive, it is possible that China could reduce its emissions to 10 billion tons by 2030, freeing up about 9 billion tons for trading.

At €25 per ton for an allowance this would mean a net inflow of €225 billion in 2030 (Fig. 3).

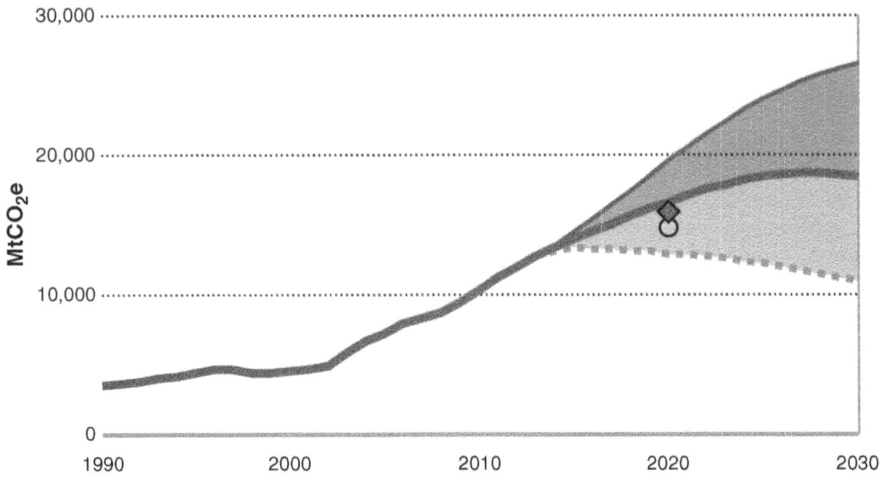

Source for data: Stockholm Environmental Institute Calculator
____ Fair Share Obligation
…….. Domestic Feasible Obligation
IIIIIII International Purchases

Fig. 3 China's fair obligation to 2030 for a weak 2 °C pathway

7 The India's Responsibility and Capacity to Pay

For India, a similar scenario could play out. India's emissions are growing as is China but from a much lower emission base of just over 1 billion tons. In 2030 emissions are projected to reach nearly 6 billion tons, a six time increase and equal to the United States' 1990 emissions. Its obligation will be to reduce emissions by 1.3 billion tons or a 20 % reduction well within feasibility. This means that India will have the potential of several billion tons to sell abroad. With a concerted effort, India could have about 6 billion tons for international trading by 2030, generating at €25 per ton about €150 billion a year of revenue for green investments (Fig. 4).

As these domestic reductions would be challenging, China and India alone may not be able to supply the international emission credits and allowances needed by Europe and the United States and other developed countries. Linking with many other economies would be needed and be inevitable as purchasing countries seek the lowest cost sources for allowances. But that said, it is highly conceivable that the United States and Europe could meet their obligations by engaging in the rigorous purchase of allowances and offsets from countries that could more easily and with less costs achieve substantial emission reductions. Even in the absence of a well-endowed international fund, the substantial flow of revenue from international trading could create a boom in low carbon emission investments in these

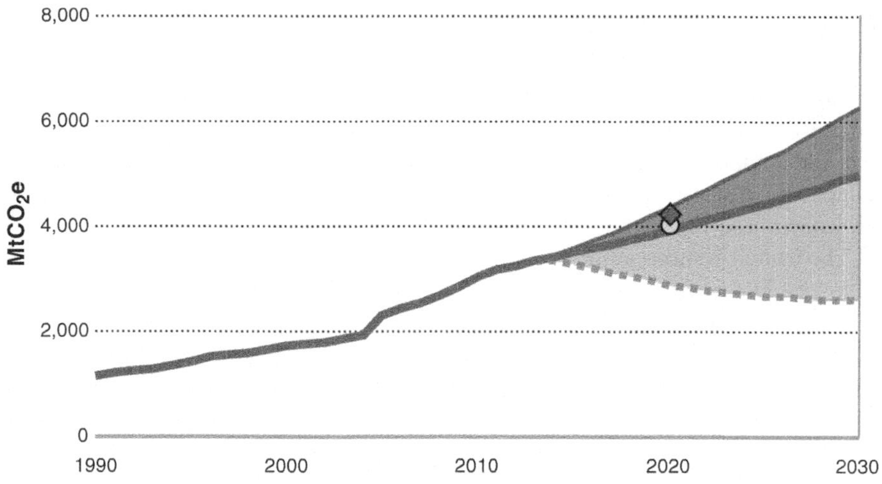

Source for data: Stockholm Environmental Institute Calculator
____ Fair Share Obligation
…….. Domestic Feasible Obligation
IIIIIII International Purchases

Fig. 4 India's fair obligation to 2030 for a weak 2 °C pathway

countries. As with the experience under the Kyoto Protocol, an international carbon market with at stake such substantial flows would draw in wholesale the private sector.

8 Enforceability

Not all countries would be willing to sign up to such a "fair" allocation of global responsibility. Those that did not would face carbon import tariffs at rates based on their carbon content of the imported good so no country would have an unfair advantage in trade. Disputes would likely arise but these could be handled under the dispute mechanism of the World Trade Organization (WTO), which has a proven record of handling disputes successfully.

Under such a regime, countries would be taxed at the border for not living up to their shared responsibility. No longer could a country escape their obligations as Canada did under the Kyoto Protocol without consequences. Countries that exceeded their responsibilities/capacity obligations would benefit by being paid for their emission reductions through international trading. As reductions to be met by industrial countries would be high, prices for carbon emission reductions are likely to be attractive, motivating a new wave of carbon reduction projects, policies and innovations.

9 Risk of Underachievement

A fully linked international market trading allowances and JI type credits would have risks that either: countries would not be achieving their emission reductions or that the underlying allowances/offsets would not correspond to real emission reductions. But as with financial securities, these risks can be assessed and the allowances and offsets rated for risk.

The United Nations could in theory be the risk assessor but given the experience with the CDM and the inherent conflict of interests built into the body, it is unlikely to get the political support from buying countries for taking on this role. Alternatively, the world could turn to independent risk assessors—the large rating agencies such as Standard and Poors, Moodys, Fitch or some smaller ones that would likely rise up to the challenge and the potential returns for selling their ratings. Regulatory bodies in buying countries could have several independent ratings to determine whether permits from any one country should be discounted for risk or prove to be so risky as to fall below a threshold for inclusion in a domestic system. Imported allowances or credits could have an internal exchange rate to domestic allowances based on the risk that the emissions were less then stated or that the source country would not fulfill its target of emission reductions.

In addition rating agencies would not be conflicted if paid from a pool of funds not tied to one country or a supplier of credits. The buying countries can set up an international fund with contributions based on their responsibility and capacity to pay, which would purchase ratings on country performance removing the bias to please the client or purchaser of the rating. Countries with stronger ratings would find more demand and prices for their allowances to be higher. If a country failed to achieve its obligated emission reductions, then the allowances from that country would be devalued in the "true-up" accounting. Forward contracts would likely have provisions for failure to deliver. It is therefore in the interest of all parties to see that the ratings are as accurate as possible.[3]

10 Wrapping It up

The Copenhagen Accord, while not a formal binding agreement, did signal that the major powers are committed to keeping global warming to below a 2° rise. Currently, no country is on a pathway of reduction consistent with this goal. If we adopt

[3]Already the World Bank has been working on such a risk rating system and may shortly ask for proposals to conduct pilot risk assessments. Some European governments have reacted sharply to this approach, either because they are still wedded to the extremely difficult task of bringing reform to the United Nations CDM process or because they know that if such a system was implemented ex-post on their own stock of emission credits much of their purchases would be devalued significantly.

reasonable criteria of responsibility and capacity to pay, both Europe and the United States would need to set a target of negative emissions, an impossible objective without international trading of emission reductions. In other words, international carbon emission trading is a necessary condition for achieving a 2° pathway.

The downside is such an international trading scheme would face risks of non-performance or free-riding. The risk of non-performance could be dealt with by independent rating from private sector agencies well versed in assessing risks. This rating would be similar to the rating of sovereign bonds where non-performance is an issue. In the case of international carbon trading, the rating body would determine whether a country is on course to achieving its pledged emission reduction as determined by responsibility and capacity to pay. Just like with bonds, such ratings would determine the value of the underlying asset, in this case allowances from the rated country.[4]

The free-rider problem could be dealt with through focused import carbon tariffs so domestic producers would not be at an unfair advantage or tempted to reestablish production in countries without a satisfactory price or tax for carbon emissions. Countries that are failing in fulfilling their fair-share obligations would face higher import duties based on the goods carbon content. The tariff rate per unit of carbon would be set based on its gap in fulfilling it target and the prevailing domestic price of a carbon allowance. The WTO could be a monitor of this process and as now, a platform for dispute resolution.

The UN would have a role in broad policy discussions and in monitoring, reporting and verification (MRV). Likewise the WTO would have an important task of ensuring that carbon tariffs did not morph into protectionism. Private rating agencies would fulfill the role of providing the needed risk assessment so countries importing credits and allowances would be better assured that their imported credits have minimal risk of not equaling ton for ton to their domestically generated reductions.

How feasible is such an outcome? Note that the option of a carbon tariff was in ever climate bill approved by the United States Congress and has been a threat pursued by some countries in Europe. While ratings are imperfect, agencies that do better in accessing risks and outcomes would be increasingly relied upon by domestic regulators and private parties.

The Paris meeting of the COP is just over 1 year away. Clearly given the progress to date, the experience under the Kyoto Protocol, and the urgency to deal with climate change, new innovative solutions must be considered which rely more heavily on the private sector and a more equitable system of country obligations, based on objective measures of responsibility and capacity to pay. Incentives must be in place to economically impact those countries that do not fulfill their responsibilities.

[4]Ideally the rating body would be paid not by the seller of permits but by a pooled fund, where the rater is not being paid by the entity being rated. The resulting rating could be used to discount the imported credit with respect to a domestic generated reduction.

Corruption of the Institutional System: Remedies

Marco D'Alberti

Abstract The usual way of conceiving corruption refers to individual behavior, such as the payment of bribes to public officers in order to obtain benefits (which could be called the "subjective' side of corruption). This is an indispensable but insufficient approach to understand and overcome corruption. It is also essential to cope with the "objective" side of corruption, which is represented by the degeneration of the institutional system and its rules. This chapter analyses some cases of "objective" corruption of the institutional system and tries to indicate possible remedies, particularly with regard to simplifying legislation, reducing administrative procedures and discretionary powers, enhancing public controls, improving transparency in public procurement. Putting in act these remedies against "objective" corruption can help reducing the incentives and occasions of "subjective" corruption.

1 The "Subjective" Approach

The relationship between corruption and the institutional system is a complex issue which can be understood only through a multidisciplinary approach. This is the reason why economists, legal scholars and political scientists have paid much attention to this topic in recent years. And this is the reason why I have proposed, together with Professor Luigi Paganetto, a national research on Corruption and Public Administration, which has been approved and funded by the Ministry of Education, University and Research and is carried out by various departments of Law, Economics and Political Science.

A premise is necessary. The usual way of conceiving corruption refers to individual behavior: particularly to the payment of bribes to public officers in order to obtain benefits. This is what one might call "subjective" corruption, the corruption of persons.

M. D'Alberti (✉)
Faculty of Law, Sapienza University of Rome, P.Le Aldo Moro 5, 00185 Rome, Italy
e-mail: marco.dalberti@cancrinipiselli.com

L. Paganetto (ed.), *Achieving Dynamism in an Anaemic Europe*,
DOI 10.1007/978-3-319-14099-5_14

As a consequence of this conception, the main approach in fighting corruption is based on a "subjective" perspective as well. The main remedies consist of preventive and repressive measures such as: penal sanctions against individuals who pay and accept bribes; codes of conduct for public officials; initiatives aimed at enhancing ethics in the public sector; plans and programs to identify the main risks of bribery in public administration and to indicate possible solutions.

This is an indispensable but, at the same time, insufficient approach. Corrupt behaviors of individuals must be sanctioned and "rotten apples" must be punished, but it is necessary to explore the underlying "objective" conditions that create corrupt incentives. In other terms, policy must address the "objective" corruption of the institutional system: otherwise, it will not produce long lasting effects (Rose-Ackerman 2006, p. xiv ff., xxxvii ff.).

2 The "Objective" Approach

In fact, the original meaning of corruption, as provided for by dictionaries, has to do with an "objective" perspective. "To corrupt" comes from the Latin verb "*corrumpere*" which stands for "to deteriorate", "to disrupt", "to degenerate". All these expressions, in classical literature, are primarily referred to things, such as waters or metals: "*aquarum fontes corrumpere*", says Sallust ("to corrupt water sources"). And "*corruptissima respublica*" ("highly corrupted polity"), in Tacitus and Seneca, refers to the corruption of institutions and rules.

The "objective" meaning of corruption comes before the personal and "subjective" aspect of corruption.

"Objective" corruption, if applied to public institutions, refers to the degeneration of the institutional system and its rules. Here lies the crucial side of corruption.

Sound institutions are capable of favoring economic and social prosperity even though affected by episodes of personal corruption. This is very well shown by Bernard Mandeville in his 18th century *Fable of the Bees* (Mandeville 1989), a clear metaphor of England, where, notwithstanding cases of personal corruption, a sound institutional system supported the industrial revolution and the economic growth. On the contrary, if institutions degenerate, prosperity is fettered and personal corruption is enhanced.

3 "Objective" Corruption to be Removed

There are many cases of "objective" corruption affecting institutions and rules. They are dangerous incentives for "subjective" corruption and should be removed. The following cases are worth considering.

3.1 Excessive and Inaccessible Legislation

It has been often stressed that many legal systems are burdened by too many statutes and regulations.[1] In addition, these statutes and regulations are often unclear: therefore, the ways of their implementation are unpredictable. Empirical evidence and economic theory underline a link between bad regulation and corruption. This emerges, for instance, if two indicators are combined: the World Bank Index on "Doing Business" and the "Corruption Perceptions" Index from Transparency International.[2] The countries that are ranked as the most corrupt ones, according to the "Corruption Perceptions" Index, are in many cases the ones that highly suffer from bad regulation under the Doing Business indicator.

Several remedies to contrast excessive and bad regulation have been put in place. For instance, the programs on "better regulation" adopted by the European Union (EU) and the Organization for Economic Cooperation and Development (OECD) have brought about useful results.[3] However, these programs have not always been implemented by the States. International and supranational remedies, such as those adopted by EU and OECD, must be flanked by national measures aimed at effectively transposing and adapting them in the various countries.

Moreover, national measures can also been independent of supranational constraints or directives. A good example of a substantial national remedy against bad legislation and regulation is the English Law Commission. Established in 1965 as a statutory independent body,[4] the Commission is composed of five full time commissioners: the Chairman is a judge from the Higher Courts of Justice, appointed up to 3 years; the other members are judges, or barristers, or academics, appointed up to 5 years. Twenty members of the Government Legal Service and a number of research assistants give support to the research and overall activity. As to its functions, the Commission reviews legislation that is unduly complicated, obsolete or unfair, and makes recommendations to the Government for reform of the legislation through, for instance, codification, consolidation of statutes, statute law repeals. Recommendations can be accompanied by draft bills. It is telling that thousands of statutes have been repealed since the establishment of the Commission, based on its proposals.[5]

The *Law Commission Act 2009* has aimed at even improving the rate at which the Commission's recommendations for reform are implemented by the

---

[1]On the negative effects of excessive and inaccessible legislation, see (Bingham 2011, p. 37 ff).

[2]The last available indexes are, respectively: World Bank Group, *Doing Business. Measuring Business Regulations*, 2014; Transparency International, *Corruption Perceptions Index*, 2014.

[3]Among the many initiatives, see: the program of the European Commission named "REFIT" (*Regulatory Fitness and Performance programme*), which aims at making EU law simpler and reducing regulatory costs, thus contributing to a clear, stable and predictable regulatory framework; for an effective synthesis of OECD efforts aimed at regulatory reform, see *Recommendation of the Council on Regulatory Policy and Governance*, 2012.

[4]Law Commission Act, 1965.

[5]The most recent Program of the Commission for the next 3 years is contained in Law Commission, *The Work of the Law Commission. Incorporating the Twelfth Programme*, October 2014.

Government. The Commission's model has been already adopted, even if in different ways, in some countries such as India and New Zealand: its further diffusion would be highly relevant.

3.2 *Cumbersome Administrative Procedures and Broad Discretionary Power*

Heavy administrative proceedings and large discretion are a substantial factor for civil servants' distorted behavior. Empirical evidence concerning Europe and Central Asia shows that too many and complex administrative barriers to market entry lead to higher corruption: for instance, authorizations or licenses to start an economic activity. The excessive scope of administrative discretion has been considered as an important factor of corruption in Europe (see Mény 1992). With regard to African countries, empirical studies underline that "vague and lax" regulations, which enlarge administrative discretion, increase the level of corruption. Where a regulation is lax, numerous and diverse solutions can be put in act for implementing it: the interested person or entity may have an incentive in paying a bribe to a public officer in order to obtain the most favorable solution (Graf Lambsdorff 2006, p. 7 ff).

As far as the possible remedies are concerned, there have been many attempts to streamline administrative procedures in various legal systems. However, the actual outcomes have been often weak. More than reducing administrative burdens on a case by case basis, general criteria and tools for reduction are needed. An important means, in this direction, is certainly the progressive reduction of authorization regimes, that has been achieved in EU law and also in US law. Decreasing administrative discretion is an objective which needs more attention. In fact, if in some economic sectors, such as banking, energy, telecommunications, administrative discretionary powers have been reduced, in many other areas, such as urban planning and the welfare sector, administrative discretion is still far from being attenuated, and a lot remains to be done.[6]

3.3 *Ineffective Public Controls*

Public controls can be an antidote to, but also an occasion of, corruption. For instance, in several countries controls and inspections are based on a case by case empirical approach. Some of them are characterized by the utmost strictness; some others, on the contrary, are particularly weak and feeble. It would be wise to put in place more homogeneous criteria. One relevant means to reach this result would be to at least reduce the fragmentation of police forces and to aim at unifying them as much

---

[6]On the reduction of discretionary power in various economic sectors, see (D'Alberti 2008, p. 99 ff).

as possible. Besides, coordination between police forces and other public administrations is a positive instrument. In addition, forms of cooperation between administrative agencies, the police and the judiciary can be highly useful, as in the case of money laundering, where effective and efficient controls have been and are put in act.

3.4 Public Contracts

There has always been a substantial connection between public contracts and corruption, particularly in the sector of public works. Over time national legislations and also EU law and international law have established provisions aimed at reinforcing the guarantees of publicity, transparency and non-discrimination of the procedures for the award of the contracts. But this has not been sufficient to overcome corrupt behaviors.

First of all, legislation on public contracts is often cumbersome and unclear. Public administrations, undertakings and the judiciary suffer from continuous uncertainties in implementing primary and subordinated norms concerning the awarding and the execution of public contracts in the field of public works, services and supplies. As has been said above, uncertainty in legislation and in its implementation is an incentive for corruption. Simplification of the legislative and regulatory framework is crucial.

Secondly, exceptions to tender procedures which the statutes provide for in case of emergency or urgency have been too widely applied. This has provoked events of collusion between public administration and undertakings, and serious cases of bribery.[7] Exceptions to tender procedures must be kept within a reasonable scope and have to be subject to an adequate reason giving obligation.

Thirdly, it has quite often happened that public controls on the execution of the contracts have been weak or inefficient. Sometimes, procedures for the award of the contract can be streamlined; exceptions to tender proceedings—as has been said—can be reasonably applied in case of urgency or emergency. As to controls on the execution of contracts and sub-contracts, a simplification is possible, but they cannot be cut off and should be efficient. There are plenty of cases where the absence or weakness of controls has caused dysfunctions and corrupt behaviors.

4 Other Cases of “Objective” Corruption to be Overcome

Weak or absent competition allows undertakings to behave unfairly with regard to new comers and consumers: an anticompetitive context is often characterized by high levels of corruption. A sound competition law is needed. It requests a good

[7]See on this point (Barbieri and Giavazzi 2014).

combination of antitrust enforcement and competition advocacy. The former punishes undertakings' infringements while the latter is aimed at promoting pro-competitive regulation: both are necessary tools against corruption.[8]

Feeble transparency in the public sector, in terms of difficult access to documents and public data, is an incentive for corrupt behavior. The British and American *Freedom of Information Acts* are certainly good models for other legal systems to enhance transparency in public policy and administration.[9] Continental European countries have weaker rules on this point.

Many cases of corruption have occurred in regional and local institutions. For instance, in continental Europe France and Italy have often suffered from cases of local corruption. Decentralization is a good tool for enhancing subnational democracy, but some proportionate limits are necessary. Some constitutional and statutory guarantees for the central government to intervene in cases of bias or failures of local authorities are needed.

5 Conclusion

Corrupt human beings will always exist and their illicit behavior must be seriously punished: the "subjective" corruption has to be vigorously contrasted. But the incentives for illicit behaviors can be dramatically reduced if the "objective" corruption, the corruption of the institutional system, is removed or attenuated.

References

Barbieri, G., and F. Giavazzi. 2014. *Corruzione a norma di legge*. Milano, Rizzoli: La lobby delle grandi opere che affonda l'Italia.

Bingham, T. 2011. *The rule of law*. London: Penguin.

D'Alberti, M. 2008. *Poteri pubblici, mercati e globalizzazione*. Bologna, Il Mulino.

Graf Lambsdorff, J. 2006. Causes and consequences of corruption: What do we know from a cross-section of countries. In *International handbook on the economics of corruption*, ed. S. Rose-Ackerman. Cheltenham: Edward Elgar.

Mandeville, B. 1989. *Fable of the bees: or, private vices, publick benefits (1724)*. London: Penguin.

Mény, Y. 1992. *La corruption de la République*. Paris: Fayard.

Rose-Ackerman, S. 2006. Introduction and overview. In *International handbook on the economics of corruption*, ed. S. Rose-Ackerman. Cheltenham: Edward Elgar.

---

[8]It is telling that the last OECD Global Forum on Competition (Paris, 27–28 February 2014) has been devoted to the theme "Fighting Corruption and Promoting Competition" and discussed how anti-competitive behavior and corruption interact in different ways: inter alia, in public procurement, or through regulation restricting business licensing and entry to market.

[9]US *Freedom of Information Act*, 1967; UK *Freedom of Information Act*, 2000.

Governance, Moral and Economic Values

Luigi Paganetto and Pasquale L. Scandizzo

Abstract As for all crimes, the cost of corruption to the perpetrator is a positive function of the probability of being detected and a negative function of the severity of the sanction. The uncertainty of the sanction and the growing importance of illegal practices in our society increases the benefits of operating illegally, while cost are reduced. This paper analyses the social costs of the activities of surveillance and sanction needed to circumvent corruption. The benefits of zonitoring and sanctioning entail both decreasing and increasing costs. There will be an optimal level of such activities, in which corruption will not be eliminated. The use of real option theory suggests, contrary to the traditional theory of law and punishment that the power of politicians and men of law both depend on uncertainty. The greater the uncertainty and the value of penalty, the greater the power of the police or the magistrate. Given this perspective it may be considered desiderable restoring the credibility of the judicial administration ,such as providing somewhat prompt extra penalties, setting up anti-corruption boards, promoting transparency and openness in governmental activities. At the same time, these policies have limited power, since moral norms and standards are delicate mechanisms that rely on trust and commitment and ensure that citizens choose to act according to principles that would not necessarily increase their wellbeing.

1 Introduction

Ethics can be defined as the economics of behavior. For rational individuals, not governed by endogenous moral norms, an act is desirable if the expected cost (consisting of the product of the probability of being discovered for the sanction if

L. Paganetto (✉) · P.L. Scandizzo
FUET, Economics Foundation, University of Rome "Tor Vergata", Rome, Italy
e-mail: luigi.paganetto@uniroma2.it

P.L. Scandizzo
e-mail: scandizzo@economia.uniroma2.it

L. Paganetto (ed.), *Achieving Dynamism in an Anaemic Europe*,
DOI 10.1007/978-3-319-14099-5_15

any), is less than the expected benefit. If we are in the presence of relative moral norms (i.e. not "categorical"), the cost is added to an endogenous component that depends on the weight that the individual gives to the same standard. This may change the terms of the problem, since the moral cost may be positively or negatively correlated with the material cost.

In the case of corruption, it is likely that the moral cost is a positive function of the probability of being detected (if this is high, it increases the degree of cognitive dissonance of an infringement). The moral cost of corruption, on the other hand, can be negatively correlated with the severity of the sanction. From the cognitive point of view, in fact, that hardness is an alternative to the autonomous moral judgment and may therefore elicit a decreased motivation to behave in a clear and fair in business, as well as to obey the laws. If a higher strength of the sanction is accompanied, as is common for economic reasons, by a reduction in resources for repression, and thus a reduction in the probability of discovering the corrupt, obedience to the law for endogenous motivation (i.e. respect social norms) is further reduced.

More easily than for the other types of crime, a theory of illegality is generated on the basis of the idea that society can "tolerate" a certain degree of corruption, as is evident from the fact that only a small part of the corruptors and corrupted are punished. If this idea of tolerance level of 1 is generalized, the number of corrupt people tend to increase, further validating the theory. Level 2 tolerance follows and then tolerance of greater and greater degree, accompanied by a crescendo of lawlessness. Since the systematic misapplication of the rule creates uncertainty among citizens, lawlessness also receive increasing support from previously "honest" citizens.

The uncertainty of the sanction and the growing space occupied by corrupt practices, in fact, increase the benefits of operating illegally, while costs are reduced. But at this point, there being a large number of parties involved in corrupt practices, even those who have tried to behave honestly, or are guilty of marginal infringements will tend to support the corrupt people's point of view. The campaigns against corruption, therefore, will not find any real support.

2 Measuring Corruption

The scientific literature has historically approached corruption as a complex phenomenon that is in large part matter of interpretation and is extremely difficult to define and measure (Wraith and Simpkins 1963). Both being immeasurable and not being measured are characteristics features of corruption that continue to represent a relevant obstacle to raising the awareness on this issue and to evaluating the effectiveness of the anti-corruption strategies adopted at the local, national and international levels.

However, the interest for the institutional aspects of development has prompted many international institutions (namely, the United Nation's agencies and the World Bank), non profit organizations (Transparency International), and research centres (Columbia University, Economist Intelligence Unit, PWC, etc.) to dedicate attention to this issue, by trying to look at it from a quantitative point of view and on a large scale.

Corruption is thus the current object of many international statistical and measurement efforts according to three main dimensions:

1. objective/subjective measurement;
2. object of measurement: level of corruption, its causes and effects;
3. level of aggregation/detail of the measure adopted.

With reference to the first point, the measurement of corruption can be classified in "objective" and "subjective" (e.g. Kaufmann et al. 2006; Sampford et al. 2006) measures. Objective measures are usually based on proxies such as large cash payments, judicial statistics, data on income elusion and evasion that are considered associated to corruption. Hence, even though they may be considered trustworthy, precise and relatively accurate according to circumstances, they have low validity (Duncan 2003) because they are essentially based on presumptions and correlations. Subjective measures are based on surveys or polls in which experts, local business people or citizens are asked to express their opinion on corruption levels in different fields and circumstances of every day life. Subjective measures may also concern the respondents' perceptions or experience (see, for example Transparency International CPI and BPI indexes). Corruption measures may also address the whole extension of the phenomenon its causes or its consequences, especially in the economic impact, as for example its impact on economic development is often measured (Kaufmann et al. 2006; Mauro 1995). Measures may also be aggregate, by attributing a score for each country such as the CPI of Transparency International or the governance indicators of the World Bank, or disaggregated by distinguishing specific economic sectors or geographic areas (as for the statistics on criminality).

Clearly all these measures, which are of increasing popularity and use in today's debate on economic development, present different ranges and operational significance. From the economic point of view, they are largely disconnected from economic theory and are often only loosely related to clear economic aggregates. Furthermore, existing measures are almost always subjective and while they may be useful from a moral and political standpoint for raising civil society and public opinion awareness on the phenomenon and for stimulating the debate, they do not provide policy indications to decision makers. The objective measures existing in Italy—mainly statistics on criminality levels and on the so called "black sector"—are incomplete and tend to confuse different phenomena such as corruption, criminality and tax evasion. In particular, again with reference to Italy, there are no well-developed instruments for measuring the economic impact of corruption (disaggregated per sector and/or territorial area), in spite of the fact that a few quantitative studies have been developed for phenomena related to corruption such as the so called *murky* sector and the organized crime (D'Antonio e Scarlato 1993; Scandizzo 2005a, Scarlato 2001).

3 Components of Corruption

From the economic point of view, corruption can be considered a contract in which two parties (the corrupter and the corrupted) agree to jointly derive a benefit from the default of another contract, to the detriment of the contractor (or contractors) of the latter not involved in the corrupt relationship. The most common context in which corruption unfolds is thus a form of contractual opportunism in which one of the main contractor— the agent, is unfaithful to the mandate received from the principal.

What are the tools to reduce corruption? The analysis of contractual opportunism has identified two main instruments of governance, which go under the name of monitoring (monitoring and sanctioning) and commitment (incentives and motivation), while the theory of crime and punishment has focused on the binomial probability-entity of the penalty. We can, however, consider the problem of punishment essentially comparable to the problem of monitoring, which is to identify the most effective ways, from the point of view of costs, to detect and punish corrupt behavior. The possibility of extending the surveillance and supervision also to external parties to the contract (or the corrupters extortionist) is in fact provided just by the intervention of the judiciary, which in this sense, tries to complete the tasks of the principals (whether a private entity or the PA) to protect their interests.

The activities of surveillance and sanction (the monitoring), however, present intrinsic difficulties and potentially high social costs. In fact, they create a division in the communities, which tend to break up into two groups: "controllers" and "controlled". The latter, even when they are not directly covered by the audit, may develop hostile and evasive behavior towards the controllers. This can be done both for solidarity with the other people controlled, and because the fact of belonging to the group of the "controlled" can lead to the conclusion that there is a positive probability of being subject to controls that are unjustified and harmful in the future. In more serious cases, such as, for example, those relating to a police state or a colonial occupation, the community developed an "anti-state" controlled subculture, which produced a specific cult of lawlessness.

Attempts to circumvent this reaction are based on indirect mechanisms, cultivating, for example, spying, further increasing the costs of monitoring. These attempts, in fact, although effective in the short term, produce, in the long term, further radicalization of the dualism controller—controlled and they foment the conflict, both through the growth of violent illegal activities, and through the multiplication of avoidance and retaliation activities.

The high costs of monitoring can also be seen, as in the literature on crime and punishment, in the dilemma posed by the binomial property of law enforcement. The literature has noted that the increase in the penalties is to be considered in the abstract more convenient from an economic standpoint, since it is able to increase the deterrent effect of law enforcement, without the expenditure of resources required by the increase in the probability of discovering the culprits. The harder penalty, however, creates indirect costs, due to the increases in the costs of prosecution—judgement error and conviction of the innocent and, from the point of view of the perpetrator, it reduces the opportunity cost of the most serious illegality. In the case of corruption, in particular, because of the pervasiveness of the phenomenon, the growth of the punishment increases the likelihood of escalation of the opportunistic agent, who, faced with the possibility of civil or criminal sanction not commensurate with the quality of the crime, decides to defy the law, setting up commensurate scenarios of illicit gain. Corruption is followed, then, by fraud, scams or other types of corruption in contracts, which threaten to undermine all confidence in market transactions.

The rising cost of prosecution and conviction of the innocent, on the other hand, is an external effect of graver sanctions, accompanied by an increase of the capacity of discrimination. This cost can be very important, because it determines an expansion of the sphere of insecurity of the individual and poses a threat to the fundamental rights of the citizen based on freedom. Given a chance of being caught and punished, in fact, an increase in the penalty increases more than proportionally the uncertainty for the innocent as well as for the culprit.

This increase is greater, the greater is the inefficiency of the judicial system and leads to the result of a greater number of violations and, correspondingly, to a higher average value of the infringements. The so-called "legal certainty" will be threatened by an implicit collective agreement, so that a level of punishment that is not commensurate with the probability of application shall be equivalent to a much lower level of punishment with a higher probability of application. This phenomenon is due to a dual effect: on the one hand, the prospect of a more serious penalty will decrease the deterrence differential among crimes, because while it is possible to increase the penalties for minor offenses, it becomes increasingly difficult to increase the penalty for felonies.

On the other hand, the burden of generalized sanctions, with equal probability of application, discourages more than proportionately minor offenses than larger ones if, as it is likely, the price elasticity (i.e. the elasticity with respect to the penalty) grows with the expected benefits of the crime. For example, it is estimated that a 10 % increase in the penalty for the offenses of corruption that promises a gain of £100 million has a larger effect of discouragement, compared to an increase of the same percentage of the penalty for offenses that promise 200 million. This effect of adverse selection is analogous to what occurs in the world of credit, when trying to distribute the loans on the basis of willingness to pay higher interest rates. Who is willing to pay more, in fact, is the bearer of positions that are, at the same time, more profitable and more risky.

Similarly, the corrupt willing to pay more in the event of conviction expects a higher gain, even if this entails a greater risk. Increases in the penalty, thus resulting in an increase in the average price of crime, preferentially select those who are willing to pay more, namely those, who are willing to take greater risks in exchange for prospects to gain more in the end.

Since the degree of tolerance implicit in the application of the penalty will increase, this will be interpreted as a value judgment on the seriousness of the offense, with the result that the dishonest will become more confident to get away and the "honest" less safe not to be unfairly prosecuted or for not having taken advantage of the circumstances to enrich the ranks of dishonest and achieve gains of uncertain illegality. The cost may increase further if the spread of the climate of impunity involves, as it seems likely, corruption in the law enforcement apparatus. Corruption, in this case, may lead to a process of degeneration of the entire system, whose institutions will be losing credibility and strength, and become "corrupt" to an increasing extent with the spread of illegal behavior in the social fabric.

The alternative to increasing the penalty is to increase the probability that it is applied appropriately. To achieve such an increase, it is first necessary to invest considerable resources, both in the investigating and in the judiciary apparatus. If this effort is carried out in an appropriate manner, the results are likely to increase the capacity for monitoring and sanctioning and, at the same time, for discriminating between the innocent and the guilty. Even in this case, however, we can expect difficulties and rising costs. Expanding the repressive apparatus, in fact, will multiply the possibilities of inefficiency: the so-called scale administrative diseconomies will make it increasingly difficult to coordinate and even control a large and pervasive bureaucracy, avoiding a logic different of its own self-assertion. A police state can also emerge that will ultimately threaten individual freedoms.

From this discussion it is evident that, since the benefits of monitoring and sanctioning entail both decreasing and increasing costs, there will generally be an optimal level of such activities, in which corruption will not be eliminated. There will be a level of "good" of corruption, that is a level below which it does not pay to reduce activity by direct repression.

4 Sanctions and Option Value

A financial option is the right, but not the obligation, to buy (in the case of so-called "call" option) or sell (for the so-called "put" option) an asset of uncertain value at a predetermined price. A real option is the analog counterpart of this definition to measure the opportunities and risks created by a "real" economic activity. Since some activities are at the same time, uncertain and irreversible, they give rise to temporary values, which depend on the particular events that may occur, the estimates of the economic operators and the degree of uncertainty (and Scandizzo 2005b). Any action or economic status can therefore be conceived as having an upstream option, since the mere possibility of undertaking it is a faculty but not an obligation. In this option, however, lies generally a contractual obligation, implied or explicit by an individual or collective counterpart. The economic freedom of a market economy, in particular, consists of a series of options that economic agents, as citizens and parties, possess. All of these options coincides with the rights that may be subject to attribution of value, exchange and detention by the individual and form the so-called "contingent wealth" of economic agents, i.e. wealth, the value of which is conditioned by the state of nature which, in turn, occurs.

An action is not, however, only subject to a contingent right that may or may not be exercised. Once implemented, every action itself tends to generate a set of options, that is, contingent rights depending on the economic origin of the action itself and on other economic agents. Some of these options are of the positive type: they represent additional opportunities for deployment of benefits to the originating agent. Others, however, are of a negative type, as they represent threats to the original agent, because of unfolding rights on the part of agents damaged by the initial actions, to obtain benefits at the expense of the original agent.

The creation of options of a negative type, or "liability options", is particularly relevant in the case of corruption, for two main reasons. First, as we have seen, corruption is a case of opportunistic behavior, i.e. an agreement between corrupt and corrupting agents to take advantage of the incompleteness of a contract at the expense of the principal. The contract between principal and agent, in other words, creates a threat by the agent, to be unfaithful in favor of a third party (in the case of corruption) or of direct arrangements with third parties (in the case of bribery), to take advantage of the contract to the detriment of principal. If this option is not exercised, the agent is honest, and if it is exercised, it enters the realm of the moral unlawfulness and, depending on the applicable law, of illegality.

Once in this area, however, a further liability option is created, which is, in turn, a threat against the dishonest and possibly corrupting agent: the option to sanction. It is an option, because, for both the moral sanction that for the legal one, there is no certainty of its automatic application. Rather, the penalty is the possibility that any society, through either informal or formal proceedings may exercise its faculty to proceed against the unfaithful agents, given the information available. With all due respect of mandatory prosecution, in other words, even the legal sanction unfolds according to individual agents who hold the option, deem it appropriate to exercise their rights, and consider the related costs bearable and useful for the prosecution and the punishment of the guilty.

If we consider both the corruption and the sanction as liability options held by different economic agents, we can infer a set of logical consequences, at least in part, unexpected. First, since the value of an option is greater the greater the uncertainty of the value of the underlying asset, both the corruption and the penalty constitute two options whose value is greater the greater the uncertainty of the basic contract. In the case of politics, for example, in a democratic regime, the principal for the politician is the sovereign people, but the mandate is surrounded by uncertainties in both motivations and objectives. We must therefore expect high opportunities to elude and twist its terms for the benefit of agents (and any of their associates), i.e. high values of the option of corruption. Correspondingly, the value of the penalty will be the greater, the greater the uncertainty relating to its application, due to the difficulty of recognizing and detecting the offense, because of the difficulty of applying the penalty. Since laws are designed and approved by politicians, moreover, we can expect a reasonable concern, in good or bad faith, that the penalty is applied for non-legitimate purposes, or that it may involve innocent parties. Consequently, the costs, but also the uncertainty of the application, will be higher.

The economic value of an ordinary asset depends positively on the difference between the relevant benefits and costs, and negatively on the risk that the difference is less than expected or negative. In contrast, the value of an option is the greater, the greater the uncertainty surrounding the realization of a net benefit. The greater the uncertainty, in fact, the greater the value of maintaining the opportunity to take action, without running the risk of actually doing so until the information collected is not sufficient. "Holding" means having an option then retains the right to proceed without exposing oneself to the risk of doing it too soon or inappropriately. The option of being corrupt, therefore, does not corrupt and does not expose the agents of the company or sanction the action of the court, but increases the value of honesty. If corruption is rampant, on the other hand, the sanction option will assume a gradually increasing value, and this will be amplified by the uncertainty on the forms, methods and objects of the penalty. In contrast to the traditional theory, the greater the possible value of the penalty, the greater it arbitrariness and, as a consequence, because of the uncertainty of its application, the more menacing the option held in the hands of the magistrate or police officer. Much greater, therefore, the sum of the powers of these officers of the state.

To conclude, real option theory suggests, contrary to the traditional theory of law and punishment, that the power of politicians and men of law both depends on an elusive force: uncertainty. In the case of democracy, in particular, this force is the basis of the implicit contract between voters and elected officials, and the possibility that it can be violated by corrupt politicians. But it is also the basis of the option of intervention in the hands of the institutions responsible for the protection of the law. The greater the uncertainty of the intervention and the value of the penalty, the greater the power of the police or the magistrate. Paradoxically, this means that in some circumstances, it may be of objective interest of political power that there is the possibility of corruption, because it gives more power to the repressive hand of the state.

5 The Costs of Repression

Corruption is a crime that involves the middle classes, professions, politicians and the bureaucracy. As sanctions are painful and uncertain, and, as we have seen in the previous section, an implicit solidarity binds the corrupt and the holder of the sanction, its suppression tends to occur in a cyclic manner and in the form of a purifying bath of the collective type. It is difficult to trace the roots of the rational collective tendency to periodically invoke strong and immediate sanctions for crimes of corruption and participate with enthusiasm to the application of these provisions. There is no doubt, however, that a common experience of all civilized countries includes periods of execution fervor in which the conviction or acquittal on the part of the public tends to precede that of the courts both in substance and in rituals. In these periods, fortunately uncommon in Western countries, together with or even before the formal processes, collective processes are celebrated, which, even in their spontaneity, have ritualistic elements: a discussion of the evidence, identification of the culprits, the contemplation of the possible penalties. Nowadays the media have come to expand social rituals on the different stages, which increasingly tend to become parallel and eventually converge with legal rituals.

In addition to ritualistic aspect, which may have common values of catharsis or reaffirmation and thus are necessarily cruel, since they assert the priority of the social over the individual, we must assume that the public expresses also instances of rational nature. In the crowd, individuals do not cease to respond to stimuli and beliefs that affect them even when they are not in the crowd: the desire for justice, for example, concerns the efficiency or honesty 'of the rulers, the fear of uncertainty and the future.

What legitimate feelings are hidden, for example, in the support for the measures of preventive detention, apparently so extensive in Italy, at least in some recent circumstances? It's not easy to say. The statistical data available clearly indicate a framework of systematic violation of human rights, which the pre-trial detention data make even more disturbing. Suffice it to cite a single alarming fact: in the last 10 years more than fifty per cent of those who were imprisoned before trial were found guilty, and this despite the fact that the use of preventive custody has received an acceleration in recent years, as a result, inter alia, of the approval of a new Code of Criminal Procedure and the opening of the front of the massive crimes against the public administration.

It should also be noted that the punitive value of preventive detention is 'far greater for uncensored citizens, whose activities' economy depends on the social reputation of honest behavior. In these cases, incarceration has the effect of irreversibly destroying a substantial amount of human capital, which can never be fully recovered by any declarations of innocence and that, in the Italian system, is substantially non-compensable. The distributional effect of preventive detention is therefore unfair and regressive, inequitable because the cost is higher for the innocent than for the guilty, regressive, because it is more expensive for those who have comparatively lower incomes.

That said, it is also fair to recognize and it can be assumed that, albeit in the absence of a clear cognitive awareness, that there are some benefits associated with preventive custody. The largest of these benefits could be that, under the current circumstances of Italy, preventive custody makes credible the prospect of a penalty that otherwise would not be. The length of the process and delays caused by claim to ensure all three levels of courts' judgement without adequate resources, create, as well as the permanent condition of injustice, an objective difference between the present values of benefits and costs of the criminal act. The remoteness in time and the slowness of criminal trials reduce the value and credibility of the threat of sanctions resulting in a more widespread lawlessness.

An insufficient amount of resources allocated to the administration of justice, thus creates a gap between the social rate of return and private rate of return of law. As a consequence, not only respect for the law is reduced, but because of the loss of credibility, penalties tend in turn to get worse, with an ensuing vicious cycle that can lead to a real system degeneration.

Given this perspective, we understand that it may be considered desirable to use a tool that somehow compensate the inefficiency of the judicial process by restoring, though improperly, the credibility of the judicial administration, such as providing somewhat prompt extra penalties. From the point of view of social welfare, however, the solution is not necessarily better than the previous one, since, in view of the reconstitution of the credibility one may create possibly higher costs, and certainly not comparable in terms of distribution, due to unrecoverable damages to the innocent unjustly imprisoned. From the point of view of justice, we risk creating a wound in the collective consciousness that is an even more serious loss of credibility of the ever delayed sanction. In addition to credibility, in fact, the penalty needs to be civil and moral dignity needs to be respected.

One can also rely, in line with our discussion on real options, that increased penalties, when they do not respond to the actual concerns of immediate protection of the community, result in a demonstration of repressive power, that does not solve the 'inherent uncertainty' of the situation, but simply restates the option of sanctioning, increasing its value through the expansion of its uncertainty of application. The penalty becomes a sword of Damocles in the hands of the authority vested with the power of sanction, which may dramatically extend its power, especially against the innocent and the weak, which are more exposed to this threat while the corrupt may engage more easily in eluding it.

Instead of relying on increased repression, a number of measures have been recommended to contain and minimize corruption (Theobald 1990; UN 1990). These include: setting up of anti-corruption boards, commissions and the like, campaign for moral regeneration or moral re-armament, strengthening controls on abuse of power and the enhancement of accountability systems, promoting transparency and openness in governmental activities, developing positive social attitudes, enforcing a code of public ethics, supporting the role of media, improving educational procedures.

To reduce corruption drastically, a number of more fundamental changes have also been advocated. These include: reducing the opportunities for corrupt transactions by cutting back state's activities; letting new centres of power emerge outside the bureaucracy; implementing far-reaching administrative reform measures that affect policy, institutional and process levels; strengthening prevention structures (Theobald 1990; UN 1990).

6 Motivations and Incentives

Greed is not the only spring for individual action. Economic theory has long identified some of the motivation mechanisms (the so-called mechanisms of commitment), which ensure that citizens choose to act according to principles that would not necessarily increase their well-being, but are beneficial to the community. Moral norms and social standards are at the origin of the most important of these mechanisms. It was, for example, suggested that investment in schools and churches is partly justified by the positive impact that these institutions have on motivations to obey the rules. In the case of corruption, we are faced, however, with rules that often are characterized by a substantial margin of ambiguity. A first ambiguity arises from a contrast typical of the production of public goods, which is the distinction between the benefit the public good offers to its users and the willingness to pay for it to be offered.

This phenomenon, which goes under the name of free riding, often means that there is a subtle distinction between the verbal support that the individual is willing to offer the dismissal or prosecution of corrupt practices and what she is willing to pay, in concrete cases that come her way, to give up the advantage that would result from corrupt transactions. The latter, in fact, often occur in the form of relatively small infractions to the rules of a very general nature, and just as the unpaid ticket by the free rider, they can be interpreted as small exceptions that are ultimately irrelevant to honest behavior. This is true at least until the escalation of individual or collective corruption does not make it impossible to continue to hold self-beliefs of honesty, even by exercising sophisticated techniques of self-deception.

A second ambiguity appears as a consequence of the fact that compliance with a moral standard is based on mechanisms of self-motivation. These, in turn, are based on the assumption that, to gain the respect of morality on the part of law-abiding citizens, there is no need to threaten more or less stringent sanctions. As many experimental psychology trials have demonstrated, a tightening of the repressive action weakens the endogenous mechanism to support the standard. In turn, this loses its endogenous support, in the sense that the individual tends to classify related behavior in the class where the burden for correct behavior is borne by society rather than the individual.

A third ambiguity, finally, depends on the elusive nature of the standard. This elusiveness is a consequence of the fact that the rule is generally supported by a common feeling (see, for example, "the common decency"), which, in turn, translates into a minimum standard, rather than in an absolute rule. This "required minimum level of honesty" varies with the level of economic development and the degree of freedom of each individual company, in the same way of other living standards such as poverty, piety, decency etc.

References

D'Antonio, M., and Scarlato, M. 1993. L'economia del crimine: parte II: la dimensione del mercato. Marsilio Editori.

Duncan, N. 2003. *When perceptions are not enough for policy*. University of East Anglia.

Kaufmann, D., Kraay, A., and M. Mastruzzi. 2006. *Measuring corruption: Myths and realities*. The World Bank.

Mauro, P. 1995. Corruption and growth. *The Quarterly Journal of Economics* 110(3): 681–712. MIT Press.

Sampford, C. J., Shacklock, A. H., Connors, C., Galtung, F. 2006 Measuring Corruption, Aldershot, UK: Ashgate.

Scarlato, M. 2001 Settore sommerso ed equilibri multipli: uno schema analitico per il Mezzogiorno. Rivistadi politica economica, 91(8), 37–60.
Scandizzo, P.L. 2005a. *L'impresa e il mercato: la teoria e i fatti*. Torino: Giappichelli.
Scandizzo, P.L. 2005b. Corruzione, Illegalità e Valori Economici. In Scritti in onore di Vincenzo Buonocore, *Vol 1, Giuffrè ed.*
Theobald, R. 1990. *Corruption development and underdevelopment*. London: Macmillan.
United Nations. 1990. *Corruption in governmen*t. Report of an interregional seminar held in the Haque, The Netherlands on 11–15 Dec. New York: The United Nations.
Wraith, R., and E. Simpkins. 1963. *Corruption in developing countries*. Crows Nest: Allen & Unwin.

The manufacturer's authorised representative in the EU is Springer Nature Customer Service Centre GmbH, Europaplatz 3, 69115 Heidelberg, Germany. If you have any concerns regarding our products, please contact ProductSafety@springernature.com

Printed and bound by CPI Group (UK) Ltd, Croydon, CR0 4YY
30/09/2026
02225234-0010